Amazons of the Huk Rebellion

NEW PERSPECTIVES IN
SOUTHEAST ASIAN STUDIES

Series Editors
Alfred W. McCoy
R. Anderson Sutton
Thongchai Winichakul

Associate Editors
Warwick H. Anderson
Katherine Bowie
Ian Coxhead
Michael Cullinane
Paul D. Hutchcroft
Courtney Johnson
Kris Olds

Amazons of the Huk Rebellion

Gender, Sex, and Revolution in the Philippines

Vina A. Lanzona

THE UNIVERSITY OF WISCONSIN PRESS

Publication of this volume has been made possible, in part,
through support from the Association for Asian Studies, Inc. and
the Center for Southeast Asian Studies at
the University of Wisconsin–Madison.

The University of Wisconsin Press
1930 Monroe Street, 3rd Floor
Madison, Wisconsin 53711-2059

www.wisc.edu/wisconsinpress/

3 Henrietta Street
London WC2E 8LU, England

1   3   5   4   2

Printed in the United States of America

Library of Congress Cataloging-in-Publication Data
Lanzona, Vina A.
Amazons of the Huk rebellion : gender, sex, and revolution in the Philippines /
Vina A. Lanzona.
p.   cm. — (New perspectives in Southeast Asian studies)
Includes bibliographical references and index.
ISBN 978-0-299-23094-4 (pbk.: alk. paper)
ISBN 978-0-299-23093-7 (e-book)
1. Hukbong Mapagpalaya ng Bayan (Philippines)
2. Women guerrillas — Philippines — History — 20th century.
3. Women in combat — Philippines — History — 20th century.
4. Insurgency — Philippines — History — 20th century.
I. Title.   II. Series.
HQ1757.L36   2009
959.9′035082 — dc22
2008040624

For Mommy and Daddy,
Virginia and Leonardo Lanzona,
who taught me the meaning of empathy and compassion,

and for the Huk women
who graciously shared their remarkable lives with me.

Contents

Illustrations

Figures

Maps

Diagrams

Preface and Acknowledgments

This book is a culmination of sorts — of my childhood in Manila, my political activism in college, and my intellectual and academic development in America. As someone who grew up in the Philippines I have been obsessed with revolution and with the part that revolutionary struggle has played in our history — the struggle against the Spanish in the Philippine Revolution, against the Americans during the Philippine-American War, and against the Japanese during World War II. As a student at Ateneo de Manila University in the 1980s, I identified with that tradition of struggle by joining highly political organizations, and by advocating for political prisoners imprisoned by the Marcos regime, prisoners I visited every week in military prisons. Like many college students who were Martial Law babies and got involved in the people power revolution against Marcos in 1986, I was inspired to join Cory Aquino's government, and to experience at first hand the problems and possibilities of working in a democracy. But the disillusionment came immediately, and I left the Philippines, escaping from politics to begin a new intellectual journey.

In America however, my political experiences continued to shape my academic endeavors, first at the New School for Social Research in New York and later at the University of Wisconsin in Madison. Studying at the New School under the guidance of Charles Tilly, my political and academic interests began to merge as Chuck reinforced my interest in Philippine revolutionary struggles with his own vast knowledge of social movements and revolutions. But unlike most scholars of the Philippines, I was less interested in the history of our first anticolonial and nationalist struggles for independence, and the preoccupation with 1896, and more interested in the struggles of the contemporary Left inside the Philippines, the struggles of the people I had visited in military prisons a decade before, men and women who were vilified as communists and socialists, and branded as subversive, godless enemies of the state. I wanted to know more about who they were and what they were fighting for, and this interest eventually led me to the Huk rebellion, and to Jeff Goodwin at New York University, whose knowledge of the

Huks, and sensitivity to the issues of gender and sexuality, inspired me to explore the topic further. When I arrived at the University of Wisconsin to study with Alfred W. McCoy, my interest in the Huks was forced to take a backseat to a broader immersion in the history of Southeast Asia. But once I began to work on my dissertation my interest in the Huks resurfaced and I began to read everything I could about the Huk rebellion. And as I worked my way through boxes of captured documents from the Politburo of the Partido Komunista ng Pilipinas (the Communist Party of the Philippines), I became more and more fascinated by their emphasis on issues generated by women's participation in the movement, and more and more struck by the almost complete silence of women in party debates and their absence from most standard accounts and histories of the Huk movement. My desire to recapture the lives, stories, and voices of women in the Huk rebellion has inspired my dissertation and this book.

This book would not have been completed without the help, support, and generosity of the many people I encountered in Manila, New York, Madison, London, Amsterdam, and Hawai'i. It would be impossible to thank everybody who has been a part of this book, but I would like to convey my heartfelt appreciation to the friends and colleagues who have helped me undertake this wonderful, though sometimes difficult, intellectual journey.

My experience at the New School made me first want to be an academic, and I was fortunate to be part of the Center for Studies of Social Change (CSSC) run by Chuck and Louise Tilly. At CSSC I benefited immensely from the presence of scholars like Louise Tilly, Eric Hobsbawm, Janet Abu-Lughod, and Diane Davis, and developed vital friendships with other graduate students, especially Tom Gold, Laima Serksnyte, Guy Baldwin, and Lizabeth Zack. When I went to the University of Wisconsin to do my doctoral work, I received tremendous support from the History Department and the Center for Southeast Asian Studies, especially Jennifer Gabrielson and the director of the center, Andy Sutton. Mike Cullinane's door (and phone line) was always open to me, and in conversations that sometimes seemed to last whole days, he would answer all my questions, give me useful comments on my work, supply me with extensive bibliographies and interesting historical tidbits (and gossip), and, most importantly, make me laugh. He has continued to be a wonderful teacher, colleague, and friend, and he, Mogi, and Liam have always made me feel welcome at their home in Madison.

At Wisconsin, I was able to assemble an ideal dissertation committee. My two outside readers, Gay Seidman and Dan Doeppers, did more than was expected of them and were always thoroughly engaged in my work. Thongchai Winichakul encouraged me to find new, exciting ways to approach my project, while Florencia Mallon offered substantial and challenging comments on my dissertation. My friends and fellow graduate students at Madison, including Amy Golden, Suzaina Kadir, Nancy Appelbaum, Mike Malley, Sean Kirkpatrick, and Steve McKay, listened to my ideas and tolerated my constant restlessness, while keeping me company during Madison's unending winters. And beyond Madison, I was fortunate to have many other good friends and colleagues, among them Rosanne Rutten, John Wiersma, Vince Boudreau, Jojo Abinales, Vince Rafael, Joyce Hermoso, Timmy Wells, Yayi Fua, Jules Dasmariñas, Eliza Fabillar, and Friedrich Huebler, who were always concerned about my work and who always helped me keep it in perspective.

I would especially like to thank Alfred McCoy and Charles Tilly. I've been very fortunate to have two such amazing mentors. By simultaneously believing in me and yet constantly challenging me, a rare combination, both of them helped me survive the rigors of American academic life. From the start, Al McCoy encouraged me to expand my intellectual horizons and inspired me with his infectious passion for Philippine history. His rigorous (and sometimes maniacal) work ethic was impossible to emulate, but I owe much of my success as a graduate student to him, and even after I moved to the University of Hawai'i, he continued to support my scholarly work. I am pleased that our relationship has evolved from that of professor and student to that of mentor and mentee and now colleague and friend.

Chuck Tilly, my very first mentor, passed away last year. I was in my early twenties when I moved from Manila to New York, and although Chuck was a towering intellectual and scholar, he immediately took me under his wing. It was he who first helped me formulate the questions that led to the dissertation on which this book is based, and I could always count on him for support and encouragement. Always so generous with his own time and help, my biggest regret is not being able to hand him this book, which germinated under his guidance, and to thank him in person. I will miss him terribly.

At the University of Hawai'i at Manoa, I have discovered the difficulties of balancing my work as a professor, researcher, and scholar with a demanding personal life. My wonderful colleagues in the History Department and the department staff have made this task easier. At the

Center for Philippine Studies, I have been fortunate to find such mentors as Lindy Aquino, Dean Alegado, Ruth Mabanglo, Terry Ramos, and Amy Agbayani, who have helped me to find my place in Philippine studies at the university and to reach out to the wider Filipino community. I would especially like to thank Barbara and Leonard Andaya, who have accepted me as a colleague in Southeast Asian studies, welcomed myself and my family into their home (and lives), and supported my work with great and genuine generosity.

I spent a total of two years in the Philippines conducting the research for this book, research I could not have undertaken without the support of many people and institutions. I first met Wilma Azarcon as I was working my way through Politburo documents in the Special Collections of the University of the Philippines Library, and because of her patience and good humor, that experience was pleasant and fruitful. Fr. Joey Cruz and Jojo Hofilena, my former teachers in the History Department at the Ateneo de Manila University, always made it easy for me to return to the Ateneo and to secure access to the Rizal Library. Mang Frank Puzon tolerated my constant (and demanding) presence at the Pardo de Tavera Collection at the Rizal Library, and helped me to find and reproduce the amazing photographs used in this book. Allan Hao Pasco patiently scanned the photos for me and Director Lourdes Vidal kindly granted me permission to use the photos. I can't imagine a better reference librarian than Merce Servida of the Lopez Library and Museum. Many thanks also to the Institute of Philippine Culture at the Ateneo, the Center for Women's Studies at Miriam College, and the Philippine Social Science Center at the University of the Philippines for inviting me to give talks that provided me with valuable suggestions about my work.

Many institutions helped to fund the graduate work and dissertation research that preceded this book. A National Science Foundation Grant (with Jeff Goodwin) made pre-dissertation research in Central Luzon possible. My master's degree at the New School was made possible by tuition scholarships and a research assistantship with Chuck Tilly. The History Department and the Graduate School at the University of Wisconsin awarded me several fellowships and travel grants. However, the most important support came from the Center for Southeast Asian Studies (through generous Henry Luce and Mellon Foundation awards), which funded my graduate study, dissertation research, and dissertation writing. As I revised my book, I received several grants from the University Research Council at the University of Hawai'i. In 2005–6,

I was a visiting scholar at the School of Oriental and African Studies (SOAS) at the University of London and a fellow at the International Institute of Asian Studies (IIAS) in Amsterdam. I would like to thank Ian Brown, Jim Richardson, Eva-Lotta Hedman, John Sidel, the IIAS staff and researchers, and my good friend Rosanne Rutten for making my stays in London and Amsterdam so wonderful and productive.

I would also like to acknowledge Gwen Walker and the University of Wisconsin Press, especially Director Sheila Leary, for their enthusiasm in getting this book published. Gwen believed in the project right away and miraculously made the review process as painless as possible. My two readers, Karen Turner and John Larkin, gave invaluable suggestions that strengthened the book. Ben Kerkvliet read my manuscript carefully, and as our foremost scholar of the Huks, his approval means a lot to me. Thongchai Winichakul and Mike Cullinane (once again) offered their unqualified support and valuable comments for this book project. Ev Wingert created the wonderful maps and Sheila Zamar improved my translations. Jan Opdyke, my copyeditor, has done a wonderfully competent job. The staff at the UW Press, including Michel Hogue and Kori Graves, saw this project through production, while Sheila Moermond skillfully (and patiently) directed its final stages. I'd also like to thank Paul Kratoska, editor of the National University of Singapore Press, and Maricor Baytion, editor of the Ateneo de Manila University Press, for their sustained enthusiasm for the book. Special thanks to the Association for Asian Studies (ASA) for a generous grant toward the publication of this book.

My heartfelt thanks go to the KaBaPa (Katipunan ng Bagong Pilipina, Association of the New Filipina), and especially to Ka Trining Domingo and the HUKVETS (Huk Veterans Organization), headed by the late Luis Taruc, which helped me make contact with former Huk women and men. Because of their introductions, finding the Huk women (who then introduced me to other Huks) was effortless and enjoyable. I first met Celia and Bill Pomeroy at their home in Richmond, England, in 1997 and they have been part of my life ever since. I have fond memories of my visits to their home in London, and their unwavering dedication to political change was and is a constant source of inspiration. My thanks to all the Huk women and men I met and interviewed in Central and Southern Luzon, and in Manila, for welcoming me into their homes, feeding me, and entrusting me with the stories of their lives, especially Ka Teofista, Ka Menang, Ka Liwayway, Ka Elang, and Ka Aida, who took care of me and treated me like their own *apo*, grandchild. These Huk women (and the men too, especially Ka Gy Alejandrino, Ka Jess Lava, and Ka Luis Taruc) were always on my mind as I wrote this book, and over the years many of these vibrant women and men have passed on. I can only hope that this book will help keep their legacy alive.

Finally I want to thank my family . . . for everything. My Mommy and Daddy have always been my biggest fans and cheerleaders. Although they didn't always understand or approve of my desire to visit military prisons or to trek around Central Luzon in search of old Communists, they always supported my personal and career decisions. My brothers and sisters, Manong Lito, Ate Cory, Butch, Ge, and Ray, my nephews and nieces, Owen and Will, and my in-laws in Manila, England, and America have provided much-needed distraction and loving support. Last but not least, I am very fortunate to have by my side Marcus Daniel. Indeed, I could not ask for a better colleague, intellectual partner, and partner in life. While Marcus has been a part of this book, our greatest collaboration is our son Miguel. Both Marcus and Miggy competed with this book for my time and attention, and although they didn't always prevail, they made completing this book both delightful and possible.

Abbreviations

AFP	Armed Forces of the Philippines
AMT	Aguman ding Malgang Talapagobra (Union of the Toiling Masses)
BCT	battalion combat team
BUDC	Sandatahang Tanod ng Bayan (Barrio United Defense Corps)
CC	Central Committee
CLB	Central Luzon Bureau
CLRC	Central Luzon Regional Command
COF	Congreso Obrero de Filipinas (Congress of Workers of the Philippines)
Comintern	Communist International
CPP	(new) Communist Party of the Philippines
CPUSA	Communist Party of the United States of America
CSSC	Center for Studies of Social Change
DA	Democratic Alliance
EDCOR	Economic Development Corps
FC	field command
Gerwani	Gerakan Wanita Indonesia (Indonesian Women's Movement)
GHQ	General Headquarters
GI	American soldier
GOMA	Guerrilla Officers Military Academy
HMB	Hukbong Mapagpalaya ng Bayan (People's Liberation Army)
Hukbalahap	Hukbo ng Bayan Laban sa Hapon (People's Anti-Japanese Liberation Army)
HUKVETS	Huk Veterans Organization
IIAS	International Institute of Asian Studies
KaBaPa	Katipunan ng Bagong Pilipina (Association of the New Filipina)
KAP	Katipunan ng mga Anakpawis sa Pilipinas (Association of Sons of Sweat in the Philippines)

KPMP	Kalipunang Pambansa ng mga Magsasaka sa Pilipinas (National Society of Peasants in the Philippines)
MPC	Military Police Command
NAW	National Assembly of Women
NCD	National Communications Division
NP	Nacionalista Party
OB	Organizational Bureau
PB	Politburo
PB In	Politburo in Manila
PB Out	Politburo outside Manila
PC	Philippine Constabulary
PKM	Pambansang Kaisahan ng mga Magbubukid (National Peasants' Union)
PKP	Partido Komunista ng Pilipinas (Communist Party of the Philippines)
Politburo	Political Bureau
PUP	Polytechnic University of the Philippines
PYC	Philippine Youth Congress
RECO	regional command
RSSP	"The Revolutionary Solution of the Sex Problem"
SEC	Secretariat
SISTERS	*Sisters in Solidarity to End Racism and Sexism* (journal)
SOAS	School of Oriental and African Studies
SPKP	Samahan ng Progresibong Kababaihan sa Pilipinas (Association of Progressive Women in the Philippines)
SPP	Sosialistang Partido ng Pilipinas (Socialist Party of the Philippines)
TNT	Tagisan ng Talino (Quiz Night)
UP	University of the Philippines
USAFFE	U.S. Armed Forces in the Far East
WAC	Women's Army Corps

Amazons of the Huk Rebellion

Map 1. Major Regions and Provinces of the Philippines. (Courtesy of Ev Wingert, University of Hawai'i at Manoa)

Introduction

Capturing the Huk Amazons

In February 1947 Remedios Gomez, known in Central Luzon as Kumander Liwayway, was captured in a major military drive against Huk guerrillas dubbed Operations Arayat. Major newspapers hailed the success of the operation, applauding the "mass capture" of the Huks and the apprehension of one of the revolutionary movement's most popular commanders. Described as a "pretty, high school senior" and "many times a queen in town festivities in Pampanga," Liwayway became an instant celebrity, and an exclusive interview with her a month later did nothing to diminish the public fascination that surrounded this Huk "Amazon":

> In the hands of her captors "Liwayway" is being given the attention that befits a heroine. She has her own room, her bed, chairs for her callers and is accessible to all and any of her relatives any time of the day. In the MPC [Military Police Command] headquarters she is even referred to as the *Joan of Arc of the Philippines* and this said not in derision or mockery now that one of the most influential enemy [*sic*] of the MPC is their captive.[1]

As the reference to Joan of Arc revealed, the attraction to Liwayway was a response not just to her beauty but to her identity as a daring female military commander who had established her reputation leading successful military attacks against the Japanese during World War II. After the war she rejoined the Huks in their struggle against the new

3

Philippine Republic, and she quickly reestablished herself as a skilled military commander, "once again leading a number of men in the mountains of Arayat but this time fighting fellow Filipinos."[2] But in 1947 the Philippine Armed Forces finally caught up with the weak and hungry Liwayway while she was resting beside a creek.[3] "If I was not sick at the time of 'Operations Arayat' and too weak to move," Liwayway later recalled, "I could have eluded capture and would still be fighting for the Huks' cause even now."[4] At the same time that she was being feted by the media the government alleged that she and other captured Huks had "unlawfully armed themselves with machine guns, rifles, and other weapons, assaulted the municipal governments" [in Magalang and Minalin, Pampanga] and exchanged fire with the police," charging her with rebellion, sedition, and insurrection.[5] Liwayway's treatment as both a dangerous enemy of the state and a former beauty queen who was "given all the treatment befitting a society star" underscored the sense of ambivalence and uncertainty that surrounded the public representation of female warriors like Liwayway in Philippine society during the late 1940s.[6]

Three years later the arrest of another Huk Amazon, Teofista Valerio, alias "Estrella," at her home in Santa Ana, Manila, also attracted great attention in the press. According to the newspapers a major raid on the Huks by the military in Laguna on August 25, 1950, had led to the capture of two teenage Huk couriers, and during interrogation the girls had revealed that they were on a mission to deliver letters from Huk leaders to a "mysterious woman in Manila named 'Ester.' This woman turned out to be Teofista Valerio, whose house in Manila was believed to be the "clearing center of Huk communications to and from the city."[7] When the police raided the house they discovered Huk papers and documents and pictures of Casto Alejandrino, the "No. 2 man in the Huk military organization," who was believed to be Teofista's lover. Teofista denied knowing Alejandrino and claimed that the father of her baby was another Huk soldier named Alamani who had "deserted her while she was in the family way."[8] After weeks of investigation the military was able to confirm that, "despite her fragile disposition," Teofista was the head of Huk communications in Manila and the common law wife of Alejandrino, although even after incessant interrogation the police were unable to extract any information from her about the Huk leader. Teofista was immediately detained at Camp Murphy with her one-year-old daughter and a month later charged with rebellion and illegal association.[9] Like Liwayway, Teofista was portrayed to the public as a bold, fearless, yet vulnerable "Amazon."

Amazon Commander Leonora Hipas and Huk Emilio Diesta both confessed that they surrendered because they wanted to "get married and live peacefully." Amazons like Leonora are invariably presented with ambiguous personas as warriors and lovers. (*Manila Times*, n.d.; Courtesy of Rizal Library, Ateneo de Manila University)

Captured women guerrillas such as Liwayway and Teofista received a great deal of publicity and attention in Philippine newspapers and magazines during the 1940s and 1950s. Almost always labeled Amazons by the press, these female guerrillas and members of the communist-led Huk movement were represented as both fearless warriors who had to be apprehended and female victims who had to be rescued. The depictions of Liwayway and Teofista in the press reflected this ambivalence. As a Joan of Arc, Liwayway was brave and impressive, and as a former beauty queen she was alluring. Teofista, on the other hand, appeared as an innocent, abandoned woman and mother, yet newspaper accounts also portrayed her as an incredibly competent and resourceful revolutionary who ran an underground communications network in Manila. These stories about Huk Amazons reflected the significance of women as agents of revolutionary struggle in the postwar Philippines, and yet most studies of the Huk rebellion have ignored the important role these women played in the movement. This book is an effort to remedy this neglect and restore these women and the issues their presence raised regarding gender, sexuality, and family to their rightful and central place in the Huk rebellion.

Stories of captured Amazons appeared on a daily basis in Philippine newspapers and magazines in the late 1940s until the late 1950s. This photo, which accompanied one such story, was described as follows: "Two pistol-packing Huk amazons—Commander Gregoria de la Cruz alias Luningning in man's uniform and Vice Commander Julia de Belen alias Norma—were being whisked away to Camp Olivas . . . Luningning was armed with two .45 cal. pistols and Norma, with one .38 cal. gun." (*Manila Times*, March 24, 1954; Courtesy of Rizal Library, Ateneo de Manila University)

The Huk Rebellion

The Huk rebellion was a result of two separate, peasant-based struggles in the Philippines. The first, which led to the formation of the Hukbo ng Bayan Laban sa Hapon (People's Anti-Japanese Liberation Army), or Hukbalahap, in March 1942, was initiated by leaders of peasant organizations and the Partido Komunista ng Pilipinas (Communist Party of the Philippines or PKP) to resist the Japanese Army during World War II.[10] The defeat of the Japanese ended this first phase of the Huk guerrilla movement, and for a time the Huks attempted to work within the political framework of the new Philippine Republic, which was established in 1946. But the new republic, still under the colonial influence of the U.S. government, was determined not to let the Left establish a political power base and launched a series of actions aimed at delegitimizing the Huk leadership and undermining its popular support.[11] By August 1946 the Huks had been forced by political repression to go underground, and its peasant members reorganized in the forests of Luzon to launch a massive resistance movement against the government.

Quickly reestablishing the Huk organization, which now became known as the Hukbong Mapagpalaya ng Bayan (People's Liberation Army), or HMB, the peasant rebellion grew in size and organizational strength between 1946 and 1950, and the number of armed Huks increased to roughly twenty thousand. Supported by an even larger number of noncombatant peasant supporters, the Huks were able to capture villages, drive out landlords, and redistribute land among the tenants while at the same time launching successful surprise attacks against the Philippine Constabulary.[12] But by the early 1950s the Huks were in disarray. As the leadership of the movement divided over policy issues and internal morale fell, the government of President Ramon Magsaysay launched agricultural reform programs and intensified military repression. As a result peasant support in the towns and barrios (villages) of Central Luzon declined, and by 1956 the Huks were in a state of terminal decline. With the surrender of leaders and followers of the Huk movement in the late 1950s and early 1960s, this phase of peasant revolution ended in the Philippines.

The Huk rebellion was the most important peasant movement in Philippine history, the most successful resistance army in Asia during World War II, and the first major communist rebellion defeated by U.S. counterinsurgency operations.[13] But the Huks were important for another, lesser-known reason: theirs was the first major political and military organization in the country to include and actively recruit women. Women played a central role in the Huk rebellion, and a significant number of Filipino women, mostly from peasant backgrounds, abandoned their traditional roles in Philippine society to participate in the struggle. Although it is impossible to determine the exact number of women who participated in the movement, former PKP secretary General Jesus Lava estimates that about one in ten active guerrillas was a woman. At its peak, then, there were about one thousand to two thousand active female Huk guerrillas, although many more women were involved as peasant supporters in the barrios.[14] These women warriors learned their communist catechism, trained as soldiers and spies, drilled in the use of weapons, and became highly skilled in the arts of war. At the same time they fell in love with the men alongside whom they fought, and in many cases they became pregnant, gave birth, and raised families amid the turmoil of the revolution. These women existed in two worlds—a world of war and a world of love—and they struggled constantly to satisfy and reconcile their personal desire for love and an affective family life with the larger impersonal and collective aims of the revolutionary Huk movement.

These women's stories remain untold, and consequently the history of the Huk rebellion remains incomplete. Drawing on oral history interviews with women who participated in the rebellion, my book examines both the political and the personal factors that led women to join the movement and shaped their lives during and after the revolution. Rather than explaining the rise and fall of the rebellion as a function of state and class formation or political ideology, I explore the movement from within through an intimate examination of women's personal and political relationships.

Gender, Sex, Family, and Revolution

The development of women's and feminist history has changed the way we understand and write about the past. Feminist scholars have pointed out the neglect of women actors in history, and this has led to the writing of women's histories and to a more general reexamination of the role played by gender in history and the social sciences.[15] And yet, according to Barbara Watson Andaya, "the historical study of women and gender in Southeast Asia," is still a "new field . . . left in the wake of the theoretical and methodological advances made in other disciplines and world areas."[16] But this is gradually changing, especially in the historiography of women and gender in twentieth-century Southeast Asia, where a wide range of source materials is readily available and scholars utilize comparative methods to understand the female experience in various contexts. Studying women and politics, and revolution, in postwar Southeast Asia, for example, necessarily explores the struggles of women not only in the Philippines, Vietnam, and Indonesia but also in other countries or regions of the world such as China, Latin America, and South Asia.

Despite this greater sensitivity to gender and the female experience, until fairly recently women's motivations for joining social and revolutionary movements were not distinguished from those of men, and it was assumed that men and women occupied a "single society" in which generalizations could be made about all participants.[17] Women were assumed to sharing male perceptions about politics and to confronting the same choices as their male counterparts. New perspectives on women and gender, however, have allowed us to see that men and women inhabit distinct social worlds that carry with them different meanings, expectations, and demands. Thus, although men and women in the Huk movement may have come from the same social class, been raised in the same village, and lived through similar experiences, they did not necessarily share the same social expectations, cultural constraints, and political opportunities. Gender shaped, or "mediated," the activist experience.[18]

Gender is therefore central to my analysis of the Huks. But this entails more than just adding the voices of women to the narratives of the revolt. Following Christina Gilmartin's work on gender in the Chinese Revolution, I define *gender* not as a synonym for *women* but rather as an essential analytical and conceptual framework for the exploration of relations between men and women.[19] *Gender* is not used in its essentialist sense as a term that defines fixed male or female physical attributes or makes these differences "simply a matter of socialized differences in behavior and attitudes between men and women."[20] Instead the term helps to organize elaborate belief systems about femininity and masculinity, ideas that are constantly altered and negotiated, defined and embedded in social structures and relations, and carry with them constraints and opportunities that shape the experiences, the knowledge, the identities, and even the dreams of men and women.

Defining and using the concept of gender in this way is important not only in differentiating the experiences of men and women in the Huk movement but in understanding the political hierarchy of the PKP, the dimensions of social and political power in the movement, competing notions of the proper place of women in public and private life, and the multiple meanings associated with masculinity and femininity.[21] As Joan Scott argues, using gender as a category of historical analysis — as a way of talking about complex systems of social, sexual, or power relations — is a way to provide "new perspectives on old questions, redefine the old questions in new terms, make women visible as active participants, and create analytic distance between the seemingly fixed language of the past and our own terminology."[22] Examining the experiences of women in the Huk revolutionary movement through the lens of gender not only augments our understanding of party politics, peasant mobilization, and collective action but "forces a shift in perspective."[23]

In some recent work feminist historians have incorporated issues of gender and sexuality into their analysis of women's participation in social and revolutionary movements. A number of works have placed issues of gender at the center of the revolutionary movements in China, Vietnam, and Latin America, although most emphasize the female subordination within these movements caused by the disjunction between revolutionary theory and practice in gender relations.[24] Feminist social scientists have also sought to remedy the largely gender-blind literature on social movements, and yet their understanding of the sexual division of labor as a product of the division between the productive and reproductive spheres fails to capture the complexities of female-male relationships in revolutionary movements such as the Huk rebellion.[25] Issues of collective action and mobilization have been more systematically explored in the social sciences, but only recently have scholars reconsidered their former emphasis on rational interests and political ideology, and many of these studies continue to rely on ahistorical and impersonal models of mobilization that fail to address the issue of gender and its role in political mobilization.[26]

My work incorporates much of this recent research on women, gender, and sexuality in social and revolutionary movements, providing a separate and distinct analytic space for women and their experiences in the Huk movement. But, just as important, this study of the Huk rebellion places culture at the forefront. While the Huk movement shared universal goals with other social and revolutionary movements, and was part of an international communist movement that promoted socialist transformation and national liberation, the actions and decisions of individual members were shaped by their own experiences within and understanding of Philippine culture. Kinship, affectual ties, and even sexual relationships were crucial to female mobilization and participation in the movement, and these personal and familial relationships were structured by notions about gender and sexuality that were deeply rooted in Philippine culture and society.

Women, Gender, and the Huk Rebellion

Studies of the Huk rebellion say virtually nothing about issues of gender, family, and sexuality within the revolutionary movement.[27] The most authoritative accounts consider the revolt as a form of peasant revolution, emphasizing its continuity with earlier peasant struggles in the Philippines. The processes of capitalist modernization, which reshaped peasant societies like those in Luzon, heightened class cleavages, increased feelings of powerlessness among the peasantry, and drew many peasants into revolutionary coalitions.[28] But this emphasis on the social basis of the Huk movement leads to conventional explanations for the mobilization and defeat of the Huks. Focusing on external pressures to elucidate peasant action, these accounts generally argue that the Huks rebelled because of economic circumstances and their movement failed because of political repression. The internal dynamics—the complex relationships between leaders and members, and especially between men and women—remain relatively unexplored.

Including women in the study of the Huk rebellion offers us a novel look at this revolutionary movement and the role of women, especially peasant women, in Philippine society. While they are recognized for their central role in peasant and domestic economies, peasant women are usually regarded and often dismissed as "conservative guardians of the status quo." They were less likely to be formally educated, less likely to have access to jobs, and usually excluded from political life.[29] And yet during the 1940s and 1950s young peasant women from Central Luzon, like the captured "Amazons," defied convention by participating in the Huk rebellion. Mobilized through complex familial and village networks, the wartime experience and political education of Huk women transformed them from the daughters and sisters of Huk men into comrades in arms and fellow revolutionaries. And a few, such as Liwayway, even assumed leadership or combatant roles within the organization, earning the epithet Amazons. Their participation in the Huk rebellion during the 1940s and 1950s led to an intense debate about the role of women in Philippine society.

In fact this debate preceded World War II. During the suffrage debates of the 1920s and 1930s, the relationship between Filipino women and political citizenship became a deeply contentious issue, and many believed women's suffrage would lead to higher levels of divorce and the decline of the Philippine family. Despite this opposition, when suffrage was granted in 1937, largely due to the efforts of elite women, the new political status of women in the Philippines seemed irreversible.[30] After World War II, however, and the establishment of the Philippine Republic the demands of rebuilding Philippine society once again relegated women to the domestic sphere. Women retained the right to vote in 1946, a crucial development, but the demands of national unity and the increasingly conservative climate of the Cold War prescribed roles for Filipino women that emphasized their domesticity and femininity.

But the image of female guerrillas such as Liwayway and Teofista disrupted the domestication of Filipinas. Whether portrayed as masculine warriors, female seducers, or wayward mothers, Huk Amazons were regarded as extraordinary and unconventional Filipinas: communist guerrillas trained to fight as soldiers against the government and women who lived in the forests, fraternized with men, and had children outside marriage. Capturing the imagination and attention of the press and the public, these Amazons played a prominent role in public discourse about the role of women in postwar Philippine society.

It was not only those outside the movement who expressed ambivalence about Huk women. Incorporating women into the movement was also difficult for its male-dominated leadership, and while the PKP was formally committed to sexual equality, sexist and patriarchal attitudes often prevented women from assuming a larger role in the rebellion. Many women guerrillas were forced to conform to traditional social roles inside the movement, doing much of the cooking, washing, and housekeeping. These contradictions created tensions, and by 1950 Huk leaders were seriously concerned about the impact of sexual and gender conflict on the morale and military effectiveness of the Huks, blaming the failings of the movement on the presence of women and the inability of rank-and-file members to control their sexual and personal passions. During the early 1950s, when the rebellion was in decline, and guerrilla squadrons faced almost daily harassment from Philippine Constabulary forces, Huk leaders repeatedly argued that the conflicts created by the presence of women contributed to the weakness of the movement. As the government declared all-out war on the Huks, pushing the guerrillas farther into the mountains and farther into isolation and despair, personal relationships within the movement became more intense and were increasingly perceived as problematic by the male-dominated Huk leadership. As a solution to these problematic relationships, the leaders imposed regulations on the sexual behavior of members, which prioritized the needs of the male cadres and reinforced the subordination of women inside the movement. Although women's rights were part of official communist doctrine all over the world after the 1920s, the Philippine Communist Party only began to discuss this issue, and then reluctantly, toward the end of the Huk rebellion in the 1950s, and its leaders rarely took this issue seriously.[31] Despite the party's formal commitment to "gender equality," women's issues only attracted attention when they seemed to hamper male military capabilities.

Among the most important problems raised by the leadership was "sex opportunism" or the "sex problem." Often separated from their own wives, many married men in the movement, including members of the PKP, took a second or "forest" wife while they were with the Huks, usually a young, single woman. These extramarital relationships were the subject of bitter criticism both inside the movement and from families in the barrios or villages, and in 1950, after an acrimonious debate, Communist Party leaders drew up a remarkable document to address this issue entitled "Revolutionary Solution of the Sex Problem." The policy set out in this document permitted married male guerrillas to have extramarital relationships with single female cadres as long as they followed strict regulations.[32] Claiming "biological necessity," the frustrated male cadre could present his problem to his superiors and attempt to convince them that either his health or his work was being adversely affected by the absence of his wife. After an unofficial review he would be allowed to take a forest wife as long as both his legal and forest wives were aware of the arrangement and he agreed to settle down with only one woman at the end of the struggle.

Huk leaders also worried greatly about what they called "the family problem," the reluctance of both women and men to join the "expansion teams," groups attempting to spread the insurgency beyond its stronghold in Central Luzon, because this meant neglecting, or even abandoning, their families. Another concern was what the party called "financial opportunism," which led men to embezzle movement funds to support their families or to buy gifts for women to whom they were sexually attracted.[33] The party's solution to these problems was to encourage the integration of spouses (especially wives) and older children into the movement and the distribution of younger children to friends and relatives not involved in the rebellion. Although they were rarely followed by action, these discussions reveal the significance of sexual and gender tensions within the Huk movement and the party's desire to regulate the sexual and family lives of the guerrillas.

This hesitant and contradictory attitude toward women compromised the commitment of individual cadres and the strength of the movement. By actively recruiting women yet relegating them to support roles, by advancing a few women to positions of command yet allowing most to serve the sexual needs of male leaders, the party fostered disaffection among both Huk men and women. By promoting patriarchal assumptions about gender and sexuality, by failing to consider how participation in the movement transformed attitudes toward gender and sexuality among Huk men and women, by encouraging a policy that ignored the complexity of personal relationships, and by initiating a system of control that was often inimical to the desires of its members, Huk leaders let an organizational strength become an organizational liability. It was not sex and passion that undermined the movement as much as the failure of the movement to tolerate and integrate the passions of its members.

Nonetheless, despite their limitations, the Huks did make the emotional and sexual lives of their male and female members part of their revolutionary agenda. In their efforts to negotiate relationships between male and female members, party officials moved issues of sex and family from the private to the public realm, weighing the "private" interests and desires of individual cadres in relation to the collective interests of the revolutionary movement. As issues of family, sex, and morality became integral to the movement's political and social goals, they became subject to bureaucratic and administrative control, and personal matters that had once been negotiated solely by individual men and women were now discussed and regulated by the revolutionary movement. Few social or revolutionary movements ever addressed such issues as directly as the Huks. Yet in the end the attitudes toward sexual and gender relations in the Huk movement were generally framed within a conventional discourse about gender and personal relationships that reflected widespread cultural beliefs and practices in Philippine society.

Voices of Huk Women

Revolutionary movements are shaped by conventional political ideology, personal relationships, and the deeply rooted ideas about sexuality and gender that shape these relationships. Yet, because political and revolutionary leaders try to suppress this information and control both the political and personal lives of their members, these issues often remain elusive, sometimes hidden to all but the participants themselves. Something can be gleaned from Communist Party documents, although these are usually written by and for men and provide only limited access to the way issues of gender and sexuality influence revolutionary organizations like that of the Huks. The memoirs and biographies of Huk leaders provide a more personal perspective on the rebellion than traditional military and political studies, but they also reflect the perspective of leaders rather than ordinary peasant members and of men rather than women.[34] While stories about "Huk Amazons" appeared daily in newspapers and magazines in the 1940s and 1950s, Huk women remain largely invisible in almost all accounts of the Huk rebellion and in discussions about women in postwar Philippine society.[35] Consequently, who these Amazons were, how and why they became involved in the movement, and how they contributed to the rebellion have remained mysteries. In order to explore the importance of these women and to connect the emotional, sexual, and political lives of the Huk guerrillas, it is necessary to listen to the voices of ordinary Huk women.

Capturing the voices of these Huk women, who have been marginalized in historical accounts and memory, presents many challenges. One of the most valuable approaches used by feminist scholars to tell "women's stories" is the biography or life history. Biographies provide an intimate look at the role of individual women in the making of history, bringing together private and public lives and enhancing our understanding of major historical events.[36] Historians have also utilized prosopography, or collective biography, to incorporate individual voices in narratives that seek to explain profound social changes and broad political movements.[37] In a complex political organization like that of the Huks prosopography allows us to trace the development of the movement through personal narratives and to trace the role of the individual guerrilla in relation to the collective movement, exploring in more detail variations in individual experience and their relationship to the broader dynamics of the movement.

Creating such individual biographies of women is highly dependent on the use of oral history. Oral history is essential, according to the Italian historian Alessandro Portelli, because it gives us information about illiterate people or social groups that, because of their relative powerlessness, either have no written records or appear in the written records produced by others in ways that distort their real experiences. Oral histories are also important because they record the daily lives of people, something usually missing from conventional historical narratives, and of particular importance to any attempt to write women's history.[38] Agnes Khoo, for example, uses oral histories to "preserve the memories, experiences and struggles" of women who were involved in the anticolonial struggles against the British and Japanese in Malaya.[39] Through oral history their stories, which had been ignored by the Malaysian and Singaporean governments, are now part of the historical record and can be integrated into the national memory. Oral histories, therefore, seek to depart from the simple presentation of facts, and to capture instead the unarticulated motivations, desires, and ideas of ordinary people, especially women who have been "hidden from history."[40]

Oral history has been essential to recovering an otherwise unrecoverable dimension of the Huk movement. In 1993-94, I began to conduct interviews with Filipina women who had participated in, or were married to participants in, the Huk rebellion. The women, mostly poor peasant women, lived for the most part in Metro Manila and the provinces of Central and Southern Luzon, including Pampanga, Nueva Ecija, Bulacan, Tarlac, Quezon, Batangas, and Laguna.[41] At first I thought it would be difficult to find these women. Unlike male Huk leaders, who had received some recognition in the historical record, female Huks remained faceless, unnamed, and unrecognized. Through the Katipunan ng Bagong Pilipina (Association of the New Filipina), or KaBaPa, a coalition of peasant women's organizations, I met women who were both former KaBaPa members and Hukbalahap guerrillas. From a few initial contacts I was able to locate many more women who were willing to tell me their stories, and I relied on these former Huk women to introduce me to their former comrades.

In 1997 I spent another year in the Philippines conducting a further round of interviews with the women I had met in 1993-94, as well as interviews with women I had met since. During that year I got to know the women more intimately. Aside from visiting them in their homes in Manila, I made trips to the villages of Central and Southern Luzon where I was able to locate former Huk women by using the same social networks that drew them into the Huk movement. Once I had one contact in a village it was easy to secure introductions to other women. I benefited tremendously from their enormous generosity, staying in their homes and cultivating friendships with them. They not only indulged my curiosity, but they also took care of me, fed me, stayed up with me, showed me around their villages, and, most important, introduced me to the community and other former Huk women. During my visits to the barrios my relationships with these women deepened, and I began to realize how central they had been to the Huk movement. I also began to interview men, mostly former Politburo leaders, who were just as gracious as the women. Although my questions about the role of women in the movement often made them uncomfortable, they tried to answer them, and some of the men even introduced me to their forest wives.

My familiarity and friendship with these women and men, who were all eager to tell me their stories, has inevitably shaped my understanding of the Huk rebellion. Most of them had been interviewed before either by government officials inquiring about their wartime experiences (and their eligibility for veteran's pensions, which few ever received) or by researchers from the Philippines and abroad who were interested in the history of the Huk rebellion. As a Filipina and a graduate student in the United States I came to the villages and homes of these former Huk women as both a cultural insider and outsider. And initially many of the women were puzzled. Why did I, a *kababayan* (compatriot), *kapatid na babae* (sister), or, more simply, somebody they saw as an *anak* (child) or even an *apo* (grandchild)—or perhaps just an overly inquisitive PhD student—have this enormous interest in them, especially given their limited role in the broad history of the Huk rebellion? But just as I patiently listened to them talk about their former lives (sometimes for hours) they were excited to talk to me and even more surprised when I expressed more interest in their personal, and sexual, lives than in their political experiences. But they readily opened these lives to me, and, although they often expressed appreciation for my interest in them, it was I who was truly touched by their openness and generosity.

I conducted my interviews in Tagalog, my native language and the language spoken in Manila and most of the provinces of Luzon.[42] My interviews started with questions about names, places and dates of birth, families, and the extent of the women's political involvement before the war. But the focus of my interviews was their experience as guerrillas and supporters in the Hukbalahap and HMB movements. Because it was important for me to understand their reasons for joining and staying in the movement I asked about their recruitment before moving on to discuss their training and day-to-day experiences. I allotted considerable time to asking about their relationships in the movement, their love affairs, marriages, and children. The women usually ended their interviews with reflections on the successes and failures of the Huk rebellion and how their experiences in the movement had affected their present outlook on life and politics. While I had prepared questions to ask, I usually listened, letting each of my respondents tell her story in her own way. Thus, the length of my interviews ranged from one to twenty hours. When interviewed my female respondents were open, candid, and surprisingly eager to share intimate aspects of their revolutionary lives. While they were highly articulate about their political convictions, they were equally keen to discuss how their political decisions fused with their personal lives. My interviews with these Huk women comprise the core of this book. Because it is important to place these women in the historical record, I have used their real names when quoting them or describing their experiences. Only two women asked me to change their names, and I have honored their requests. All in all I conducted formal interviews with over a hundred former Huk guerrillas and supporters, seventy women and thirty-two men, although during the course of my research I talked informally with many more women. From these women I was able to collect extraordinary oral histories and life stories.

But oral history has both strengths and weaknesses. Because it is based on memory, the past is usually constructed not as a depository of facts but, as Portelli states, as "an active process of creation of meanings."[43] My male and female respondents ranged in age from sixty-two to eighty-eight. Many were therefore confused about actual dates, events, and people and sometimes suffered from lapses of memory. At the same time they often interpreted their past experiences in the Huk movement through their subsequent and present political and personal lives. Rather than simply telling me what they had done and thought, their oral stories also told me what they had wanted to do and what they thought about their actions in the past. A sense of nostalgia was often evident in the recollections of their past lives. While many still recalled how much they had suffered during and after the war, most Huk female veterans talked about their former comrades and their experiences in generally positive terms. Almost everybody told me that they had no regrets. Reading between the lines, paying close attention to their facial expressions, and listening not only to their words but also to their silences became part of my work as a biographer and researcher.

Issues regarding the tensions of the public and the private, so central to the lives of the women in the Huk movement, also influenced my own position with regard to this work. As a historian I wished to write a history of the rebellion that allowed Huk women to speak for themselves. But at the same time I was aware that their voices, the voices of people who graciously welcomed me into their lives and generously told me their stories, were shaped by my own voice and my desire to maintain a critical and intellectual distance from them. Ultimately I was the one who was writing a new history of the Huk rebellion, one that I hoped placed the women at the center but at the same time was not simply a recollection of their experiences. As I interviewed these women I therefore had to navigate between two poles: a distancing objectivity that transformed them into my subjects and threatened to betray their understanding of events and an excessive familiarity and suspension of skepticism that collapsed history into recollection. I like to think that I was generally successful, although it was often difficult to mask my empathy for these women. The credibility of my account and my book, which results from the complex interaction of my subjectivity and the subjectivity of the Huk women I interviewed, must ultimately be decided by the reader.

I have therefore used other sources to create a more complete picture of the past and to supplement these interviews. The most useful documents I used are the captured documents of the Politburo (Political Bureau) of the PKP, which have been declassified and are available at the University of the Philippines. Issued as directives to the Huk guerrillas, these documents disclose the movement's official goals and strategies, but reading them "against the grain" and remaining alert to issues of gender provided revealing glimpses of the sexual and gender culture of the Huk revolutionary movement. Contemporary newspapers and magazines, which reported the capture of Huk Amazons on an almost daily basis in the 1940s and 1950s, were also immensely useful, adding a new dimension to my work and helping me to relate my study to broader discussions about gender in postwar Philippine society.[44]

Using these oral and written sources, this book not only retells the story of the Huk rebellion but it also provides a historical space for these remarkable Huk women who have almost but not quite passed into historical oblivion. Chapter 1 introduces the women who joined the Huk guerrilla struggle against the Japanese during World War II with roles and cultural norms ascribed to them by their families, communities, and society. Mobilized through familial and village networks, these women underwent ideological and military training and became full-fledged Huk members. As a result, the Huks emerged as one of the most successful guerrilla armies in World War II. While the Japanese Occupation has always been an important theme in Philippine history, there has never been a systematic study of the contribution made by women to collective resistance during the war. This chapter probes how and why these women joined the Huk guerrilla movement.

After the victory against the Japanese, the Huks continued their struggle against the postwar Philippine Republic. In this second and more explicitly communist phase of the movement, women underwent more intense political education and faced larger and more challenging responsibilities as underground guerrillas. Chapter 2 explores how and why women remained in the Huk communist struggle. While most Huk women assumed traditional roles in the rebellion, doing much of the cooking, washing, and housecleaning, some emerged as top-rank communist leaders and military commanders. Chapter 3 focuses on the place of these Huk Amazons in broader debates about gender and the role of women in postwar Philippine society. It also highlights the lives and experiences of the few, exceptional women who emerged as leaders and military commanders in the male-dominated organization. Issues of gender, family, and sexuality are also central to chapter 4, which discusses more deeply the sexual relations of men and women in the Huk movement and the conflicts these relations created, as well as how party leaders responded to what they called the "sex problem." These issues of sexuality and family life led to a radical reconfiguration of revolutionary policies and efforts by the party leadership to extend control over the personal and emotional lives of ordinary Huk members. Chapter 5 brings these issues together, examining the profound transformation these women experienced from ordinary peasants to Huk revolutionaries and the challenges they faced in their postrevolutionary lives. It also reevaluates the decline of the rebellion and the dilemmas the Huks faced because of gender and sexual conflict inside the revolutionary movement.

Drawing on individual and collective biographies and the oral histories of women who participated in the Huk rebellion, this book examines both the political and the personal factors that led women to join the movement and shaped their lives during and after the rebellion. These women's lives and words reveal how central feelings and experiences associated with gender, family, and sex are to revolutionary movements like that of the Huks. My book seeks to reverse the usual bias in studies of social and revolutionary movements, which privilege the political over the personal and the male over the female, by giving direct expression to the voices of Huk women. But, while introducing Huk women into the written record is an important step toward correcting the gender-blind practice of Philippine historical writing, this study goes beyond women's history, bringing men and women together in a common analytical framework informed by the concept of gender. By looking at the intimate political and personal lives of Huk Amazons through the voices of Huk women themselves, my book recasts our understanding of this rebellion and restores these women to their rightful place in Philippine history.

1

Women at War

Huk Women and the Japanese Occupation

Filomena Tolentino was a twenty-two-year-old girl in Pampanga when the Japanese invaded the Philippines in World War II. One of five children, she left school after the third grade and sold rice at an early age to help her struggling extended family of peasants and vendors. Her family suffered from successive tragedies when she was very young; four of her siblings died, probably in an epidemic, and her mother, unable to cope, suffered a mental breakdown. It was up to Filomena and her older sister to sustain the family. She was raised by relatives who lived nearby, becoming another child in her aunt's family, a family that already contained eighteen people.[1] Despite Filomena's high grades and her teachers' encouragement, her aunt stopped sending her to school. She resented the way her family discouraged her education and assumed she was only a girl who would get married eventually anyway. Like other girls in peasant families, Filomena quickly learned to work in the fields. In the late 1930s she worked in one of her aunt's *sari-sari* (food) stores in the local town of Floridablanca. When the war began Filomena and her family abandoned their store and settled in the barrio, fleeing the Japanese, who stationed themselves in the local towns. Here Filomena first encountered the Huk guerrillas, an encounter that changed her life.

Elang Santa Ana's life was also transformed when the war reached San Ricardo, Talavera, her village in Nueva Ecija. Like Filomena she grew up in a family of peasants and left school in the third grade to help her impoverished family. Her father, she recalled, "had nothing" but nevertheless became a peasant leader, helping to organize associations and strikes in support of peasants' rights in Central Luzon. Because of his activities he was in and out of prison during much of Elang's childhood. But he transmitted his political commitment to his daughter, who became involved at a young age in a youth organization in her village that was affiliated with the peasant movement. By the time the war began, her father had become a Huk leader, and within a few weeks he summoned his daughter to join him in the mountains with the other guerrillas. Still only fourteen years old, Elang obliged.[2]

As Huk guerrillas Filomena and Elang soon met one another and other female members like themselves—young, single girls with limited educations, mostly from peasant backgrounds. While most Huk women had never left their villages before the war, they did not lead isolated lives in Central Luzon and traveled within extended kin and village networks. Although many of these women were already politically aware and some, like Elang, were involved in political organizations before they became Huks, most seemed destined to live within the confines of the home and the village as peasant wives and mothers, much like their mothers before them. Although they attended school, most assumed they would marry before they finished their education, and even Elang assumed that her early interest in politics would end once she was married. But their experiences during the war and their participation in the Huk movement gave women such as Filomena and Elang a chance to transcend the limitations of their class and gender and to carve out a different path for themselves. These women's lives intersected in the Huk movement, and their involvement with the Huks and one another transformed their lives and their sense of identity. This chapter explores the prewar lives of Huk women, including the political and social realities and cultural values that shaped their world and their involvement in the Hukbalahap.

Growing Up in Central Luzon

Young girls growing up in Central Luzon in the 1930s and 1940s, such as Filomena and Elang, were not shielded from the daily struggles of their peasant families and the communities around them. Central Luzon, located to the immediate north of the capital, Manila, is an extensive lowland area, the largest and most populated region in the Philippines (see maps 1 and 2).[3] At the time it was also a region of extreme inequality where most residents were peasants who worked on land

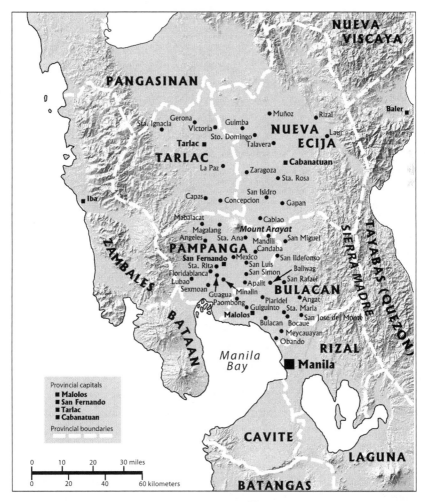

Map 2. Major Cities and Villages of Central and Southern Luzon (Huk Areas), circa the 1940s-1950s. (Courtesy of Ev Wingert, University of Hawai'i at Manoa, and Benedict Kerkvliet)

owned by a handful of powerful landowners. Central Luzon's history was marked by sporadic yet sustained conflicts between landlords and peasants.

Before the 1950s the economy of Central Luzon was based on agriculture and was dominated by rice and sugarcane production. The commercialization of the Central Luzon economy, which began with the opening of the port of Manila to foreign trade in the early nineteenth century, made its land and resources available for the development of commercial and export crops, including rice, sugar, and tobacco.[4] As the hacienda (plantation) system grew in the late nineteenth and early twentieth centuries, landlords made more stringent demands on small farmers, renting parcels of land to tenants in exchange for annual rents and a percentage of the tenants' annual yield.[5] *Katiwala* (overseers) were hired to act as intermediaries, collecting rents and pressuring tenants for higher yields on behalf of landlords, who had left their haciendas and moved to Manila and other cities. Most tenants were powerless to resist the extractions of the landlord, the overseer, and the Chinese merchants who operated the rice mills in the villages. By the 1930s more than half the farmers of Central Luzon were share tenants.[6]

Elena Sawit's family was typical. Born in Pampanga, Central Luzon, both of her parents came from peasant backgrounds, and their lives and livelihoods revolved around the cultivation of the land. She considered her father's family better off than her mother's because they owned a parcel of land and were not sharecroppers. But around 1938, after incurring enormous debts, her father lost his land and was reduced to the status of a tenant farmer. Elena grew up on the brink of poverty, and her family was sustained only by the vegetables they grew on their small plot of land. That same year, she lost her mother and had to discontinue her education. By the time the war arrived in 1941 she was working as a dressmaker to augment her family's income.[7]

Peasant families in Central Luzon resented the erosion of the traditional social ties between peasants and landlords as much as the loss of land.[8] In the traditional tenancy system landowners relied on their loyal clientele to pioneer the land and were personally involved with the peasantry's well-being. But as land became a more valuable commodity landlords began employing modern techniques to generate profits, transforming their once paternalistic ties with peasants into business relationships. In the old fixed-rent system, "the landowner had no reason to concern himself with the efficiency of a tenant as long as he paid," but the new sharecropping system "gave the landlord an incentive to evict any tenant who was aged, widowed or inefficient."[9] Rental agreements also became a source of contention between landlords and tenants. Generally the landlord furnished the land and space for the tenant's dwelling while the tenant and his family supplied the labor, plowing and harrowing the land.[10] While landlords should have been responsible for supplying and maintaining irrigation pumps and farm implements, in practice they often required tenants to share in both the capital and operating costs of the farm, and it was a common practice for tenants to receive loans or advances from the landlord in the form of cash or *palay* (unhusked rice). Thus, any profit tenants gleaned from the harvest usually went back to the landlord in the form of loan payments, often at exorbitant rates of interest. Ultimately, tenants earned little income and fell into a recurring pattern of debt and dependence on the landlord.[11]

This new system of share tenancy created serious social conflicts in Central Luzon's villages, and foremost among them were disputes over land. Peasants accused landlords of obtaining land by fraudulent means and charging illegal rates of interest on loans.[12] Although they continued to make their rent payments, peasants such as Elena's family lost more and more of their land while the haciendas grew larger and the gap between the landlords and landless peasants grew wider. While the large landowners prospered during a rice and sugar boom, building homes in the provinces and urban centers, dressing in the latest fashions, and sending their children to elite schools and universities in Manila and abroad, the peasants had barely enough for subsistence.[13] The geographical and social distance between landlords and peasants produced mutual suspicion and distrust.[14] Landlords accused peasants of theft and neglect of crops while peasants believed that they had been cheated out of the profits they deserved. Peasants also lost the economic security they had once enjoyed, which had enabled them to survive despite poor harvests or sickness.[15] The introduction of overseers similarly destroyed the former relationship of mutual trust between the landlord and his peasants. As absentee landlordism increased, the peasant had no one to turn to, and his place in the social system was threatened.

The realities of poverty and conflict pervaded the childhood memories of Filomena, Elang, and Elena. Elang remembered a childhood filled with days when they "had nothing, *walang-wala*," and lived a "hand-to-mouth existence." Everybody in their families contributed to the household because their peasant fathers, even after a harvest, were barely able to provide basic necessities. They knew that their families worked for wealthy *hacenderos*, but they did not remember having any personal relationships with the family of the landlord. This poverty, they believed, limited their chances to leave home. Despite the existence of public schools in the village, most peasants, lacking income and cash, were unable to educate their children past the second or third grade. But, although Filomena and Elang reached only the third grade, they valued their brief educational experience and considered themselves more fortunate than their parents and grandparents, who had never attended school. Having to leave school because of poverty was one of the most difficult moments of their childhoods. And yet, despite the enormous poverty of peasant families, parents still tried to provide a good life for their children. As girls growing up in Central Luzon's provinces, Filomena, Elang, and Elena remembered happy childhoods, playing with other children in the barrios, cared for by extended village networks, and participating in community activities. They always found comfort and security in their relationships with their families and their larger communities.

Peasant life in Central and Southern Luzon, as in most rural societies in the Philippines, was organized around significant kinship networks. While the *mag-anak* (family) was central to the kinship structure, intensive and extensive interpersonal relationships went beyond kindred, as relatives, friends, and nonkin also shaped village life.[16] Ritual kinship based on *compadrinazgo*, in which ritual bonds are forged through baptism, confirmation, and marriage, extended social relations to relatives, friends, and neighbors.[17] The men and women of Central Luzon, as residents of particular barrios, were embedded in strong kinship networks that provided mutual alliances and aid at the same time as they imposed a whole series of particularistic claims and obligations.[18] Within the real and ritual kin group each person had a role to play (as father, mother, son, daughter, sister, brother, and so on) with corresponding obligations shaped by social values such as *utang na loob* (debt of gratitude), *hiya* (shame), and *pakikisama* (yielding to the majority of the kin group).[19] By adhering to these obligations members received complementary affection, loyalty, and assistance from the kin group. The fabric of rural society depended on these relations of interdependence and reciprocity, which were supported by sentiments of gratitude and positive regard.

In Central and Southern Luzon kinship was often the only source of social support and security in times of hardship for poor peasants and sharecroppers.[20] Peasant families lived in close proximity, enabling them to develop strong group thoughts, feelings, and habits and a sense of security. Social contact between men and women was frequent, face to face, and intimate. A relatively high degree of community consciousness and loyalty was therefore attained through these close interactions.[21] With the widening of class divisions between landlords and landless peasants, residents of Central Luzon became even more reliant on their kin—their families, extended families, and other villagers. The highly personalized social networks in their villages enabled peasants to cope with limited resources and unforeseen economic difficulties.[22]

This sense of community and loyalty, as well as shared experiences of poverty and exploitation, helped bond the peasants and peasant families of Central and Southern Luzon. Landlessness, indebtedness, hunger, and poverty forced them to realize that only by coming together could they improve their situation. As they would never be able to restore the traditional tenancy system in their villages, peasants increasingly regarded landlords not as venerable patrons but as exploiters. "Without the landlord and his personal concern for their welfare," writes John Larkin, "the tenants started to sense for the first time the inequities of the system under which they labored."[23] Peasants believed that they should "take the land, refuse to pay more rent, and renounce their debts."[24] They were the "real" farmers, and since the landlords played no part in production they had no right to its fruits. This radical ideology led peasants to believe that there was no more hope in the system and only their collective efforts could bring about change.

The World Outside

The 1930s was marked by a series of transformations in Philippine politics and society. In 1935 the U.S. colonial government set up the Philippine Commonwealth as the precursor of the modern, independent Philippine state. Under the leadership of Commonwealth president Manuel Quezon, political consolidation became the primary goal during this "transitional" stage toward the full implementation of Philippine sovereignty, which the Americans promised would commence in 1946.[25] From the early years of U.S. rule Filipinos became eligible and competed for bureaucratic positions in almost all layers of government. The Americans, however, continued to rely on Filipino elites as collaborators in state-building efforts in the country.[26] Women's movements and others, both peasant and working class, that had been marginalized during the Spanish colonial period took advantage of the opening of political space and opportunity during the 1930s to challenge elite dominance and play a central role in defining the emergent nation. One effect of this transformation in public life was to revitalize what would become the U.S. colonial government's foremost political challenger in the Philippines—the Left.

By the 1930s Manila was the political center of the Philippine labor movement, a movement dominated by socialist ideas and leaders such as Crisanto Evangelista. Evangelista, who was heavily influenced by Marxism after a trip to the United States as a member of the first Philippine independence mission, became the secretary of Congreso Obrero de Filipinas (Congress of Workers of the Philippines), or COF, the "biggest and best organized" labor federation in the country for nearly two decades.[27] In 1929 he was elected the executive secretary of a new working-class party, the Katipunan ng mga Anakpawis sa Pilipinas (Association of Sons of Sweat in the Philippines), or KAP,[28] and on August 26, 1930, at the thirty-fourth anniversary of the "Cry of Balintawak," sixty labor and peasant leaders set up the Partido Komunista ng Pilipinas (Communist Party of the Philippines), or PKP, and elected the first Political Bureau (Politburo), with Evangelista as secretary general.[29] Finally, on November 7, 1930, five thousand people gathered at Plaza Moriones, the heart of Manila's working-class district, to attend the official launch of the new Communist Party, ushering in a new era in the political history of the Philippines.[30]

While Manila was the political capital of organized labor the countryside of Central Luzon was the heart of the peasant movement. In 1932 a new party was born—the Sosialistang Partido ng Pilipinas (Socialist Party of the Philippines), or SPP—founded by Pedro Abad Santos, a wealthy doctor and lawyer who devoted his life to leading the peasant movement in San Fernando, Pampanga. The SPP quickly established the Aguman ding Malgang Talapagobra (Union of the Toiling Masses) or AMT, a union in Pampanga that mobilized peasants and organized strikes and mass demonstrations. Luis Taruc, who soon became part of the inner circle around Abad Santos, drafted the constitution of the party, became its general secretary, and was later elected secretary of the Socialist Party.[31] In the 1930s a unified peasant movement was created across Central Luzon when a committee was set up to coordinate the activities of the AMT and the Kalipunang Pambansa ng mga Magsasaka sa Pilipinas (National Society of Peasants in the Philippines), or KPMP, based in Nueva Ecija, a larger and more established organization directed by the highly regarded peasant leaders Mateo del Castillo and Juan Feleo.

The political activism of their peasant fathers figured prominently in the lives of many young girls in Central Luzon. Both Filomena Tolentino and Elang Santa Ana were aware of the activities of the AMT and KPMP because their fathers were local leaders of these organizations. Filomena sang and campaigned for peasant and socialist leaders in Pampanga, although she admitted, "I did not know that our activities were political then."[32] Like other young girls in her situation, Filomena engaged in political activities because of her influential relatives and in order to socialize with other young people in the village, and she might not have understood the class politics of the society that surrounded her. Elang was more politically aware, probably because her father, a well-known peasant leader of the KPMP in Nueva Ecija, was imprisoned several times for his politics. She joined a youth organization affiliated with the peasant movement, attended rallies, campaigned for peasant leaders, and went house-to-house eliciting support.

Like Filomena and Elang, Marcosa de la Rosa grew up in a poor peasant family in San Miguel, Bulacan. Her father, Lope de la Rosa, was a national peasant leader and one of the founding members of the AMT. When she was only sixteen, Marcosa participated in youth activities organized by the AMT. Like Elang's father, Lope de la Rosa was frequently in prison, and this prompted the young Marcosa to play a more public role in the peasant organization. As she recalled, "My father was touted as the *Hari ng mga Bandido*, 'King of the Bandits,' in major newspapers because he often fought for peasants' rights against the *hacenderos*. I often spoke in political rallies, and even though I was very young then I was not ashamed because I wanted to refute the things they said about my father."[33] Marcosa remembered how her family suffered because of her father's constant absence, yet she never lost faith in him and attributed her early politicization to his influence. He had made her aware of the "struggle between the landlords and peasants."[34]

On November 7, 1938, the Socialist Party and the Communist Party merged, believing that they would be more effective if their political efforts were united.[35] The merger was ratified at a public gathering of Communists at the Central Opera House in Manila, and Crisanto Evangelista was named chairman and Pedro Abad Santos vice chairman of the new PKP (Merger of the Communist and Socialist Parties).[36] The immediate program advanced by the party called for a popular national and united front of all labor and peasant organizations against fascism and the perceived threat of Japanese aggression in the region. By this point it was becoming clear that Japan, the foremost imperial power in Asia, was forging alliances with fascist regimes in Europe and seeking to advance its interests. The freedom enjoyed by the Communist Party was supported by Manuel Quezon's Commonwealth administration, which believed a united Philippines was needed to thwart Japanese aggression. Although the organizational merger of the two parties came gradually, by 1940 the Left had become a powerful force in the country.

The merger also increased the influence of the Communist Party in Central Luzon, where the PKP promoted itself as the "champion of the masses," who were neglected by the elite interests and politics of the Commonwealth government. The peasantry in Central Luzon responded vigorously, engaging in strikes and joining the various peasant organizations. Between 1939 and 1940 five to twenty thousand villagers, mostly members of the KPMP, marched throughout Nueva Ecija demanding that landlords divide the harvest fairly and stop evicting their tenants. In other parts of Central Luzon, such as Pampanga and Bulacan, several thousand farmers demonstrated, protested, and refused to pay rent. These public displays of discontent and peasant unity culminated in 1939 with a huge parade in Nueva Ecija that celebrated the merger of the two biggest peasant organizations at that time—the KPMP and AMT.[37] Marcosa remembered those demonstrations well:

> I was only sixteen years old when I became active in the peasant organization founded by my father. I was always with many other girls, even though there was no women's movement then. We always went to rallies. And we had a uniform—a white shirt and a red skirt. We also fixed our hair a certain way. And we always wore this during demonstrations. We all dressed alike, we all walked together, we all sang and cheered together.[38]

Toward the end of the 1930s peasants in Central Luzon realized that their power lay in their numbers, peasant organizations contributed to their economic security, and protests and demonstrations were their most viable weapons. But the coming of the war would disrupt this peasant mobilization and put the solidarity of the peasants to its ultimate test.

The Japanese Occupation

In 1931 Japan occupied Manchuria and established a zone of economic and political dominance throughout the region.[39] Through the ideology of what it termed the Greater East Asia Co-prosperity Sphere, Japan saw its occupation of Asia as an opportunity not only to control the region's vastly rich resources of oil, tin, rubber, and other valuable commodities but, perhaps more important, to free Asia from Western rule.[40] On December 7, 1941, Japan bombed Pearl Harbor in Hawaii, neutralizing the American Pacific Fleet, and in rapid succession occupied the Philippines, Borneo, Malaya (later Malaysia), Singapore, South Burma, and the Dutch East Indies (later Indonesia). In the early morning hours of December 8 the Japanese army intensified its invasion of the Philippines by attacking U.S. bases in Bataan, Pampanga, Zambales, Baguio, and Davao in Mindanao. At Clark Air Force Base in Pampanga American aircraft were destroyed. These attacks effectively eliminated the air defenses of the Philippines and crippled the U.S. Armed Forces in the Far East (USAFFE).[41]

On January 2, 1942, the Japanese entered the capital city of Manila and immediately took control.[42] Within a few days, according to Teodoro Agoncillo, the city "looked like an orphan," with about one-sixth of the six hundred thousand inhabitants abandoning their homes and fleeing for refuge to the provinces.[43] Government offices were shut down, schools and universities were closed, transportation was halted, and other public facilities were neglected, leading to a blackout of the city. People rushed to the banks to withdraw their money while storeowners raised the prices of prime commodities to astronomical levels. All emergency hospitals were put on alert.[44] There was confusion everywhere as people attempted to survive amid the air raids and chaos.

From the beginning, the Commonwealth government and Filipinos resisted the Japanese Occupation, regarding the invasion not as "liberation from Western rule," as Japanese propaganda insisted, but as a threat to their long-coveted dream of independence. This dream seemingly vanished when, faced with the inevitability of defeat, Commonwealth president Quezon, along with General Douglas MacArthur, the commanding general of USAFFE, evacuated the Philippines in March 1942.[45] With their departure American and Filipino military forces, left to fend for themselves, consolidated their defenses in Bataan and Corregidor. The Japanese, with fresh reinforcements and new military plans, mounted attacks on these bases, and by May 6, 1942, after three months of fighting, the USAFFE had surrendered and all organized resistance in the Philippines ended.[46] The country was now under Japanese control. After defeating the United States in the Philippines and other Western colonial governments in Southeast Asia, the Japanese began transforming the military, political, and economic structures within their occupied territories.[47]

In October 1943 Jose P. Laurel became president of the Second Philippine Republic, and he soon called on other prominent elites to join him in the new regime. But this "Filipino" government was under the firm control of the Japanese, who ruled the Philippines through a military police organization called the Kempei Tai.[48] Filipinos everywhere feared the Kempei Tai, which used coercive measures to enforce every aspect of the occupation.[49] Most of the Kempei Tai soldiers behaved in a "most insolent manner" toward the Filipinos, and incidents such as plundering homes, abusing and raping of women, bayoneting those who refused to salute, and slapping faces were dreaded by locals as routine activities of the Japanese.[50] Their harsh methods were designed to intimidate Filipinos who refused to cooperate. But it was not only the Kempei Tai that instilled fear and resentment among Filipinos. A group of pro-Japanese Filipinos welcomed and supported the Japanese military in their drive to occupy the country. In the barrios the Sakdals, a mass-based group that had fought against the Americans in the 1930s, reorganized and renamed the Ganap, acted as the intelligence arm of the Japanese military. While some Ganap members were opportunists who sought to profit from collaboration, many were fervent nationalists who had been critical of the Quezon administration and truly believed that the Japanese would give the Philippines its independence.[51]

The Japanese and their collaborators almost immediately gained a reputation for being brutal and inhumane, and by mid-1942, 625,800 Japanese soldiers were stationed in the Philippines to control the population through propaganda, "forced labor, starvation, torture, insult, plunder, violence and deprivation of human rights."[52] Many Filipinos believed that leaving the cities was the most effective way to avoid the Japanese, and evacuees from Manila, for example, sought refuge in Bulacan, Pampanga, Tarlac, Batangas, Laguna, and Tayabas in Central and Southern Luzon.[53] But it soon became apparent that Central Luzon would not provide much refuge. Because of its proximity to the capital, it was probably the most policed region in the Philippines. Pampanga and Bataan, where U.S. military headquarters were located, were the first provinces to fall under Japanese control. In Talavera, Nueva Ecija, Japanese troops began arriving shortly after Christmas 1941 and stormed the town center in January 1942.[54]

Women were the most vulnerable to the abuses of the Japanese Army. Unable to flee, Filipina women in Manila and in Central and

Southern Luzon were confronted with incredibly difficult circumstances. Rosenda Torres was a sixteen-year-old student in Arenas, Pampanga, when the Japanese invaded. She remembered villagers talking constantly about the coming of the Japanese, but she never expected to experience their brutality firsthand. Her brother, a soldier in the Philippine Armed Forces, participated in the infamous Death March, which took place after the fall of Bataan on April 9, 1942, when about seventy thousand captured American and Filipino soldiers were forced to march more than a hundred kilometers from Bataan to Tarlac with hardly any food or water and under the brutal bayonets of the Japanese.[55] Hundreds died on the march, including Rosenda's brother. In June the Japanese arrived in Rosenda's barrio and immediately set about harassing and arresting villagers who refused to welcome them, including Rosenda's father, another brother, and some cousins. Both her father and brother were imprisoned and subjected to the "water cure" treatment, a method of torture that involved forcing them to swallow several gallons of water before pumping their stomachs, causing water and blood to flow from different orifices in their bodies.[56] Although they survived the ordeal, Rosenda's cousin was shot by the Japanese, and she became convinced of the arbitrariness, irrationality, and brutality of Japanese rule.[57]

When the war began, Filomena Tolentino expected to continue selling fruits and vegetables in her village in Floridablanca, Pampanga. But in June 1942 she had her first encounter with the Japanese. While she was walking around the town center with friends, Japanese soldiers forced the women to bow down and salute them. When they failed to salute properly, the soldiers slapped and threatened them with bayonets. When a Filipino man intervened and explained to the soldiers that the women did not understand their orders, they were spared. Nonetheless, they were forced to stand in the sun for three hours, and the soldiers taunted them as prostitutes and threatened to rape them. The experience, which brought tears to Filomena's eyes fifty years later, confirmed the stories she had already heard about the brutality of Japanese soldiers, especially with regard to women. She recalled:

> The women were being captured by the Japanese, raped, and forced to serve the Japanese. The men were forced to give them rice and their carabaos and pull their carts for them. If they don't do it, they'll kill them. We heard that the Americans already surrendered and that the Japanese were killing people wherever they encountered them.[58]

Like Filomena, Felisa Cuyugan, who was twenty-five at the time of the Japanese occupation, vividly remembered running and crossing rivers around Central Luzon to escape the oncoming troops. Her husband, Vivencio Cuyugan, a socialist mayor from San Fernando, Pampanga, refused to collaborate with the Japanese even though they offered him the governorship of the province. Instead he gathered arms and ammunition from his municipality and recruited men to resist the Japanese advance. But, as Felisa recalled, when news reached them that "hundreds of soldiers" were coming to arrest him, they headed for the mountains. She later heard that the Japanese killed men in their town in retaliation.[59]

Puring Bulatao, like Felisa, was also harassed by the Japanese because her husband, Rosendo Feleo, was a peasant leader and the son of Juan Feleo, a well-known peasant and communist leader of the 1920s and 1930s. Puring wrote her own version of the events during the war:

In May 1943, [Rosendo] Feleo was taken by the Japanese Imperial Army, and was released after 5 days. Japanese intelligence officers took him to the province of Nueva Ecija to speak at public meetings in support of the Japanese. But after a month or so, while at another rally, he escaped. The Japanese Army then took me and my own father to Fort Santiago where we were detained for two nights and three days. The Japanese Army released me after they realized that Feleo was under their authority when he escaped and that I and my family did not have any knowledge of the whole thing. Their next step was to get me and [so they] took me to the province of Nueva Ecija and like Rosendo, I was ordered to speak before public meetings, where I was introduced as the wife of Rosendo and the daughter-in-law of Juan Feleo. I was there to plead for their surrender to the Japanese government. I attended at least 4 times and after the meetings, I was slapped by a Japanese soldier. Apparently, they came to know that I did not plead for the surrender of the two men and that they were using me to get to Rosendo. They continued their hunt and eventually they found him. An intelligence officer took me to see him. Rosendo had blooded eyes and he was black and blue all over. They allowed us to stay together for one night and one day. After a week or so, Rosendo came home. The Japanese military decided to bring the entire family of Juan Feleo to Cabiao, Nueva Ecija as hostages—we were seven in all. We lived in the big house about five houses away from the Japanese headquarters. We were never allowed to go out of the house. The general idea I believe was to keep us totally *incommunicado*. We stayed in their custody for at least six months.[60]

While most women were not imprisoned in their homes by Japanese soldiers, they had similar stories of personal abuse and violence during the war.

Stories, rumors, and gossip played an important role in shaping popular perceptions of Japanese rule in the Philippines.[61] From the beginning of the occupation, cities and villages were rife with rumors about the Japanese. In Manila, the circulation of rumor functioned, according to Vicente Rafael, to both "displace truth" about the war and "shape the texture of everyday life."[62] Agoncillo, himself a World War II survivor, left several dramatic accounts of life under the Japanese. He wrote:

> Life seemed to be at a standstill. . . . The people generally kept indoors, exchanged news or rumors, and waited for developments. Rumors of alleged Japanese bestiality committed in the towns through which they passed on their way to Manila gave shivers to women, for it was bruited about that many comely women in the provinces were raped by the Japanese soldiers. True or not, the Filipinos in Manila looked at the Japanese with extreme suspicion.[63]

Rumors about death, disaster, and Japanese cruelty reflected the grim reality of the war, but at the same time they provided an ideological justification for Filipinos to challenge the hierarchy between the new colonizer and the colonized.[64]

As the war progressed rumors became even more central to the everyday lives of Filipinos. The circulation of news regarding enemy activities was aided, in part, by the Japanese government's efforts to spread propaganda and gain support within Philippine society. Central to the Japanese war effort was persuading Filipinos to end their political and psychological dependence on the United States and assist the Japanese, their fellow Asians, in the war effort.[65] They therefore sought the participation of native elites in the administration of the government, giving them primary responsibility for running the affairs of the country.[66] In attempting to erase Western cultural legacies in the Philippines, the Japanese also promoted the use of native languages, customs, and practices. They allowed existing religious organizations and neighborhood associations to flourish in many areas of the Philippines in the hope that this would win them some goodwill.[67] Despite the grim reality surrounding them, meetings of these associations were often festive, although they were punctuated by required (and monitored) political slogans praising Japanese rule.[68]

Many villagers, especially in Central Luzon, used these meetings to gather and exchange stories about the Japanese. Women were convinced of the "inhumanity of the invaders" based on stories they heard from other people whether they were true or not. Felisa Cuyugan stressed that "the women in the villages had to look ugly. Why? Because the Japanese were raping them. If not, then they hide in the forest."[69] This perception during the war was confirmed by Maxima San Pedro, a young peasant woman from Talavera, Nueva Ecija:

> Women were in a dangerous position because the Japanese were raping them. We were very scared of the Japanese. Even though we were ugly, the Japanese wanted us. But especially when you were still young and pretty, you cannot escape them. So we were very scared.[70]

Luz del Castillo recalled that her family had to hide in the mountains for nine days because they got word that the Japanese were about to raid their town in Pampanga. "We were trapped there for nine days," she narrated, "but when we went down to the village, we did not see any trace of a Japanese raid." However she still believed that they successfully "hid from the Japanese who tried to attack us."[71] Although reality and fiction were often intertwined in rumors, women and their families took these rumors seriously.[72]

For many of the women in Central Luzon the truth of the rumors was irrelevant. Hearing and then telling stories about other people's experiences with the Japanese justified the fear and hatred they felt toward the colonizers and at the same time allowed them to commiserate with the suffering of other Filipinos. Even after many years the memory of the war remained fresh in their minds. While they had known hardship at a young age, the suffering they experienced under the Japanese was incomparable. True or not, these women believed that they had two choices in the war: be victimized by the Japanese or resist them. As a result many women in Central Luzon decided to fight.

The Hukbo ng Bayan Laban sa Hapon

On March 29, 1942, peasant guerrillas marched from every direction in Central Luzon to "a clearing in the great forest that joins the corners of

Pampanga, Tarlac and Nueva Ecija," and established the Hukbalahap.[73] The Hukbalahap (People's Anti-Japanese Liberation Army) was created by officers of the Communist Party (after its merger with the Socialist Party) and leaders of peasant organizations in Central Luzon.[74] The setting and ceremony marking its founding were simple. Around a small, wooden table, guerrillas delivered enraged speeches against the Japanese, who at that moment were defeating the armies of the United States and the Philippines. While the men feasted on carabao the Huks devised a set of guiding principles and a military program for the anti-Japanese movement. From the beginning, they believed that the movement should extend beyond the Communist Party and its affiliated organizations, which had already suffered great setbacks.[75] The leaders of the (merged) Communist Party, PKP — Crisanto Evangelista and Pedro Abad Santos — fell early in the war. On January 25, 1942, both were arrested by the Japanese in Manila and imprisoned in Fort Santiago. Evangelista was executed in May 1943. Abad Santos was released after two years in prison but remained extremely weak and died in Pampanga in early 1945.[76] The Hukbalahap needed new leadership and a new strategy. At the end of the weeklong conference, a Military Committee was elected composed of Luis Taruc, Casto Alejandrino, Bernardo Poblete, and the lone female guerrilla leader Felipa Culala (Dayang-Dayang). Luis Taruc was chosen as the military leader of the Hukbalahap, a position that earned him the title of Huk Supremo (Supreme Leader). Members of the Hukbalahap were simply called the Huks, a name Taruc knew "would live in Philippine History."[77]

From that forest clearing the Huks launched an intensive campaign to organize effective mass resistance against the Japanese. First, the leadership conceived of an armed force to harass and attack the enemy. The arming of the Huks, however, proved to be difficult. When the Japanese first attacked the Philippines, the party had issued an appeal for the formation of a united anti-Japanese front and urged the arming of the people, but President Quezon and General MacArthur ignored their proposals. The Huks therefore had to scavenge weapons abandoned by American and Philippine military units to fight the Japanese, although later they conducted raids against Japanese garrisons to secure more arms and ammunition. In addition to raising an army, the Hukbalahap set out to create a mass-based alliance of mostly peasants and laborers against the Japanese and their collaborators. It welcomed different groups — peasants, workers, youth, women, and even landlords — into their organization. As part of this "united front" policy the Huks avoided peasant-landlord confrontations despite the fact that many peasants believed the "rich people were pro-Japanese."[78] The Japanese did court Filipino elites, and in Central Luzon the Japanese government made no moves to seize the landlords' properties. But the Huks defined resistance to the Japanese as a nationalist war and believed success depended on Filipinos—from all classes, rich and poor—coming together. In some areas in Central Luzon, however, where landlords openly collaborated with the Japanese or abandoned their property to flee to the cities the Huks provided protection to peasants who occupied abandoned lands and refused to pay rent.[79]

In early February 1942 leaders and members of the PKP, the Popular Front Party, the League for the Defense of Democracy, and peasant and labor organizations such as KPMP, AMT, and KAP convened in Cabiao, Nueva Ecija, to create a structure for unified resistance to the Japanese.[80] At this meeting the Hukbalahap was recognized as the citizen's army, and the Central Luzon Bureau (CLB) was established to lead the resistance. Dr. Vicente Lava, a world-renowned scientist who had assumed the leadership of the PKP after Evangelista's arrest, was elected head of the CLB.[81] At its inception, the Hukbalahap adopted a political structure that resembled that of a military organization (see diagram 1).[82] The elected leaders of the Military Committee, Supremo Luis Taruc, and Vice Commander Casto Alejandrino assumed the highest authority and took command of the army regiments. Other elected officers included Mateo del Castillo, head of Organization and Communication, which was responsible for coordinating the relationship between the leadership and its support base; Juan Feleo, head of the United Front, which was responsible for propaganda and mobilizing support for the guerrilla movement; Primitivo Arrogante, head of Intelligence and Education, which was in charge of political education and providing information on enemy activity; and Emeterio Timban, head of Finance (Provision and Management), which was responsible for supplying provisions and other necessities to the guerrillas. According to Alfredo Saulo, the CLB was the "wartime version of the [Communist] party's politburo."[83] Indeed, leaders of the Hukbalahap were commonly (and perhaps mistakenly) referred to as the Politburo. While PKP officers did assume important responsibilities in the Hukbalahap leadership, the resistance movement encompassed more than members of the Communist Party and its affiliated organizations.[84]

Once organized the Huks established camps in various locations from the forests near Arayat, Pampanga, to the clearings in Bulacan and

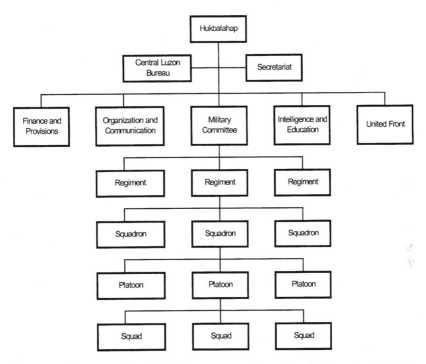

Diagram 1. Structure of the Hukbalahap, ca. 1943. (From Teresita Maceda, *Mga Tinig Mula sa Ibaba*, 120; and Politburo Exhibit O-180-253, "Milestones in the History of the Communist Party of the Philippines")

the mountains of the Sierra Madre (see map 2). The forest camps were temporary bases distant from the villages and the reach of the Japanese military where the Huks built makeshift huts to concentrate their numbers, plan and organize attacks, and recuperate after battles against the Japanese. These camps quickly became headquarters for the Huk-balahap where leaders of the movement discussed and formulated poli-cies for the resistance movement. The nature of the guerrilla struggle made it hard to establish any permanent Huk headquarters during the Japanese Occupation, although as the resistance movement gathered strength semipermanent camps were built, located mostly in Pampanga.

Most support for the Huks, however, came from the villages of Central and Southern Luzon, and it was leaders from the largest peasant organizations in the country, such as the KPMP and the AMT, who formed the core of the Hukbalahap.[85] They summoned their members, who willingly gave their support to the resistance movement. But Huk leaders knew that mobilizing villagers, who were under constant surveillance by the Japanese and their collaborators, required careful planning and organization. The guerrillas saw the Japanese-sponsored neighborhood associations formed as part of their imperial policy of encouraging native rule and generating support for the occupation as the most effective avenues for mobilization. The Huk leadership urged its members to form Sandatahang Tanod ng Bayan (Barrio United Defense Corps), or BUDCs, under the guise of these neighborhood organizations. These BUDCs, composed of KPMP and AMT members and ordinary peasant villagers, organized popular support for the Huks, set up local governments, shielded the harvest from the Japanese, and attacked Filipino collaborators.[86] The BUDCs rapidly transformed many of the barrios of Central and Southern Luzon into protected zones and safe havens for guerrilla resistance, and Huk guerrillas moved constantly between the forest camps and these secure villages.

According to Benedict Kerkvliet the growth of the Hukbalahap in 1942–43 was remarkable. In April 1942 it had less than three hundred guerrillas. Less than a year later it claimed over ten thousand members, and by the war's end about twelve thousand guerrillas had joined the Huk ranks. Between 1942 and 1944 the Huk army expanded from five squadrons to seventy-six.[87] But this military force was only a partial reflection of the Huks' influence. While first and foremost it was an armed force, Bill Pomeroy wrote, in the popular mind the Hukbalahap "had become synonymous with the Philippine liberation movement."[88] By the end of the war the Hukbalahap had developed from an army into a movement with an aggregation of forces that included peasant unions, trade unions, nationalist and progressive organizations, and mass support in the barrios.[89] Village networks in Central and Southern Luzon sustained this movement by providing much-needed recruits and supporters. In the end the Hukbalahap was not just an organized army—it was a movement that claimed thousands of supporters.

The First Mobilization of Huk Women

At first the Huks did not have a systematic plan for recruitment, especially for the recruitment of women. When the Huk Military Committee was established in March 1942 its strategy was to recruit male peasants to be trained as soldiers. Although this strategy of targeting young men who could easily leave their homes was successful, the predominantly male Huk leadership soon recognized that the male-dominated military alone could not win the war.[90] Women could also provide a crucial base of support for the Huk movement, and despite the absence of a formal recruitment strategy women quickly became an important part of the national liberation movement.[91]

A significant number of women joined the movement after its formation and forced the leadership to reconsider its gendered recruitment policy. Women themselves placed the issue of their participation on the agenda of the Huk movement. Outraged by stories, and in many cases direct experience, of Japanese brutality, and sometimes fearful for their personal safety, many young women from Central and Southern Luzon and even Manila responded to the call for mobilization. Most were between the ages of fifteen and thirty-five, single, and lived in peasant households. Some responded by joining the Huk camps and donating their services directly to the guerrilla movement. But most stayed in the villages, working within the BUDCs to collect supplies, money, and information for the guerrillas.[92] These village-based BUDCs became important sites for female mobilization and politicization where women, operating under the nominal protection of the Japanese, could communicate with other villagers, discreetly gather information about the Japanese, and organize support for guerrilla activities without attracting suspicion.

Seventeen-year-old Maxima San Pedro hated the Japanese. While she did not join the Huks in their forest camps, their presence made her feel secure in her barrio San Ricardo in Talavera, Nueva Ecija, and she remained a Huk sympathizer throughout the war.[93] On the other hand Teofista Valerio, a twenty-two-year-old peasant woman from Cabiao, Nueva Ecija, chose to live in the Huk camps when the Japanese military began to patrol her town and a soldier began to pursue her relentlessly. Fearing for her life, she joined the Huks and did not return home until after the war.[94] Japanese brutality also inspired reluctant recruits such as Avelina Santos from Anao, Mexico, Pampanga, to join the guerrillas. Although she had thought she could continue to make a living as a seamstress during the occupation, when a Japanese raid led to the death of a friend's father and uncle and the burning of several houses in her village she left the barrio for the mountains. Scared when she left home, she immediately felt safe and secure among the Huk guerrillas.[95]

Women who joined and supported the Hukbalahap shared the experiences of Maxima, Avelina, and Teofista. When the Japanese rounded up about 150 men in their barrio, Maria and Felicidad Angeles of Santa Rosa, Nueva Ecija, saw their relatives killed by the Japanese, including their father and brother, and many other women lost relatives and neighbors during the systematic and arbitrary raids the Japanese conducted in the villages of Central Luzon.[96] In mid-1942 Candelaria Pangan from Santa Ana, Pampanga, was working as a teacher in her village when the Japanese arrived. She remembered:

> Even before the Japanese came . . . I was teaching reading to children in our barrio. One day, a Japanese soldier suddenly entered my classroom and asked me what I was hiding. I told him nothing, but he just slapped my face repeatedly. He was insisting that there were guerrillas in our barrio and that I should reveal their identities. I told him I did not know what he was talking about. He slapped me some more and let me go.[97]

The abuse did not end there. After two weeks the Japanese once again raided her village, and when Candelaria heard machine-gun fire and stepped onto her patio she was instantly hit by a stray bullet. Although the wound was minor, the incident convinced her and her parents to seek refuge with the Huk guerrillas at Mount Arayat. After three weeks Candelaria returned to her village, but she continued to support the guerrillas. "Of course, I knew who the guerrillas were," she recalled, laughing, "but there was no way I would ever reveal their names and betray them."[98] As the war dragged on, more and more women joined the Huks as fighters and supporters, determined not to end up as victims of the Japanese.

But traumatic personal experience of Japanese brutality does not fully explain the decision of these women to join the guerrilla movement. Although Japanese repression drove many women to join the Huks, their recruitment was shaped by much broader social networks. Foremost among these were women's political ties with established peasant and leftist movements such as the KPMP, AMT, PKM (Pambansang Kaisahan ng mga Magbubukid, or National Peasants' Union), and Communist Party. Women who were already members of these radical organizations often viewed joining the Huks as a logical continuation of their prewar activism. Elang Santa Ana was one of these women. Politicized by her father, she believed, like him, that "the system in the farms consisted of a master and slave relationship."[99] As a leader of a KPMP-affiliated youth organization her main task was to encourage other young people to support the movement, debate national issues, and attend rallies. When the war broke out, she received a letter from her father, who had joined the Hukbalahap, urging her to do the same. Already an activist, Elang wanted to continue her political activities and willingly joined the Huks. Although she was disappointed not to be reunited with her father when she arrived in the camps, she continued to work for the Hukbalahap, and by the time she was reunited with her father in 1944 she was a full-fledged Huk cadre.[100]

Like Elang, Puring Bulatao, a student at the University of the Philippines, was also an experienced activist. Born in Caloocan City in Manila, her father was a militant labor leader, and when she enrolled at the university in 1937 she was swept up in the highly political atmosphere. She immediately joined two radical student organizations, the National Students' Union and the League for the Defense of Democracy, where she met equally radical students who campaigned for political rights and debated the threat of fascism in Asia. Her activism deepened when she married Rosendo Feleo, the son of peasant leader Juan Feleo. After her brief imprisonment and several months of house arrest caused by her association with the Feleos, she joined the Hukbalahap, convinced that the only way to fight Japanese imperialism was "for the people to be united."[101] While she joined the guerrilla movement because of constant harassment by the Japanese, Puring's political connections also inspired her. The hard life of the Huk guerrillas, who shared her political convictions, was a much more attractive prospect than being imprisoned again by the Japanese.

Many other women joined the Hukbalahap for explicitly political reasons. Juana Fajardo from Gapan, Nueva Ecija, an active member of a youth group affiliated with the KPMP, her parents' peasant organization, heeded her group's call to join the Hukbalahap.[102] Cion Amorao, a peasant from Nueva Ecija and a member of the youth and women's division of the Socialist Party of the Philippines, to which her father belonged, also decided to follow the lead of the young men and women who belonged to her prewar political organization and join the Huk guerrillas.[103] Vicenta Lacanilao, from San Miguel, Bulacan, was also a youth supporter of the PKM and joined the Huks along with the other PKM youth members.[104] Others, such as Marcosa de la Rosa, Felisa Cuyugan, and Maxima San Pedro, were already involved in the small women's division of the KPMP and the Communist Party. As Teofista Valerio explained, the Huks did not have a difficult time recruiting people to their organization:

Wherever the Huks came, people responded well. Before the Japanese came, there were already organizations all over Central

Luzon, with many sympathizers and many demonstrations happening. All we had to do as Huks was to organize the people, and in the end they were all united.[105]

While these women had not exercised leadership roles in prewar leftist and peasant organizations, their prior activist experience helped them in their new roles as members of the Hukbalahap.

But it was personal and extended family networks that played the most important role in recruiting women to the Hukbalahap. Kinship relations, crucial to survival and security in Philippine rural societies, became even more important during the Japanese Occupation. Familial and village networks formed the core of the Hukbalahap and BUDCs as families and neighbors provided mutual protection from the Japanese and their collaborators and assisted each other in the daily battle for survival. Men who joined the Hukbalahap did not come to the movement by themselves but took with them other members of their families, including wives, sisters, and even mothers. Many women became part of the Hukbalahap because they had close links with male members. Networks of family, relatives, friends, and close neighbors ensured a regular flow of women ready and able to work for the Hukbalahap.

Most of the young women who joined the movement were recruited by their fathers, the majority of whom belonged to the PKP and peasant organizations such as the KPMP and AMT in Central Luzon. These PKP and peasant leaders left behind homes and possessions in the city and the village to settle in the forest camps and often reconstituted their homes in the Huk barrios and camps, bringing their spouses and children with them. Mateo del Castillo was a labor union leader in Manila who became an officer of the Communist Party and subsequently a top political adviser in the Hukbalahap.[106] Born the son of a Spanish landowner in Batangas, Southern Luzon, del Castillo sold the land he inherited from his father and moved to Manila where he invested in a restaurant, boardinghouses, and other real estate. In the 1930s he provided lodging in his boardinghouse in Manila for peasant leaders and labor union members and frequently participated in the peasant movement, speaking at demonstrations, lobbying Congress on behalf of tenants' rights, and writing in English to communicate their demands to government officials. Arrested several times for his political activities, he lost his land, property, and business interests because of his involvement in the movement but remained a committed labor and peasant leader and a communist.[107] Despite their hardships, del Castillo's wife and six children understood his political commitments and supported his activism, and from early on his children were educated about the inequalities in Philippine society and encouraged to join youth organizations allied with the Communist Party. When the war began, the entire family left Manila for Pampanga where they joined the Hukbalahap, including del Castillo's daughters, Luz and Zenaida.

Zenaida was del Castillo's youngest child, only eleven at the time of the Japanese Occupation, yet she was already aware of her father's politics.[108] She knew her father's radical friends by name—Feleo, Capadocia, Robles, Manahan—all national figures who had frequented their restaurant and transformed it into a labor headquarters. While she understood that her father's financial ruin was a result of his "devotion" to the movement, she was devastated when her father was arrested for his political activities. She later recalled:

> I did not really join the movement. . . . The whole family was always involved. I was born there. I have no other way but to exist within. I was already there. When I was captured [in the late 1940s] and asked, "Why did you join?" I answered, "Actually, I did not join. I was born there."[109]

During the war, members of the del Castillo family were constantly separated from one another and the children rarely saw their father, but, as Zenaida explained, "we were not so affected that we were all separated since we already grew up that way. I was already formed by the movement, so I did not question it anymore. I am part of this, so I work accordingly." She added poignantly, "We all loved our father. We all followed his work and ideology because we wanted to be united in our family."[110] Eventually Zenaida assumed her own role and responsibilities within the revolutionary movement.

Luz del Castillo, her sister, was eighteen years old when the war began and had a much more sophisticated understanding of her father's politics and the Hukbalahap. She had always believed what her father taught her, that "all strata in society should be involved in the struggle for social reform," so she joined a youth organization and later the Philippine Students' Union, where she worked against tuition hikes and supported the issue of land reform in solidarity with the peasant movement.[111] According to Luz the family had been "wanted by the Japanese and their spies" even before the decision was made to join the Hukbalahap, but the decision was not taken merely to protect themselves. To Luz becoming a Huk meant continuing to fight for the rights of Filipinos, and "the enemy was not only the Japanese, but also the many Filipinos who collaborated with the Japanese, who followed whatever the Japanese wanted."[112] Luz clearly understood and believed in the Hukbalahap movement, and, although she rarely saw members of her family while working as a Huk, she accepted these sacrifices. For both Luz and Zenaida the goal "to help the oppressed and fight the foreign enemy" was strong, but family loyalty and their desire to support their beloved father also made them devoted Hukbalahap women. Luz recalled:

> My father made me realize these things. . . . Even though we were not born poor or we were not oppressed, the heart of my father went to the ones who were oppressed. This was what he was fighting for, and he got all of us involved. So we were all convinced that he was right. So all of us joined him, helped him.[113]

Marcosa de la Rosa was also inspired by her father, Lope de la Rosa, who was a well-known peasant leader of the KPMP before the war.[114] When the Japanese invaded the Philippines Marcosa's father quickly became a squadron commander of the Hukbalahap. Marcosa, who lived in Bulacan, was already married and had a child when the Hukbalahap was organized, but she did not hesitate to join the Huks, leaving her baby with her mother. She never regretted the decision to join both her father and her husband in the camps. Marcosa attributed her political involvement to her father, who convinced her to join the peasant movement and tirelessly explained the need for peasants to band together.[115] Bella Simpauco's father, Alejandro Simpauco, was a leader of Pedro Abad Santos's Socialist Party of the Philippines and moved on to assume a leadership post in the Hukbalahap. She remembered her father fondly and his willingness to risk his life for the sake of the peasants. When her father summoned her from their home in Tarlac, she did not hesitate to join him among the guerrillas.[116]

But it was not only Communist and peasant leaders who recruited their children to the Hukbalahap. Ordinary members of these political organizations also recruited their kin to the movement. Maria Manalang, for example, was recruited at the age of fifteen by her peasant father, a member of the Socialist Party and a Huk guerrilla. Like many girls she rarely saw her father in the forest camps, but she never doubted his cause as she worked willingly for the Hukbalahap.[117] Both Vicenta Soliman from San Miguel, Bulacan, and Anita Laban-Laban from Kalayaan, Laguna, joined the Hukbalahap because their peasant fathers had joined. At first they thought their fathers just wanted to protect them from the Japanese, but they soon realized that their fathers, who were both members of prewar peasant organizations, believed their daughters could make a significant contribution to the resistance movement in Luzon. Vicenta and Anita stayed in the Hukbalahap until the end of the war.[118]

Araceli Mallari's relationship with her parents, especially her father, also convinced her to join the guerrillas. Born to a middle-class family in Manila, she was a sophomore studying at the University of Santo Tomas when the war began. Her father was very strict with her, never allowed her to talk to men, and constantly monitored her activities. Just before the war her friend Puring Bulatao introduced her to the League for the Defense of Democracy, an organization composed of radical students and intellectuals. Although she wanted to be more active in the group, her father prevented her from leaving the house, and after an incident in which her father hit her with a bamboo stick she decided to run away from home. With the help of Puring she made contact with the Hukbalahap, and two days later she packed her belongings, met her guide in Tutuban in Manila, took the train to Bulacan, and trekked to the Huk camps in Candaba, Pampanga. The day after she disappeared her photograph appeared in several major newspapers under the headline "Wanted: For 200 Pesos." Although initially inspired to join the Huks by her desire to escape her strict father, Araceli remained with the guerrillas throughout the wartime period.[119]

Husbands as well as fathers convinced women to become Huks.[120] As demonstrated by the experiences of Pasencia David, whose husband was a Huk commander, and Felisa Cuyugan, whose husband was the former mayor of Pampanga and a Huk member, women often joined the movement to be close to their husbands. Pasencia David from San Fernando, Pampanga, was only eighteen when she married Fajardo David, a peasant member of the Socialist Party. Pasencia became involved in the organization, attending meetings and rallies with other peasant men and women, and when her husband became a soldier in Huk Squadron No. 1 she also joined the Hukbalahap.[121] Felisa Cuyugan also joined the Huks to support her husband, Vivencio Cuyugan, and when he became ill during the war she stayed to tend him in the Huk camps.[122]

Many women became guerrillas and active supporters because their husbands were already officers and soldiers in the Hukbalahap. Like Felisa, Elena Gonzales from Santo Rosario, Mexico, Pampanga, followed her husband into the Hukbalahap after he was detained and tortured by the Japanese along with several other men in their town. By pleading with the Japanese officers Elena was able to secure her husband's release, and after she nursed him back to health he joined his cousins as a soldier in a Hukbalahap squadron. Elena stayed in the barrio to supply food and medicine to the guerrillas. Elena rarely saw her husband and often walked for hours to attend meetings in the Huk camps, leaving her children with neighbors, but she accepted these sacrifices not only to fight "the enemy she detested" but also to be closer to her Huk husband.[123]

Silvestre Liwanag was already an active member of the Socialist-affiliated peasant organization AMT when he and Rosita Manuel, also from Lubao, Pampanga, were married before the war. Both their fathers were peasant leaders who fought landlords to lower tenants' rents. They were also orphaned early, leaving Silvestre to assume his father's farming responsibilities while at the same time taking a leadership role in the Socialist Party. During the war he became the commander of a Hukbalahap squadron. Since their elopement (and marriage), Rosita had actively supported her husband's political activities, and her life had been unpredictable and even dangerous. However, she accepted and understood her husband's commitment to the peasant cause."[124] Although she described herself as not very political, in the end she decided that the best way to support her husband's cause was to join the Hukbalahap and to stay with Liwanag whenever he was in the camps. "How can you not join," she explained, "when you know that your husband possessed those principles? You will believe what he believes and follow him. Of course he was my husband. Whether they were fighting against the Japanese or for the peasants, I understood him."[125] Rosita's testimony, which reflected views shared by many Huk women, reveals the value that women like her placed on their personal relationships (over their political intentions). Although Rosita always understood the political implications of her actions, her loyalty to the Huk movement began and ended with her devotion to her husband.

For women not yet married during the war, networks of family and friends provided crucial links to the Huk organization. Leonila Sayco was seventeen when the war disrupted her schooling and forced her to spend most of her time at home in San Rafael, Pampanga. When her brother, who had already joined the Huks and was afraid Leonila might be victimized by the Japanese, asked her to join him, she agreed and accompanied him to the Huk camps in Arayat. Although she rarely saw her brother for the remainder of the war, she stayed in the movement.[126] At the start of the war, Elena Sawit gave up her job as a dressmaker in

Manila and moved back home to Licab, Nueva Ecija, to help her family. Although she "hated the Japanese," she admitted that she was "not political." But her life in the barrio and her exposure to the Huks changed her. Outraged by stories of Japanese atrocities, she discovered that her male cousins were already part of the Hukbalahap and decided to join the resistance. Together with a female cousin, Elena first became a Huk sympathizer in the barrio, attending meetings, gathering information for the guerrillas, and occasionally helping them in the camps. But she felt she was among family with the Huks and soon joined her cousins in the camps.[127] Similarly, the Valerio sisters, Belen and Amparo, became Huk supporters after their sister Teofista joined the guerrillas. While they stayed at their home in the barrio, they supported the Hukbalahap by providing food and supplies to the guerrillas. The sisters rarely saw or heard from Teofista, but in their minds their support meant helping not only the Huks but also their brave Huk sister.[128] Ana Sula's father, who was a peasant leader before the war, was too old to become a Huk guerrilla by 1942, and he relied on his neighbors to help protect Ana. It was they who recruited her to the Hukbalahap. She recalled attending meetings led by people she knew intimately, and it was this sense of familiarity that gave her the confidence to become a guerrilla and eventually to lead Huk meetings herself. Because everyone in their town was a sympathizer she had no misgivings about joining the Hukbalahap.[129] In provinces that were Huk strongholds villagers recalled that all their neighbors were Huks like themselves, and even after many years they still recognized each other and reminisced about their days as Huks.[130]

Araceli Mallari explained how the Huks mobilized village supporters and built strongholds in Central Luzon:

> In the towns, we tell [people] that the military cannot exist without the masses. It was like the fish in the water: *parang isda at tubig iyan. Ang isda hindi mabubuhay kung wala sa tubig. Kaya, ang tubig ay ang masa, ang gerilya, ang militar ang isda.* [The fish will not survive if not in water. So, water pertains to the masses and the guerrillas are the fish. So, if you will not organize the masses, the guerrilla could not exist.] Where will you hide? Who will feed you?[131]

Indeed, the success of the Huk military operations would have been impossible without the networks of kin, relatives, friends, and neighbors that were such a central part of peasant and rural life in the villages of Central and Southern Luzon.

Women of the Hukbalahap

When women joined the Hukbalahap in the camps and barrios they attended what most of them called the Forest School. Here women and men received an orientation and learned about the goals, organization, and methods of the Hukbalahap. Instructors delivered lectures on a number of different topics, including "Fundamental Spirit," "Military Discipline," "Guerrilla Tactics," and the "United Front." The Huks also organized study meetings in every squadron in which each individual was encouraged to ask questions. Since members of the Hukbalahap came from different backgrounds, with varying degrees of education and political experience, an individual's orientation was carefully planned to cater to his or her needs and abilities. Aside from lessons on the Huk organization, women also learned how to administer first aid. They came to realize that the Hukbalahap was a complex organization. As an army it needed to teach its soldiers "iron discipline" and military techniques. As a movement it desired to transform its recruits into cadres who possessed the skills needed to organize political and practical support in the barrios.

For this reason the most important lecture, "Fundamental Spirit," laid out the guiding principles of the organization and, according to Luis Taruc, "established the character of a revolutionary army, and emphasized the differences between a people's army and the ordinary hired army of the ruling classes."[132] The fundamental spirit of a revolutionary army, insisted the leaders of the Hukbalahap, involved equality between officers and soldiers and the values of comradeship and unity. The core text of the lecture emphasized that

> people with the same political will are called comrades. . . . Comrades should be friendly to one another. Friendship brings about precious mutual help. Unity is strength. The stronger the unity, the greater will the strength be. . . . In order to defeat the enemy, we must be stronger than the enemy. . . . Our officers and soldiers should be friendly to one another, and they will be united into one body.[133]

Although lectures like this one were written principally for the men who comprised the majority of the Huk army, because the leadership allowed women to receive their ideological and practical training alongside men this language of comradeship and equality was implicitly extended to them. Many women remembered the ideas contained in the

"Fundamental Spirit" as the foundation of the Hukbalahap, and these ideas made a deep impression on them.[134] Although she has forgotten the duration of her "schooling," Araceli Mallari remembers that she "learned so much those days" and the "fundamental spirit" was crucial to her development as a Huk cadre.[135]

One part of the "Fundamental Spirit," which described how to enter and leave a barrio, how to work with villagers, and how to spread Huk ideas, had a particular impact on the women. "A revolutionary army" it declared, "should not only love and protect the people. . . . It should help the people wherever it goes." The Huks were expected to do more than fight and protect the people. The requirements were laid out clearly:

> Clean the houses provided by the people. . . . Speak in a friendly tone. . . . Buy and sell things fairly. . . . Return the things we borrow. . . . Pay for the things we destroy. . . . Do not do, and even refuse to do, things which may harm the people. All actions that may encroach upon or harm the people are forbidden. Any offender of this rule will be severely punished. Forcing the people to work for the army is forbidden. Coercion, beating or insulting the people are forbidden. Rape and robbery are forbidden. These are not the actions of a revolutionary army. They are criminal acts. Help the people in plowing, transplanting, harvesting or in cutting wood whenever it does not hinder the actions of the army. Help the people organize, and support the organizations of the people.[136]

As these commands made clear, the Hukbalahap was more than just an army; it was a movement embedded in the community, a fact that was enormously important to Huk women. Both men and women embraced these principles of service, which were designed to break down the distinction and distance between the guerrillas and their peasant supporters. Villagers would feed guerrillas who helped them plant and grow their vegetables. They would hide guerrillas who vowed to stay away when danger was imminent. Preserving and encouraging the bond between Huk soldiers and the communities from which they came not only reflected the social logic of the Huk movement but also made it impossible for the Japanese to distinguish a friend from an enemy, and thus it was impossible for them to wage a successful war of occupation.

The Forest School was often a crucial turning point for women. No longer were they simply the daughters, wives, sisters, or friends of Huk men; they had become cadres and revolutionaries. Through her education in the Forest School, Filomena Tolentino came to understand the larger revolutionary purpose of the Hukbalahap. Almost immediately she felt a new sense of purpose and self-importance, realizing that the Huks needed her "to fight the war and to transform Philippine society."[137] Avelina Santos compared her training to attending a military school as she learned about "military tactics and strategies." Bella Simpauco had similar recollections. The lectures convinced her that she could be a good guerrilla even without any prior experience. Ana Sula, like Bella, remembered studying guerrilla tactics and learning how to ask for food from barrio people. Virginia Calma, who was recruited by her family and friends in the barrio, at first had no idea that the Hukbalahap was a formal organization with goals, principles, and strategies to pursue, but after her schooling she became a committed Huk. When she performed her duties for the movement, she was not just following orders but also acting on her beliefs, and, like most women who joined the Hukbalahap, she remembered, "I felt that I was an essential part of a national liberation movement."[138]

After their schooling, new recruits were immediately integrated into the Hukbalahap structure to perform specific roles in the guerrilla movement. Men were trained to fulfill the roles of political cadres and military soldiers in the squadrons, which occupied the pivotal place within the military-organizational structure (see diagram. 1). Most women did not fit easily into this structure because Huk leaders did not originally intend to recruit and train them as soldiers, underestimating the response of women to the movement and the way familial networks and prewar organizations drew women into it. Thus, while men's roles were clearly defined, women's were ambiguous. Men were immediately given arms and sent to the front line as soldiers and officers where they conducted raids and attacked Japanese garrisons to secure weapons, ambushed enemy soldiers and harassed Japanese collaborators, including landlords and Ganap members. In contrast, when women joined the Huks they were explicitly excluded from combat duty and participated primarily in the support networks of the Hukbalahap.[139]

At first women were assigned to the service divisions of the Hukbalahap, including propaganda, medical, communication (courier duties), organization, intelligence, secretarial, and education. The Huk leadership created these divisions in order to harness support for the resistance movement. The intelligence network monitored Japanese movements inside the barrios, communication workers were responsible for carrying messages and information among guerrillas and between them and the villagers, and organizational teams visited different villages to muster support, often accompanied by propaganda workers who tried to boost popular morale and support through songs and dramatic skits. Those belonging to the educational division gave lectures to other guerrillas about the goals and tactics of the movement. Members of the medical group worked as nurses and caregivers, tending to the sick and wounded, and those who stayed in the Huk camps worked as clerks or secretaries for the Huk leaders. While the official structure emphasized its military arm, these support committees, made up mostly of women, were vital to the success of the Hukbalahap military resistance and to the broader social movement on which it rested.

Members of the education department, who were responsible for the political instruction of Huk members, underwent intensive training. Women who became instructors had to have several weeks of schooling and be able to read and write in Tagalog, Kapampangan, or another regional language.[140] Because of their limited education and political experience only a few women met these standards. Rosenda Torres was one. She was chosen because she had some education and was a skilled lecturer. She recalled:

> I went to the mass schools so I can be trained to educate. . . . Since I had some education before I joined, they trained me so I can educate the others. We constantly attended lectures, and these same lectures were the ones I relayed to the other members, most especially the soldiers. As an educator, I taught the others about what we are fighting for, about our goals, about discipline and dedication to the movement.[141]

On several occasions Rosenda was sent to the barrios to lecture. Initially she was not sure she could perform this daunting task, but widespread sympathy and the support she received from other Huk comrades and barrio people made it easier. She explained:

> I went down to the barrios and gave lectures. I was educating different kinds of people—from ordinary folks to Huk members. There were groups [called *buklod*] in the barrios, and I educated and trained them. I even trained my brother and relatives. Even though I was a young person giving lectures,

everyone was receptive. They were listening to me. We discussed many things from the peace and order situation to problems in their areas such as gambling and the lack of food.[142]

Working in the education department required commitment, patience, and hard work. When Leonila Sayco joined the Huks it quickly became apparent to her instructor (who noticed how attentive she was to the lectures) that she enjoyed the forest school, and he asked her to become his assistant. Because she "loved learning" Leonila agreed, and thus began the arduous work of preparing lectures for the Huk soldiers. Leonila never complained about her work but accepted its challenges. As part of the education department, "First, you need to teach the leaders how they will deal with the masses, for example, when you go to a house, you just cannot act the way you want, you need to adjust. Then, we also teach them about our enemy, the Japanese and how to fight them, including guerrilla tactics."[143] Virginia Calma was also part of the education department, although her responsibilities differed from those of Rosenda and Leonila. As part of the translation team she translated official Huk documents from English to Tagalog or Kapampangan.[144] Members of the education department also had the task of publishing official documents and news updates in the revolutionary newspaper *Katubusan ng Bayan* (Redemption of the Nation). These articles, though few and brief, were essential to the Huk movement and described the state of the guerrilla war, the political situation, and military strategy. Most were written by Hukbalahap (or Politburo) leaders, and circulated only among Huk cadres. Because the Huks moved constantly from one camp or village to the next these articles were a crucial means of communication, especially during the most difficult periods of the war.[145]

The organization department was the core of the Hukbalahap movement. From the outset the leadership realized that the guerrilla army would not be able to thrive without popular support. But to create this support, the Huks needed skilled organizers to enter the barrios, spend time with the people, talk to them, and elicit their cooperation. Luis Taruc explained:

Starting with a handful of organizers . . . we created our own schools to teach the technique of organization. These Mass Schools, as we called them, were held throughout the war and turned out hundreds of mass workers. They were schooled in the methods of underground work, in the ways of bringing about unity between all kinds of organizations and guerrilla groups, in the principles of democracy and of our traditions of struggle for national liberation and in how to penetrate and combat the [pro-Japanese] Neighborhood Associations, the PC [Philippine Constabulary] and the Ganaps. These were the people who went into the field singly and in twos and threes and laid the basis for our expansion.[146]

Although Taruc emphasized the significance of the organization department, he focused on the men, ignoring the fact that many women played an important part in "leading the organization and mobilization of the masses."[147]

Women's prewar experience in peasant movements in Central Luzon made them ideal organizers for the Hukbalahap. Often appearing inconspicuously, women were less suspicious in the eyes of the Japanese and moved freely around the villages, ostensibly just talking to people but actually exchanging information on guerrilla activities. Organizers such as Teofista Valerio and Elang Santa Ana understood that they were representatives of the People's Liberation Army in the barrios. As an organizer, Teofista recalled,

> I met with the leaders of the barrios to talk about the situation and strategize what to do when the Japanese arrive in the barrios. I also specified tasks they can do to help the guerrillas—for example, doing informal intelligence work for them, giving them food and washing their clothes, and especially caring for the sick and wounded. I traveled from one barrio to the other. I never had any difficulty in dealing with the people, especially when we tell them that we are Huks.[148]

Elang Santa Ana also traveled to different barrios to tell the villagers "what the Hukbalahap was all about and why we needed their *tulong at sakripisyo,* help and sacrifice." When the Huks organized these people, their homes became "safe houses." Elang added:

> I also monitored our organization's progress in the barrios as an organizer. I made sure that the leadership in the barrios was following the national policy of the Huks. If someone committed a violation, I made sure that I report this to the higher authorities to confer with them what should be done. I should always make

sure that the leadership in the local level was towing the party line.[149]

Entering a new territory was not always easy or safe, and there were times when women risked their lives to perform their organizational tasks.[150] Huk organizers had to be careful about the presence of pro-Japanese sentiment in the barrios, and often the organizers brought along Huk army members to protect them and intimidate Filipino spies and collaborators.

Among the organizational workers were the so-called checkers. According to Godofredo Mallari, these checkers went to the barrios to make sure the policies of the Hukbalahap were being implemented smoothly.[151] Their goal was to make sure the barrios remained anti-Japanese and that residents were protected from enemy attacks and remained firmly committed to the Huk cause. Luz del Castillo compared her work in the barrios to *parang nagdidilig ng halaman* (watering plants):

> You organized the people in the barrios, but it does not mean that once they are organized your work there is over. You need to take care of these BUDCs like you are always watering the plants. *Didiligin mo iyan hanggang sa yumabong iyan* [You will always water the plants until they flourish]. So from time to time we visit these barrios. And we always teach them and uplift their spirits and educate them. We constantly needed to boost their morale during the war.[152]

Other women in the organization department, including Ana Sula, Elena Sawit, and Marcosa de la Rosa, were filled with nostalgia when they recalled how being a Huk organizer allowed them to interact with barrio people. "Despite our sacrifices and separation from families," Ana explained, their contacts with villagers inspired them to keep on with their work.

Women also made up the majority of another crucial division of the Hukbalahap, the Propaganda Core, sometimes called the cultural division, which was responsible for the propaganda campaigns the Huks conducted in the barrios to win the hearts and minds of ordinary Filipinos. Through songs and short plays propaganda workers created a mood of camaraderie and festivity among the Huks and their village supporters, helping them feel safe, protected, and eager to help the cause. Propaganda was closely linked to the organizational work of the Hukbalahap, and propagandists and organizers usually traveled to the villages together. Having women as organizers and propagandists was clearly an important part of placing a friendly face on the guerrilla movement as the Huks established a presence in the barrios. While organizers lectured on the basics of the "fundamental spirit," propagandists performed songs to boost the morale of barrio supporters. By encouraging villagers to join them in song, the Huks sought to identify themselves with village supporters. One of the most popular songs of the Hukbalahap was this call for a united front:

Ang pagkakaisang hanay ay itinatag
Sa sinapupunan ng ating bayang sinta
Upang ang bayan ay magkaisa
Laban sa Hapong pasista.

The United Front was founded
In the womb of our beloved country
So our nation shall be united
Against the Fascist Japanese.

Mayaman, mahirap dapat magtulungan
Matalino't mangmang dapat magkaisa sa pakikipaglaban
Mga malalakas, mga bata, mga matapang
Kailangan natin sa larangan
Ang intelehente sa organisasyong makabayan
Lahat ng inyong katangian
Iabuloy para sa kinabukasan.

The rich and the poor must work together
The learned and the uneducated must be united in this fight
The strong, the young, and the brave
We need them on our side
The intellectual in nationalist organizations
Must offer everything they have
For the future of our land.

Music was an important part of village life, and songs like this gave the movement popular appeal.[153] Performed at the beginning and end of most barrio meetings was the theme song of the cultural division or Propaganda Core:

Narito na ang lingkod ninyo ngayon
Nagpupugay sa inyong lahat ang Cultural Division
Kung mabawasan sa langit ang tala't bituin
Narito sasamahan natin

Here we are, your servants
Greeting you all from the cultural division
Though the light and stars diminish in the sky
We shall remain here to keep you company

Magsibaba na kayo at mabigyan ang aliw	Join us so we can entertain you
At saya na di magmamaliw.	And your happiness shall not cease.
Kay saya nga nitong bayan ngayon	The nation is indeed joyful
Nang matampok ang Cultural Division	With the cultural division in our midst
May marangal itong nilalayon	It has a noble goal
Kalayan ay ating ibangon.	To restore freedom in our land.
Dati noon, ang laya ay pangarap sa ligayang minimithi	Freedom used to be but a long-awaited dream
Ngunit ngayon, ang Cultural Division ang tutulong sa kanyang lunggati.	But now the cultural division will help end our misery.
May marangal itong nilalayon	It has a noble goal
Kalayaan ay ating ibangon.	To restore freedom in our land.
Cultural Division ay nagpapaalam	Cultural division bids you farewell
At nag-iiwan ng gintong aral	Leaving you all a golden lesson
Cultural Division ay tangkilikin	Support the cultural division
Mabuhay ang Cultural Division.	Long live the cultural division.

Cultural workers often taught supporters the words and melodies of songs like these, hoping they would find strength in them. Years after the rebellion ended Hukbalahap members and their barrio supporters still knew these songs by heart. Teresita Maceda believes that these songs, preserved in the oral tradition of the peasants who sang them, demonstrated the guerrillas' revolutionary zeal and that the emotions that they invoked—pity, sorrow, happiness, love, hatred, and strength—inspired not only the villagers but the revolutionaries themselves.[154] The women who were part of the Propaganda Core were enthusiastic about their work and very effective in harnessing popular support for the movement. Zenaida del Castillo described the typical work of a *propagandista*:

> We were presenting dramas and poetry—all anti-Japanese. For example, we usually have a story about *Inang Bayan*, our Mother

Philippines, represented by a woman dressed in black, blind-folded and her hands tied at the back. We present her to the villagers and tell them that she was bound because the Japanese had enslaved us, had taken advantage of our women, and were punishing all of us. What they are doing to us was against the honor of *Inang Bayan*, our Mother Philippines. Then we always end up singing anti-Japanese songs.[155]

Anti-Japanese songs, like this one recorded by Maceda, were central to the propaganda efforts of the Hukbalahap:

Mga Hapon na dito lumusob	The Japanese who attacked
Itong Pilipinas nais nilang masakop	the Philippines they sought to conquer
Sa tanikala nais nilang igapos	With chains, they wanted to bind us
Sa kaalipnan at pagkabusabos.	in servitude and slavery.
Kaya tayong mga anak ng Tinubuan	We, the children of our Motherland,
Magkaisa tayo at lumaban	must unite and fight
Di tayo dapat paalipin pa	That we would no longer be enslaved
At sa panginoon di na titingala.	And end our worship of a false god.
Mahigit sa tatlong daang taong kahaba	For more than three hundred years
Ang pananakop dito ng mga Kastila	the Spanish ruled our land
At sa mga Amerikano lubos tayong nakulong	And under the Americans, we were denied freedom
Ngayon, sa Hapon, tayo kaya'y payag pa?	Are we now going to bend to Japanese conquerors again?
Gumising ka na Pilipinas	Arise, Philippines
Pilipino tayong lahat	We are all Filipinos
Ibangon ang dangal	Raise the honor
Ng Bayan nating pinakamahal...	Of our beloved land.

Just like the organizers, propaganda workers such as Filomena Tolentino, Dominga Centeno, Crisanta Abejera, and Felisa Pineda recalled their experiences with great fondness, largely because of the opportunity the work provided to interact with local townspeople. Filomena was part of the "choral group" and often acted in zarzuelas (*sarswelas* in Filipino), Spanish-influenced dramatic presentations with spoken and sung scenes and dances often depicting stories of the battle between good and evil.[156] The Huk *sarswelas* were invariably anti-Japanese. According to Zenaida del Castillo, the guerrillas usually performed their "cultural presentations" at night. Filomena concurred, stating, "Those Japanese were dumb [*nakatanga*]. They just stand and watch our performances. They thought we were just having a fiesta, a good time. But we were really organizing the people by making them stand up against the Japanese."[157] Zenaida elaborated:

> We go from barrio to barrio. . . . And then we sing and make cultural presentations, including drama, poetry, etc. Propaganda work aims to motivate the barrio to support the Huk movement. The barrio was the base, and the people, in the mornings they were farming and at night, they join the Hukbalahap movement.[158]

Even in the midst of war, these women believed that their songs, and especially their presence, provided comfort to the people of Central Luzon.

Unlike the organizers and propaganda workers, who felt secure among village sympathizers, those women who worked as couriers for the Huks in the communication department did more dangerous work. According to Luis Taruc, the Hukbalahap communications system was "very intricate" and relied on two types of couriers: the direct and the relay.[159] The swiftest way to send important messages was through direct couriers, who always traveled a definite, mapped route, usually transporting messages from the Huk headquarters to another Huk location or a specific Huk leader. The relay system was more circuitous, with one courier passing a message to another as it made its way to the final recipient. Both Huk men and women remembered the courier system as highly reliable and effective during the war. Despite their modern radios and telephones, the Japanese could not keep pace with the Huk couriers.[160] Almost all the women in the Hukbalahap served as couriers at one point or another during the war.

Women were ideal couriers, and Huk leaders quickly recognized their potential, skill, and willingness to carry out this hazardous task. In the eyes of the Japanese, women were innocuous and unthreatening, figures whose presence in the barrios, usually with baskets of fruit and vegetables, gossiping mindlessly with their neighbors, was unremarkable. These impressions allowed women to travel from one barrio to another rarely suspected of being guerrillas. Leonila Monteverde recalled:

> As a courier . . . I used to walk from Quezon to Pampanga to Manila. I brought with me letters and documents. I bring these materials from one leadership group to another. It was a very difficult job; there were many times that I was almost captured by the Japanese. Because I was always successful despite the risks, I was considered as a very important courier.[161]

Huk women described the different methods they used to hide and transmit important letters. Most of the time they hid these messages in their baskets, but sometimes they hid them in their blouses or under their skirts. Lutgarda Gana recalled with a smile, "Sometimes I looked pregnant because of all those letters and documents that I kept in my belly, inside my blouse."[162] But courier work was very serious. Belen Valerio remembered walking miles out of her way just to deliver a letter from a Huk leader to a woman in the next village. As part of the relay system she rarely knew the final recipients of the messages she carried.[163] This work also required a good memory as couriers were often instructed to memorize the letters they were delivering just in case they were caught by the Japanese or their collaborators. When the enemy got too close, some women recalled swallowing their letters to prevent guerrilla correspondence from falling into Japanese hands.

Courier work required tenacity and courage, and women couriers had to be resourceful. Marcosa de la Rosa, for example, was delivering an important letter to a peasant leader when she saw Japanese soldiers approaching. Thinking quickly, she opened the basket she was carrying, took out some fruit and started to eat where she was standing. The soldiers passed by without bothering her.[164] Elena Sawit believed her knowledge of the villages and towns made her a good courier, and it helped that she was inconspicuous and ordinary looking. "Men would not have been good couriers," she believes, "because they were more distrusted by the Japanese and easily lost their heads in difficult situations."[165]

Women also played a major role in the intelligence networks, the part of the communication division that gathered information about the activities of the Japanese in the barrios. Like courier work, intelligence gathering looked effortless but was often risky. However, people who were part of the BUDCs were always willing to do it. Loreta Betangkul insisted that the Japanese and their spies thought women were idle, sitting around in their homes and gossiping the whole day. They did not realize that these women were collecting information about Japanese plans and relaying it to the Huks. Sometimes referred to as the "signal corps," men and women responsible for monitoring Japanese activity would employ different methods to communicate with the Huk army: flashes of light or open lit windows at night, flags, banners, or clothes hung on a line in the daytime. Hanging a white blanket from a window was one of the favorite signals used by villagers to warn the Huks of a Japanese presence in the barrios. As Belen Valerio recalled:

> Even when you are a woman or still a child you already know what you had to do. For example, you are taught that when the Japanese approach a barrio you should hang a *puting kumot*, a white blanket, in your window to alert the Huks that they are coming. The people in the next towns, upon seeing this signal, will then follow. The Huks were therefore warned and prepared for any action.[166]

This type of work often exposed organized villages to enemy retaliation. When Japanese plans against the guerrillas were foiled because of the intelligence work of barrio women, residents were often tortured and beaten. Sometimes villagers were forced to reveal the identities of guerrilla leaders, and some were even killed. Amparo Valerio remembered an incident in which truckloads of Japanese soldiers arrived in her barrio, presumably to fight the Huk guerrillas. She and other neighbors immediately hung white blankets outside their windows. The Japanese realized what was going on, and when the guerrillas failed to show up they took some of the village men and forced them to admit their support for the guerrillas. Since she was only a teenager Amparo was spared. Although the men came home alive, they definitely suffered the wrath of the Japanese.[167]

Japanese retaliation, instead of frightening villagers, often strengthened local support for the Huks. Luis Taruc underscored the success of these intelligence networks:

> In the beginning, the zeal of the people to pass on everything that occurred produced amazing reports. We were given the position of every *carabao* in the fields, the number of chickens and pigs in the vicinity, and an account of all births, deaths, marriages, and

family quarrels, as well as the details of enemy movements. The *barrio* intelligence was as its best, however, in the observation and investigation of strangers; it was our most effective way of combating spies and enemy agents.[168]

By 1943, he reported, it was almost impossible for pro-Japanese spies to penetrate Huk territory. Unfortunately, women who worked as couriers and communications agents were still considered to be performing "subsidiary" work for the Hukbalahap.[169] Since many believed this work did not require much training or decision making, it was generally perceived by both male and even female Huks as secondary to the activities of the

Luis Taruc, Supremo of the Hukbalahap, is flanked by relatives and friends to show the success of the Huk leader in eluding enemies during the war because "his friends tip him off by courier or by signs (flashlight, at night), giving him ample head start." Note the number of women around Taruc who acted as couriers and intelligence agents during the Hukbalahap period but probably never received the recognition that they deserved. (*Manila Times*, 1947; Courtesy of Lopez Museum Collection)

military soldiers and leaders. Despite Taruc's admiration for the intelligence work of the Huks, he paid little attention to the women who did much of this work.[170]

Huks not only operated in the organized villages. As an army, they conducted military actions against the Japanese. Since situations in which guerrillas were killed or wounded were common, the Huks organized a medical division composed mostly of women who worked as nurses and caretakers. Just as in the mainstream society, most if not all nurses in the Hukbalahap were women. Many women embraced this responsibility, believing that they were best equipped to care for and nurture their comrades. These women felt they needed little if any training to perform the tasks of caring for comrades and attending to the sick. Many would have agreed with Prima Sobrevinas, who remarked that women "have been trained their whole lives for this work."[171]

As makeshift nurses, these women administered first aid, used herbs to cure diseases, and gave shots for malaria, the most common sickness found among comrades in the mountains. Although she never had any medical education, Maxima San Pedro became a Huk nurse after attending an intensive seminar on basic medicine. She soon found herself near combat areas treating wounded guerrillas. First aid workers, Maxima remembered, "cleaned the wounded, cured those with fever, and gave medicines provided by sympathizers. Doctors who supported the Huks taught us how to treat the sick and how to give injections so when they were not around we can still do the job."[172] Rosita Manuel joined the Huks because her husband, Silvestre Liwanag, was one of its top squadron commanders. But when her husband fell ill in the camps Rosita took care of him and later became a member of the Huk medical corps. Although she thought she was "too weak" to treat the wounded, eventually she got used to the work, giving injections to comrades and at one point even helping to deliver a baby.[173] When the Huks were not able to get medicines from the villages, they had to use whatever they could find in the forest. Other women used their knowledge of traditional medicine and methods of healing to treat the sick and wounded. Candelaria Pangan, for instance, recalled the many times she used certain types of leaves to heal the wounds of comrades. Avelina Santos remembered that when she stayed in the camps soldiers often came to recuperate from the wounds they received on the battlefield. "They came in wounded from shots, sharp objects in the forest, or because they fell down running," she said, "and we always treated them. I used to boil guava leaves and placed them above their wounds. They were surprisingly effective."[174] For many of these women, who never went to school, the experience of working as nurses and medics tapped an inner potential and courage they never thought they possessed.

When the Huks were not conducting military operations or organizing villages, they stayed in temporary camps scattered around Central and Southern Luzon. These camps usually had a main office, where male leaders gathered, and sleeping quarters for the guerrillas. Aside from the male leaders, most of those who attended to the administration of the Huks were women working as clerks and secretaries. Since administrative tasks required special skills such as reading, writing, and transcribing, women who had some education usually filled these roles. Unintentionally, a division developed between women from Manila, who were usually more educated and middle class and were typically assigned to the camp headquarters with the leaders, and peasant women from Central and Southern Luzon who worked directly with the barrio population.

When Araceli Mallari's college education was disrupted by the war she joined the Hukbalahap and immediately became the secretary to Jose Lava, who was then the chairman of the organization department. Coming from Manila, she admits that she was a "petit bourgeois" who did not have the skills or experience needed to work as a barrio organizer. But she was educated and knew how to read and write, unlike most of her female and male comrades. She explained:

> I did not involve myself with the *masa*, the masses; I just stayed in the headquarters, where I worked as secretary of Jose Lava, responsible for noting down all correspondence within the leadership. I also transcribed letters coming from the couriers. Whenever there were meetings, Lava always came prepared because I organized all his notes.[175]

Secretarial work was considered a special task reserved for educated women such as Araceli. Most of the women who worked in the headquarters served as clerks. Elena Sawit remembers typing documents written by and for Politburo leaders. Belen Simpauco arranged the movement's paperwork. Celia Reyes and Avelina Santos worked as treasurers in their respective camps. They usually handled money for the movement, making sure that they had enough funds to give the guerrillas what they needed, especially food.

A major part of women's work in the camps was housekeeping, which included cleaning and tidying up, cooking for the guerrillas, and washing their clothes. But since Hukbalahap guerrillas often found safe havens in the villages much of this type of support, especially the provision of food, beds, and clothing, came from barrio supporters. In general there were no fixed headquarters during the Japanese Occupation, and once the Huks had organized a village and declared it "safe" from the enemy and their collaborators, they would transfer operations from the forest camps to the barrio bases. Women, most of them left behind by husbands, fathers, or brothers who had joined the Hukbalahap, played an important role in these organized communities. Their homes became the homes of Huks, and their most important task was gathering supplies, including money, food, and medicines. Without these female supporters the Huks would have found it extremely hard to organize resistance in the barrios. Jesus Lava observed in his memoir that "no guerrilla could survive without the voluntary and sympathetic support of the masses," and, as Araceli Mallari remarked, "the Huk is to the people as fish is to water."[176] Although Lava never emphasized the role of women in the guerrilla movement, women were these bodies of water and an indispensable part of the popular base of support for the Huks.

The End of the War

In the desperate months leading up to the end of the war the Japanese military "decided to launch an intensive drive, hoping to destroy the Hukbalahap."[177] But by 1944 most Huks knew that victory was at hand. In October of that year the Allied forces under General Douglas MacArthur landed in Leyte in the southern Philippines and began the long campaign to retake the country from the Japanese. The months of fighting culminated in the Battle of Leyte Gulf, which ended in a total defeat for the Japanese navy. In January 1945 U.S. forces finally landed in Luzon, launching operations in Lingayen, Pangasinan, and Pampanga that eventually led to the surrender of the Japanese. But the Japanese continued to fight in Manila, and many areas of the Philippines became major battlefields. On February 3, 1945, just over three years after the Japanese occupied Manila, U.S. forces reentered the capital city, sparking a monthlong battle that left the city devastated. As Ricardo Jose writes, "[T]he Japanese, knowing they would not come out alive, vented their anger on the hapless residents of Manila, burned buildings, blasted all the bridges across the Pasig and committed an orgy of rape and murder."[178] As the U.S. Air Force pounded the city, Filipinos once again evacuated the capital. By the time American and Filipino forces had regained control of Manila the city lay in ruins and about one hundred thousand Filipino civilians were dead.[179]

The Japanese occupation of Central Luzon ended bloodily in late 1944 and early 1945 with major battles between Hukbalahap squadrons and Japanese troops. In their last efforts to preserve control, the Japanese army and its collaborators in the Bureau of Constabulary (BC) waged war on the civilian population of the region.[180] In Talavera, Nueva Ecija, for example, Japanese and BC troops conducted *zona* raids, rounding up over a hundred people suspected of being in the Hukbalahap, and took them to a chapel for interrogation.[181] Retreating Japanese forces routinely exacted revenge on village populations, committing more massacres and atrocities. But the Hukbalahap continued to fight vigorously, declaring victory in several provinces of Central and Southern Luzon. By the end of the Japanese Occupation, the Huks had come close to establishing a de facto civilian government in Central Luzon with the support of a large peasant base.

Following the collapse of Japanese resistance in southern Manila in February 1945, General MacArthur turned over the reins of government to President Sergio Osmeña, the successor of Commonwealth president Manuel Quezon, who had died in exile in August 1944 without realizing his lifelong dream of an independent Philippine Republic. Japan formally surrendered to the Allies on September 2, 1945, in ceremonies held aboard the battleship *Missouri* in Tokyo Bay. Proud of the role they had played in the liberation of the Philippines, the Huk guerrillas initially welcomed the returning Americans and joined the nation in celebration.

For many Huk women the defeat of Japan meant the end of separation from their families. When the war ended Marcosa de la Rosa was immediately reunited with her husband, a Huk commander who had been arrested by the Japanese in 1943 and was eventually released by the Huks, and her five-year-old daughter, who had been left with her mother. Zenaida del Castillo, who was separated from her father and siblings throughout the occupation, was reunited with them when the war ended. The early days of peace were a period of great happiness, and many women recalled a great sense of euphoria and celebration as guerrilla fighters returned to the barrios and families were reunited. For most of them the destruction of the war was nothing compared to the return of peace, freedom, and the prospect of national independence.

The Huk Woman and the Huk Legacy

In his memoir on the Huk revolt the American soldier Bill Pomeroy, who arrived in the country with U.S. forces in 1944 and later became a Huk, encapsulated the status of the Filipino woman in a few sentences. "In a colonial country," he observed, "she is bowed under a double weight. She lacks the independence of her nationality, and she lacks the independence of her sex."[182] Mired in the dull monotony of barrio life, the Filipina had no distractions and her future was settled at sixteen or seventeen when she married. The Huk movement, Pomeroy wrote, offered her hope:

> Hope for what? For the tremendous release of her personality that is found in the equality of life in our camps. For the chance to contribute to her country more than just the act of giving it sons. In the Huks she is a Filipino, whose purpose is the nation and not the mere confines of a single home and of a single man.[183]

Pomeroy's statement reflected the struggles of the Filipino peasant woman.[184] Before the war most peasant women in Central and Southern Luzon were largely excluded from political life, and even after the introduction of public education under American colonial rule most had little or no education. This lack of education deprived them of employment options and opportunities for social mobility. Like peasant women from previous generations the women of Central and Southern Luzon focused on maintaining and supporting their households. As Filomena Tolentino stated, if peasant women like her had not joined the Huk movement they would have ended up as "teenage peasant wives," and instead of doing revolutionary work they "would be nursing our babies or taking care of our parents."[185] The Huks gave them a new sense of purpose.

Until the middle of the twentieth century the rightful place of the Filipina was the home, and her duty to the country was to produce sons who would eventually become its most productive citizens. The disruptions of the war, however, and the powerful continuities of peasant society and kinship in Central and Southern Luzon had given women a chance to become part of the Hukbalahap despite the cultural limitations placed on women. Ironically, the nature of the peasant societies in Central and Southern Luzon had, in many ways, facilitated women's entry into the Hukbalahap. Most women joined because their fathers, husbands, brothers, or friends were already part of the movement or because of their involvement in prewar political and radical organizations, which were themselves the product of kin networks. In the villages of Central and Southern Luzon the reins of Japanese control were also looser, providing space for interactions. The close-knit social relations among villagers, their common experience of suffering, and their feelings of solidarity, which had already characterized rural life before the war, drew many women into the guerrilla movement.

The experience of Huk women highlights the importance of social organizations and networks in the mobilization of social and revolutionary movements.[186] Activists are typically recruited into movements by one or more members with whom they have a preexisting, extra-movement, or interpersonal tie. Recruitment among acquaintances, friends, and kin is generally more successful than recruitment among strangers.[187] In a "high-risk" social and revolutionary movement such as the Hukbalahap, familial and social networks, as well as contact with other activists, are even more crucial for effective recruitment.[188] Whether through kin, friends, neighbors, or organizational acquaintances, prior contacts with other activists facilitated mobilization in the Hukbalahap.

Nevertheless, we cannot discount female agency and the important role individual choice played in women's decisions to join the Huks. Most Huk women acknowledged both the influence of kinship and friendship and their own principled motivations to explain why they joined.[189] Male mentors such as fathers, brothers, and husbands were indeed crucial, but Huk women were also deeply committed to the cause of anti-Japanese resistance. Although they were often separated from their male relatives once they joined the Huks, they still managed to carve out their own space within the movement. At the same time most women were very much aware of the cultural limitations imposed by their gender.

The same social relations that mobilized peasant women in Central and Southern Luzon shaped and eventually limited their involvement. Kinship relations came with particularistic claims and obligations for every kin member, and thus women, despite their role as guerrillas, continued to act as the wives and daughters of Huk men. Women who followed their husbands and fathers into the movement usually ended up taking care of their needs, as well as the needs of other male members. Indeed, their deference to their husbands, or other men, sometimes limited their role in the movement. In the forest camps and barrio bases they were expected to do the kind of work they normally did in their households such as housekeeping, cooking, and washing clothes. For the most part they obeyed the orders of the Huk men, and even after many years in the movement most women were kept out of leadership positions and their work was frequently described and disparaged as no more than support for the main task: military combat. As Sofia Logarta observed, "[W]omen in the Huk movement did the cooking, washing and sewing" and "performed traditional tasks of females"; only occasionally did they do "things not tied to their sex role."[190] Most women did not question these duties, and even if they assumed other responsibilities in the movement they accepted that their primary role was to take care of the men.

Gender influenced not only the recruitment process but also the role of women within the organization.[191] Just as cultural prejudices influence (and limit) female mobilization, preconceived notions of femininity also shape the roles of women in revolution. In many societies, including that of the Philippines, men control public life while women dominate the "domestic" space. Since women are linked to the "natural" sphere of reproduction, through activities such as childbearing, the socialization of children, and the care of family members, they are relegated to domestic roles. When women accomplish work outside the home they are still expected to do reproductive work.[192] It is therefore not surprising that the Huk female revolutionaries themselves often interpreted their domestic tasks as their foremost duty in the movement.

This sexual division of labor, a direct result of the division between the productive and reproductive spheres, is manifested in different realms of social life and even in armed or revolutionary movements. Like established military institutions, revolutionary armies are run by men according to masculine ideas and usually rely heavily on male social power. As Cynthia Enloe argues, however, women are essential to maintaining the military and the values of male culture and masculinity. Women who support and depend on the military are directly and indirectly "maneuvered" into accepting the institution's values and its notions of femininity and masculinity as normal, acceptable, and even necessary. Militarization shapes what is acceptable masculinity and in the process creates femininity. These patriarchal ideologies are fundamental to the operation and success of militarized institutions, including liberation armies. Women—from mothers who allow their children to join armies to the loyal wife who waits and works while her soldier husband is gone and the female military nurse who tends and supports the men—and their identities are militarized, but they are still dismissed as what

Enloe calls "camp followers," those who enable military institutions to exist and survive but whose roles are not recognized as essential.[193]

As a military organization, the Hukbalahap separated the roles of men and women, mirroring a hierarchical structure that dichotomizes the "public" and "private" spheres. Despite the expectation that liberation or revolutionary armies should be more or less sensitive to women's immediate needs and issues of gender equality, the fact that most of these movements are controlled by men indicates that the same conventional ideologies that limit women's role in the military persist in revolutionary movements and guerrilla armies.[194] "Barriers to women's participation in guerilla struggle," writes Linda Reif, "include the structural constraint of women's role in reproductive activities and the ideological constraints which define women's roles."[195] Women therefore face organizational constraints imposed by radical social and political movements themselves, including male dominance and agendas that neglect issues important to women.[196]

The Hukbalahap, like the Philippine military, had a formal policy of excluding female guerrillas from combat duty. This practice defined the guerrilla army as a male institution, which reinforced the idea that "men are the defenders, women the defended," in effect perpetuating a dichotomous ideology of men as strong, women as weak.[197] Despite the presence of women in the villages and on the battlefields, the "reconstruction of gender hierarchy" inside the Hukbalahap, in common with many other revolutionary movements, rendered women invisible and defined them as "outside combat."[198] Of course female Huks themselves expressed ambivalence about combat. Many believed it was properly *trabaho ng lalaki* (men's work) while others admitted that they were afraid of guns and lacked the "ability to shoot." Thirty years later women in the New People's Party (NPA), the armed guerrilla group established by the new Communist Party of the Philippines, would offer similar observations. Anne-Marie Hilsdon explained that women in the NPA, "combatants by definition," used weapons primarily in self-defense, preferring "interactive, non-combative approaches particularly towards civilians."[199]

According to Enloe, "The . . . notion of 'combat' plays such a central role in the consciousness of concepts of 'manhood' and justifications of the superiority of maleness in the social structure. . . . [T]o be a soldier means possibly to experience 'combat,' and only in combat lies the ultimate test of man's masculinity."[200] Nancy Gallagher explains that women are perceived as "more caring and compassionate, more concerned with preserving interpersonal relationships," and less willing to believe that "might makes right."[201] Thus, within revolutionary armies women's work is concentrated in administrative, medical, and support units. This male-female distinction comes as no surprise. The roles women play in social and revolutionary movements like the Huk rebellion usually reproduce the sexual division of labor that exists in their communities and in society in general.[202] And in Philippine society the home is considered the Filipino woman's "sphere of greatest influence." Consequently, while men as "heads of households" and "citizens" dominate the workplace and shape public life, women's (house)work, which is focused on reproduction and child rearing, is considered nonproductive labor and invites stereotyping of women as nurturers.[203] "Inevitably," concludes Hilsdon, "women have been excluded from many social roles through the division of functions into public-private and productive-reproductive."[204] In the Huk movement women focused on "support committees," which was perceived as "private, reproductive" work, as opposed to the men, who engaged in the "public, productive" work of combat.

But revolutionary movements do not simply reproduce the sexual division of labor embedded in society. Despite the structures that consign women to support roles and "free" men to fight, the strict division between the battlefront and the home front is hard to maintain in guerrilla armies and revolutionary movements.[205] Like Huk women, women in liberation armies in Vietnam and Latin America performed traditional tasks such as cooking, nursing, cleaning, and laundering for the guerrillas, but they also fought alongside men on the battlefront, challenging conventional boundaries between male and female military roles.[206] Women therefore have more opportunities to challenge and stretch the traditional limits on their roles in revolutionary movements primarily because of their exposure to combat and recognition of their indispensable supportive responsibilities.[207] In many ways, such movements are not conventional military organizations. The Hukbalahap was a nationalist, radical movement that was also committed to the liberation of women. By recruiting and promoting women the Huks actually recognized their role in fighting for the nation. And part of their challenge to conventional ideas about gender was to allow women to serve as guerrillas.

In reality Huk women possessed a radical idea of the home that extended beyond the parameters of the immediate family, albeit with strict, unambiguous roles for men and women. The means by which they were recruited into the movement, usually facilitated by male mentors, and the freedom they experienced inside it, often independent of men, further reinforced their idea of the home as dynamic, open, and limitless. Although confined mostly to domestic duties, female guerrillas and supporters perceived and redefined these roles as productive, indeed central, to the Huk organization.[208]

Women's capacity for nurturing, as well as ideas about femininity, shaped their role as nurses and medical practitioners in the Huk movement. But "it is the female nurse or doctor," asserts Karen Turner, "who operates within an ambiguous space, between domestic and military arenas."[209] In the Vietnamese revolution, like the Huk movement, women made up the majority of the medical corps because of the common belief that women were by nature nurturers, had the patience and agile hands to treat injuries, and had sweet, caring voices that could bring the wounded back to health. But, as Turner argues, although women were "expected to render the kind of unselfish care mothers give naturally," they were also expected to "perform efficiently amidst a world of carnage and violence believed to be men's unique province."[210] As nurses and medics, women in the Vietnamese and Huk movements, however, witnessed up close the "blood, gore, and indignity—and the costs—of war."[211] And in performing their seemingly feminine role, these nurses and caretakers often crossed the boundary between nurturer and fighter, female and male.

The roles and responsibilities of women ultimately transformed the Huk movement and challenged conventional understandings of femininity and masculinity. By joining the Huks these women became part of a revolutionary, nationalist movement. They left the "traditional" home but redefined it to include their extended relations in the guerrilla camps, a liberating experience for Filipino, and especially peasant, women. They performed extraordinary tasks—organizing and educating people, nursing the wounded, transmitting information, conducting intelligence work, and boosting morale—and were transformed by the experience. But their experiences also transformed the Hukbalahap. While originally conceived as an army of men, it became a guerrilla movement that created new space for women. Women provided the revolutionary organization with able teachers, propagandists, organizers, nurses, and couriers, and the success of the Hukbalahap would not have been possible without the women who defied their traditional gender roles, redefined notions of the home and community, and participated in the resistance against the Japanese.

A married couple with a folded U.S. flag holds up the Philippine flag in a patriotic pose after the war. The text that appeared with the photo, "Tarlac guerrillas wave the flag for which they fought so bravely," also identified Major Lopez of the Philippine Army and his wife, Mercedes, the "Captain of the Luzon Guerrilla forces." While being a military captain was a rare role for women, this photo acknowledges women's central role in the resistance movement against the Japanese. (n.d., Courtesy of Lopez Museum Collection)

As a result, the Hukbalahap was able to mount the most effective guerrilla resistance to Japanese imperial power in Asia.[212] And women played a crucial role in this resistance movement, paving the way for Philippine liberation. The Huks, Marcosa de la Rosa insisted, helped the "hopeless and helpless Filipinos free themselves from Japanese rule."[213] Despite all the sufferings her family experienced, including the death of her brother in combat, Luz del Castillo had no regrets about being part of the Hukbalahap. She believed in the Huk leadership but especially in its members and ordinary supporters. "The Huks truly gave their lives for the movement," she asserted. She was proud to know many of them and to have "witnessed a lot of people who had discipline, who had consciousness and love for the movement and its leaders." But for her, and for other Huks, it was the barrio people, those who protected them "even at the risk of their own lives," whose "love and dedication" to the guerrillas "truly liberated the Philippines."[214] Almost all the women who were part of the Hukbalahap agreed with Luz that their lives were enriched by their revolutionary experience. By becoming Huks, they had learned to play new and significant roles beyond the boundaries of their homes and villages. And for many this was just the start of a lifelong engagement with Philippine politics.

2

Comrades in Arms

Huk Women, Nationalism, and Communist Revolution

At the age of sixty-five Zenaida del Castillo could still remember the words to the songs she sang as a member of the propaganda division of the Hukbalahap. Initially drawn into the movement as the daughter of the peasant and Communist Party leader Mateo del Castillo at the start of the Japanese Occupation, by late 1943 she was very much her own revolutionary. After her training in the party school she joined other members of the propaganda division in the barrios, performing plays and skits, reciting poems, and singing revolutionary songs. By early 1944, she remembered, most of the songs she and Huk supporters were singing in Central Luzon sounded a victorious note.

Bayang nagtiis sa kasakitan	My country you have endured pain
Sumisikat na ang iyong kalayaan	But now your freedom is awakened
Ang matagal mo nang pinakahihintay	Your long-awaited dream is here
Tagumpay nitong Lupang Tinubuan.	Victory for your motherland.

At kung inaalipin ka	If you are oppressed
Binubusabos ng lahing pasista	Enslaved by the fascist race
Halika, sumama ka na	Come, join us
Sa paraiso ng ligaya.	To the paradise of happiness.

Sa ilalim ng HUKBALAHAP	Under the HUKBALAHAP
Makisama at yumakap	Join us and embrace
Ang makulay niyang pangarap	the colorful dream
Ng ating Inang Bayang Pilipinas.	of our Motherland the
	Philippines.[1]

The dream, according to Zenaida and other Huk members, was to free their beloved Philippines from Japanese occupation. The Huks had been fighting continuously since 1942, and by 1945 the Japanese had been defeated by both the U.S. military and Hukbalahap forces.

On July 4, 1946, the United States established the Philippine Republic, marking the colonial nature of its relationship with the Philippines even as it granted independence. From the very beginning there was no suggestion that the postwar Philippine Republic was willing to share power with the Huks or even to recognize the role they had played in defeating the Japanese. Soon after independence the Huks once again returned to the hills, this time not to fight the invading Japanese but to launch a massive resistance movement against government troops and landlords, who had initiated repressive measures to restore prewar land arrangements in Central and Southern Luzon. Thus began the Huk rebellion in the Philippines, the revolutionary movement that grew out of the anti-Japanese resistance and a determination to resist the efforts of the U.S.-supported postwar government to restore the prewar social order in the countryside. Under former leaders of the PKP and peasant organizations the Huks, with a new name, the Hukbong Mapagpalaya ng Bayan (People's Liberation Army), or HMB, once again mobilized the peasantry in Central and Southern Luzon to support its cause.[2]

When the Huks returned to guerrilla warfare the Hukbalahap women also returned, although many left the movement in order "to live in peace," returning to their prewar roles in peasant society as wives and women devoted to maintaining their households. Because the enemy was now the Philippine state and military rather than a foreign enemy, the HMB called for a much greater radical commitment, and the women who continued in the struggle were more formally trained as cadres and communists. In addition to exploring the reasons why women left the movement, this chapter traces the transformation of those who remained from reluctant rebels to cadres and revolutionaries.

The Huks and the Postwar Philippine Republic

The war and the Japanese Occupation left the Philippines in a "state of exhaustion, devastation and chaos."[3] "After the initial jubilation of the liberation from Japanese rule" Ricardo Jose writes, "came the grim task of confronting the losses, estimating the costs of rehabilitation, seeking justice for war crimes, rewarding the heroes and punishing the villains, and picking up the pieces."[4] The damage to transportation, communication, medical, and sanitation facilities was enormous, and the urban and rural economies were paralyzed as factories shut down and agricultural land became "a veritable wasteland."[5] Most of Manila was destroyed, many houses had been razed, and basic necessities such as clothing, medicine, and especially food were hard to come by. It took a long time for most businesses and institutions — universities, banks, hospitals, libraries, offices, hotels, and printing presses — to resume operations, and when the U.S. Pacific commander, Douglas MacArthur, left the Philippines for new challenges in Japan, "Filipinos were left limping through the rubble, their cities and their government alike in shambles."[6]

Immediately after the war Sergio Osmeña, who had succeeded Manuel Quezon as interim president, restored the Commonwealth government and the Philippine Congress pending scheduled presidential elections later that same year. One of the most immediate problems facing the new leadership was the dilemma of what to do with wartime collaborators, many of whom were respected politicians, bureaucrats, and parliamentary leaders.[7] Under pressure from the Americans, Osmeña and his government turned a blind eye to collaborators, believing the task of rebuilding a war-damaged society required unity and cooperation among national leaders. Manuel Roxas, who was involved in the collaborationist wartime government, was absolved by his prewar friend and patron MacArthur, who supported his bid for the presidency. In April 1946 Roxas became president of the new Philippine Republic, winning by a modest majority over the old and weary Osmeña.[8] On July 4, 1946, Manuel Roxas became the first president of the independent Republic of the Philippines. As president he was forced to deal with a country badly damaged by war, a bankrupt economy deeply dependent on the United States, a corrupt bureaucracy, continuing conflict in the countryside, and the geopolitics of the cold war.

The unprecedented wartime destruction in the country and the great burden of restoring order in postwar society made the newly independent Philippine Republic greatly reliant on its former colonial master and "tutor of development," the United States.[9] The United States, which did not want to abandon its economic and political interests in the Pacific, persuaded Philippine leaders to accept postwar aid in return for permitting the establishment of U.S. military bases and parity rights for American companies operating freely in the country.[10] In order to create a sense of "normalcy" in Philippine society the new state restored prewar political and economic institutions that reinforced Philippine dependence on the United States in economic, political, and military terms.

Deeply skeptical about continued American influence in the Philippines, the Huks nevertheless joined the new government in the task of nation building. Wartime Huk commanders tried to negotiate agreements with the Philippine government to secure the surrender of arms, but the refusal of the government to consider peasant problems and implement a genuine program of land reform made progress difficult. Instead the government launched a series of military actions that aimed to disarm the Huks, delegitimize its leaders, and harass its supporters. Harassment of Hukbalahap veterans and peasant union participants by landlord-financed security forces and government troops intensified, starting with the violent suppression of labor and peasant organizations. Acting under official government orders, the Philippine Constabulary systematically ransacked the headquarters of the Pambansang Kaisahan ng mga Magbubukid (National Peasants' Union), or PKM, the largest peasant organization in the country.[11] At the national level Roxas and the Philippine Congress prevented congressmen from Central Luzon who had been elected on the Democratic Alliance (DA) ticket, including Luis Taruc, Jesus Lava, and Alejandro Simpauco, all former Hukbalahap leaders, from taking their seats in Congress, alleging that they had used terror and other illegal means to win.[12] The refusal to seat these representatives, coupled with the Roxas administration's zeal for the use of military force, resulted in more violence in Central Luzon and drove an increasing number of peasants to return to the military underground. According to Benedict Kerkvliet, the last straw was the disappearance and death of Juan Feleo, a popular and highly effective peasant leader, on August 24, 1946.[13] His killing signaled the beginning of a new rebellion. By this time the Huk leaders were convinced that no truce or pacification settlement could be achieved, and soon they returned to the hills to launch a massive resistance movement against government troops and landlords.

The death of Roxas on April 15, 1948, elevated his vice president, Elpidio Quirino, to the presidency, and he moved quickly to quell the "agrarian unrest" in Central and Southern Luzon by proposing land reform programs and amnesty for all Huks who surrendered their weapons. But the Huks' previous experience with the government had left them deeply distrustful, and when the negotiations collapsed they declared all-out war on the Philippine state. Between 1946 and early 1950 the Huk movement gained momentum, claiming at its height between fifteen and twenty thousand armed guerrillas and perhaps one hundred thousand active peasant supporters.[14] Cold war politics and American hostility to communism ensured that the Huks would be excluded from the shaping of the new nation.[15]

Whether the anticommunism of the Philippine government and the United States was justified or not, the history of the Huk movement is inextricably bound up with the history of communism in the Philippines, and most leaders of the Hukbalahap and the HMB were also high-ranking members of the PKP. During World War II the PKP adopted a worldwide (communist) policy of a "united front" in its struggle against the Japanese Occupation.[16] In 1946, as the PKP gained more experience in organization, its leaders promoted principles promulgated by international communism, including historical and dialectical materialism, democratic centralism, and iron discipline, which all required a high level of political awareness among members.[17] In reality, however, many if not most members never reached the level of political consciousness required of Communist Party ideologues.

To advance their communist agenda, the party adopted a new constitution and a new structure (see diagram 2).[18] Party organization was highly centralized, and at the peak of the hierarchy were the Central Committee, which acted as the directing body of the party, and the Political Bureau, or Politburo, its think tank and policy-making organ. From 1945 to 1947 the new Politburo was dominated by Jose Lava (general secretary), Jesus Lava (political commissar), Federico Maclang (organizational chairman), Peregrino Taruc (educational chairman), Ramon Espiritu (finance chairman), Luis Taruc (military chairman), and Casto Alejandrino (assistant military chairman), all of whom had occupied prominent positions in the Hukbalahap.[19] Indeed, in terms of leadership the two organizations were almost identical. The command structure of the Huk movement was thus closely integrated into the PKP. Huk operations in Manila were governed by the "PB In," the Politburo operating inside Manila, and those in Central and Southern Luzon by the "PB Out," the Politburo operating outside Manila.[20]

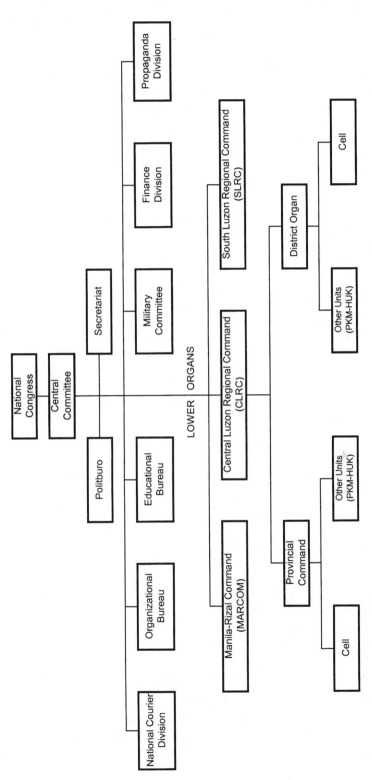

Diagram 2. Structure of the Partido Komunista ng Pilipinas (Communist Party of the Philippines), 1946. (From Department of National Defense, *Handbook on the Communist Party of the Philippines*, 74; and Politburo Exhibit GG, "Organizational Chart of the PKP")

Official histories of the PKP emphasize the role of the Huk rebellion in the prolonged struggle for communism in the Philippines, and, despite the claim of some scholars that the HMB was first and foremost a peasant struggle, its relationship with the PKP remained strong.[21] Although peasants joined the Huks for self-preservation and "to fight for national liberation, freedom from persecution, and social justice," the leaders of the movement remained Communist Party members until the end.[22] And when the party abandoned its United Front policy after World War II for a strategy of more exclusive recruitment and confrontation with the class enemy, Huk leaders immediately set up schools to train their members in the eternal principles of communism and the more fluid principles of the Comintern. The guiding principle of the PKP was democratic centralism, a policy that enabled the party "to act as a whole regardless of unresolved theoretical differences."[23] While every member was given the right to elect delegates to the party congress and to participate in political debates within the party, the rank-and-file members were expected to comply with the decisions of party leaders, a principle that allowed the Politburo to exercise tremendous power in the movement.[24]

Although the Politburo constantly reminded Huk cadres about their duty as communists, they also emphasized the nationalist and agrarian goals of the movement. The People's Liberation Army of the Huks, according to the party, was formed "by the people because of the people," and its primary aim was "to fight against the American Imperialists" and the feudalism that caused "pity, poverty, hardships and death of millions of farmers."[25] While the Huks were waging an ideological battle against American imperialism and Philippine feudalism and capitalism they were also promoting respect for the poor, who they believed had been abandoned by the state. Peasant followers were especially made aware of the practical goals of Huk and Communist ideology, including better agricultural conditions, a larger share of the crop, easier access to credit, and the extension of landownership.[26]

To the Americans and the Philippine government it was not this practical appeal but the promise of a communist society that explained the success of the Huk movement and the threat it posed to the political order. While the government acknowledged the poverty and "general atmosphere of illiteracy, poor health, and stagnancy in the rural communities," it believed the communists who "undertook the organization of the restive agricultural workers in Central Luzon" were encouraging economic illusions and exploiting the "antagonistic attitudes" of peasants toward the government "in order to incite lawlessness and disorder."[27] Consistent with cold war ideology and policy the Philippine and U.S. governments accused the Communist Party of destroying the country's freedom and prescribed a military solution to the rebellion. Since the Huks were "plain Communists who sought only to overthrow democracy and the Philippine government, and to brainwash the poor peasantry that their economic and social problems can be solved through bloodshed, violence and revolution," the solution to the peasant problem proposed by the two governments was repression and the defeat of the armed rebels.[28] Not surprisingly, the Communist Party agreed with the Philippine government that its role in the rebellion was pivotal.[29] But while the government dismissed the Huks as "plain communists," the party believed the social injustices created by the Philippine economy and American colonialism were the most immediate cause of peasant unrest. "The best way to expose American imperialism," the party argued, "is to force them to intervene in aid of the much hated puppets, without giving any justifiable cause." Only in this way could "the myth of American altruism be shattered."[30]

Party intellectuals such as William Pomeroy, the American soldier and writer who joined the Huk movement in the 1940s, believed Huk members and the Communist Party found common ground in the postwar struggle.[31] According to his memoir *The Forest*, in 1944:

> I came to the Philippines as a soldier myself. It was in the midst of a war against fascism, a war in which I believed deeply. We had come, I thought, as liberators, to oust an invader that was ravaging the country. I was not prepared for what I found.[32]

What Pomeroy found was the "finest of all Filipino guerrilla movements, the Hukbalahap," whose leaders had been arrested by the American-supported Philippine government and whose squadron members were regularly shot to death. He also saw American military forces acting in the interest of big landlords to suppress the peasant movement. Pomeroy therefore found an additional reason to stay. He recalled:

> To my intense shame, I was not a member of an army bringing freedom; I was a member of an army reestablishing an imperialist rule. I swore to myself then that I would not rest until I had done all that I could to correct that wrong, until I had wiped

from my own hands the moral stain that had been placed there, until I had put my American strength on the side of those who had suffered from American imperialism.[33]

While Pomeroy recognized that most peasants did not have a full grasp of communist ideology, he believed they had a basic understanding of economic justice, as the words of one ordinary peasant, Ka Pedring, revealed:

> You know, today it is the landlord who is the power. No job is given in my town without the approval of the landlords. Jobs are favors given to those who are loyal or subservient to the landlords' interests. . . . If a peasant goes to the Constabulary for protection against the landlord, they laugh at him or slap him. The peasant, well, you know the peasant is made to be the slave of the landlord.[34]

And when Pomeroy asked him, "What does taking of power mean to you?" Ka Pedring had a ready reply:

> I think I will have more to eat. I think I will have shoes. I think I will have a better house to live in. My kids will go to school, to all the grades. We will all have good education. I think there will be more of those things for everybody because most of the money will go for our good and not to the landlord or to his crooked henchmen politicians or to foreigners who take it out of the country.[35]

While Pomeroy framed such sentiments himself, he always believed that peasants in Central Luzon possessed both ideological and practical motives for participating in the Huk rebellion. Luis Taruc, a Hukbala-hap leader and the son of a tenant farmer in Pampanga, believed that the merger of the Socialist and the Communist parties played a crucial role in mobilizing the peasants and workers against the Japanese and subsequently against the state and landlords.[36] The Huk leader Jesus Lava, who became secretary-general of the PKP, returned "to the mountains" in July 1946 convinced that the Philippine government had no intention of fulfilling its promise to share power with the Huks and sought only to intimidate peasants in the countryside.[37] According to ordinary Huk members, government repression increased peasant frustration and pushed them back toward rebellion. Instead of instituting social reform programs to address peasant grievances, the government opted to "crush" and "eliminate" the rebels using military force. Faced with such repression, peasants had little choice but to flee to the mountains.[38]

But what about the women? While women are largely invisible in most accounts of the Huk rebellion, their experience allows us to go beyond purely political, economic, and ideological interpretations of the revolt. The voices of Huk women make clear that cultural and social relations and the relationships between the Huks, their families, and their communities are as crucial as political ideology to an understanding of their demobilization or continued mobilization after 1945.

The Mobilization and Demobilization of Huk Women

Most accounts of the Huk rebellion written by men who were involved in both the Hukbalahap and HMB movements treat the postwar revolt as the continuation of the struggle against foreign—first Japanese and later American—imperialism, implicitly assuming that the Huk organization remained essentially the same.[39] In this narrative of the postwar Huk rebellion the beliefs and behavior of Huk men (and implicitly women) were mere extensions of their roles in the wartime phase of the revolutionary struggle. Other interpretations of the Huk rebellion recognize it as a culmination of the long-standing tradition of peasant resistance in Philippine history.[40] But placing women in the history of the rebellion produces a rather different picture, revealing both continuity and discontinuity in the Hukbalahap and other peasant struggles. While a considerable number of women remained in the HMB, many female rebels left the movement at the end of the war. The incorporation of women's experience in the history of the rebellion also shows that, in contrast to the views of the leadership, there were major differences between Communist Party mobilization in the Japanese period and under the postwar Philippine Republic. Women understood these differences intimately, and this awareness shaped their decisions about whether or not to leave the Huk movement.[41]

Araceli Mallari, who had assumed a prominent position in the Hukbalahap organization during the war, working as secretary to Jose Lava, a Politburo member and later secretary-general of the Communist Party, decided not to join the HMB after the war, claiming that "the people were already tired after the war, and you cannot make them revolt just like that."[42] Contrary to what the party advocated, Araceli was convinced that there was no revolutionary situation in the Philippines ("not at that moment, during that time, and even until now") that most people yearned for peace after years of suffering during the war. She remembered that people were just anxious to put their lives back in order. "The people were not yet ready for the taking up of power—because people were still eating," she explained, and as long as basic necessities such as food were provided for them there was no need for the guerrillas to take up arms again. Many Huks would find such convictions problematic, especially coming from someone like Araceli, who returned to her middle-class life in Manila after the war. But it is also possible that Araceli felt conflicted about not joining her former comrades in the struggle and therefore used her disagreement with official party policy to justify her reluctance. While it is not certain that Araceli's views were shared by many Huk peasants, Avelina Santos from Pampanga, who worked as a Huk nurse during the war, nevertheless shared her desire to live peacefully after the hardships of the Japanese Occupation. During the final days of the war she ate nothing substantial for more than a month, and her life was threatened daily by bombing raids. By the end of the war all she wanted to do was to return home to her family.[43] Both Araceli and Avelina were lukewarm about resuming their revolutionary lives in the HMB.

Many Huk women felt the same way, and many had to return to work to support their families. Manila youth leader Puring Bulatao was very active in the Hukbalahap and was imprisoned by the Japanese because of her political activities. But despite being married to Rosendo Feleo, the son of slain peasant leader Juan Feleo, Puring decided to "lie low" after the war. When her husband became sick after being tortured by the Japanese, they decided to withdraw from the movement, a decision Puring believed was understood by her former comrades. She moved to Manila where she worked "for survival" at a government agency, the Philippine Employees Association.[44] The Valerio sisters, Amparo and Belen, who had wholeheartedly supported the wartime Hukbalahap army, also decided not to join the postwar HMB. Amparo wanted to go back to high school, and Belen had to take care of their elderly parents after the war. Both decided to stay in Cabiao, Nueva Ecija, and since their village continued to be a Huk stronghold they continued to support the HMB guerrillas who frequented their village, although they had doubts about the wisdom of continuing the rebellion.[45] Although Felisa Cuyugan wanted to join her Huk comrades in the mountains, she and her husband opted to limit their involvement because of the trauma they had endured during the war. Her husband's health shattered, they left the Huk camps before the war ended only to be arrested by the Japanese once again. Although they survived their ordeals, the war permanently damaged their lives. Physically and emotionally, Felisa was unable to continue her revolutionary involvement, realizing that the postwar HMB struggle would be even more difficult than the struggle against the Japanese.[46]

Ana Sula, a prewar socialist and Huk organizer from Pampanga who had been very active in the wartime Hukbalahap, also hesitated to join the HMB, especially when her husband decided to join his fellow Huk comrades and become part of an expansion team sent to the Visayas. Instead she decided to stay in their home in Central Luzon to give a semblance of normalcy to their young children's lives. As a result she rarely saw her husband, who was eventually killed in an encounter between Huk guerrillas and the Philippine army.[47] Like Ana, most Huk women were ambivalent about joining the HMB because the Huks were no longer fighting foreign aggressors but fellow Filipinos. Despite the official Communist rhetoric, which presented the Huk rebellion as a continuation of the national liberation struggle and a class war against the wealth and privilege of the rich, many women were unconvinced. They had viewed the Hukbalahap movement as primarily a war for national self-preservation, a struggle against a brutal foreign invader. But with independence in 1946 the situation changed and the enemy was now fellow Filipinos. Many women believed there was much less popular enthusiasm for the Communist-led HMB than there had been for the Hukbalahap, and the erosion of support in the villages of Central Luzon had a powerful impact on women whose commitment to the Hukbalahap had been grounded in their sense of community affiliation.

Leonila Sayco, the daughter of a peasant family in Pampanga who served in the education department of the Hukbalahap, lost her husband before the war ended. Like everybody else she went hungry for days and spent nights sleeping with no roof over her head. Although she understood the objectives of the HMB and sympathized with the guerrillas who continued the struggle, she was too sick and heartbroken to rejoin her former comrades. She also admitted that the postwar struggle was harder to justify because "*ibang-iba na* [the HMB was very different]." Whereas literally everyone in the villages supported the Huks during the Japanese Occupation, it was "more difficult to join the HMB because they were no longer fighting the Japanese." The issue of class struggle—war between rich landlords and poor peasants—did not strike the same chord with many women. "We've had that war forever," clarified Leonila, "but that was harder to fight than the Japanese."[48]

Huk organizer Filomena Tolentino also believed that the HMB struggle was more complex and difficult, but she did not completely agree with Leonila. "Yes, the Japanese were gone," she reasoned, "but do we truly have our own *kalayaan,* freedom? No, not yet. First, the Americans were still here. They still controlled our economy and our politics. That was not yet freedom."[49] Together with her husband, Filomena supported the Huks by participating in peasant organizations and giving money to the movement, but despite her belief ("How can you not believe? We knew they were fighting for the liberation of the peasants and the workers.") she did not go back to the mountains to fight with her comrades. Like Filomena, hundreds of men and women in Central Luzon supported the HMB despite their decision not to take up arms again, and, although many former Hukbalahap women decided not to remain Huks, they understood why the rebellion had to continue. Women such as Marcosa de la Rosa, Luz del Castillo, and Elang Santa Ana chose to live relatively peaceful lives after the war, but they fully supported the Huk cause and felt the only choice left for their former comrades was rebellion.

These women's reasons for not joining the HMB were largely practical and personal rather than political, although the line between what was personal and what was political was often crossed. Many women, for example, were forced to temporarily abandon the struggle to raise their families. Elang Santa Ana lived and worked as a vendor in Manila, but despite her poverty she allowed her husband, Federico Maclang, to fight with the Huks and contributed whatever she could to the movement.[50] Similarly, Marcosa de la Rosa, daughter of the Huk and Communist leader Lope de la Rosa, left the Hukbalahap and moved back to Manila after the war to look after her children. Although she did not take up arms again, Marcosa kept in touch with her Huk comrades and risked her personal safety many times to help the HMB movement.[51] She considered the postwar period a time of "civil war" in the Philippines when there was no real peace, when "all organizations that stood for the interests of the poor were suspect, and when the government dismissed her comrades as Communists so it could continue to support the U.S. interests and exploit the people." Since no change was possible through the government, she believed the Huks had to explore all possible means to achieve their goals and "that is why the party organized the HMB."[52] On a more practical level, she pointed out that the Huks were pushed to the wall and had no choice but to declare a revolution since they were being killed and their organizations had been declared illegal. Although she did not officially become an HMB cadre, Marcosa's convictions show that even those who left the movement remained deeply sympathetic with its aims.

Luz del Castillo, daughter of the well-known peasant leader Mateo del Castillo, who married and started a family soon after the war, believed many Huks had little choice but to rejoin the rebellion. Although attempts to recruit her were unsuccessful, she needed no persuasion

In a rare photograph, Luz del Castillo is shown here with fellow Huk female cadre Felisa Cuyugan, along with male Huk leaders and members. While Luz and Felisa were never formally part of the HMB, they belonged to the extensive support network of the Huks and the Communists, who were briefly arrested as "Huk and communist suspects," although they were eventually released. (n.d. [late 1940s or early 1950s]; Courtesy of Rizal Library, Ateneo de Manila University)

challenging political environment that existed in postwar Central and Southern Luzon. But it also hindered the movement, making it easier for the government to argue that the HMB did not have popular support and harder for the HMB to mobilize the same sources of support in the barrios that had been available to the Hukbalahap, especially among barrio women. Women such as Tomasa Arnao, for example, who donated her land to the movement to express her support for the goals of the Huk struggle, were crucial to the survival of the HMB.[76] Building popular trust and support, however, became increasingly difficult because of government propaganda and the daily reports in Philippine newspapers about the "abuses" of the Huks, including intimidation, looting, rape, and even murder. According to the *Philippines Free Press*, villagers were caught in the middle of a war between ruthless Communist guerrillas and unsympathetic and occasionally brutal members of the Philippine Constabulary:

> If the peasants refuse to give the Huks what they want (like food and clothing), the latter beat them up and perhaps kill them. There have been such tragic incidents. . . . A farmer declared: Can a farmer refuse to give food to hungry Huks who come during the night with a gun? We are helpless. The trouble with the Constabulary [is that] . . . after their operations, they go back to their quarters leaving us at the mercy of the Huks. And yet whenever they receive rumors that Huks have passed by our homes, they (the PCs) slap our faces, kick us around, beat us with the butts of their rifles and sometimes shoot us. What can we do?[77]

Because newspapers published disturbing reports about the guerrillas and because their mere presence in the barrios, often pursued by military patrols, created an atmosphere of fear and intimidation for ordinary villagers, the Huks had to be extremely careful about soliciting donations and not alienating their supporters.

Respect for villagers was mandated by the principles of the HMB organization, and, as official Party documents emphasize, cadres were encouraged to cultivate popular support and respect in the barrios. The Constitution of the PKP outlined the moral qualities expected of a cadre. "A revolutionary and lover of freedom," it declared, should be a "good teacher and leader" who is "concerned and loving to comrades, friendly and gets along well with neighbors and the masses," but who does not believe in "Bahala Na" (Leave it to God). Cadres were warned not to "indulge in vices (gambling, drinking, and *women*)" and never about the justice of the Huk cause. As part of a political family whose siblings, mother, and father left Manila to return to the mountains of Central and Southern Luzon, she expressed strong support for the Huks:

> The Huks participated in the elections because they wanted democracy, so they can serve the country legally. But those in power knew that if they allowed them to sit, they would protect the rights of the poor. Of course the landlords and the rich people wouldn't want that and since they didn't want to face them or fight with them legally, the Huks were outlawed, even killed. Feleo was my father's friend and comrade. They also wanted to kill my father during what they called the Pacification Campaign (when they were telling the Huks to surrender their weapons). So the Huks who thought that we had a democracy and wanted to have quiet lives became hunted and therefore had to go back to the mountains.[53]

While personal circumstances prevented women such as Elang, Marcosa, and Luz from rejoining the Huks, they continued to support the mission of the HMB and, like most former Hukbalahap women, usually became part of its extensive support network.

But a significant number of women did become full-time members of the HMB, and the issue of female agency plays an even more important part in their decisions to join the struggle. While influential male figures remained important in the lives of Huk women, the decision to become an active guerrilla after the war depended more on women's own convictions and desires. During the Hukbalahap struggle, women had often been encouraged by men to join the guerrillas, but during the postwar transition many men encouraged women to leave the HMB and resume their conventional place in the home. The women who decided to stay in the movement therefore had to have compelling reasons to continue, and in general these women, steeled by wartime experience, military training, and a communist education, were no longer political novices. Almost all the women who served in the HMB remembered the postwar struggle as having been more difficult and recalled the enormous demands it placed on their physical bodies and emotional lives. The more complex (and hazardous) nature of the postwar struggle required greater political and ideological sophistication from all its male and female members, and as the HMB was transformed into a more exclusive organization women were forced to become more conscious of the movement's political and ideological goals.

Women such as Rosenda Torres, Teofista Valerio, and Zenaida del Castillo, who had played major roles in the Hukbalahap, responded immediately and with varying degrees of enthusiasm when the predominantly male leadership called for a return to revolution. For them there was no question that the Huks should take up arms once again. Rosenda Torres, a dedicated Hukbalahap educator and Communist Party member from Pampanga, at first wanted to finish her education, but a chance encounter with one of the Huk leaders convinced her to rejoin the underground struggle. Restless at school and disturbed by the volatile political situation in the country, Rosenda was deeply angered by the government's attitude toward the Huks and by the murder of Juan Feleo and Manuel Joven. "I was ambitious," she recalled. "I wanted to learn more." But she only "really decided [to rejoin the Huks] when they were already killing us. They killed our leaders. If they were not threatened, then they might not have fled to the mountains."[54] Rosenda, who was still only twenty at that time, decided to abandon her studies and "learn in the university of life" under the HMB. Virginia Calma, another Huk educator from Pampanga, believed "there was still a struggle to be waged against those who refused to grant the poor their rights." Together with her husband, who was also a Huk cadre, she returned to the movement's headquarters in the mountains, although she admitted that popular support for the Huks had diminished. She was also only eighteen when she joined the HMB, but her experiences hastened her political maturity.[55]

For a short period, Teofista Valerio resumed life with her family in Nueva Ecija, but she quickly left to work full time for the HMB. Serving as the youth and female representative of the Partido Nacionalista, she witnessed firsthand how the Huks were attacked by the government, their elected representatives unseated and their organizations driven underground. When the government branded members of the Hukbalahap as "*bandido,* or plain bandits," Teofista felt personally threatened and immediately went into hiding. After witnessing a "Huk guerrilla dragged to his death during the so-called pacification program of the government" in 1946, she attended a party meeting at which the Huks decided to continue the struggle.[56] In October 1947 she became part of the Central Luzon Committee of the Communist Party and worked full time at the Huk headquarters. As she later recalled, her decision was shaped by anger and fear for her safety:

> Because I was scared to be arrested and it was clear to me what we were fighting for—they [the Philippine government] did not

recognize the Hukbalahap. We fought against the Japanese, but we were not recognized. They also ignored our demands and our rights. We wanted to struggle as parliamentarians, like Dr. Lava, Luis Taruc, but the government did not let them sit [in Congress]. So, I decided to join the Huks again. We continued what we were fighting for.[57]

For Teofista there was no distinction between the Hukbalahap and the HMB, but she realized that for most people in Central Luzon the continuity of the struggle was harder to grasp. She explained:

During the Japanese period . . . everyone was fighting against the Japanese. Everyone was united as comrades. When the Japanese left, you realized that your friends were really your enemies. You did not know. There were many selfish people. They wanted others to suffer and only improve their own lives. During the Japanese time, when you pass by a barrio, they will protect and take care of you even though they don't know you. During the HMB, you do not know whether the person facing you is a supporter or an enemy. People had a *mababang kaalaman* [very limited understanding] of what you were doing. They will say, "The Japanese are no longer here, so what else were you fighting for?" Many people did not understand what the HMB was fighting for.[58]

While it was more difficult to explain to the Central Luzon villagers the rationale behind the new rebellion, Teofista never tired of trying. She argued:

We are fighting against the government. We are fighting for the peasants so that they will be given land to till. We want the tuition lowered so those that needed to go to school will go to school. The teachers' salaries should go up, and the workers should have their rights and higher salaries. The prices of goods should be lowered. And the government was not doing any of these.[59]

But despite her efforts to evangelize for the Huks Teofista was aware that many peasants remained skeptical, and she understood why most women who had served in the Hukbalahap chose not to continue the fight after 1945. "The enemy was the Japanese before the war," she explained, "but now it was Filipino versus Filipino."

Even after all those years Teofista was unapologetic about her revolutionary activities, and her motivations remained clear and fresh in her mind.[60] But other women who continued to serve in the HMB, such as Zenaida del Castillo, were more skeptical about the postwar struggle. An energetic Hukbalahap guerrilla, Zenaida recognized that the Huks had been pushed into a corner. Instead of being honored for their role during the war they were being disarmed, killed, and treated worse than Japanese collaborators. And yet Zenaida later wondered whether the Huks' call to arms in 1946 played into the government's hands, allowing it to delegitimize the movement, brand the rebels "communists," and isolate them from the people who had once supported them. Although Zenaida, like most other Huks who rejoined the struggle, fled to escape arrest and persecution, she sometimes wondered whether armed resistance was the best way to fight the government.[61]

Not all HMB women came from the ranks of the wartime guerrillas, and some became Huks only in the postwar period. Despite a more selective process of recruitment, the Huks continued to mobilize supporters in the villages, and while men were still the priority the movement continued to welcome women. Linda Ayala and Belen Bagul-Bagul were just two of the women who were too young to fight during the Japanese Occupation but joined the Huks during the postwar struggle. Linda Ayala, who came from a peasant family, first encountered the Huks in her village in Tayabas during the war. When they returned to her barrio after the war, she was immediately attracted to their goals, which were, she remembered, "to defend the oppressed and the poor — so we will all have equal rights." Realizing that the Huks were not the bandits portrayed in the press, Linda joined the movement, and after a brief period of schooling in the forest she became convinced of the justice of their cause. She explained:

> I knew by then what the movement was all about. I knew they were right. The government was siding with the Americans. And what did the Americans do to us — except exploit us? So I understood it. I accepted that the Huks were fighting for our rights, our rights as citizens, to drive out those who were oppressing us. And I knew that even though I will die in the movement these principles would be intact.[62]

Belen Bagul-Bagul, who was from a militant peasant family, was also a young girl when the Japanese invaded the Philippines, but after the war she joined a clandestine youth organization in her village and attended discussions about the political situation in the country. Cadres of the HMB often held meetings in her village, and she later recalled being scared of the Philippine Constabulary, which monitored villagers' actions and constantly pursued the Huk guerrillas. In 1948 she decided to join the HMB, believing that the only way to empower poor people was to mobilize them for revolution. Outraged by the way people in power, especially the police, "abused, harassed, and threatened villagers," Belen was convinced that the Huks offered the poor their only chance "to stand up to their oppressors."[63]

According to Belen her political convictions inspired her to join the HMB, but for most others kinship networks continued to play a significant role in recruitment, and most of the women who stayed and worked in the Huk camps after the war were the wives of male soldiers. Elena Sawit, for example, a Huk organizer from Nueva Ecija, was married to Communist Party leader Felicisimo Macapagal and joined him in the Huk camps in the Sierra Madre in Laguna soon after the war.[64] Her primary motive was to be with her husband for she believed it was a wife's duty to stay with her husband wherever he might be. But she also served the Huk movement wholeheartedly, and when her husband was assigned to the Visayas as part of the Huks' "expansion work" Elena joined him.[65]

Rosita Manuel, who was married to Silvestre Liwanag, a peasant and Huk squadron commander from Pampanga, chose not to challenge her husband's decision to join the HMB. She even made the difficult decision to leave their children with her parents so she could accompany her husband to the mountains. She poignantly said, years later:

> How can I not accept [the rebellion]? . . . Of course, because we were already there and my husband was part of it. When we were together I did not think that we should rest or stop for a while. I never told him that. I never questioned him. Even though we were young, I already knew who he was. I never told him to leave the movement.[66]

Was Rosita more dedicated to her husband than the HMB movement? While there is no straightforward answer to this question, what was clear in Rosita's mind was that the Huks, including her husband, and their principles were inseparable. Another Huk leader, Peregrino Taruc (head of the educational division and brother of Luis Taruc), and his wife, Gloria Aquino, lived in the Huk camps together, at times with several of their children. Although Gloria always reiterated that she "was not very political" when she was growing up, her marriage to Taruc in 1943 inevitably drew her into the revolutionary movement.

But, like Rosita, Gloria's commitment to the movement may have begun—and probably ended—with her commitment to her husband, and despite her contribution to the movement she always considered the Huk struggle to be her husband's.[67] Dominga Centeno claimed that she also became a Huk "because my husband was part of the HMB." Although she was in the Hukbalahap in Nueva Ecija, Dominga initially stayed aloof from the HMB struggle, confessing that she did not understand the need to continue the armed struggle after 1945. "Why have the HMB when there were no more Japanese in the country?" she asked. Eventually however, she came to appreciate the position of her husband and the other Huks who "were not happy" about government harassment and repression. When her husband and his comrades, who were already "wanted" by the government, left for the Sierra Madre, she realized that her life was also in danger, and once in the camps she developed a deeper sense of loyalty not only to her husband but also to the Huk movement.[68]

While personal networks were crucial to the mobilization of many women, these same kinship relations also explained their demobilization. Since most women who served in the Hukbalahap were young and single, becoming guerrillas did not create significant conflicts with their familial obligations. But by the time of the HMB mobilization many of these women, now in their twenties, were married and expected to have children. These women faced enormous pressures to quit the movement and concentrate on their families, and despite their experiences as guerrillas most continued to believe that their primary responsibility and identity as women revolved around nurturing a family.[69] Luz del Castillo, for example, decided to support the HMB only indirectly after 1945. While her father, Mateo del Castillo, and other family members escaped to the camps of Southern Luzon, Luz stayed with her newly wed husband in Manila. The birth of a child soon after the war made it doubly hard for her to resume the life of a revolutionary.[70] Filomena Tolentino was in an even more difficult situation. When she accepted the proposal of a Huk suitor, she had to choose between being a Huk or a wife and mother, especially as her husband had children from a previous marriage. Despite her belief in the Huk cause, Filomena decided to stay at home, take care of the children, and support the guerrillas in whatever way she could.[71] The same tension shaped the decision of peasant leader Leonila Sayco, who had served as a Huk educator during the war but believed that caring for a family was more important than her commitment to the movement. She believed that joining the HMB would mark her failure as a woman and a mother, and, like many Hukbalahap women, she chose to raise a family after the war and limit her involvement in the movement.[72]

For the most part the Huk leadership did nothing to discourage women like Leonila from leaving the movement, thus reinforcing the broader climate of antagonism to women's political involvement that operated in postwar Philippine society. Many of the young, single women who had joined the Hukbalahap feared their social reputations had been tarnished by their close association with its mostly male members and their independence from parental authority. They felt great pressure to reclaim their identity as women after the war and regain the respect of their families and communities. The best way to do this was to marry and have children. The refusal of many women to sacrifice the sources of their femininity—marriage and children—played a crucial role in limiting their involvement, and the lack of aggressive female recruitment and retention within the HMB reinforced the cultural conservatism that discouraged women from participating in the movement.

In her work on women in the postwar Greek resistance movement, a movement also led by communists, Janet Hart argues that women's demobilization was closely linked to the intensity of government repression (including torture, sexual violation, homelessness, and unemployment) and to the imposition of cultural taboos on women who engaged in political activities.[73] In Greece, the state launched a full-scale ideological offensive depicting female revolutionaries as "moral degenerates" who were "dangerous to public welfare" to make sure they returned home and stayed there. Hukbalahap women were exposed to similar repressive, ideological pressures designed to prevent their recruitment in the next stage of the Huk rebellion. Political repression and government propaganda that portrayed guerrillas as immoral and unpatriotic, and guerrilla women as "unnatural" mothers or threatening Amazons, played a key role in deterring women. As many women testified, the government assault on the Huks—unseating their elected representatives, delegitimizing their organizations, harassing their supporters, and even killing the rebels themselves—instilled fear and uncertainty in many of the movement's female supporters. And for many choosing a "peaceful" life was not a choice but the only way to guarantee the safety of their families. But political repression and heavy-handed government propaganda was a double-edged sword, and if it deterred female participation it also provided a legitimate reason to take up arms again. Thus, despite intense political repression and the absence of effective recruitment policies in the HMB, women such as Rosenda, Teofista, and Zenaida, who decided to join the HMB and its underground networks, and women such as Luz, Filomena, and Marcosa, who indirectly supported the Huks, remained dedicated to the revolutionary principles of the movement and what they believed was the abandonment of the poor by the postwar Philippine Republic.

New Roles and Responsibilities in the HMB

By 1946 the HMB had launched a revolutionary war against the new Philippine Republic and the government had mobilized both the military and the Philippine Constabulary against these "Communist guerrillas." In this new political context the HMB movement had to create new strategies to elicit peasant support in Central and Southern Luzon. Because Communist Party policy was no longer shaped by the need to create a united front against the Japanese and was now directed toward class enemies in the countryside, the Huks were more careful about entering villages to mobilize supporters and more wary about their degree of support among the peasantry.[74] This was reflected in the internal reorganization of the Huk movement. During the war the Hukbalahap was organized to build a broadly based and popular resistance army that had the support of all Filipinos. In contrast, during the postwar period the organization of the HMB was less ad hoc and designed to create a more exclusive and disciplined military and political movement that could operate in a socially divisive and polarized countryside. Superficially, however, the HMB functioned much like the Hukbalahap. The Secretariat served the administrative needs of the Politburo, the Organizational Bureau was concerned with the recruitment of cadres, the Finance Unit was responsible for the procurement of needed supplies, and the Propaganda Bureau handled the problem of creating a mass base for the movement. The rank and file of the Huk organization—mostly cadres and soldiers—obeyed the directives of the leadership, and each member had particular functions: to carry out propaganda and organizational work; to enforce party programs and decisions; to act as a liaison between the party and the masses; and to absorb new members, collect fees, educate party members, and enforce discipline.[75] Most Huks belonged to one or more of these bodies, and, just as in the Hukbalahap, most women served in the support units of the HMB.

Creating a more disciplined and exclusive organization thus reflected the changing political goals of the Huk movement and more

to be individualistic, selfish, or "blinded by money and worldliness."[78] Although the Constitution applied to all cadres, it is clear from its language — the use of the word *lalaki* (men) and *babae* (women) in the Tagalog version, and the constant use of *he/his* in the English version — that these principles were directed toward men. Both male and female members, however, believed it was their adherence to this particular set of ethical principles and their respect for people that ensured continued loyalty in the villages. Former Hukbalahap guerrillas such as Felisa Cuyugan believed the Huks were always "upright, trustworthy, and loyal" to the cause of the peasants, and even though Felisa decided to "lie low" after the war in order to care for her sick husband she welcomed the Huks to her house in San Fernando, Pampanga, which became an informal headquarters for the movement. Throughout the rebellion she stayed in contact with Huk leaders such as Casto Alejandrino and the Lavas and periodically sent doctors and medicines to the mountain camps.[79]

Women sustained much of the Huk underground network not only in the provinces but also in Manila. Although Araceli Mallari did not fully agree with the leadership's decision to launch another revolution, she continued to support her former comrades, and her house in Caloocan also became an informal headquarters for Huk leaders when they met in Manila. She later recalled the heated discussions among leaders that transpired in her living room. In addition to accommodating the leaders, in 1947 Araceli founded the Philippine Women's Society in Manila, a women's organization that was affiliated with the PKP. She attended rallies in support of the HMB in the early postwar years and delivered speeches at Plaza Miranda in the heart of Manila, activities she was forced to suspend when government repression intensified in 1950.[80] Marcosa de la Rosa also provided temporary shelter to Huk cadres in Manila and, together with her husband, became part of a neighborhood association that was affiliated with the Left.[81] Rosenda and Cesar Torres, part of the HMB's education division, both worked in a clandestine printing office in Manila. Because they were educated, their main assignment was writing and reviewing articles for the movement's revolutionary newspapers, *Titis* (Spark) and *Ang Komunista* (Communist). But on several occasions Rosenda resumed her former work as a Hukbalahap guerrilla and was sent to the barrios to educate and train HMB recruits.[82]

Women, in other words, were as central to the organization of the HMB as they had been to the Hukbalahap, serving on almost all the

This group of young, mostly peasant women from Pampanga was arrested by the police as "Huk suspects," although they were eventually released. This image is instructive in two ways. First, it shows how ordinary barrio women were easily suspected as part of the Huk network, and second, it shows not only how extensive Huk support was in the barrios but also how women formed an integral part of that network. (*Manila Times*, November 7, 1949; Courtesy of Rizal Library, Ateneo de Manila University)

support and service committees and performing a multiplicity of roles inside the HMB. But they also contributed to the organizational efficiency of the Huk movement by mobilizing popular support for the underground movement in Manila and the barrios of Central Luzon. As Sofia Logarta states, the women's primary role in the movement was to form a "strong link between the guerrillas and their mass support."[83] Like their predecessors in the Hukbalahap, women played a key role at the margins of the movement, mediating between the Huk army and its thousands of peasant and working-class supporters.

Life in the Camps

At the center of the Huk movement, however, the revolutionary struggle changed after 1945. No longer able to establish bases in the villages of Central Luzon, HMB guerrillas lived mostly in forest camps located in the Sierra Madre, close to the villages but a safe distance from the military authorities. William Pomeroy considered these Huk camps, composed of several huts built on a series of heavily wooded ridges, as the nerve center of the revolution.[84] On the outer ridges were security huts and on the inner ridges were camp households, each housing a particular division of the movement. Most camps also included a school and a social hall where guerrillas could gather for meetings. Women who lived in the camps remembered them as bustling centers of activity alive with the buzz of constant meetings to strategize about the movement's goals and directions. Couriers came and went, soldiers moved hurriedly from one assignment to the next, and party educators labored at typewriters and mimeograph machines, churning out articles for *Titis* or preparing lesson plans for new and old recruits. According to Pomeroy there were literally hundreds of such camps, housing 10 to 150 Huks each, scattered in "mountains, in forests, in swamps, [and] in the grassland areas" of Luzon and other parts of the Philippines, giving shelter to perhaps 10,000 Huks.[85]

Most women who were married to HMB leaders and soldiers lived in these forest camps. While some were assigned roles in the movement, others remained on the periphery performing housekeeping duties. Indeed, most women recalled that their main contribution to the movement was household work—cooking, cleaning, and washing clothes. Gloria Aquino, for instance, spent most of her time cooking and cleaning, and so did Rosita Manuel and Dominga Centeno, who believed such work was not only essential but also gave a sense of normalcy to their otherwise unstable revolutionary lives. But sustaining households in the camps was not easy. Perhaps the biggest challenge women faced was feeding the guerrillas without adequate supplies of food. Rosita recalled that during the latter part of the rebellion she "used to boil root crops, or guava leaves, and anything [I] found in the forest to feed [my] fellow Huks."[86] Living in the mountains became a test of endurance, she exclaimed: "If you were not strong, you would have died easily." Dominga, along with many other women in the camps, also worked hard to ensure that the Huks were as well fed and clothed as possible. But she missed going to the barrios to interact with people as she had done in the Hukbalahap:

> Most of us women did not do many things in the mountains of Sierra Madre. You cannot because you cannot organize people anymore. The leaders were constantly meeting there. But we were not included there, only officials were meeting. So, what did I do? Well, I washed clothes, and I cooked rice, if there was rice. If not, I just cook whatever was there. When there were no activities in the camps, I did production work that mostly involved looking for food, for example, unearthing sweet potatoes. There were many huts there, and we built our own huts in the mountains. We had to make sure that the households were maintained in the forests. Sometimes we had dances in our common playground.[87]

"I only followed my husband," added Dominga. "I did not have any responsibility in the group. How can I have a role when those who were there were carrying guns?" Since she was not an "armed guerrilla," she claimed that no responsibilities were assigned to her other than household work, although eventually she was taught how to administer first aid, used as a courier, and asked to raise supplies in the barrios. For women who did not consider themselves political this experience was typical, although even Dominga gradually supplemented her primary task of taking care of her husband and other men with a more varied range of activities.

Women not only performed household work but also participated in the common life and activities of the camps. Belen Bagul-Bagul remembered life in the camps as *maraming trabaho* (always busy) and *masaya* (lively, happy), at least during the early years of the rebellion. During the mornings and afternoons cadres attended Forest School, exercised, cooked and ate meals together, and then completed homework, assignments, and tasks such as typing documents. Belen especially enjoyed the evenings when the Huks got together after dinner to tell stories, sing songs, report news from the "outside," and sometimes hold open forums to discuss organizational problems. "I especially loved," she fondly recalled, "TNT or *Tagisan ng Talino*," quiz nights, when different groups battled each other using their knowledge of political events and the Huk organization. "In order to prepare for these competitions, participants needed to read a lot of materials, especially concerning current events," Belen continued, "but in the process, I always acquired new knowledge." Because the Huks were instructed to be alert and keep up with what was happening in the movement and the world outside the forest, she "never got bored in the camps."[88]

Most women in the HMB did courier work. Women had also played a key role as couriers in the Hukbalahap period, and in recognition of the importance of communications to the success of its revolutionary activities the party reorganized its postwar courier network into a separate group, the National Communications Division (NCD), which ensured close and regular coordination between the party and its far-flung guerrilla units. The regular and timely flow of information and orders was imperative to the success of the Huk military campaigns. The Politburo depended on the NCD to deliver orders, provisions, and letters and to supply it with reports from the rank and file. The NCD was also the only means of communication between guerrillas and their families as the government's postal system was deemed unsafe.[89]

Just as in the Hukbalahap and other revolutionary movements, courier work in the HMB was highly gendered and relied on the invisibility and innocuousness of women, who were commonly perceived as focused on mundane, day-to-day activities within the narrow boundaries of the home and the village.[90] Cadres themselves believed courier work suited women because it did not require much skill. And yet being a courier involved a great deal of intelligence and was often risky. Women couriers had to infiltrate unfamiliar villages and communities, interact with local people, and locate party contacts without inviting suspicion. They had to possess intelligence, a good memory, a capacity for quick decisions, courage, and unflinching loyalty to the movement, and they had to be prepared at any moment to sacrifice their lives to preserve the secrets of the movement.[91] Linda Ayala knew how difficult and dangerous courier work could be:

> As a courier, I constantly trekked from Quezon to Pampanga and back. It was *mahirap talaga,* a [very] difficult job. Sometimes you don't eat at all, such as the time in Quezon when I lived a whole month with hardly any food. Many comrades also got caught because of our dangerous mission. There were several times that plainclothesmen followed me, and I myself was almost caught. But I always eluded them since sympathetic supporters always warned me about men who were always looking for me. I carried documents, letters, materials, and mostly reports from the camps. Sometimes I also carried money such as

the time when I hid P10,000 [pesos] in a can of fruits to give to the camp leaders.[92]

When the situation got worse toward the end of the rebellion, Linda's work became even more dangerous. During that time she said there were "many couriers who surrendered," and many more were caught and interrogated. Linda, who was never caught, was convinced she would not have betrayed the Huks. "There was no doubt," she insisted. "I know I will sacrifice my life for our cause."[93] Such loyalty reflected Linda's remarkably strong political convictions, her sense of worth, and the value she placed on her work in the revolutionary struggle, work some of her fellow Huks probably dismissed as the contribution of a "mere courier."

Belen Bagul-Bagul managed to elude the authorities many times during the height of the Huk rebellion. When she joined the HMB she was sent to Manila for her training, where she learned about the Huk movement and communist ideology. After her schooling she became a courier, traveling between the forest headquarters, Manila, and the provinces of Central Luzon, delivering messages and materials from the leadership to the rank and file. She memorized and delivered her messages orally so she would be carrying no incriminating evidence if she were arrested. Most women couriers however, particularly the wives of party leaders, did not get much training and became communications workers solely because of their involvement in the movement and their willingness to work. Elena Sawit, for example, worked as a courier, often making the trek from the camps of the Sierra Madre to the villages of Central Luzon, and Rosita Manuel did courier work as well whenever she needed to go down to the barrios.

The key role played by women in party communications was reflected in the appointment of Illuminda "Luming" Calonje as chairman of the National Communications Division.[94] An active Hukbalahap organizer, Luming gained a reputation for bravery and efficiency and was immediately recruited into the party. Although she effectively ran the NCD, she never became a member of the Central Committee. In a letter dated June 8, 1949, Luis Taruc expressed his deep admiration for Luming:

My Dear Sister Luming:
    We must write to each other in English from now on. I want you to revive and practice your knowledge—all what you learned in school. I want you to improve further—to increase

continuously what you know now. You have the brains, the guts and the determination. You have the burning flame of our cause in your heart. You have . . . the millions of oppressed toilers to avenge and lead to victory in the ranks of party leadership — and you have your kids to reap that victory.[95]

Taruc ended his letter by thanking Luming for sending much-needed supplies, including "soap, crackers and medicines," for the guerrillas in the field.

Not all letters addressed to Luming expressed such appreciation. Others complained about the lack of supplies and couriers from the NCD. One letter to the party attacked Luming's handling of her responsibilities:

> I want you to know that one of our comrades was making us look stupid here. I am referring to Com[rade] Luming. The reason for this was whenever she instructs Com. Belen, she never bothers to inform us of her plans. If we did not question her, then we would not even know where she was sending Belen. We found out that she sent Com. Belen to Com. Rene without telling us, when we needed to also send something to Rene. These errors should be changed so that our work for our dear movement will go smoothly.[96]

Luming was not entirely responsible for the inadequacies of the courier system. Recruiting couriers with the necessary qualifications was one of the biggest problems facing the NCD. Ideally, couriers were required to undergo intensive training, which included courses on communist ideology and technical training in NCD intelligence methods and techniques. However, the urgency of putting the NCD into immediate operation resulted in the recruitment of many unqualified and untrained couriers. By the early 1950s the party had even reduced the requirements to "a person not wanted by the enemy, of good moral character, with some knowledge of intelligence techniques, and capable of learning and developing *himself* into the ideal courier."[97] But despite this it was still difficult to recruit capable couriers. Thus, when the letter writer was not informed of the actions of a particular courier that he needed himself he blamed Luming for her handling of the communications crisis.

In a report published by the Philippine government's Department of National Defense in 1950, the top couriers listed as crucial to the operations of the Huk organization were all women. Aside from Calonje, women who played a prominent role in the NCD's activities included Aurelia Cayetano (alias Rosario Vda. [widow of] de Santos), Elsie Ramirez, Rosalina Quizon, Esperanza Pasco (alias Naty Cruz), Aurora Garcia (alias Dalisay), Armanda Cruz (alias Amante), Juana Acuesa (alias Aurora), and Mrs. Mario del Castillo (alias Manay). Cayetano, vice chairman of the NCD, was an efficient assistant and courier who transported important messages to high-ranking leaders. With the exception of Elsie Ramirez, all of these women were later arrested, tried, and sentenced in connection with their work for the Huks.[98] Even the government believed that the success of Huk operations depended heavily on the competence of the courier system and the women who organized it.

Aside from courier work, the task of attending to sick and wounded guerrillas almost always fell to the female Huks. Linda Ayala, already an indispensable courier, also learned how to administer first aid. So did Belen Bagul-Bagul, who spent her remaining years in the HMB as a nurse when it became too difficult to work as a courier. Rosita Manuel also trained as a nurse. These women studied first aid and learned to administer injections and medicines. Belen worked mostly in the camp clinic but sometimes traveled with soldiers to treat the wounded in other Huk outposts, nursing sick guerrillas back to health, giving them medicines, and feeding them. Malaria was the most common illness, and once Huk members were infected the women could do little other than treat the symptoms and nurse the victims. As the rebellion stretched from weeks into months and finally years, these female nurses bore the brunt of treating those who were wounded in government attacks as medicines became increasingly scarce. Nevertheless, many female Huks shared Rosita's sentiment: "I thought I would die in the camps with the other guerrillas," but until the end "I took care of them, protected them."[99]

A few women with some education or previous organizational experience were given major responsibilities in the movement. By 1946 Teofista Valerio, who had fought with the Hukbalahap and worked for the Partido Nacionalista (Nationalist Party) after the war, was no longer a political novice. Although she had little formal education, her political experience made her an ideal leader in the HMB, and as early as 1947 she was assigned as a supply and finance officer to the Central Luzon Committee, tracking the movement's financial resources and distributing money to Huk units and camps in various locales. She sometimes collected contributions from supporters in the villages and Manila, but most of the time she received funds from other collectors and distributed it according to the directives of the Central Committee. From her position at the center of the Huk's supply system, Teofista witnessed the slow decline of the HMB as the Huks became increasingly isolated from outside supporters and had to fend for themselves, coping with diminishing supplies of food and money. "I just never gave up," she recalled, as she relentlessly sought support of various kinds, especially during these periods of isolation, a testament to her skill and intelligence.[100]

Virginia Calma and Zenaida del Castillo also assumed important roles in the HMB movement. Virginia worked at the Huks' General Headquarters in the Sierra Madre, resuming her wartime role in the education division, translating documents from English, the preferred written language of the Politburo members, into Tagalog and Kapampangan for the perusal of ordinary rank-and-file members. Zenaida also worked in the education division, but her primary task was to review, type, and translate newspaper reports on the contemporary political situation, which were then distributed to guerrilla units. The tasks of Virginia and Zenaida underscore the crucial role women played as intermediaries within and outside the organization, with Virginia translating Politburo documents for the rank and file and Zenaida distributing news stories intended to keep fellow comrades up to date about the world outside the Sierra Madre.

Whether the women worked in the camps, the barrios, or Manila, almost all of them remembered their involvement in the HMB as challenging and dangerous but ultimately life enhancing. The postwar Huk rebellion, unlike the Hukbalahap during the Japanese Occupation, required more ideological understanding of women and imposed more challenging duties on them largely because of the more tentative nature of popular support in the villages and the increasingly repressive nature of government action. The political commitment required to serve in the HMB thus reached new heights. No longer mere extensions of Huk men, these women of the HMB were transformed from political novices to highly self-conscious political cadres who embraced the Huk struggle as their own.

The Changing Identities of Huk Women

Narcisa Reyes was only fifteen when her neighbors recruited her to join the Hukbalahap in 1942. By the age of nineteen she had finished her training at the Forest School, worked as a Huk educator, attended countless Communist Party meetings, and become one of the most important organizers in the Huk movement. Narcisa admitted that she was *ta-tanga-tanga* (just a naive little girl) when she "foolishly" joined the Huks, *parang laro lang* (like a game) since this was what other young people in her barrio were doing. But, although she joined the Huks because of her brother and her village friends, as her involvement grew she became increasingly frustrated because she was *walang alam* (not in the know) and was excluded from crucial Huk meetings and the decision-making process. After the war, despite some misgivings about the hardships of guerrilla life, Narcisa rejoined her former comrades in the mountains. Her youth had previously limited her involvement, so she struggled and studied hard until she was invited to join the Communist Party, becoming a full-fledged HMB cadre at the age of twenty-one. As we have seen, although social networks often facilitated mobilization, these same networks did not guarantee continued participation in the movement, and the involvement of women such as Narcisa in fact reflected the powerful new sense of self and identity these women had developed, a sense of themselves as capable and committed revolutionaries that allowed them to resist the pull of traditional social roles for women — as wives, sisters, and daughters — and the tug of village social networks. The transformation of these women into cadres and revolutionaries was shaped by the complex interaction of individual and collective identity within the Huk rebellion.

Issues of personal and collective identity are central to understanding why men and women participate in social and revolutionary movements and reflect their own definitions of who they are in relation to categories of ethnicity, class, race, gender, national identity, religion, and sexuality, which are collective in character and shaped by the social environment. Categories of identity, in other words, are not fixed or innate because, as Charles Tilly argues, people "actually live in deeply relational worlds" where their identities are constantly changed and renegotiated by their repeated interactions with others. Thus, people possess not only individual but also collective identities, which are constantly defined and redefined through symbols, discourses, and practices. In social and revolutionary movements identity itself becomes the locus of struggle. The changing, and sometimes contested, identities of Huk women demonstrate the transformative nature of the revolutionary movement.[101]

In the Huk rebellion class identity framed the struggle between the economic elites, the wealthy landowners, their agents in the state and police, and the peasants and working-class inhabitants of Central and Southern Luzon. In their directives to members Huk leaders constantly emphasized the class consciousness of the predominantly peasant rank and file. And yet most Huk guerrillas, particularly women, defined themselves in ways that went beyond class or material interests and expressed a new sense of nationalism—fighting for the "Filipino" against the "Japanese" and later "American" enemy to establish their country's liberation and right to self-determination. Although they rarely articulated these identities explicitly, women in the Hukbalahap developed feelings of nationalism, *pag-ibig sa bayan* (literally, "love for the nation"). Their experiences in the Huk movement deepened this sense of nationalist commitment and identity, which found expression in cultural symbols such as revolutionary songs and literature.

In her work on the history of the Left in the Philippines, Teresita Maceda places great emphasis on the role of revolutionary songs in the Huk movement. In the absence of formal education, popular cultural forms such as songs were an important vehicle for the expression of political beliefs and ideas. These songs, often composed by the guerrillas themselves, revealed their nationalist aspirations, their solidarity with poor Filipino farmers, and their anger toward Filipino collaborators and the Japanese. These songs called on Filipinos to unite with and join the Huk guerrillas, who were willing to die in defense of the Philippines. According to Maceda leaders of the movement used songs to arouse emotions and mobilize people for the collective struggle.[102] The songs made the feelings of the revolutionaries apparent, and it is this openness that attracted supporters to embrace the guerrillas.

One song, originally written and sung in Kapampangan, the regional language of Pampanga, depicted a guerrilla comforting the nation, weeping and in chains. "My country," the song goes, "do not lament. Wipe your flowing tears." The guerrilla, "your child who loves you," "will defend you till the end." The tune of the song changes as the guerrilla summons the country "to smile and be glad," promising that "your chains will be shattered" and "tomorrow you will reign in freedom and other nations will praise you."[103] The song invoked Christian hymns by highlighting themes of pain and resurrection. But instead of calling on Christ to save the country from suffering the song cast the Huk rebel as the source of salvation, summoning "the lovely children of the nation to defend their country suffering from the clutches of the Japanese." "Now is the time to rise up, abandon retreat, and give praise to the Hukbalahap, the model of the bravery of the Filipino" the song informs its listeners, ending with a cheer: "Long Live the Hukbalahap! Guerrillas, the hope of our land."[104] Both Huk men and women recalled how proud they were to sing this song as an expression of Filipino patriotism and a celebration of the Huk movement.

According to Maceda, for the Filipino Huks the reality of the song and the reality of their struggle were one and the same.[105] One popular song, which most Huks still remember, encapsulated the hardships of a guerrilla's life:

O kay hirap, buhay ng gerilya	Oh, how difficult, the life of a guerrilla
Hirap, lungkot, kaulayaw tuwina	Suffering, grief, our constant companions
Mahal sa buhay pag naalaala	Remembering our loved ones
Maglalandas ang luha sa mga mata.	brings tears to our eyes.
Dahil sa paglaya ng bayan kong api	For the freedom of my oppressed land
Iwinaksing lahat ang pansarili	selfishness was forsaken
Lungkot, gutom, uhaw di mananatili	Sadness, hunger, thirst won't last
Sa araw ng bukas hangga't may duhagi.	For tomorrow shall bring hope.

A special verse was written for women:

Lalo na ang mga babae, sinumpa nilang matibay	Women, especially, their promise is firm
Kahit maubos man, mahahango ang buhay	To give up their lives
Matubos lang nila ang nasira mong puri	Just to save your broken honor
Kahit sa labanan, para silang lalaki.	Even in battle, they are like men.[106]

This song not only acknowledged women's participation in the Huk movement but also made them central to the revolution. Just like men, women were prepared to defend their country, no longer simply mothers who wept for their children but warriors who were prepared to suffer and fight "like men." Women's spirit of private self-sacrifice was transformed here into a public virtue, an essential attribute of citizenship and masculinity. And yet, even as it praised women, the song subordinated them to men and male notions of honor and bravery, suggesting that women could become productive citizens only after abandoning their femininity. Songs like these treated female guerrillas as distinct from Filipino women in general. They shared space with men and possessed "masculine" capabilities that made them ideal freedom fighters. In all these songs women expressed a sense of their worth in the revolution and asserted their place in the defense of the nation.

Most women in the Hukbalahap knew these revolutionary songs by heart and performed them in the villages they visited. Even after many years Zenaida del Castillo and Filomena Tolentino could still sing Huk songs from memory. One extremely popular song, "Babaeng Walang Kibo" (The Timid Woman), had particular resonance for the women of both the Hukbalahap and HMB movements:

O babaing walang kibo	Oh woman so timid
Magnilay ka at mag-isip	Reflect and realize that
Malaon ka nang inaapi	You've been oppressed for so long
At malaon ka nang nilulupig.	And you've been shackled for so long.
Bakit hindi ka magtanggol	Why don't you protect
May anak kang nagugutom	Your child who is starving
Bunso mo ay umiiyak	Your youngest who is weeping
Natitiis mo sa hirap	You endure with your suffering
Ano't hindi ka magbalikwas	Why don't you act
Kung ina kang may damdamin at paglingap?	As a mother full of feeling and affection?[107]

Sung in a melodic and romantic style, this song appealed to the emotions and maternal instincts of peasant women. As mothers and prospective mothers, the song urged them to protect their children from economic injustice and to cast off their timidity in an act of revolutionary sacrifice. The song then moves from a tone of melancholy to a forceful insistence on the need for direct, revolutionary action:

Labanan mo ng lubusan magnanakaw na puhunan	Fight to the end the thieves of wealth
Lagi nang inaapi ang tanang kababaihan	Women are always oppressed

Alipin nang ganap tayo, alipin na   All of us are slaves, even freedom
   pati laya   was enslaved
Na siniil at binigti demokrasya   Our nation's democracy shackled.
   nitong bansa.

Upang ating mapadali labanan ng   We must hasten our collective
   mga uri   struggle
Tibayan ang mga puso, alisin ang   Harden your heart, cast away your
   pagkakimi   fears
O babaeng walang kibo, gumising   Oh timid woman, arise and be
   na at magtindi   strong
Sabay-sabay na sumigaw,   Together let us raise our voices,
Mabuhay ang anak-pawis.   Long live the toiling masses.[108]

This song was significant on many levels. Instructing the Filipino mother to harden her heart, the song called on women to abandon their traditional feminine timidity and become part of a revolutionary movement. In a sense they had to cease being women to be revolutionaries, and yet the appeal to revolutionary action is rooted in their maternal instincts as women. As Huks they were called on to identify their familial interests with the interests of a larger family defined by class and nationhood. Moreover, their own liberation is explicitly connected to the liberation of the nation as a whole.

For women like Narcisa, Zenaida, and Virginia, songs such as this one captured the inner turmoil they experienced as part of a revolutionary movement. As women they were oppressed, forced to give up their personal dreams and to sacrifice for the sake of their families. And as women in the Philippines they had endured centuries of injustice under a colonial system that deprived all Filipinos of independence and freedom. Revolutionary songs therefore helped to connect their experiences as peasant women to the politics of Philippine nationalism. Since women had little formal education and were unable to read many of the political manifestos and historical treatises produced by Huk leaders and the Communist Party, songs provided them with a framework for understanding their relationship to the Huk cause and for expressing their will to struggle. But while most of these songs were highly nationalistic in tone, they were also deeply radical, consistently emphasizing the oppression that existed within Philippine society and advocating internal revolution as a solution.

As this suggests, women in the HMB understood the Huk rebellion not only as a nationalist struggle but also a revolutionary war and embraced a political identity that was shaped by their knowledge of socialism and communism. This is not to argue that they were all orthodox Marxists-Leninists, although the Communist Party leadership did its best to require all cadres to subscribe to an officially sanctioned communist ideology and adopted strict rules of membership that required cadres to receive their communist catechism with subjects that included dialectical materialism, Marxism-Leninism, and the state and revolution.[109] To what extent were the ideas of Huk women shaped by such communist pedagogy? While most accounts of the Huk rebellion emphasize the important link between male leaders and the Communist Party, the general neglect of women's participation in the history of the Left, and of the Huk movement in particular, is based on and reinforces a perception that women joined the movement not because of their ideological commitment but because of their relationships with more ideological men.[110] Indeed, the belief that women were incapable of understanding the complexities of communist ideology has been used to both explain and justify male domination within the Huk leadership.[111] But the accounts of women themselves after 1945 lead to a different conclusion. In fact Huk women, especially those who moved on to the HMB struggle, were well versed in communist ideas and well informed about the role of the Communist Party in the movement.

Felisa Cuyugan, for example, was already a member of the Communist Party when she met her socialist husband in the late 1930s. As an active Communist Party member who attended party meetings, conventions, and rallies, she was easily mobilized by the Hukbalahap, and, although she decided not to join the HMB movement directly, she continued to support the HMB and the Communist Party. She understood clearly that "the struggle for economic justice in the Philippines did not end with World War II." Felisa recalled:

> Before the war . . . there was already a struggle between the *may ari ng lupa* [landlord] and the *uring magsasaka* [peasant class]. The rich owned land. When you owe something to the landlord, you had to pay him more than double your debt. There were even some landlords who raped the children of the peasants. They can get any woman they want, sometimes as payment for a debt. The socialists and communists sought to remove these conditions—they united the poor peasants and organized them. They sought revenge from the evil landlord.[112]

For Felisa, this was what communism meant. Teofista Valerio was also politically active before the war, having joined the Hukbalahap before becoming a member of the Communist Party. While she was not initially aware that her prewar youth organization was affiliated with the Communist Party, she soon discovered the connection, and, although she "never sought out the Communists," when they attempted to recruit her after the war she was flattered. "They said," she recalled, "that the skills I demonstrated in organizing should be put to good use so others can benefit from them. The party knows that I can work very well and the organization in general should benefit from my talents."[113] Since her goal was "to help people, to serve my country," she "decided to join," although she confessed that she never quite understood the arcane subtleties of communist doctrine:

I did not have any schooling, but they did explain to me what communism is. They showed Russia as an example in which the leaders were from the Communist Party. In Russia *walang mahirap* [there are no poor people], and *walang mayaman* [no rich people]. People respected each other, and their resources and food supply are the same for everyone. So if you desire that there will no longer be poor people in your country then you should join the communists.[114]

Many Huk women shared Teofista's basic understanding of communism, and, although many of them attended the party school, few could explain the formal tenets of communist ideology. When asked to explain dialectical materialism, for example, Virginia Calma responded, "This was only about how you should not be *materioso* [materialistic] in life. You should not only think of material things. Unlike now, people always want material things." The communists, she continued, preached that communism meant *simpleng pamumuhay* (simple living) and having simple needs. She concluded: "That was how I remembered the teaching on the dialectics of materialism—that you should not be materialistic, you should not want material things." Although most Huk women remembered being taught dialectical materialism, few could explain what the term meant.[115] Like Felisa, Luz del Castillo understood communism simply as a class struggle between the rich and the poor. According to her the Huks wanted to replace an unjust system with one that gave the poor more rights and privileges. While she described communist ideas as "very theoretical," she believed that the goals of the

Communist Party were plain: "to protect the rights of the poor."[116] Rosenda Torres embraced the same beliefs and fondly remembered the simple oath-taking ceremony that marked her induction into the Communist Party. As she recalled, "I became a communist. Just like that. After a few lectures, I made an oath to the party."[117] Belen Bagul-Bagul became a member in 1950, convinced that being a party member was a critical part of her work in the HMB, and she could still sing the "Internationale" years later.[118] The family background of Zenaida del Castillo, whose father, Mateo del Castillo, was a leader of the PKP, provided her with an intimate knowledge of communism and the Communist Party. Though later hesitant to admit she was a *komunista,* she considered the PKP "the political arm of the workers and peasants." As a member of the HMB movement, she explained, "I knew then that I was part of the *uring manggagawa* [working class], and the political party of the working class is the Communist Party. Colonialism is truly the enemy. In the fight against colonialism, nationalism and communism are *nagkakaisa* [united]."[119] While the Philippine and American governments were trying to separate communism and nationalism, Zenaida believed that nationalism and the rights of oppressed peasants and workers were connected. She eventually joined the party because she knew that "the working classes will not attain liberation without the guidance of a strong party—the party of the proletariat."[120]

During the war against the Japanese, peasant women such as Maxima San Pedro, Leonila Sayco, and Filomena Tolentino had no idea that the leaders of the Huks were communists, and most women, despite their wartime involvement and their intimate relations with party leaders, did not join the party. Elang Santa Ana and Dominga Centeno were both married to men who were leaders of the PKP, but neither was recruited to the party. In fact, Elang claimed that she only found out that her husband, Federico Maclang, was a communist when he was arrested. "Even though you were married in the movement," she commented, "if you know that you are not in the same level of understanding, then even your spouse will not recruit you to the party."[121] However, she admitted that her husband tirelessly explained the principles of communism to her and that she remained an ardent sympathizer of the HMB until the end. When Maclang was sentenced to death Elang remained loyal to both her husband and his communist beliefs. Similarly, Dominga Centeno never questioned her husband's Communist Party membership. "Why should I care," she said, "when these people were good people?"[122] Like Elang and Dominga, many women regarded the goals of the Huk movement as more important than the issue of party membership. Rosenda Torres summed up this point of view:

> For me it was immaterial to be a party member. The important thing is, how you can fight the enemy, how you can help the movement? There were two kinds of membership in the Huk movement—those who wanted to act for the country and those who joined because they wanted to be instruments of the party.[123]

Rosenda's comments revealed an inner tension within the Huk movement. Although she did not much care whether people were members of the party or not, party membership was not that important to her either. Like many women in the movement she had a distant intellectual relationship with "the party." All the women she knew who were party members had joined the Huks because of a "belief in the larger cause of nationalism and social justice" not because of a blind adherence to communist ideology. While this might not reflect the "official" position of the Politburo, Rosenda believed that this was the general sentiment of the members of the Huk movement.

Once again a commitment to socialism and communism can be traced in the revolutionary songs of the Huks. While nationalism is a central theme in most Huk songs, several songs that deal with communism were important during the HMB struggle. The same themes that pervade the songs of the Hukbalahap—freedom, democracy, struggle, and sacrifice—appeared in the HMB period, but new and sometimes controversial ideas were also introduced. One of the HMB songs celebrated the movement's connections with communism and the vital contribution of communism to the liberation of the poor:

Kalayaa't demokrasya,	Freedom and democracy,
islogan sa pakikibaka	slogans of struggle
Malaon nang minimithi ngunit hindi matamasa	Long desired but never attained
Nang dahil sa paghihintay ng mga oportunista	Because opportunists don't act but wait
Tangi lamang ang sandata ang titiyak sa paglaya.	Only the sword can guarantee liberation.

Lupa para sa gumagawa ang	Land for those who toil our
dakilang adhika	noble goal
Nagnanais mapasagana ang buhay	Desiring to improve the lives
ng mga manggagawa	of the working classes
At iba pang kauri sa loob ng bansa	And other toiling masses in the
	land
Nang ang bayang Pilipinas ganap	That the Philippines would fully
na mapariwasa.	prosper.
Kaming Hukbong Mapagpalaya	We are the People's Liberation
ng Bayan	Army
HMB kung tagurian, lubhang	The HMB, such an appropriate
angkop na pangalan	name
Anak kaming maralita na	We are Children of the poor
kayo ang pinanggalingan	we are your children
Nagtatanggol sa mga api,	Defending the oppressed,
dinusta ng kalaban,	mocked by the enemy,
Inihain aming buhay	Laying down our lives
Baya'y guminhawa lamang.	for the country's welfare.
Mabuhay ang HMB (Mabuhay!)	Long live the HMB!
Mabuhay ang Pilipinas (Mabuhay!)	Long live the Philippines!
Mabuhay ang uring api	Long live the oppressed
Sa daigdig ay nagkaisa	In this world, we are united
Mabuhay ang Komunista	Long live the Communists
Na patnugot nating lahat	Light, guide of us all
Mabuhay ang Pilipinas!	Long live the Philippines!
Tagumpay ay natitiyak.	Victory is certain.[124]

Casting the communist rebels as "children of the poor," this song calls for the people to recognize and support those who sacrifice their lives to create a better society. A song written by Communist Party leader Casto Alejandrino also appealed to the people to recognize the sacrifices and bravery of the communists, declaring that they must "rise from their enslavement" and "not to forget the ones who oppress them" and imploring the nation to "depend on your children, the communists, who will not stop fighting until you are free."[125]

But despite their willingness to acknowledge communism as an important part of the Huk struggle, women such as Zenaida del Castillo and Felisa Cuyugan later showed a palpable reluctance to admit that they were communists and openly discuss their past activities. Like many Filipinos these women perceived a stigma surrounding communism and often tried to separate their legacies from communist ideology. Some of this is clearly retrospective and reflects the development of anticommunist and cold war politics after the 1950s. As the Huk songs reveal, allegiance to communism was part of both the official and popular culture of the Huk movement. And it is at least possible that even the women's avowed incomprehension of the tenets of communism may have been a way to disguise their past political sympathies.

Women involved in communist-led struggles in countries such as Nicaragua, Vietnam, and China also often interpreted their political roles as a function of familial identity rather than communist ideology. Women in the Nicaraguan revolution, for example, called themselves "Sandino's daughters" to dramatize the familial character of the Sandinista revolution. And women in Vietnam identified with "Uncle Ho" Chi Minh, who summoned them to join the revolution in the belief that the struggle could not be won without the participation of Vietnam's daughters. During the Long March, Chinese women relied on their "brotherly and sisterly" comrades to survive death, hunger, exhaustion, and the perils of their revolutionary trek through the Chinese countryside. Many teenage girls who joined the march purposefully escaped their "evil" in-laws to become part of this new "red" family of revolutionaries.[126] Like the Huks, women in other revolutionary struggles often defined themselves in personal and familial terms, finding the meaning in their involvement through their intimate relations with other members. Their commitment to the struggle was not to its avowed communist goals but to the people who fought with them.

By the end of the rebellion most of the women who had been mobilized by the Huks were in their late twenties or early thirties. But they were not only older. Their experiences in the movement had transformed them politically, socially, and emotionally. As they admit, they were often young and naive when they first joined the Huks and were drawn into the movement because of their relationships with the more experienced men who recruited them. But their experience as guerrillas transformed them into nationalists, and after the war their nationalism was transformed into an ardent desire for change. For some Huk women this meant adopting the principles of communism and socialism.

From Reluctant Rebels to Revolutionaries

In 1946, when the Philippines formally established an independent republic, leaders and members of the wartime Hukbalahap declared a second revolution and called on its former guerrillas to resume the armed struggle. Many women who had served in the Hukbalahap during the war heeded the call and embraced the new goals of the movement, making the struggle their own. These women developed a deep ideological commitment to the liberation struggle, embracing new identities as nationalists, communists, and revolutionaries.

Female mobilization after World War II revealed the dramatic differences among Huk women. Some came from urban, middle-class families, particularly in Manila, but most came from rural families. Some had advanced educations, but most never went beyond elementary school. Women from urban areas generally made a conscious decision to join the Huks, often because of their involvement in political and student organizations, while most peasant women were mobilized through the social relations of village life. Inside the Huk organization these differences shaped the roles of women. Those who came with husbands and partners tended to stay close to the camps, while single women had more freedom to move around and performed multiple tasks. Varying degrees of political experience and education inspired some women to join the Communist Party, while others remained aloof. All of these differences add complexity to female involvement in the Huk movement, yet such variations were generally lost on the party leadership and Huk men. Most viewed Huk women as a group characterized by political immaturity that needed the protection and guidance provided by more sophisticated male members.

But women's commitment and contribution to the revolution did not go completely unnoticed, and eventually the party realized that it needed to place more emphasis on the training and political education of women. While women were still ignored in the recruitment of Huk soldiers, their participation in the HMB was discussed as part of official party policy:

The most important underground activities that our women's movement can undertake to help the armed struggle are to recruit and train young women who can serve as first aiders; solicit contributions of money, office supplies, medicines, clothes, shoes, etc. for the armed forces; [act] as intelligence agents; and serve as couriers.[127]

According to this Politburo document, women could also play an active role by investigating the living conditions of "women and children from the poorer classes" in order "to expose the anomalies of the existing system." But, while party doctrine acknowledged a place for women in the movement, official party pronouncements placed clear limits on how they could serve. As nurses and suppliers of money, medicine, food and clothing they were welcome, and they could even perform valuable work as intelligence agents and couriers, but they had no legitimate role in combat. "Because of the increasing mobility that our armed forces will have to adopt due to increasing and intensified enemy suppression," argued the party leadership, the movement could not expect women "to endure the physical hardships incident to the rank and file guerrilla soldiers." Official documents and male party leaders frequently described women's work in the Huk movement as "secondary" or "subsidiary," reinforcing a gender ideology that placed women in subordinate positions to men. Some Huk women internalized these limitations, calling themselves "appendixes" to the movement.[128]

The transformation of Huk women thus clashed with male assumptions about women's roles and femininity, and while women defined themselves as revolutionaries and cadres they remained wives, daughters, and sisters to many Huk men. In the camps women often remained on the outskirts, performing housekeeping and domestic tasks, and no matter how vital these tasks were most never assumed leadership posts. Most of the time it seemed that women's purpose in the movement was to support the men and "make them happy."[129] The leadership rarely listened to women's ideas or asked for their opinions. It is therefore not surprising that many of the most committed female guerrillas of the Hukbalahap failed to join the HMB and only a handful of women were invited to join the Communist Party. Marginalized because they were not primarily soldiers and leaders of the movement, they still valued their experiences and their comrades in the Hukbalahap and the HMB. It is a testament to their political commitment and consciousness that however obscure their role at the time they remained loyal to the movement and however little recognition they later received in accounts of the Huk rebellion they remained faithful to its collective history.

3

Women on Top

Amazons and Leaders in the Huk Movement

The story of female commander Dayang-Dayang still captivates the people of Central Luzon and illustrates well the mythology surrounding the Huk women commanders. Dayang-Dayang, a name Felipa Culala took in honor of a Muslim princess who came from a long line of fighters against Spanish colonizers in the southern Philippines, was a former peasant activist who led one of the first guerrilla detachments against the Japanese. From her hometown in Pampanga, Barrio Mandili, she enlisted thirty-five men and armed them with weapons obtained from fleeing landlords. While gathering *palay* (rice plant) one day at the start of the war her detachment was surprised by enemy police who arrested 8 of the guerrillas. In response, Dayang-Dayang meticulously planned an assault on the jail to free her guerrilla comrades. On March 8, 1942, she led her command into Candaba, Pampanga, captured the municipal building, freed the prisoners, and retreated to Mandili. When a Japanese patrol accompanied by the collaborating Filipino police forces launched operations to punish the barrio, Dayang-Dayang and the 130 guerrillas under her command were ready. The guerrilla army ambushed the enemy on their approach and killed thirty-nine to forty Japanese along with sixty-eight members of the police, captured many weapons, and forced the Japanese to retreat from the barrio.[1] The battle of Mandili marked a turning point in the Huk rebellion, proving that the guerrilla movement could defeat a powerful enemy and pose a serious threat to the Japanese. According to Huk Supremo (supreme leader) Luis Taruc, other guerrilla detachments quickly emerged in a similar fashion across Central Luzon.[2]

When the guerrilla army of the Hukbalahap was founded, Dayang-Dayang and about a hundred of her men, still proud of their success in Mandili, immediately enlisted. Along with top Huk leaders Casto Alejandrino, Bernardo Poblete, and Luis Taruc, Culala was elected one of the four members of the Military Committee of the Hukbalahap, which organized the guerrilla operations of the movement. She was the only woman ever elected to the committee—indeed, the only woman to achieve comparable rank in any Philippine military organization.[3]

But soon after her election, disturbing reports about Dayang-Dayang reached other Huk leaders. According to Taruc she disliked taking orders from the other leaders, encouraged her soldiers to call her "*Generala*," and built a little hierarchy in the squadrons under her command. Her actions provoked complaints from local barrio people, who alleged that she wanted to be "treated like a queen in the barrios, calling for pigs and chickens to be killed and cooked upon her arrival."[4] By 1943 numerous complaints about Dayang-Dayang had reached the Huk leadership, including accusations about the theft of food, fishnets, *carabaos*, and even money and jewelry. After an investigation, the leadership concluded that Dayang-Dayang had used her rank to accumulate wealth and commit abuses. Summoned by the Politburo, she was disarmed, arrested, and later that year court-martialed, found guilty of her crimes, and shot by a firing squad.[5] But, despite her notoriety, Dayang-Dayang remained a legend in Central Luzon and embodied the image of the true "Amazon." Huk women such as Dayang-Dayang, who were fighting alongside men and carried guns, elicited awe and admiration in the popular press and occupied a central place in the discourse on the role of Filipino women in postwar Philippine society. In this chapter, we will look more closely at these "amazing Amazons" through the lives of prominent female leaders and military commanders and the larger roles they played inside and outside the revolutionary movement.

Gender in the New Nation

The story of Dayang-Dayang elucidates the role of gender in the Huk movement and, more generally, the situation of women in Filipino society. Dayang-Dayang, and Huk women in general, achieved prominence in the press and the popular imagination in the 1940s not only because of their extraordinary experiences but because they deviated from the conventional image of Filipino peasant women. Peasant women were usually regarded in Philippine society as conservative guardians of the status quo: traditional, passive, religious wives who were timid in public, lacked social and political consciousness, and were more used to enduring their sufferings than fighting back. But during World War II and the postwar rebellion peasant women defied tradition and convention to become Huks. The presence of women fighting in a revolutionary army helped shape the ongoing public controversy about the role of women in the postwar Philippines.

The height of the Huk rebellion—the late 1940s and early 1950s—coincided with a period of great transformation in Philippine society. The country had been devastated during World War II and, perhaps more significant, after almost four hundred years of colonial occupation was granted independence by the United States and formally became a republic. Independence not only marked the end of colonialism but further intensified debates regarding nationalism and modernity in the Philippines.[6] Women occupied a central place in the definition of this new republic. In the 1920s and 1930s Filipino women, particularly elite women, energized the political scene by campaigning for suffrage, and American tutelary efforts led to an expansion of public education for women.[7] For the first time a significant number of women went to school, and, while only a few obtained college degrees, education opened up new employment opportunities for many women.[8] Yet many areas of public life remained exclusively male. Although women occupied positions within the colonial bureaucracy, they were restricted to its lowest ranks, working primarily as clerks and secretaries. Most significant, Filipinas were not allowed to vote, and for the most part the colonial state resisted extending political power to women.

But as more and more women came to share public space with men issues of female political representation became crucial within Philippine society and middle-class women began to question their exclusion from public debate and the denial of their right to vote. Under Spanish and American rule the vote was an exclusively male privilege and voting requirements were strict: men had to be twenty-one years old, pay taxes of thirty pesos annually, and own property worth at least five hundred pesos. In addition, they had to be literate in at least one language or have held political office before 1898.[9] During the early years of its rule, the U.S. colonial government sought to protect this male monopoly over political power by limiting women's participation in public life to the classroom, charitable institutions, the church, and voluntary organizations where their nurturing qualities could benefit the whole community. This exclusion inspired a group of upper-class Filipinas, including Pura Villanueva Kalaw, Encarnacion Alzona, Paz Mendoza-Guanzon, Josefa Llanes-Escoda, Natividad Almeda-Lopez, Maria Ventura, Concepcion Felix Rodriguez, and Pilar Hidalgo-Lim, to demand suffrage and create the most important women's movement in the early-twentieth century Philippines.[10] The women's organizations they established initially waged campaigns for women's rights by addressing issues such as family health, support for childrearing, and better conditions for working women, including maternity leave.[11] But these campaigns gradually became more overtly political as women's associations and social clubs recruited members, undertook advocacy work, and coordinated nationwide efforts to enfranchise the Filipina.[12] All of these activities created a lively debate in Manila, where suffragists won support from American administrators and even the Commonwealth president, Manuel Quezon, who declared, "I have always been and always will be in favor of woman suffrage."[13] But Philippine society in general was divided on the issue. The pioneer Pilar Hidalgo Lim explained:

> The Filipino women had been agitating for participation in elections. But perhaps because of the indifference of the majority of women still steeped in the idea that women's place is only inside the house, or because there was no organized or concerted action among them, bills granting women the right to vote were always tabled and buried.[14]

To prepare for eventual independence a Constitutional Convention was held in 1931, which renewed the debate for and against women's suffrage. At this crucial juncture, as the country was preparing for independence and drafting a constitution, different groups in society competed to define the relationship between the new nation and Filipino women. According to Mina Roces the public hearings featuring suffragists revealed sharp conflicts about citizenship and nationalism. At the center of the suffrage debates was the broader issue of which cultural construction of the feminine—and Filipino women—should be endorsed in the new nation. Should Filipinas be Spanish influenced—that is, pious, religious women confined to the domestic sphere—or Americanized, English speaking, university educated, and professional with the right to vote?[15] By engaging in these debates and campaigning for suffrage rights women in the Philippines stretched the limits of female citizenship beyond the boundaries of family life for the first time.[16] While elite women welcomed the idea of the educated "modern" woman, many Filipino men opposed women's suffrage, deeply anxious that allowing Filipinas to enter politics would lead to "the neglect and detriment of husband, children and household."[17] They feared women's suffrage would drain public finances, lead to divorce, and destroy the moral fiber of Philippine society. While higher education and the professions were already open to women, Filipino politicians, who were mostly male, wished to limit women's public activities to charitable institutions and volunteer work. They were supported by the Manila press, which was vitriolic in its opposition to women's suffrage and called for women to concentrate on social work and abandon their preoccupation with politics.

But the debates themselves "unwittingly recognized the critical leadership role that women play in the national arena," and by the end of 1936 a compromise bill had been passed granting women the vote provided that 300,000 out of the 497,000 potential women voters approved it in a national plebiscite.[18] Women's associations united to form the National Council of Women, whose members pledged to work to pass the women's suffrage measure.[19] Legislative, educational, and public campaigns ensued in Manila and the provinces to encourage women to say yes on plebiscite day. As a result more than 450,000, or about 90 percent of eligible voters, turned out to vote in favor of women's suffrage. A year later, in 1937, Congress passed a bill granting suffrage to all women who were twenty-one years old and could read and write. As Mary Grace Ampil Tirona writes, "For Lim and the rest of the *panuelo* activists that the Filipina was the first Oriental woman to win the right to vote and be elected into office was a crowning achievement."[20]

The efforts of elite women, particularly during the suffrage debates, demonstrated the significance of gender and women's issues in Philippine society during the 1930s. For the first time in Philippine history Filipinas were actively involved in nation-building efforts and in ushering their country into modernity. Mina Roces argues that the debate on suffrage was a "site where cultural constructions of 'the Filipino woman' were raised and negotiated" and highlighted the fact that women, despite male reluctance, could play an active role in the shaping of the new nation.[21] By campaigning for and gaining suffrage elite Filipinas not only effectively expanded their political role but also declared that they were major participants in the process of nation building. Their participation in the political arena seemed irreversible, and they assumed they would never again be marginalized in Philippine political life.

But while the suffrage movement signaled a change in the Philippine polity the struggle to establish equal rights for women was far from over. Women were able to carve out their own political space through the suffrage campaigns, but they were still excluded from other areas of social life as the Philippine state and society continued to define separate domains for men and women. Unfortunately, the process of negotiating and increasing female political participation was abruptly cut short when the Japanese invaded the Philippines in December 1941. World War II radically changed the political context for Filipino women and not only left the exploration of the "cultural construction of the Filipina" unfinished but in many ways reversed women's progress toward political participation.

After the war the Philippine state and society, as reflected in public discourse, called for national unity and prescribed new roles for Filipino women. The new state embraced a masculine ideology for postwar reconstruction and nation building, effectively marginalizing public discussion about the political role of women. The new nation needed mothers, sisters, and daughters to heal the wounds of war and support its men as they began the difficult task of rebuilding. In a country traumatized by war, loss, and suffering and overwhelmed by the desire for national unity, the image of the Filipina was once again closely linked to the domestic sphere, and much of the momentum Filipino women had gained before the war was lost.[22] This domestication of the Filipina was best encapsulated by then first lady Trinidad Roxas who stated that the "first and most important service" the women of the Philippines could offer the nation was the "proper care of the children, of their health, education and morality." Women had the valuable mission not only to build "*kaaya-aya at kasiya-siyang tahanan* [a fine and happy home]" but also to make it a "temple of *kabutihan* [goodness], *kagalingan* [excellence], *kagitingan* [bravery], and *kasipagan* [industry]."[23] Articles in newspapers and magazines during the postwar period emphasized the dual role of the Filipino woman as nation builder and homemaker and echoed the belief of First Lady Roxas that the woman's role in building the nation was intimately tied to her role as a homemaker, one "whose main concern is maintaining a well-knit and orderly family."[24] This image of Philippine womanhood proved to be remarkably influential. Despite the personal and political advances of women, argues Amaryllis T. Torres, the "ideal woman" in Philippine literature is still

a loving and loyal mate to her husband; she is responsible for keeping the marriage intact by her patience, hard work, submission, and virtue. Aside from whatever outside employment she may hold, she is also expected to be a diligent housekeeper and budgets the money [for] family and household needs. The husband has the larger voice in decisions involving the family. He is not expected to do household chores, except for occasional repairs to allow time for more "manly" activities like relaxing, drinking, and socializing with friends outside the home.[25]

The dominant image of the Filipino woman in the postwar period positioned her firmly in the home, but this did not mean she was completely excluded from the public sphere. Women, for one, retained the right to vote, an important achievement. Women were also an essential part of an official and quasi-official "culture of consent" designed to demonstrate that Filipinos supported the continued involvement of the United States in the Philippines and shared its cultural values. American-style magazines and newspapers proliferated in the country and played a key role in defining the new nation and the role of Filipino women. According to Georgina Reyes Encanto, "[T]he Filipina was bombarded with advertisements that propagated the American lifestyle as the standard to be desired."[26] Middle-class Filipina readers were enticed by Western ideals of femininity that valued glamorous (and often Caucasian-looking) women who ran their households efficiently. The "New Filipina" propagated in the postwar press and print culture was no longer the modern, educated, and professional Filipina of the prewar years but the carnival queen and domestic goddess. As Encanto argues, the press "dished out fantasy to women," offering them "a weekly escape from their mundane concerns to an ideal world where all women, regardless of class, could attain the ideals of physical beauty, harmonious relationships within the home and the workplace, [and] romance in the distant exotic places that were the settings of the romantic novels."[27]

Alfred W. McCoy contends that this ideal of femininity and masculinity shaped many institutions in the immediate postwar Philippines, including the military and the educational system. In military institutions, for example, women were barred from drill but recruited as "sponsors to appear in formal, frilly gowns at full dress parades."[28] The Philippine military, with the total exclusion of women from its ranks and its valorization of masculine strength, further contributed to what Anne-Marie Hilsdon calls the "oppositional relationship" between men, who possessed strength, and "womenandchildren" [*sic*], who were "weak and in need of protection."[29] In the military, McCoy states, "[W]omen remained the ultimate opposite, an alluring, defining, antithesis."[30] This masculinized ideology, central to the practices of the military, further reinforced male hegemony in the public sphere and discouraged direct challenges from women, whose sense of place and security remained entrenched in the home.[31]

While the home was reaffirmed as the proper domain of the middle-class Filipino woman, the economic distress created by the war forced Filipinas of lower social status back into the workplace. But their prospects were limited. During the first few years after the war the Philippine economy was still closely tied to that of the United States and favored "capital-intensive, large-scale, urban-based industries," which increased industrial production but diminished the jobs available to women and encouraged the masculinization of the labor force. In rural areas growing economic pressures, such as unemployment and landlessness, pushed women back into the home, making them largely dependent on male incomes.[32] Peasant women were strongly tied to their traditional roles as mother, wife, and housekeeper, but they contributed to the family economy in other ways such as selling in the marketplace, washing clothes, or working as domestics for richer families. But according to Carolyn Sobritchea the priorities of women in the villages did not differ much from those of the urban middle-class. "Marriage and raising a family," she wrote, "are among the most important and, in fact, more easily attainable career paths."[33] With limited formal schooling and few "occupational skills" most poor women had few employment options. Instead they continued to focus on having children as a way to safeguard the family regardless of the economic constraints. This strategy affected the economic opportunities available to family members, especially women.

For women in the postwar Philippines the tension in public discourse between the home and society and domestic and the public space echoed earlier debates about women's suffrage. Writing in 1951 the suffragist Maria Paz Mendoza-Guazon reflected on "the development and progress of the Filipino woman" after winning the vote and voiced her concern about the "Filipino woman of tomorrow." "Will she be completely westernized," she asked, or "must she stick to the rigid Victorian notion of propriety, with an admixture of Chinese conservatism and the oriental fatalism of the past, or shall she follow the new standard that sprang into being as the result of the World War?" Mendoza-Guazon and other elite women wanted Filipino women to embrace an American understanding of the modern woman as one who was educated, English speaking, and active in "matters of education, sanitation, commerce and home industries."[34] Women had a role to play in politics and the public sphere, and during the early postwar years women, argues Mina Roces, "were pivotal in charity and civic works organizations— although many were founded and run by wives and female kin of politicians with the goal of boosting their husband's civic profile."[35] But through their roles in civic and charitable organizations, community work, beauty contests, and other social activities women further reinforced their domestic roles in public.[36] For example, the Women's Auxiliary of the Liberal Party, established in 1946, and the National Political Party for Women, founded in 1951, were composed primarily of wives of party and congressional members, and acted as support groups for male-dominated political parties as well as focusing on "social welfare work."[37] Their activities attracted attention in the popular press, but this coverage rarely challenged the cultural constructions of the woman as wife and mother, beauty queen, and civic worker. Indeed, the public persona of these women was an extension rather than a repudiation of their domesticity.

A handful of women also became politicians in the postwar years, but, according to Roces, "their path to official political power was through women's activities in civic organizations or women's reputations as beauty queens." "A close look at women politicians in the postwar years," she continues, "reveals a clear pattern of association either with civic work or beauty titles. Female power was still associated with the woman as beauty queen and the woman as moral guardian. Women were still defined as 'wife and mother.'" Filipino women therefore "did not oppose the view that the 'home' was women's primary sphere although they did argue that women needed to go outside the home and perform civic work in order to become better homemakers."[38] The suffrage movement, or what Roces calls the "first wave" of Philippine feminism, had succeeded in giving women political power but not in radically altering nineteenth-century definitions of the feminine. According to Hilsdon, however, the cultural construction of the Filipino woman in the postwar period was not limited to her role as wife and mother. The militarization of postwar Philippine society, which promoted masculinized ideologies of strong states and strong men, had cast women "primarily in marginalized or stigmatized roles such as mistress, whore and Eve, and passive roles such as wife, virgin and Mary."[39] Such cultural constructions played a role in preventing women from assuming a more active role in the public sphere. Indeed, not until the 1970s and 1980s, when a new women's movement emerged that was more attuned to the worldwide feminist movement, did women begin to assert themselves in public life once again.[40]

Roces challenges what she perceives as established scholarship that "sees only women activists or women's movements as representing politically active or empowered women." She argues that a focus on women activists as "*sublime* [emphasis in original] examples of empowered women" is misplaced in the Philippines, where women "have shunned kinship politics" and as a result have been "marginalized from official power by the male leadership of the radical organizations." "Deprived of official power and refusing to exercise unofficial power," she concludes, "women activists were practically impotent."[41] Although this argument has some merit, the experience of Huk women challenges some of its assumptions. The activism of women in the Huk movement was profoundly shaped by kinship relations and politics, and their marginalization was not a product of "shunning" kinship politics but of the challenges their involvement created to kinship and patriarchal politics. While Roces is generally willing to grant political agency to elite women, she undermines the efforts of lower class women to define power in Philippine society. In fact Huk women challenged the image of the Filipina as an efficient, committed, and subordinate wife, mother, and homemaker, confronting more conservative cultural constructions of Filipino women with the image of the Huk Amazon.

Huk Amazons

Immediately after World War II the Huk movement and guerrillas were widely recognized for their role in the anti-Japanese resistance movement. But postwar ideology and the atmosphere of the cold war soon turned these war heroes into enemies, relentlessly vilified by the government as communists. But the public was more ambivalent about the Huks, and this was reflected in attitudes toward women fighters, who assumed increasing prominence in print culture. Indiscriminately labeled *amasonas* (amazons) in the Filipino vernacular, the actions of these female guerrillas were followed with intense curiosity and scrutiny in the press, and women warriors elicited awe and admiration, as well as fear and hostility, in popular newspapers and magazines in the postwar period.

The phenomenon of the Amazon or "warrior woman" in the postwar period was not new to Philippine history. Folktales and mythological stories portraying women who possessed "male" martial skills existed in precolonial indigenous society. And during the colonial period Amazons became part of the nationalist imagination, playing a role in anticolonial struggles against the Spanish and American governments. Female shamans and healers, the *babaylans* of the precolonial Philippines, whose power was undermined by the Catholic Church, were never integrated into colonial society and survived within messianic organizations that tried to preserve their central and uncontested spiritual role in peasant society.[42]

The dominant image of the Amazon in the eighteenth and nineteenth centuries was embodied by Gabriela Silang, a female "general" who assumed control of her husband's revolutionary army after he was slain by the Spanish. Gabriela rode horses, wielded bolos and spears, and led attacks against the Spanish, but she remained a feminine figure. Images of her usually portrayed a statuesque woman with long, free-flowing hair, wearing a long dress, and mounted on a horse with her left breast partially exposed as she wielded a bolo in her right hand. She was eventually arrested and hanged by the Spanish.[43] Women also played a role in the Katipunan movement, which recognized the indispensability of women in the struggle against Spain and acknowledged their rights and privileges but largely excluded them from the revolutionary army.[44] Nonetheless, out of a small group of women, including Josefa Rizal, Marina Dizon, Angelica Lopez, and Marcella Agoncillo, who worked for the Katipunan and the revolution, there emerged a number of prominent female heroes, among them Tandang Sora, who took care of the rebels; Trinidad Tecson, who procured arms for the revolution; Agueda Kahabagan, a freedom fighter and soldier from Batangas; and Teresa Magbanua, reputed to be the first woman from Visayas to join the revolution. Gregoria de Jesus, the wife of Katipunan founder Andres Bonifacio, was said to be constantly at his side, even in battle. Several historians have argued that the Katipunan and the Philippine Revolution opened the door for Filipina women to engage in political and revolutionary affairs, and in recent years feminist historians have rescued these women from obscurity and restored them to nationalist narratives of the revolution.[45]

Female rebels also emerged from the dissident and millenarian movements that challenged American colonial rule in the 1930s, most notably the Sakdal ("accuse" in Tagalog) movement, which advocated tax reductions, land reforms, the breakup of the large estates or haciendas, and an end to American rule in the Philippines. On May 2, 1933, armed Sakdalistas mounted an uprising in Southern Luzon and seized municipal buildings in fourteen towns. The uprising was crushed the next day, but one woman, Salud Algabre, emerged as an important rebel figure. Her fellow comrades called her Generala, a title the scholar David Sturtevant believes was well deserved:

> During fifteen hours of turbulence . . . she oversaw the placing of tires across the main rail line south from Manila, supervised the cutting of telephone and telegraph wires, ordered and assisted the *bolo* wielders who felled trees across the pavement of the south highway, assumed command of the resulting roadblock, stopped and searched all vehicles bound for Manila, and confiscated one scout car after disarming its occupants—four United States Marines. It was an excellent night's work for a ninety-pound mother of five.[46]

Salud Algabre was not the only woman arrested after the Sakdal uprising. In official and press reports about the Sakdalistas, however, women were usually lauded for their bravery but also dismissed as impulsive and misguided fanatics.[47]

This same fascination with women warriors characterized press accounts of Huk women. When the Huks declared war against the new Philippine Republic, Manila's major newspapers reported daily on the battles between the so-called dissidents and government forces, and, while the deaths of male guerrillas were considered secondary stories and were usually ignored or featured in the middle pages of the newspaper, the capture of women warriors was almost always headline news. Typical headlines included: "Amazon captured," "20 Armed Amazons Captured by PC Men," "Huk Amazon Unit Encountered by PC," "Huk Amazon Mother Captured with Baby," "Woman Huk Commander Facing Trial for Sedition," "Pretty Girl Amazon Denies Any Huk Connection," and "Huk Amazons Welcome New Life."[48] These headlines, which featured Huk women as soldiers, mothers, pretty girls, and suspects, capture the complex and contested representations of these women warriors.[49] Indeed, while the image of women as warriors was already a well-established part of Philippine revolutionary history, the treatment of Huk Amazons brought it to a new, heightened level of recognition and importance in both the press and the public imagination.

The capture of Huk Amazons was almost always accompanied by sensational stories such as the reports in the *Manila Times* and *Philippines Free Press* about the arrest of Leonila Monteverde, alias "Ningning" ("sparkle" or "glow" in Filipino), in March 1948. According to the papers the military hailed her capture as part of a major victory, the result of three weeks of close surveillance of a village in Southern Luzon where the Huks had been operating. Leonila, a college student, was the chairman of the regional educational department in Southern Luzon, had been trained in the Huk school, and served as a lecturer in a training camp in the Sierra Madre. The headlines described her capture in dramatic terms. Military officers surprised Leonila while she was bathing in a river and, chivalrously, waited for her to finish bathing and dressing before they took her into custody. Although she was reportedly carrying a .22 caliber pistol, she did not resist and denied possessing firearms. She also refused to tell officers the whereabouts of her husband, a certain Commander Algo, with whom she had been living for more than ten years and with whom she had two children. Leonila was then taken to the military stockade for interrogation and detention.[50]

In September 1948 several newspapers ran headlines about the discovery of an Amazon combat unit by the Philippine military in Central Luzon. One story read:

> A startling report received from the *Manila Times* correspondent in Nueva Ecija yesterday disclosed the participation of 80 women, allegedly members of the Double Star Squadron under Commander Mahinhin ["shy, demure" in Filipino], against the Huk-PC [Philippine Constabulary] in Nueva Ecija. After a half-hour skirmish, the strange army of Huk Amazons retreated in confusion leaving a dead woman soldier and two others wounded. One carbine was seized from the withdrawing Huks. During the investigation the woman captives—one Sulpicia, 19, the other, Adelaida, 16—showed a meager education but spoke English. They confessed they joined the Huk army since liberation in the capacity of "first-aiders" but later transferred to a combat unit. . . . The two Huk captives further revealed another Huk squadron composed mostly of women were bivouacked four kilometers west of Guimba.[51]

A few days later, the *Manila Times* ran another story on Amazons in combat:

> Eighty-three Huks, including one major and five women fighters of an Amazon unit, were slain in an encounter with government forces, believed to be the bloodiest fighting in Central Luzon so far. Two special policemen were killed when five women Huks fired at them from their hideout.[52]

These reports may have sensationalized the military activities of Huk women in order to justify using *Amazon* to describe them, a term that highlighted their participation in the traditionally male activity of war. Originating from Greek mythology, Amazons were women who lived in exclusively female societies separated from men and engaged in hunting, pillaging, and killing them.[53] These mythological women warriors assumed undeniably masculine roles. They lived outdoors, wielded weapons, rode horses, and fought ruthlessly. While they occasionally had sexual relations with men, they refused to live with them. Figures of fascination and repulsion, these warrior women were usually thought to be "as beautiful as they were cruel."[54]

The press played an important role for bringing the presence of Amazons among men in the Huk movement into public attention. From the mid-1940s to late 1950s, the capture of Huk Amazons became a matter of great public interest. Leonila Dizon, who was captured in 1948 at the age of 18, was described as "a pretty girl or beautiful barrio lass" who, despite her denials, held a top position as secretary to Huk Supremo Luis Taruc.[55] Rosa Carlos, who was only sixteen at the time of her capture, had already been administering first aid to wounded Huks.[56] A report in 1953 recounted the capture of four Amazons who were part of a military combat team that surrendered 148 rounds of .30 caliber ammunition after an encounter with the Philippine Armed Forces in Laguna.[57] In the same year another Huk Amazon, Aurelia Calma, alias Commander Auring, who was the wife of a Huk leader in Central Luzon Command No. 5 and was alleged to be the Huks' finance officer, was arrested on her way to solicit funds from sympathizers.[58] In 1953 police intelligence officers in Manila believed they had broken "the backbone of the Huk message service in Manila" by arresting three female couriers and confiscating "dissident documents and letters addressed to the Huk members." One of these couriers, Julia Reyes, alias Lucy, was married to a member of the Huk Central Committee in Southern Luzon. Although she initially denied membership in the Huk organization, she eventually "broke down and said she was forced to join the movement." She had previously been arrested but was released for lack of evidence, and this time the police believed they had stopped her dissident activities for good.[59] Journalists made few distinctions among Huk women. While many of the captured women held significant positions in the Huk movement, any woman associated with the Huks was immediately labeled an Amazon.

Journalists and reporters who covered the Huk rebellion found it difficult to hide their fascination. "These women like their male counterparts," wrote one sympathetic journalist from the *Philippines Free Press,* "lived and slept with death, underwent much physical suffering and risked all in the name of the love of country."[60] But, although he praised them for their bravery in fighting the Japanese, he also invoked their femininity, emphasizing that, while some perished in the struggle, "the majority stayed behind the front lines, educated their fellow cadres, uplifted the morale of ordinary townspeople, or nursed their ailing comrades who had either been wounded in combat or stricken with malaria—the dreaded menace in the hills that the guerrillas feared even more than death itself."[61] Not all commentators highlighted the feminine qualities of Huk women. One reporter was clearly impressed by their masculine virtues and image as Amazon women, describing them as ruthless and daring soldiers, women who "faced bullets, instead of mirrors, explosive powders, instead of face powder," Amazons who acted "like real men" not "summer soldiers or sunshine patriots."[62] Like men, he cautioned, "[T]hese women should be feared. They must be treated as men, because in the art of guerrilla warfare, these women are men."[63] As this description reveals, while these masculine traits were admired by many male journalists they also created an undercurrent of trepidation and anxiety, and in other newspaper accounts reporters tried to assimilate these women into more traditional female roles, portraying them as innocent female victims. Described as a "pretty girl," a "charming woman," a "girl secretary," an "innocent girl of 16," a "mere wife," and so on, these were women who needed to be rescued and whose femininity was at odds with their participation in the Huk rebellion. These women were commonly described as "former beauty pageant winners," which reveals the importance of the beauty pageant in defining women's place in postwar Philippine society.[64] Such contradictory responses betrayed a deep fascination with these female rebels against traditional gender roles but also a desire to bring them back into the fold of tradition and convention as "lovers," "mothers," and "innocent girls" who had to be protected by men.

The story of Waling-Waling reflects this ambivalence about women as agents of revolutionary struggle. For several weeks in May 1952, a number of newspapers ran stories about the arrest of Coronacion Chival, alias Waling-Waling (the name of a rare Philippine orchid), who was described by the army as the highest-ranking Huk woman in the

Visayas. One story described her as "smartly dressed in a man's worsted shirt and blue denim trousers with a .38 caliber revolver tucked in her belt" when she was captured, adding that she was accompanied by "two male Huk bodyguards, who carried a carbine, a rifle and a hand grenade." The wife of another famous Huk commander, Andres, she was confined in army headquarters where the guards were doubled "to control the crowd of curious people who want to take a look at the beauteous Waling-Waling" and were attracted by the capture of an Amazon who appeared to be as ruthless as she was beautiful.[65]

Huk women who fought alongside male comrades were often captured, wounded, or even killed. In September 1948 a woman "Huk entertainer," Filomena Divina, alias Kundiman ("lullaby" in Tagalog), was found dying from bullet wounds after a clash with Philippine Constabulary forces.[66] Another Huk woman, described in newspaper accounts as "having mestiza features and lugging a .38-caliber pistol," was

The same fascination around the capture of Waling-Waling surrounded the arrest of Commander Betty, shown here in a wheelchair after being wounded in a battle with military forces in 1952. Not much was written about Commander Betty except that she was "beautiful and fragile," and she was constantly hounded by "the press and radio representatives from Manila," who were captivated by her sexual aura and military prowess. (*Manila Times*, May 9, 1952; Courtesy of Rizal Library, Ateneo de Manila University)

stopped by the police when she "tried to whip out her pistol" and "was beaten to the draw." She was mortally wounded in the chest.[67] The death of Corazon de Castro, alias Nora Rey, was featured prominently in several news accounts in 1948. "Miss Castro," who was killed by the military,

> was the best known woman Huk in Bulacan. . . . As secretary to Dr. Jesus Lava, overall commander of the Huks in Bulacan, she ranked third in the organization. . . . She is a charming woman

This dramatic photo shows that Huk Amazons were never that far away from danger and death. The caption in the accompanying article, which expressed a fascination with guns and Amazons, described the scene: "Photo shows some of the 15 slain Huks including several Amazons who were killed yesterday in Candaba swamps . . . who were among the 250 dissidents under the command of Luis Taruc who planned to stage a general attack against government centers in preparation for the March 29 celebration of the Huks. Among the newly-imported foreign made firearms seized were automatic carbines." (*Manila Times*, March 23, 1951; Courtesy of Rizal Library, Ateneo de Manila University)

of 27, a convincing speaker and an able debater. Affiliated with many movements even before the last war, her name had become a household word in many a village home. . . . In her possession at the time of her death were numerous Huk documents including minutes of meetings and instructions to Huk commanders.[68]

The unsympathetic response to the death of the Huk Amazons was purposeful, conveying a belief that female rebels, by virtue of their unwomanly behavior, deserved gruesome deaths just as the men. Most female Huks, like Filomena and Corazon, were portrayed by the press as fearless dissidents who could not be trusted. Commander Cinderella, for example, despite her feminine name was depicted as the ruthless leader of a group of thirty armed women when she was involved in a clash with the Philippine Constabulary. Described as a "former nightclub hostess in Manila," the press expressed no sympathy for a woman who "ruthlessly killed the police with automatic fire" and, "facilitated by total darkness," successfully escaped into the mountains of Central Luzon.[69] A later report describing her pursuit by armed troops commented sarcastically that "Commander Cinderella fled bare-footed, wearing only her underwear, leaving her rubber shoes and hunting knife."[70] The description of her humiliating flight literally stripped the dignity normally associated with her femininity.

But the most serious charge against Huk women was not that they were unnatural women but that they were unnatural mothers. Newspaper reports of captured Amazons were often accompanied by stories of captured "Huklings," children who were abandoned by their Huk parents during military encounters, "rescued" by military authorities, and raised in military orphanages. A fascinating report appeared in the *Philippines Free Press* in 1952:

> Unmistakable proof that the dissidents are definitely "on the run" is the capture of Huk babies who, it is believed, were abandoned by their hard-pressed parents so that they could move faster. One captured Huk confessed that their camp had 50 Huk Amazons and Huklings. But once the camp was attacked, the Amazons and most of the Huklings had already left. Those Huklings left behind all had chafed feet and were under-nourished. And every one of them was suffering from skin diseases. They smelled badly as they looked. The children seemed to have an instinctive fear or hatred of anybody in khaki or army fatigue.

A government nurse at Camp Murphy feeds the children of Huk guerrillas. In a series of published photographs, the government aimed to show its benevolence by taking care of these abandoned children at the same time as it launched a propaganda campaign aimed at Huk women to leave the mountains so they could reunite with their children. (*Philippines Free Press*, n.d. [early 1950s]; Courtesy of Rizal Library, Ateneo de Manila University)

Accompanying this report were photographs of the "innocent" babies with their angelic but scared faces and their thin bodies dressed in tattered clothes. The message of the report and images was clear: these beautiful children had been abandoned by their heartless mothers who left them to starve or die in the forest. The current state of their bodies and clothes revealed that they had not been cared for by their parents. The report was quick to highlight how the state had rescued these children, who then received the care and love they deserved:

> These children were placed in a Children's nursery at Camp Murphy. Each child has a bed of his own, complete with mattress and bedsheets. During the first days, they refused to eat their bread and drink their milk. They kept asking for rice porridge and coconut meat—their staples in the forest. But after a few

Another captivating photograph of the "Huklings." The original caption describes "Ms. Teresita Magsaysay, daughter of the President, Saturday morning, May 29 [1954], [who] visited the Hukling nursery at Camp Murphy as part of her birthday activities. The Huklings are shown singing a nursery song 'I Have Two Hands.'" The benevolence of the state, here epitomized by the lovely presidential daughter, was again highlighted by this image. (*Philippines Free Press*, May 29, 1954; Courtesy of Rizal Library, Ateneo de Manila University)

days, they began to like bread and candy and cookies. They have
gained weight since their capture.

And yet, despite the attention bestowed on them by the military, these
children were now orphaned. And the reporter made sure to emphasize
that the Huk women must be feeling intense shame, and especially
guilt, for abandoning their children:

Very often they cry themselves to sleep. But on the whole, the
children are happy. Those of them who can talk tell their nurses
that they want to stay. But no matter how well they are being

Despite the realities of abandonment and possibly death, soldiers obviously wanted to
show their compassionate side against the heartless Huk parents who fled ironically to
save their babies from the threats posed by the military. According to this photo's
original caption, "TWO 'HUKLINGS,' abandoned children of Huk parents, are in the
hands of 20th BCT men who came across the babies . . . in Bulacan. Lieut. Margate
(*left*) holds the six-month-old daughter of a Huk commander while Capt. Masungsong
tries to feed the two-month-old baby girl held by an unidentified soldier." (*Manila
Times*, June 18, 1953; Courtesy of Rizal Library, Ateneo de Manila University)

taken care of in their new home, these innocent children miss their own mothers.

Finally the article stated:

Military investigations reveal that the Huk policy was to abandon the children if they proved a hindrance to the speedy movement of the Huks on forced marches or hasty retreats, and to

Not only were children brought back to the folds of the state and society but they were also welcomed back to the Church, an institution that promotes forgiveness and reconciliation. The caption accompanying this photograph read: "Huklings, abandoned children of Huks, now under the custody of the Armed Forces of the Philippines in Camp Murphy, were baptized Monday morning at the camp chapel with Father Antonio Vera, camp chaplain, officiating." (*Manila Times*, July 25, 1952; Courtesy of Rizal Library, Ateneo de Manila University)

liquidate those who, by their crying, might reveal the position or otherwise endanger the security of other dissidents while in hiding.[71]

Although many newspaper articles discussed the so-called liquidation policy of the Huks, there is no evidence they pursued such a policy. The stories about captured Huklings created a highly critical portrait of Huk Amazons as women who went to war, had sex in the forest, got pregnant, and sacrificed their children to the goals of the revolution.[72] These stories about the capture of Huk babies presented Huk women in particular as neglectful, uncaring, and selfish mothers who had betrayed the nation and their duty as mothers by abandoning their young, who as "innocent" orphans were then adopted and placed under the benevolent care of the new Philippine state.[73]

It is easy to see why the Amazons—whether they were depicted as brave fighters, alluring women, or neglectful mothers—captured public attention. During the 1940s and into the 1950s, at the time of the Huk rebellion, most women in the Philippines, despite their role in the earlier suffrage campaigns and the rebuilding of postwar society, were marginalized in public and national life. They did not assume prominent political roles and lower class women, such as most Huks, had limited formal education and assumed traditional roles within and outside the home. But women guerrillas such as Leonila Monteverde, Waling-Waling, Commander Cinderella, and those who belonged to the Amazon combat unit defied conventional roles and directly challenged the dominant postwar images of the Filipina as domestic goddess, carnival queen, social worker, and homemaker. These women were comrades, leaders, and commanders—women who challenged both the image of the modern Filipina and the largely male command structure of the Huk organization. They subverted the ideal of the "man as strong, woman as weak," and a surprising number of the Huk squadrons were commanded by women who attained formidable reputations as aggressive fighters. The emergence of these women leaders and commanders was unprecedented in Philippine revolutionary and military history. Women such as Celia Mariano, the only woman ever elected to the Central Committee of the PKP; Remedios Gomez, known as Kumander Liwayway (Commander Dawn); and Simeona Punzalan, known as Kumander Guerrero (Warrior) broke with traditional women's roles and became successful and important guerrilla leaders and commanders. At a time when women played minor roles in the Philippine political arena and were excluded from all state and military activities, the Huk army created radically new roles for Filipino women.

How were these women able to emerge from the male-dominated structure of the Huk organization to become Politburo members and military leaders? What circumstances made their mobilization and rise within the revolutionary hierarchy possible? The lives of Celia Mariano, Remedios Gomez, and Simeona Punzalan reflected the struggles of Huk Amazon women to redefine sexual and gender politics both within and outside the Huk movement.

The Awakening of Celia Mariano

Celia Mariano was born a middle child of six children on June 18, 1915, in Tondo, the historic home of Manila's working class and its radical movements.[74] Calling herself a "city girl," she grew up in an urban middle-class family, the daughter of a treasurer-registrar at the University of the Philippines and a homemaker. But, having been raised among proletarian families in Tondo, she understood early on the importance of social class. Like many lower middle class families, hers subsisted on her father's salary but managed to invest in two small homesteads in the town of Tanay, Rizal, then a hilly farming community about two hours from Manila. Unlike most Huk women, Celia did not trace her political beginnings to her largely nonpolitical family. In hindsight she had reason to believe that her father was a nationalist since he baptized all his children in the Filipino Independent Church, also known as the Aglipayan, rather than the predominant Catholic Church. But when Celia recalled her childhood she traced her early political convictions to her observations of working-class life:

> When I was ten years old, I used to come with my mother around Tondo and at that stage already I began to be appalled by the poverty of the people, and I always wondered, "Why are there so many poor people here while we live in better circumstances?" I began to wonder why there are poor people, why there are middle-class people, and why there are so very few rich people. That was a question in my mind that tagged on my conscience for a long, long time, . . . I was conscious of the fact that these people live in such outrageous conditions. But how could they tolerate it? They had no running water, no electricity, and no

This photo was taken the day after Celia Mariano was captured by military forces during a major drive in April 1952. Celia never kept a photograph of herself while a member of the Huks and the Communist party, but with her arrest, her face became a prominent fixture in major Manila newspapers and magazines. (Courtesy of Celia Pomeroy)

toilets. How could they live that way? I began to wonder, but I did not know how to answer my own questions.[75]

Her comfortable situation did not encourage her to seek radical answers to these questions. As a young woman Celia benefited from an excellent education at the University of the Philippines (UP), where she obtained a bachelor of science degree in education. As a college student in the early 1930s she regarded her education as both a means of achieving social mobility and an opportunity for intellectual advancement. She fondly remembered her study of sociology and history, subjects taught by progressive professors who stimulated her interest in learning about the world around her. But the climate at the UP also encouraged her political awakening. University life at the time was marked by intense political discussions about the vital issues affecting the country, in particular the growth of fascism in Asia and the growing threat that Japanese imperialism posed to the region, and Celia began to think for the first time about political problems and to become both an activist and a nationalist.

After graduating in 1935 Celia became a high school teacher, and a year later she took the civil service examinations. Civil service posts were much sought after, especially by women, but despite the intense competition she did well enough to secure a post as an examiner in the Bureau of Civil Service. Although she was devoted to her career as a government bureaucrat, she continued to seek answers to the questions that had troubled her since childhood. In 1936 she attended a lecture on the situation in the Philippine countryside delivered by Pedro Abad Santos, a prominent leader of the peasant movement and founder of the Socialist Party of the Philippines. When members of the Philippine Youth Congress (PYC), impressed with Celia's apparent enthusiasm and curiosity about social and political issues, urged her to join their organization, she agreed to attend their meetings although she knew little about the group.

Thus began the political courtship of Celia. In 1937 she joined the PYC formally and quickly became an active member. Appointed as treasurer, she met with senators and congressmen to solicit donations and at the same time continued her political education, for example attending a lecture by a Japanese American visiting professor at the UP, Kenneth Kurihara, on imperialism, socialism, and communism, her first exposure to these concepts. She devoured the readings on fascism and the Philippine Communist Party that her friends in the PYC lent to her. She recalled that her earliest education about fascism and communism was derived from reading two books given to her by fellow PYC members: Amleto Vespa's *Secret Agent of Japan* and Edgar Snow's *Red Star over China*.

Celia's colleagues in the PYC made sure she understood that her political education was just beginning, and soon they began to visit regularly at her home to discuss political issues, particularly the impending threat of fascism in Asia. At that time Celia was in awe of these young people (all men, including Jesus Lava, Jorge Frianeza, Bayani Alcala, and Pacifico Puti) who seemed to know so much more than her about politics and international issues. She welcomed them into her home and fraternized with them, not realizing that their visits were part of a plan to recruit her to the Partido Komunista ng Pilipinas (Communist Party of the Philippines), or PKP. According to Celia she was in the PYC for four or five years before her colleagues told her about the PKP, and before this revelation she admitted her views were conventionally anticommunist. When her friends told her that they were communists, however, her views began to change:

> They counteracted all my beliefs about anticommunism. They told me what communism really is and why Catholics and the press are always hammering on communism. I can understand why—because the press . . . even our president of the Philippines . . . and the Church were controlled by imperialists. And they explained to me so many things about the blind, mistaken thoughts I have . . . and I can believe them because I can see they are true, in real life they are true, so this feeling of anticommunism vanished away, and in fact I felt sympathy for the Communist Party.[76]

She felt sympathy but not commitment. True to herself, Celia decided to learn more about the party before joining. Again her friends worked tirelessly to win her to their cause, encouraging her to attend their meetings as an observer. This phase of the courtship did not take long. The coming of the war hastened and deepened Celia's involvement, and two months before war broke out in 1941 she decided to join the Communist Party. As she later admitted however, joining the party at that time did not make her a full-fledged communist. Her commitment to the party and its cause grew gradually, nurtured by her friends and comrades.

When the Japanese attacked the Philippines in December 1941 members of the PYC, who had been convinced for some time that "the rise of militarism in Japan would lead to a Japanese invasion of the Philippines" called for vigilance.[77] On December 18, as chaos descended on Manila, Celia's supervisor at the Bureau of Civil Service announced that government offices would close indefinitely; with her mother, father, brother, and sister, Celia hastily evacuated Manila for the family farm in Tanay, Rizal. But the war failed to disrupt her political activities. Soon after settling in Tanay, comrades from Manila, including Geruncio Lacuesta and Isabelo Caballero, began to visit her, and during one of their visits they began to devise a plan of action in response to the Japanese Occupation. Eliciting cooperation from her parents, Celia and her PKP comrades started to organize the farm as a base for guerrilla operations against the Japanese. Determined to assist the nascent revolutionary organization in Rizal, the party sent Pedro Penino, a veteran of the International Brigade, which had fought in Spain against Franco, and Mariano Balgos, a well-known trade union leader, to organize a meeting of the "United Front" at Tanay. "We asked the people of Tanay for assistance," Celia recalled, "stating that a guerrilla movement would require money, food, medicine, clothing, and arms. The guerrilla unit would be kept secret and therefore needed to be self-sufficient. The people of Tanay were very positive." Tanay eventually became a United Front stronghold, harboring guerrillas and acting as a center from which the party could direct its anti-Japanese activities.

Celia's leadership and dedication to the movement did not go unnoticed, and a few months later Dr. Vicente Lava, the secretary-general of the PKP, invited her to move to Central Luzon to join the guerrilla movement, the Hukbalahap. Believing that education was critical to the resistance movement, Lava assigned Celia as educator to the guerrillas and the villagers. Hundreds of people had already joined the Huks, but few members had the ability to organize and educate them. Celia was Lava's ideal choice for this mission. He also recommended that the Military Committee officially recognize the guerrilla unit in Tanay as part of the Hukbalahap. Celia, who considered herself a young and inexperienced political worker, was pleased with this achievement. Taking the alias Loleng, she proceeded to Bulacan, where she took up residence with the Lavas and was introduced to Ida Santos, a good friend of the Lava family who had served as the chief campaign officer for Jesus Lava when he ran for Congress in Bulacan in 1941.[78] Together with Ida, Celia traveled, usually on foot, to the villages of Meycauayan, Plaridel, Taal, Guiginto, Paombong, and Hagonoy to deliver lectures on the nature of Japanese fascism and the need to organize resistance under the auspices

of the United Front. After this first assignment Celia was asked to educate members of the resistance movement in Nueva Ecija, visiting the
villages of Cabiao, Cabanatuan, and San Carlos, under the alias Lydia,
and helping to organize the Barrio United Defense Corps (BUDC).
Dressed in borrowed peasant clothing and with uncut hair, she resembled a barrio lass, concealing her Manila origins from both Japanese soldiers and their Filipino collaborators. She was always amazed by how
efficiently the villagers were organized. "At one point," she narrated, "I
hid out in the Candaba swamps—that area had creeks in a mazelike
formation—and the BUDC built for me a small hut that could not be
detected in the swamps."

During her time as a Hukbalahap guerrilla, Celia came face to face
with the Japanese on many occasions, narrowly escaping arrest and torture. She encountered the Japanese on the streets of Manila and in the
villages of Central Luzon, but she always managed to elude them. During a meeting with Comrade Dading, the son of peasant leader Mateo
del Castillo, the Japanese Army entered the barrio where they were staying. "I had to hide in a bamboo grove in order to escape capture," Celia
recalled, "but Dading was unfortunately caught on his way to Manila
and was later tortured to death." A number of times Japanese soldiers
came looking for her at home or in the villages, but she was always one
step ahead of them. Her family was forced to move back to Manila in
1943 to escape increasing surveillance and harassment. But Celia trusted
the people around her, and they repaid this trust, protecting her from
the Japanese often at great risk to their own lives. One of the highlights
of her involvement with the peasants was what Celia called the Harvest
Struggle, when the Huks encouraged villagers to withhold food supplies
from the Japanese soldiers with slogans such as "No rice for the enemy!"
and "Keep the food of the people." Protected by the guerrillas, peasants
would harvest and hide the rice in the hollow bamboo poles of their
houses and concealed warehouses or bury it underground to keep it out
of the hands of the Japanese collection agency. The success of this campaign increased Celia's nationalist fervor and gave her a tremendous
sense of faith in the Huks and their peasant supporters.[79]

This faith was reciprocal, and in 1943 Celia became the editor of the
revolutionary newspaper *Katubusan ng Bayan* (Redemption of the Nation). Under a new alias, Alicia Garces, she became even more deeply
involved in the Huk movement, continuing her educational activities as
well as translating documents from Huk leaders into Tagalog and writing articles for *Katubusan*.[80] A year later she was reassigned once again,

becoming educational secretary of the Central Luzon Bureau, where she supervised five Huk provincial committees in Bulacan, Nueva Ecija, Pampanga, Tarlac, and Pangasinan and was responsible for operating schools in the region. Celia later recalled her early experiences as an educator as her most memorable, and she prided herself on having taught many of the men and women who later achieved prominence in the Huk movement, including Remedios Gomez, who became Kumander Liwayway.

By early 1944 the Communist Party knew that the Americans, under the command of General Douglas MacArthur, were advancing toward the Philippines. Like most Huks, Celia believed that it was the Huks — then the strongest, most militant guerrilla organization in the country — who had done the most to pave the way for Philippine liberation. According to her they "sustained, augmented and increased their resistance campaign against the Japanese from the fall of Manila, unlike other movements who were attached to MacArthur's forces," engaging in ambushes, sabotage, and attacks on Japanese property with the support of the Philippine peasantry and therefore "earning a fearsome reputation among the Japanese."[81]

On September 22, 1944, American forces bombed Manila. At this critical juncture the Communist Party's secretary-general, Vicente Lava, assigned Celia to inform the leaders of the Southern Luzon Bureau that Huk squadrons would be joined by the Chinese Squadron, which was then a Huk ally, to fight against the Japanese and facilitate the entry of the Americans in Luzon. Conveying this message was a crucial assignment, and Celia still remembers that Lava told her, "You must not allow yourself to be caught."[82] With her comrade, Ely, Celia set off to deliver the message, stopping in Manila to warn her family that the city would soon become a battleground between the United States and Japan and instructing them to leave immediately. The Marianos moved to San Juan, Pampanga, where Celia's comrades took care of them. Months later she recalled how moved she was when "the peasants said that, as 'Lydia' educated them, they should look after the Marianos." In part because of Celia's success in delivering her message, the Huks were able to coordinate their northern and southern forces, and "the Huks fought the Japanese to clear the way for the U.S. forces throughout Central Luzon until the Americans reached Manila."[83] Like most Filipinos, Celia welcomed the end of the war and the independence of the Philippines, and she dreamed of going home to her family and starting a new life in Manila. But the celebration did not last long, and for Celia the postwar period was far from the blissful life she had envisioned.

The Story of Kumander Liwayway, the "Joan of Arc of the Philippines"

Remedios Gomez grew up in a relatively affluent peasant family in Pampanga. Her father, Basilio Gomez, was a peasant leader who, because of his sympathetic stance toward the peasantry's plight, was elected mayor of the town of Mexico, Pampanga, between 1930 and 1940. According to Remedios, the local land system was unjust and repressive, where a few *hacenderos* (landowners) controlled practically all of Pampanga's farms. Her family was one of the very few lucky enough to own a small parcel of land. Growing up, she remembered how their lives revolved around the land and how intimately connected they were to the other peasants who worked the land. Indeed, despite her family's relative wealth, her father emphasized to her the plight of the poor peasants and involved her in his political activities.[84] The demands of maintaining the household prevented Remedios from finishing high school. But she was "educated in life," as she repeatedly emphasized, by her active role in her town's youth and peasant organizations. As a young and beautiful teenager she was constantly invited to participate in social activities, although she never assumed a leadership role in these organizations. While Remedios helped support her family, working in various small businesses such as selling rice and baby dresses, she also gave her time and talents to the peasant organizations. The arrival of the Japanese however, dramatically changed her life.

When the Japanese entered Remedios's village of Anao, in Mexico, Pampanga, in January 1942, her father, who was then the vice mayor, instructed his constituents to resist the "foreign invaders" and gather the town's arms and ammunition. But they did not stand a chance, and for his efforts to spark resistance Remedios's father was pursued by the Japanese, quickly captured, mercilessly tortured, executed, and finally displayed in public as a warning against noncooperation with the new Japanese-controlled government. He was the first casualty in their village. "What saddens me greatly," Remedios later recalled, "is the fact that when we asked for the remains of our murdered father they would not even give them to us."[85] After being threatened further by the Japanese, Remedios and her family decided to leave Pampanga in March 1942.

The alluring, well-dressed, and well-groomed Remedios Gomez. Most members of the Central Luzon Huks knew Remedios for her beauty and poise but were nevertheless aware that this woman was also the "dangerous" and highly efficient commander Liwayway. (n.d., Courtesy of Rizal Library, Ateneo de Manila University)

The decision to join the Huks was an easy one for Remedios. "Rather than die without putting up resistance," she remembered, "we had to defend ourselves."[86] The Japanese were after her family, and her capture would surely have meant death. Moving with the aid of clandestine village networks, the family arrived safely at their relatives' house in Tarlac, although that did not provide a safe haven and Remedios still felt that their lives were in jeopardy. Although at first she feared the guerrillas who appeared in the barrio after dark, she was already familiar with their activities and soon agreed to meet with them. The courtship between Remedios and the Huk guerrillas was not a protracted one. At the foot of Mount Arayat she met with Eusebio Aquino, who introduced himself as her father's friend and quickly convinced her and her brother to join the movement. He told her that joining the Huk movement was the only way to protect her family and her femininity against the Japanese, who by then were rumored to be kidnapping and raping Filipina women at random. Remedios soon found herself living at the Huk headquarters in Tarlac. She attended party schools where she was taught various topics such as "fundamental spirit," "dialectical and historical materialism," "communism," and "guerrilla strategies and tactics." Although she still finds some of these concepts puzzling, her studies convinced her not only that the struggle against the Japanese was necessary but also that a struggle against the inequities of the agricultural system was inevitable.

After she completed her Huk training and had been baptized Liwayway, Remedios was assigned to the medical team, where she treated the wounds of the guerrillas and took care of the sick. After several months their group in Tarlac decided to form Squadron 3-V, and Liwayway, who must have already demonstrated her bravery and personal resourcefulness, was immediately picked as its new commander. The men under her "were raring to fight," but they did not have enough arms and ammunition, and it was only when "another woman Huk organizer in Zambales heard of a certain Liwayway" and immediately "sent her extra arms and ammunitions" that her squadron got its chance to fight.[87] Not quite realizing how extraordinary women commanders were in the movement, Liwayway felt encouraged and vowed to make her squadron a major force in the Hukbalahap.

Initially her role was to persuade people from nearby towns to support the Huks. But as she became more confident as a military commander she began to organize military training sessions for her troops. At the Guerrilla Officers Military Academy (GOMA), Liwayway received weapons training and instruction in basic military tactics and strategy. "Our schooling in GOMA," she later observed, "taught us how to fight—for example, what to do in the firing line, how to measure your distance from the enemy, what's your positioning, how to shoot a gun when you are standing or when you are sprawled to the ground. I was taught that timing is the most important thing in an encounter."[88] While many male soldiers had received prior military training under the government conscription program, the guerrilla tactics of the Huk

movement were decidedly different. Unlike the Philippine and Japanese military, guerrillas had to learn how to ambush the enemy and position themselves to fight a military truck or tank with minimal equipment and tactical support. The Huks also had to learn how to retreat
when overwhelmed by enemy troops. Liwayway later asserted, speaking
like a true military veteran, that "guerrilla tactics can be learned, but
only perfected through actual encounters." Most women were not actively involved in military combat, but many received training in basic
guerrilla tactics.

After her training Liwayway knew she was ready to lead a squadron.
Her routine tasks included supervising meetings and planning sessions
for military operations against the Japanese. "We did a lot in our squad,"
she later recalled, including raiding military camps and "talking to the
people in the barrio to elicit their participation in either giving us information on where the arms of the rich and the army were hidden or in se-
curing the arms themselves." Acquiring weapons and ammunition was
never a problem, according to Liwayway, as her team could "steal guns,
assemble and fix guns," as well as "use them." At one point, she claimed
she had about two hundred men under her command, and her military
prowess in Tarlac and Pampanga became well known, especially after
her most famous encounter with the Japanese, the "Battle of Kamansi."
She led Squadron 3-V with about one hundred men and later recalled:

> I was one of the commanders who were assigned to attack the
> Japanese. Because we were outnumbered, the lead commander,
> Eusebio Aquino, called for a retreat. But my men and I stayed.
> We did not retreat. By the time the reinforcements came, we
> were very near to overcoming the Japanese and their allies from
> the Philippine Constabulary. In the end, the enemy retreated
> and I was commended for fighting even though the other com-
> manders already gave up.[89]

But leading dramatic battles was not her most typical task. As chief
of the military provision division assigned to procure food and supplies
for the guerrillas, and as a conduit between the barrio supporters and
the Huk leadership, most of her daily operations were routine. But
there were times when she doubted her abilities and encountered dis-
comfort, danger, and even the threat of death. "Being a Huk," she recalled, "entailed sleeping in the forests and eating whatever was available, vastly different from my past life of sleeping on a real bed and
eating three full meals a day." However, the dedication of the other

guerrillas and the support she and her squadron secured from the villagers inspired her to accept the consequences of her revolutionary commitment. Perhaps because the dangers she and her troops faced in fighting the Japanese had long since passed, Remedios tended to recall those days of fighting with nostalgia and a sense of pride, blending her identity seamlessly with that of the fearless Commander Liwayway.

The Huk Supremo, Luis Taruc, had only praise for Liwayway, who negotiated her masculine tasks without sacrificing her feminine allure. He wrote that she

> preserved her feminine charms under the most difficult of circumstances. . . . The character of Liwayway . . . belied her mannerisms. She was not flighty and superficial. Our movement consumed all her energies and dominated her thoughts and speech. She did not talk of dresses, dancing or perfumes; she talked of the work to be done, our organizational tasks, of the obstacles to be overcome.[90]

Her efforts to preserve her femininity while assuming a "masculine" role in the movement endowed Liwayway with an aura of respect and authority. One of the best-known and amusing stories about Liwayway, and one that endured for many years after the war, was about the fact that she always combed her hair, manicured and polished her nails, and applied lipstick before going into battle. She acknowledged the truth of these stories, explaining that it gave the guerrillas under her command greater confidence when they saw her well groomed and wearing lipstick and convinced them that their commander was fearless and calm. But, as Taruc recorded in his memoir, she had another explanation for her behavior: "I am also fighting for the right to be myself."[91] Until the end of the war, Taruc noted, Liwayway spoke of nothing "but the welfare of other comrades and of the directions of the resistance."[92] The press was captivated by her enigmatic personality. As one newspaper article described it:

> Just before the arrival of the Japanese when "Liwayway" was a high school senior in Pampanga nobody suspected that this very effeminate (every inch a woman) student would one day ride a horse through creeks and mountain fastnesses, whip .45 cal. pistols with the dexterity of a professional gun wielder and lead a sizeable number of men to destroy an invading Japanese army and avenge the cruel death of her father, and later preach a doctrine of

brotherhood among Central Luzon peasants and work for the improvement of the lot of these peasants.[93]

Journalists frequently invoked the image of Joan of Arc to describe Liwayway, and she readily embraced this image. If being an Amazon meant "carrying a gun, fighting with men against the enemy, and sacrificing my life for the cause of freedom," she said, then "I am proud to be a Huk Amazon."[94]

Military Leaders in the Hukbalahap

Remedios Gomez was not the first female military commander of the Huks. This distinction, as already discussed, belonged to the commander Dayang-Dayang. Another woman who gained a reputation as a fearless female Huk commander was Simeona Punzalan. Like Remedios, Simeona came from a peasant family that owned a small parcel of land in San Simon, Pampanga. Her father was a farmer and fisherman and an active member of the peasant coalition in their barrio before the war. Simeona grew up heavily influenced by her father's politics and involved herself in solidarity activities with Central Luzon peasants without fully understanding the historical and colonial roots of their exploitation. In San Simon she became first an active youth member and later an organizer of the Kalipunang Pambansa ng mga Magsasaka sa Pilipinas (National Society of Peasants in the Philippines), or KPMP. Like Liwayway the coming of the Japanese further deepened Simeona's political commitments.[95]

Simeona was convinced by her neighbors and relatives that she must join the guerrillas or face the possibility of being tortured and raped by the Japanese. She admitted that she was pro-American then and fought against the Japanese partly because she "loved the Americans," a sentiment that conflicted with her later commitment to the revolution.[96] Her recruitment was relatively easy since the Huks were already actively involved in her village. Simeona volunteered that Luis Taruc himself talked to her about contributing to the liberation movement, and in 1942, during the first year of the Hukbalahap, Simeona decided to join. While she joined the Huks because of her anti-Japanese, pro-American feelings, she eventually embraced the communist ideology of her comrades. Her political education occurred in the party school, or Stalin University, as she called it, where she learned about United Front, dialectical and historical materialism, and guerrilla strategies and tactics.

But her commitment to the Huk movement was not grounded in communist ideology, as she later explained, but on her support for the peasantry. She stated:

> I was not a full-fledged communist. . . . But I saw how oppressive the present system was. The poor become poorer. And the rich become richer. The rich had everything—they had education, they had money—so they can easily become richer. And the government is like a spider's web—it captures the small flies, the small farmers. And the big flies destroy the web and get away with anything. And the poor get nothing and are oppressed.[97]

If siding with the poor meant believing in communism, then Simeona was prepared to be called a communist even if it meant abandoning her affection for the Americans. The poverty and exploitation of Filipinos, especially poor peasants like her family, led her to realize that imperialism—whether Japanese or American—was always unjust and an ally of the rich.

But Simeona regarded her experiences with ordinary Huk soldiers as the most crucial part of her revolutionary education. Soon after she finished her training she began to work full time as an organizer for the Hukbalahap. Her main assignment was to keep townspeople informed about the struggle against the Japanese and to elicit their support for the guerrillas. Although she was captured and briefly imprisoned during one Japanese Army operation, her arrest and imprisonment did nothing to dampen her revolutionary spirit, and she immediately returned to the hills to become part of Apalit Squadron 104, one of the Hukbalahap's most respected squadrons.[98] It was during this period that she acquired the name Kumander Guerrero. But despite her title Simeona was not the platoon commander; she acted more as a political director whose primary responsibility was to raise the political consciousness of the soldiers and to boost their morale as they prepared for battle. Nevertheless, Guerrero, like Kumander Liwayway, was involved in several military battles, planned combat operations, and on many occasions led her squadron in raids to secure ammunition and other supplies from the enemy. Taruc described her as "adept at handling an automatic rifle," someone who could be relied on to fight and had often "commanded on the firing line."[99] Guerrero admitted that guns never scared her. She felt at ease with weapons and before long had gained a reputation as a fearless commander.

This photo, originally published with the headline "SIX-FOOT AMAZON," shows "Simeona Pun[z]alan, alias Major 'Guerrero,' and commander of Squadron 104, surrendering recently to Governor Jose B. Lingad . . . with her .45 calibre revolver. A six-footer, Guerrero said her husband, 'Montemayor,' was slain in the Candaba operations while her own squadron was annihilated in a series of clashes with the constabulary. She promised to contact fellow Huks and ask them to surrender." Much of this story, including Guerrero's surrender and her plea to contact Huks to follow her lead, may have been fabricated by the press and by government authorities to demonstrate the Huk's declining influence. But what was certain was the interest that surrounded the capture of this formidable and intimidating female commander. (*Manila Times*, December 6, 1948; Courtesy of Rizal Library, Ateneo de Manila University)

Kumander Guerrero took under her protection another woman warrior, Gloria Rivera, also from San Simon, Pampanga. Gloria was preparing to evacuate to Manila because of the sexual advances of a Japanese soldier when Guerrero convinced her to join the Hukbalahap. Like other Huk women, Gloria learned about movement ideology, as well as military strategy and guerrilla tactics, in the Huk Forest School. She was also taught how to handle weapons. While she was personally acquainted with the Huks who organized in her hometown, only after her forest schooling did she truly understand the guerrilla movement. As she later recalled, the Huks "awakened in her a revolutionary determination to fight the Japanese and protect the rights of Filipinos."[100] Gloria took the alias Luzviminda, or Kumander Luz, when she joined the military department.[101] Like Guerrero she worked primarily as a political director, instructing troops on guerrilla tactics and strategies and encouraging villagers to support the Hukbalahap. She eventually rose to become the commander of Squadron 104 with the "rank of captain," a rank extremely unusual for women. Accompanied by fifteen to twenty men, Gloria often participated in attacks on Japanese garrisons to secure arms and ammunition. On many occasions she recalled that she "used her 'feminine charms' to gather information about the enemy's strength and strategy." According to her, enemy soldiers were often "caught off guard when a seemingly demure barrio lass would suddenly order her troops to seize their weapons." Like Liwayway and Guerrero, Gloria relished her extraordinary experiences as a commander of the Hukbalahap, often crediting these experiences for her "bravery and strong belief in herself."[102]

While only a few women became military commanders in the Hukbalahap, it was more common for ordinary female guerrillas to bear arms. Almost all Huk guerrillas carried guns, and women usually used either .38 or .45 caliber pistols for self-defense. When the Huk Amazon Leonila Monteverde was arrested the military looked for her ".38 caliber gun," failing to find it only because she "managed to throw her gun in a forest bush."[103] According to her those women who wanted and knew how to use guns were given them. "Of course not everybody," she explained, "but many of us had guns."[104] Pasencia David, who joined her Huk husband in the camps, remembered that she had a "short gun." "We were taught how to shoot the gun," she said, but she added with a smile, "I never really had an opportunity to use it."[105]

The fact that women carried guns fascinated both the press and the Philippine public. As a soldier and a war correspondent, William Pomeroy remembered encountering an armed unit of young Hukbalahap women in a Southern Luzon camp:

> The Women's Unit was drilling in a clearing when we arrived. There were seventeen of them, marching in formation and deploying in the tall grass. They looked like small American WACs [Women's Army Corps] with a tropical tan. All had American carbines, which were kept in perfect condition and handled expertly. They were dressed in shirts and trousers and had fatigue hats slanted on their heads.[106]

According to Pomeroy the average age of these women was eighteen, and "all of them were daughters of peasants." The commander was

a nineteen-year-old woman named Neri, a Huk member since its establishment who had participated in several encounters with government
troops. Other women had also been in combat units. Pomeroy noted
that these women had a "fanatical devotion to their cause" and "would
not be led into temptation by the offer of candies or gifts." When he left
Pomeroy looked back at the girls, and "they raised their carbines aloft in
a soldier's gesture of farewell."[107] Indeed, it was their ability to pose as
men, and especially their skill at handling weapons, that earned the
women of the Hukbalahap the epithet Amazons.

Despite the attention these women warriors received in the press,
military commanders such as Dayang-Dayang, Liwayway, Guerrero,
and Luz were considered relatively rare in the Huk movement. Men,
who composed the majority of the Huk membership, were all trained as
soldiers and many were promoted as commanders while most women
served in support units and remained subordinate to men. Despite their
"military training and education" most Huk women were effectively
excluded from combat duty and discouraged from engaging in direct
military action. But, although the emergence of women military leaders was exceptional, it highlights the revolutionary impact of the Huk
movement. By recruiting women as soldiers and combat commanders
the movement subverted the conventional military roles of men as protectors and women as protected. And by defying traditional, stereotypi-
cal female roles in a male-dominated military organization Kumanders
Liwayway, Guerrero, and Luz, among others, redefined these conventionally masculine roles, making it possible for women to thrive in the
Huk movement. Their rise as military commanders demonstrated the
openness of the Huk movement to women and the opportunities it
created for women to fashion new roles for themselves, opportunities
many of them seized with enthusiasm and determination.

New Lives and Roles in the HMB

After World War II many Hukbalahap women left the movement to resume their prewar lives and to focus on their families. Although most of
them were trained cadres, many were reluctant to join the postwar communist struggle waged by the HMB. But women such as Celia, Remedios, Simeona, and Luz did not abandon their commitment to the revolution and refused to accept the victory over the Japanese as the end of
the struggle. Moreover, because they had occupied significant leadership
and military positions during the war, these women expected recognition

within the movement and a role in the revolutionary hierarchy during the postwar struggle. Such expectations were not shared by the predominantly male leadership of the Huk movement.

By the time the war ended Celia Mariano, Remedios Gomez, and Simeona Punzalan could no longer be considered political novices. In the party schools they attended they had acquired a thorough grounding in Marxism-Leninism and Communist Party ideology. But it was their experience of war and revolution that enabled them to understand these political concepts in very personal terms. Although Celia Mariano was always able to discuss the tenets of communist ideology, when asked to explain her political convictions she described them in deceptively simple, unadorned language:

> What influenced me to join the Communist Party . . . was its emphasis on ridding the country of poverty—which was what really had disturbed me since the age of ten—the poverty in the Philippines. And it is the PKP that explained how to do it. You have to fight imperialism. You cannot fight imperialism frontally; you have to do a lot of organizational work, political work, propaganda work, writing, talking, and delivering speeches, to make people understand. . . . We are poor, and our people did not know that they are poor because they are being exploited by these imperialist forces. You do not see them, it's invisible, but they manipulate, they control people, even the most important people in the Philippines. They are so rich, so influential, and so powerful. I did not see it at first, but [it was] when I began to read and think, and only when these communists began to explain it to me, that I understood it. I was convinced to work with the communists, who will really help me conquer poverty. To me, poverty is the greatest scourge in our country and all countries in the world.[108]

Celia, who initially thought of herself as politically inexperienced, was changed by the war and the people and comrades who fought alongside her in Central Luzon. After the war she yearned to lead a quieter life, so she briefly rejoined her family in Manila. But the fight against poverty constantly beckoned, leading her to reaffirm her commitment to the Communist Party.

Celia and her fellow communists also realized that the U.S.-backed Philippine government would never permit the Huks, a nationalist and anti-imperialist movement led by communists, to play a significant role in Philippine political life. As the campaign of suppression against the Huks and their peasant supporters in Central Luzon developed, and as the guerrillas themselves were harassed, intimidated, and arrested, Huks such as Celia had no choice but to take up arms again in self-defense.[109] Celia wholeheartedly supported the party's decision to launch another revolution, and shortly after Philippine independence in 1946 she, along with other comrades, returned to the mountains and the life of a revolutionary.

The plight of Celia's family further intensified her political commitment. They lost their home and possessions in Tanay, and their land was burned by the Japanese, who suspected it was a guerrilla base. They eventually resettled in Manila, returning to their old neighborhood in Tondo, where Celia briefly stayed with them in a one-room house with no toilet, electricity, or running water. She did not need to adjust to this life; she had already lived it among the peasants of Central Luzon, and these hardships only strengthened her resolve to improve the lives of the poor. She decided to work full time for the Communist Party. In a lecture delivered in the 1990s, Celia recalled her personal motivations for joining the Huk rebellion:

> The war and my experiences in Central Luzon had changed my whole outlook. Gone were my dreams of building for myself someday a big beautiful house and to travel abroad to see lovely places. What was disturbing me then was the plight of those kind, hospitable peasants, who even in their poverty shared with me the last bit of rice they had in their pantry. At the back of my mind I felt the drabness and emptiness of their lives, the hopelessness of their futures. Working with the cadres of the Hukbalahap, I sensed that their thrust was to alleviate and eventually eliminate the deprivation and wretched misery of workers and peasants who are the underdogs of society. I felt a strong identification with them and thereby I decided I would stick it out with the Hukbalahap.[110]

The peasant leaders also impressed her. They were not formally educated, yet they had a sophisticated understanding of how to improve life in their communities. In the end, she recalled, "I developed a new purpose in life: you must serve society. Working with people with the same objectives, one can get somewhere. I decided to become a full-time revolutionary and to dedicate my life to working to improve the life of the peasants." When asked why she returned to the struggle after the war, she insisted, "It was the right thing to do."[111] But the decision must have been a difficult one, and during the first few months of her postwar political involvement Celia missed her family and usually cried herself to sleep. It was clear that her life would never be the same again.

And yet she had been transformed. Communism did not confuse or frighten her anymore. Indeed, she believed it enabled her to understand how politics and society worked and gave her a new sense of vitality and purpose. Describing herself as quiet, reticent, and "sort of lethargic" when she became a communist, she said, "I felt very alive; there was a lot of vigor in myself, as though the learning of these things was stimulating me as a person."[112] She wanted to learn much more, so she read a lot, engaged in discussions, and became even more sociable. The Communist Party knew that a dedicated revolutionary such as Celia was a valuable asset, but it did not know how to deal with her, a woman of unquestionable commitment and intelligence. A male cadre with similar political experience would surely have assumed a leadership position in the Huk organization, but even after many years as a party member Celia was excluded from party decision making. And while her male comrades recognized her abilities they did not encourage her to be more assertive, speak her mind, or question party policy. Indeed, while being the only woman in party meetings made her feel awkward and frustrated, she waited patiently for an opportunity to exert greater influence.

That opportunity came when Celia joined forces with her husband, William Pomeroy. An American soldier who had arrived in the Philippines with General Douglas MacArthur's forces during the Leyte invasion in October 1944, Pomeroy fell in love with the country and returned to the Philippines in 1947 to work as a freelance journalist.[113] He wanted to write a history of the Hukbalahap movement, and Celia was assigned by the party to accompany him as an interpreter and help him interview Huks in Central and Southern Luzon. During that trip Pomeroy fell in love with Celia, and before long he had also embraced the Huk cause and joined its underground struggle. When he proposed Celia was reluctant to marry someone she had known so briefly, but she accepted, moved by Pomeroy's promise to be her partner in everything: in the home, at work, and, most important, in the revolutionary struggle.

During their first years of marriage, Celia and William (known as Bill) lived in Manila, where she worked full time for the party and he studied at the University of the Philippines. But the armed struggle of the HMB made underground work for a cause outlawed by the government extremely dangerous, and as the situation in Manila became more precarious for the PKP's top intellectuals Bill and Celia were assigned to work in the education department, which had its headquarters in the mountains of Laguna Province. In April 1950, therefore, they abandoned their home in Manila for life in the forest.

In the dense forest of Laguna they took up residence in a small, thatched, bamboo hut where they and other comrades mapped out a long-term plan for the movement. Bill, alias Ka Bob, was placed in charge of the propaganda division, and Celia, who became known as Ka Rene, became head of the national school division. In the two years Celia and Bill lived in the forest their commitment to the struggle and each other deepened as they faced numerous challenges, including malaria, hunger, cold, wet weather, leeches, and, of course, "the enemy," the Philippine Armed Forces. Yet, those years were also the most productive for Celia, as she later recalled:

> For a period of two years, 1950 to 1952, working under very rough conditions in small makeshift huts and living on very scanty rations of rice and dried fish or rice and mung beans, which our HMB comrades transported on their backs over long distances from towns below, we turned out leaflets and pamphlets and a newspaper called *Titis* [Spark]. We conducted monthlong schools that frequently had to move from place to place to avoid enemy raids. We wrote our own textbooks. Our educational materials were distributed to the various far-flung regional organizations of our movement.[114]

As a revolutionary and a woman Celia was torn between her commitment to the movement and her personal desires, including having and raising children. Yet because of her unique position as a woman leader she had to abandon such desires for the demands of the revolution.

Celia always had to exhibit strength no matter how much physical or emotional pain she suffered. She had to be decisive even in moments of utter confusion. Not only were her mind and emotions often in conflict, but her body, "soft and feminine," as Pomeroy described it, also endured punishment. At a time when she needed intimacy and expressions of love were as important as expressions of principle, Bill and Celia had to suppress their emotions. While they lived in the forest they were careful not to show affection in front of their comrades. They even slept apart so they would not arouse jealousy. In one story in his memoir Pomeroy described a rare "day of rest" and privacy with Celia:

This is the first time that we have been alone in all these months. There is no privacy in the camp, where we sleep with others like one giant body upon the floor, and where we move always in the vision of others. Now we have found a room of our own in the forest, a green wall of trees on either side, a blue ceiling, a white floor with a strip of blue carpet running upon it . . . We take off our clothes and are strangely pale, like the growth under leaf mold on the forest floor. . . . We splash in the water and our laughter echoes along the forest wall. . . . We sit closely, talking quietly of our lives together. . . . It is not long. The shadows of the trees creep over the beach toward us, reclaiming us. Our afternoon is over. We rise and go, back into the forest and affairs and all.[115]

This is the only intimate passage in Pomeroy's memoir, and most of his account focuses on the larger political purpose that defined their existence in the forest. At times Celia had doubts about sacrificing her personal desires to what she believed were the higher purposes of the revolution. But for the most part she put such thoughts aside.

Just like her marriage and her relationship, Celia did not own her body. Whatever her body needed had to be evaluated as her commitment was always measured by her ability to go on with the struggle. She never asked for anything more than what others received. She had to forgo even simple pleasures such as a bath, a good meal, hot coffee, and cold water. The revolution called for endurance and sacrifice—and this is what Celia offered. And as Bill and Celia, along with other Huks, moved deeper into the forest to escape the enemy they endured days and weeks without food and sleep. Bill wrote:

It is two weeks now since we have eaten anything of substance. . . . Prior to that there were months of semi-starvation. . . . Celia is a wasted figure, dark loops beneath the eyes, the full breasts almost disappeared; for two months, in the cold rivers, her menstruation has not occurred. For weeks neither of us has had a bowel movement. I did not know that the human body could take such a punishment.[116]

Celia constantly had to suppress her most basic needs and exert her body beyond its usual physical limitations. Living up to what she believed were the standards of a true revolutionary meant not allowing herself to exhibit vulnerability. She wholeheartedly believed what her top comrades preached—that the Huk cause was far more important than her individual desires. In a sense she believed that sacrifice entailed acting like a man, and as a woman in a predominantly male movement she was always careful that her actions would not set her apart from her male comrades. Pomeroy recalled one incident in which Celia used her strength, and her comrades' assumptions about female weakness, to goad them on:

> There is a morning when the comrades in a security unit say they cannot stand, cannot stand, cannot go any further. Celia, my wife, her face like a frail flower on a thin stalk, hardly able to walk herself, goes into their shelter. What are you? she says. Do you call yourselves men? Must I, a woman, carry you? They look at her with weak pained expressions, holding to the rifles with the butts upon the ground. Ka Rene, they say. Please don't say those things. They pull themselves up, stagger into line, and we go on.[117]

Life in the forest for Celia was, therefore, an unending test of strength and commitment, and while there were many things she valued in her life—Bill, her family, and her future—she struggled not to let her personal comfort and desires cloud her commitment to the revolutionary cause.

As we have seen, other female guerrillas in the HMB faced the same predicament as Celia. Most experienced a similar sense of conflict about whether to stay or leave the Huks, but such conflicts were even more acute for female leaders and commanders who recognized their unique place in the movement. Liwayway initially resumed her duties as a military commander while Guerrero continued the struggle, although she assumed a more organizational role in the movement. Both women also went through more intensive schooling, which, according to them, gave them a "deeper understanding of Marxism and of the role of the Communist Party in the overall struggle of the proletariat and the peasantry."[118] Like many former Huks, Liwayway felt that she had no choice but to go back to the mountains, "What can you do," she said, "when the government was hostile to you—arresting you, raiding your offices?" Believing Philippine democracy was a "farce," she decided she had to continue her struggle "for genuine freedom through justice and democracy."[119] Joining the Huk military department once again, she was assigned to Tarlac and Pampanga where she supervised military forces and trained soldiers for the new struggle.

In 1947 Liwayway was captured by the Philippine army in Tarlac

while she was on her way to Manila to be treated for malaria. Betrayed
by a comrade and imprisoned by government soldiers, she immediately
became a media sensation. The press was fascinated by the beauty and
grace of someone who was labeled a dangerous Amazon by the military
and accused of unlawfully arming herself and successfully assaulting
the local police. Within a month she was charged with the crimes of
rebellion, sedition, and insurrection. The formal charges included the
following:

1. Public uprising
2. Taking up arms against the constituted power of the
   government
3. Inflicting an act of hate or revenge upon the military police
4. Committing for political and social ends an act of hate against
   landowners in the provinces and capitalists
5. Attempting to overthrow the existing government.[120]

Liwayway's notoriety led to a face-to-face meeting with the newly
elected president, Manuel Roxas, who accused her and the Huks of ter-
rorizing innocent civilians. When Roxas denounced the Huks as terror-
ists who wanted to seize the government, she defended herself and the
movement:

> No, Mr. President, you are wrong. . . . We are only fighting for a
> decent livelihood and are only for the democratic treatment in
> our plight. Who are the Huks, Mr. President? Ninety-five per-
> cent are families of peasants, so I cannot see any reason why the
> Huks will terrorize their own families or why the parents will be
> afraid of their own children. We, the Huks, champion the rights
> of the peasants.[121]

For her irreverence to the president Liwayway was placed in a prison
cell incommunicado. After a writ of habeas corpus was issued on her
behalf she was released, and her case was dismissed when the court
found no concrete evidence against her.[122] After her release she rejoined
the Huks, and in 1948, with her husband, Bani Paraiso, she became part
of an expansion force in the Visayas. As the struggle wore on, however,
her commitment began to waver, and like many Huks she disliked
fighting other Filipinos. The birth of a son also made it more and more
difficult to balance her participation in the struggle with caring for a
family, and she struggled internally as she witnessed some of her former
female comrades leaving the movement to start families.

In the end she accepted the double life of a mother and revolutionary. But living in the Visayas, so far from her home in Central Luzon, made Liwayway feel isolated from her closest comrades and supporters. Working to build the revolutionary movement in the unorganized communities of Iloilo proved to be a difficult task. Liwayway was used to relying on popular support, but working underground in Iloilo she and her husband were constantly in danger because they could not completely trust the people around them. Indeed, in 1948 Liwayway's life was shattered when she and her husband were betrayed once again by a fellow Huk. When the Philippine Constabulary raided their meeting place, Liwayway was captured and her husband was killed.

Imprisoned for the second time in a provincial jail in Iloilo, Liwayway was placed in solitary confinement and not allowed to see her family or friends, although eventually her young son was allowed to join her in prison. The court advised her to plead guilty to rebellion to ensure a minimum sentence, but pleading guilty meant admitting the truth of the government's accusations of rebellion, murder, theft, and arson, which would tarnish her name and the reputation of the Huk movement. Convinced that the justice system would not look favorably on an unrepentant communist, she followed her lawyer's advice and chose a more traditional defense, claiming that she had joined the Huks only to be a loyal wife to her husband. "Being a wife is not a crime," she recalled saying at her trial, and "I should not be charged of the accusations against my husband." Her defense was revealing. As Liwayway herself confessed, her commitment to the revolution was closely entwined with her commitment to her husband, and she did rejoin the movement partly because she wanted to support him. In this sense, her zeal was very much tied to her identity not only as a revolutionary but also as a wife. But this traditional defense also exhibited Liwayway's political acumen. Certain she would not get a fair trial because of her association with the Communist Party, she used the system of values that both condemned her as a revolutionary and professed to pity and protect her as a woman. Indeed, by presenting herself as a traditional wife and mother she orchestrated her own release.

Her imprisonment and the death of her husband had a powerful impact on Liwayway's subsequent political involvement. After her acquittal she decided to lie low. Constantly watched by the government authorities, she needed time to recuperate and restore her belief in the revolution. In the end she did not rejoin the Huk movement again. But, although Liwayway regretted not having a normal family life and having to raise her only child alone, she never regretted being a part of the Huk movement.

While Liwayway was sent to the Visayas, Simeona Punzalan stayed in Central Luzon. The decision to join the HMB was not a difficult one for her. "How can I not join," she pointed out, "when everyone knew you were part of the Hukbalahap and the government will look for and kill you?" Initially she took a job in a factory after the war, but she soon returned to the mountains as a revolutionary. Like Celia and Remedios, Simeona believed that "the fight for social justice did not stop with the war" and even after the defeat of the Japanese "the country was not yet free and the peasants were still oppressed."[123] Although she retained the name Kumander Guerrero, Simeona did not serve as a military commander during the HMB period. Instead she became part of the Central Luzon Regional Command (CLRC) where she worked as an inspector based in Bataan. Her main responsibility was to monitor the different divisions and report to the CLRC on the general situation of the movement. When problems in the different divisions arose, Guerrero helped units to resolve them or brought them to the attention of the CLRC leadership. Like Liwayway, she remembered the HMB period as much more difficult than the Hukbalahap days. In the HMB she had to be more cautious about the people because it was harder to determine who was the enemy. She also began to sense that many of her Huk comrades were becoming disillusioned with the HMB, tensions that were reflected in the emergence of factions within the Huk leadership. In 1947 Simeona married another Hukbalahap cadre named Tapang. But, like Liwayway, her husband was killed in battle in 1948 while she was in Manila giving birth to their first child. Originally Simeona intended to leave her child with her parents and "return to the mountains" with her husband. But after his death she decided to remain in the barrio with her child. While the press celebrated the capture of the "six-foot Amazon," the Huk movement suffered another casualty.

Gloria Rivera, Kumander Luz, faced the same dilemma as Guerrero. While still in the Hukbalahap she met and married another Huk commander, Guillermo Sagum. Even before the war ended the couple had a child, yet Gloria resumed her work in the Hukbalahap. But during the HMB mobilization she made the difficult but not uncommon choice to leave the movement to support her growing family. While her husband Sagum rose to a high position in the revolutionary organization, Gloria worked on their farm and raised her young children. Separated from her guerrilla husband for twenty years while Sagum lived in the mountains and spent time in prison, Gloria acted as both father and mother to their children. Perhaps partly out of respect for her husband's decision, her belief in the Huk movement never diminished. She supported the guerrillas every time they needed her help and allowed her husband to participate in the movement at the expense of their family. This was her sacrifice to the revolutionary cause. Indeed, women such as Celia, Liwayway, Guerrero, and Luz faced the same dilemmas as most other Huk women, but their prominence in the movement—as intellectuals and military commanders—accorded them the added and more demanding responsibility to intensify their revolutionary commitment.

Rising Up the Ranks: On Leaders and Amazons

As Celia Mariano became more involved in the movement, her leadership qualities became apparent to everyone. But, although the party wanted her to be more active and gave her increasingly challenging tasks, it continued to deny her a leadership role, and eventually she had to assert herself and demand that the party recognize her capacity for leadership. During the war Celia became a member of the Bulacan Provincial Committee of the Hukbalahap, meeting for the first time with leaders of the party, including Pedro Castro and Jose Lava, who later became secretaries-general of the PKP. Although she was given no major personal responsibilities, she now attended meetings at which the Provincial Committee devised strategies against the Japanese, and she was sent to the National Party School, where she received further training in communist ideology and policy. In 1944 a general meeting of the Communist Party was called to draw up a plan of action to help liberate the Philippines and assist the Americans against the Japanese. Among the twenty-five leaders in attendance, Celia was one of only three women. "When they asked for volunteers to deliver a message to the Central and Southern Luzon guerrilla units," she later recalled, "I raised my hand with absolutely no reluctance."[124] Convinced of her commitment and value to the party, her comrades elected her to the Central Committee of the Communist Party, the first woman ever to assume such a post. Her first major task was to unite the Hukbalahap's Southern Luzon squadrons with the Chinese Squadron, a move that helped defeat the Japanese Army in Laguna and facilitate the entrance of the Americans into Luzon.

As the only female member of the Central Committee, Celia took advantage of her position to promote a new approach to women's issues and to make suggestions about changes in party policy. For example, she lost no time in establishing a women's division to educate women in the movement. But, while the Politburo tolerated Celia's efforts, it was consistently lukewarm about women's issues. However, her leadership was becoming more and more indispensable to the Communist Party, and at a conference of the Central Committee in December 1950 she was elected to the Politburo of the PKP, the policy-making organ of the party.[125] This move was unprecedented. Never before in the party's history had a woman been elected to the Politburo. Assuming a position of power in the movement represented for both Celia and the party an act of liberation.

Celia always believed that she became a Politburo member because of her dedication, and she offered the following explanation for her rise:

> It depends on your achievements and on what you have done for the movement—that is always the criteria. If you have done enough to get the attention of the Politburo and the higher organs, they will notice you. They will promote you, as they have promoted me. You are chosen because of what you have done, whether you are a man or a woman. If a woman has not risen to the rank that I have, it is because she did not do as much work as I or she did not show enough talent to help the movement as I did.[126]

In reality however, dedication was not enough. Many Huk women exhibited the same commitment to the movement but were never promoted to positions of leadership. One important factor in Celia's promotion was her education. She had graduated from the University of the Philippines, one of the country's most prestigious schools, she wrote and spoke in English, she grasped the subtleties of communist ideology, she spoke eloquently, and she was smart, thorough, and articulate. In a movement in which the average level of education, for both men and women, was the fourth grade, Celia stood out. While peasant men with no education had access to power through organizational experience, women in the movement, mostly from peasant backgrounds, remained at the margins. Celia explained:

> When I became a Central Committee member . . . there were two other women who were present in the CC [Central Committee] meetings—Remedios [Liwayway] Gomez and Teofista

Valerio. But when we sat in the meetings they didn't say anything, while I gave contributions. I questioned what they said, I disputed with the other members, and I gave suggestions. And these two women, they just sat there and said nothing. So who will be noticed? I was also the one who took minutes of meetings. They could not do that. They did not have any education. Liwayway reached only the seventh grade and Teofista only the fourth grade.[127]

Celia understood that it was not the fault of Huk women that they were undervalued in the movement. "The women," she explained, "were deterred by the attitudes of society, of men, towards them." But she also criticized them for their passivity, for failing to question their status as followers, and for not aspiring to be leaders. To Celia these women accepted too readily the belief that they should be subservient to men. "I was not deterred by that," she concluded, "because I had already emancipated myself." Celia's explanation for her rise expressed her sense of loyalty to the Huk movement. Justifiably frustrated by the party's lukewarm promotion of women, she seemed to think that women were partly to blame for this and that their reticence and lack of confidence explained why they did not rise in the ranks. The movement and its leadership would have recognized women more, she believed, if they had asserted themselves more forcefully as she did. Whether this was fair or not, Celia clearly saw her own recognition as part of a larger battle within the Huk organization.

But, as Celia knew well, obstacles to women's advance, even in revolutionary movements, were not easily surmountable. As the experience of Liwayway and Guerrero showed, gender played a large part in shaping the revolutionary culture of the Huk movement. While boldness and competence in combat were expected of men, women who assumed the role of warriors were regarded as sexually ambiguous. Dayang-Dayang, for example, was frequently described by other Huks as a woman who possessed a somewhat "masculine personality with a commanding demeanor" or as a "huge woman, very masculine of appearance."[128] Luis Taruc observed that men were afraid of her while Dayang-Dayang, like a real man, feared nothing.[129] Attributes normally associated with women were never used to describe Dayang-Dayang and unsurprisingly, when she was tried and executed by her Huk comrades, she was depicted as ruthless and uncaring, depictions that made it easier to condemn her. Her masculine persona and her male acts warranted a masculine punishment: the firing squad.

Descriptions of Commander Guerrero echo those of Dayang-Dayang. Celia herself commented that Guerrero was a "big-bodied woman with masculine demeanor," who would probably be mistaken for a "lesbian" these days.[130] Taruc described her as "a big-bodied woman with a man's strength, who was fond of wearing men's clothes."[131] A newspaper account that covered her capture called her "the six-foot Amazon," and Guerrero described herself as "tomboyish." When asked why she had become a commander, she did not provide a specific answer, saying only that she was always fond of physical activities and liked to fight with boys even when she was young.

The fact that both Dayang-Dayang and Guerrero were seen as sexually ambiguous reveals how skeptically women with masculine traits and women who assumed roles as military commanders are regarded in revolutionary organizations like that of the Huks. On the one hand women who took military and leadership roles in the movement had to behave and act like men. On the other hand their masculine behavior raised questions about their femininity that male Huks found unsettling. This reality reinforced the patriarchal structure of the Huk organization. Since men were the ones who led the movement women could become commanders as long as they looked and acted like men. Men, or masculine-looking women, were still the warriors who protected women. Indeed, in memoirs and conversations with other Huks the masculine demeanor of these female commanders was almost always offered as an explanation of their military prowess and role as military leaders.

In this context, Liwayway's ascent as a commander becomes all the more interesting. At the time of her capture she was described as a "pretty, high school senior and many times a queen in her hometown."[132] Indeed, the emergence of a "pretty woman, soft-spoken, and fond of stylish clothes, perfume and dancing" as an important military commander was something of an enigma.[133] Even Taruc was puzzled at the way Liwayway preserved her feminine charm under the most difficult of circumstances.[134] Gomez herself speculated on the subject:

> They picked me as a commander because they thought that I would not abandon my responsibilities. My father was killed by the Japanese, so they thought that I had enough revenge in me to

lead a squad against the Japanese. They were right—I did not complain because I wanted to avenge my father's death.[135]

A journalist's account of Liwayway's capture supports this explanation:

> The signal for a drastic change of life in "Liwayway" from "queening" in barrio festivals to that of a guerrilla squadron commander was sounded when the savage enemy stepped arrogantly on Central Luzon soil and got her father, Basilio Gomez, who refused to cooperate with the Japanese, imprisoned him, maltreated him and paraded him in many plazas "as an example to those who refuse to work for the Japanese," until the life in that robust manhood was snapped out.[136]

By becoming a commander did Liwayway seek to restore her father's lost masculinity? The promotion of Liwayway highlighted the internal contradictions within the Huk organization, and the explanations offered for it reveal the apprehension of her male comrades. She became a commander because she possessed feelings of revenge and bravery brought about by the death of her father. In the Huk gender ideology these emotions were intrinsically masculine, as men were expected to fight for dignity, honor, and vengeance. For her male comrades powerful feelings of revenge—regarded as a masculine emotion—counteracted Liwayway's natural femininity and made her an effective female commander. But whether or not this "masculine" thirst for revenge fueled Liwayway's rise as a military commander it certainly inspired the respect of her male comrades. Certainly she was good at what she did, and her bravery and competence in combat put to rest whatever doubts her comrades might have had. But women like Celia, Remedios, and Guerrero remained exceptional, and most women in the Huk movement found their place serving on support committees. For most male cadres and leaders women's service was not deemed crucial to the movement's military success, and with some important exceptions patriarchy and the division of the sexes were reproduced as faithfully in the hills of Central Luzon as in the rest of Philippine society.

Gender, Nationalism, and Revolution

At the end of World War II different groups in Philippine society enthusiastically participated in defining the new Philippine nation, a process that many believed had begun during the revolution against Spain but was interrupted by American colonization and the Japanese Occupation.[137] In this process of imagining and creating the nation political elites, government bureaucrats, industrial workers, peasants, and the Huks themselves offered different, and sometimes competing, perspectives on the definition of this new nation. For the Huk movement the transformation of Philippine society required the new state to sever its colonial relationship with the United States and to champion the rights of the peasantry and the poor. These ideas represented a revolutionary challenge to the Philippine state and provoked official retaliation and repression. The challenge to the existing order posed by the Huks' incorporation of women into the movement was less dramatic but no less profound.

Women occupied a central place in the nationalist discourse of postwar Philippine society. As Partha Chatterjee argues, women and the "woman question" are central to modern nation building. In many postcolonial nations, political and social modernization and, more specifically, the entry of women into public life are closely linked to the exercise of colonial power as it is often colonial governments that initiate policies such as public education and female suffrage that enable women to play a more important part in the public sphere. In contrast, nationalist politics, according to Chatterjee, often glorify the precolonial past and tend to defend everything that predates colonization as part of a traditional culture. Changes to local customs that aim to emancipate women are therefore "seen as the aping of Western manners and thereby regarded with suspicion."[138] But as nations become independent and free of colonial control the role of women in the discourse of nationhood often shifts once again as the leaders of postcolonial states regard gender equality as a signifier of a modern nation and progress in that direction as essential to establishing the international legitimacy of the new nation-state. And yet defining the role women occupy as citizens of a new nation has always been complicated because, as Janet Hart argues, the "political norm for citizenship" in many societies "has been made in the male image."[139] While male citizenship is closely tied to the development of radical ideas about democracy, female citizenship is not. According to Hart,

> There is no set of clothes available for the female citizen, no vision available within political theory of the new democratic woman. Women have always been incorporated into the civil orders as "women," as subordinates or lesser men, and democratic

theories have not yet formatted any alternative. All that is clear is that if women are to be citizens as women, as autonomous, equal, yet sexually different beings from men, democratic theory and practice has to undergo a radical transformation.[140]

During the 1930s the role of Filipino women in the emerging nation had been highly contested, and the suffrage debates before the war had confirmed that women, despite male reluctance, could play an active role in building and shaping the new nation. But the war cut short these debates, and in the postwar Philippine Republic the advancement of women's issues was firmly subordinated to the demand for national unity. Traumatized by war and suffering and moved by the desire for national reconciliation, nationalist discourse required Filipinas to return to the home and preside over the restoration of male authority and familial tranquility in the domestic sphere.[141] It seems that the "radical transformation" of women as political citizens, which Hart argues was necessary in a new and democratic nation, did not find much resonance in the immediate postwar Philippine society.

Domesticating women after periods of war and revolution is not unique to the Philippines. During Indonesia's anticolonial struggle against the Dutch, political parties and movements called on women to join the nationalist cause and help give birth to the new nation.[142] But after the war was won in 1949 and the Dutch colonizers driven out, a "process of restoration of male power" took place. Women's voices were once again drowned out as men urged them to "leave politics and return to their homes and social clubs," effectively claiming the field of politics for themselves and "leaving the social terrain to women."[143] At the same time the new Republic of Indonesia promoted what Susan Blackburn calls a "state gender ideology" that defined men as primary breadwinners and women as child rearers and housewives.[144] The *wanita* (woman) in Indonesia should be the bearer of societal norms and values, the one who maintains harmony and traditions in the family and community, and a docile partner of men.[145] Although these assumptions about gender are contested in Indonesian society, official policy and deeply entrenched ideas about gender have continued to ensure the subordination of women in public and political life.[146]

Women in the postwar (and postcolonial) Philippines were also subjects of male power and control. As in Indonesia the newly independent Philippine Republic urged women to return to their homes and focus on becoming ideal wives and mothers to the (implicitly male) citizens of

the new nation. But the presence of Huk Amazons in popular print culture challenged the image of the domesticated and proper Filipina. Huk
women did not fall into either of the two dominant categories that defined Filipinas in the prewar and postwar periods: they were neither the
educated, professional, and English-speaking "New Women" nor the
traditional, pious, passive, and devout Catholic Filipina. Instead they
were revolutionaries who lived and fraternized with men, who had
left conventional lives to live in the forest, and who sacrificed their family lives for an organization that, at least formally, was committed to
women's emancipation from bourgeois domesticity. Women like Liwayway, Guerrero, and Celia took on roles that normally define masculinity, blurring the gender divisions in the movement and exposing the
false dichotomy of the "public" and "private" space in revolutionary
movements. The Huk revolutionary movement, by subverting conventional roles of women inside the organization, presented a competing
discourse on the role of women in the new Philippine nation.

The emergence of the female Amazons—as leaders and warriors—
also exposed the contradictions that existed within the Huk movement.
In discussing the role of women in the 1896 Philippine Revolution
against Spain, Barbara Andaya observes that "warrior women" were
perceived as extraordinary precisely because "they had stepped outside
the accepted boundaries of female behavior."[147] Female Huk commanders also had to demonstrate "male" qualities such as leadership and courage in battle. It was this incorporation of masculinity—whether physical or emotional—into the female body that legitimized their role as
participants in and leaders of the armed resistance.[148] Yet women had to
be careful not to overstep these boundaries. Liwayway's application of
makeup before military encounters was at least in part an effort to de-
fuse charges that she was too masculine, although she clearly enjoyed
heightening the contrast between her feminine appearance and her
masculine role. For Liwayway, then, being an Amazon meant emphasizing her feminine attributes. But even "masculine-looking" Huk
women did not abandon their sexuality and femininity, including Guerrero, who left the movement to marry and have children. Negotiating
issues of femininity and masculinity was a difficult task for many of
these women, and the difficulties and contradictions were especially apparent in the careers of Celia Mariano and Dayang-Dayang.

As studies of women in revolutionary contexts have shown, female
leaders rarely achieved status in the movement on their own, and their
roles were often legitimized by marriage to men who were prominent

party leaders.[149] According to Christina Gilmartin, the unwritten requirement for the advancement of women in the Chinese Communist Party was marriage or a consensual union with an important Communist leader, and most key women in the party were the partners of male leaders. Consequently, women were rarely able to command the status and legitimacy of their male partners because their access to authority was dependent on their sexual liaisons.[150] Indeed, the most important determinant of a woman's high political status in Communist institutions was not political accomplishment but the political rank of her partner.[151]

In some respects Celia's experience in the Huk movement can be compared to that of Chinese Communist women. Like them, her male partner, Bill Pomeroy, was a respected member of the Communist Party of the United States who eventually became a leading intellectual in the PKP. The respect Pomeroy enjoyed among his male comrades may have been extended to Celia, who was given a more prominent role in the party after their marriage. But Celia's ascent to the party leadership was more complicated than this suggests. Years before Celia joined the Communist Party, she was already a war hero who had achieved prominence in the movement, and it is possible that it was Celia who facilitated Bill's acceptance as a party intellectual. Celia cannot be seen simply as an appendage to a powerful man.

Celia Mariano's ascendance in the party hierarchy was not totally surprising. She was highly educated; she belonged to the urban middle class, from which most of the male members of the Politburo came; she was outspoken and articulate; and she seems to have been encouraged from the start by comrades who realized how valuable she could be to the Communist Party. She also distinguished herself from other Huk women. While she admonished her male comrades for their sexist attitudes, she also blamed women themselves for their passivity, avoiding housework and admitting that she did not discuss political questions with women but exchanged ideas more easily with men. Her class position may have set her apart from working-class and peasant Huk women, and her ideas about women's liberation probably reflected her middle-class background and advanced political education as much as her interactions with other women. Her experiences highlight the importance not only of gender but also of class divisions within the Huk movement.

Dayang-Dayang's case also underscores the double standard among men and women in the Huk movement. She was the first Huk female commander and the only person of her rank executed by her own comrades, although some male commanders also had dubious records.

While many Huks felt that her punishment was justified, her execution raised many questions about equality in the movement. As Dayang-Dayang became more influential, her power seriously threatened male dominance in the Huk movement. Removing her ensured the uncontested authority of the male leaders, and female commanders that followed her, even Liwayway and Guerrero, would never possess as much power as had Dayang-Dayang.

The treatment of women such as Celia, Dayang-Dayang, Liwayway, and Guerrero by the press and within the Huk movement illustrates the difficulties confronted by women who challenged traditional gender roles in Philippine society. Seen as exceptional yet anomalous, they, as well as other Huk women warriors, deviated from the dominant portrait of the Filipina immediately after the war. Certainly the Huk Amazon was not embraced as the model of the new Filipina as she has rejected her femininity and lived with men outside of marriage. At the same time she could not be emulated as the "mother of the new nation" since she had abandoned her children. The widespread public interest in the Huk Amazons demonstrated both a fascination with and a fear of female sexuality and power, reinforcing the dominant role of men over women even in discourses on gender and revolution.[152] The Huk Amazon was a myth created and perpetuated by men within and outside the movement to explain the phenomenon of women warriors and leaders, which ultimately bolstered men's sense of superiority and domination. Portraying these women guerrillas as Amazons made their actions and behavior anomalous and therefore preserved the "essential masculinity" of warfare.[153] At the same time it has allowed the restoration of most women to their "rightful" place: the home.

But it was also a myth that was appropriated and celebrated by women because it provided them with an image of female political power, military prowess, and autonomy, an image that was embraced by politically active Filipinas in the 1970s to the 1990s. Even after the decline of the Huk rebellion in the mid-1950s, therefore, the legacy of the revolutionary Huk woman endured among the activists of the feminist movement and guerrillas of a new, much stronger revolutionary movement, the New People's Army.[154] Huk Amazons paved the way for these revolutionary Filipinas. The rise of these Amazons—and indeed their treatment in the press and the popular imagination—marked a turning point in Philippine revolutionary history. These women left their traditional homes to re-create, and expand, their familial and political relationships in a military and revolutionary organization that was both outlawed and dominated by men. By joining the Huks they became active, political members of society and in a significant, though limited, way transformed the Huk movement into a site for political and personal change. The efforts of the Huk Amazons therefore consti-tute an important contribution to the structural and cultural transfor-mation of postwar Philippine society.

4

Love and Sex
in the Time of Revolution

Men-Women Relations
in the Huk Movement

In 1954 the *Manila Times, Manila Chronicle,* and *Philippines Free Press* headlined the capture of the Huk Amazon Leonora Hipas. Several articles told the love story of sixteen-year-old Leonora, alias Kumander Linda de Villa, and twenty-one-year-old Emilio, alias Kumander Oscar, both members of Huk Field Command 104, who were married the day after their capture in a temporary wedding hall constructed in the Philippine Constabulary barracks.[1] According to the reports the "Huk bride had escaped from the brutal clutches of the HMB with her sweetheart" because she wanted to get married and live a peaceful life but was prevented by the Huk commander Villapando, "who was allegedly courting and interested in her."[2] "Dressed in an immaculate, silvery bridal gown," the story continued, "the comely 16-year-old Leonora was given away in marriage by Provincial Governor Dominador Mangubat" and walked to the improvised altar with her beaming bridegroom. "Misty-eyed and pretty, she bore little resemblance to the young Huk Amazon reputed to be a dead shot with a pistol."[3] The reporter made clear the message of the wedding:

The couple met first in 1950. Only recently did they declare their love. But neither wanted to get married while leading the life of the hunted. On September 7, they surrendered. As a sign of good faith, they turned over three carbines, two pistols, and a Thompson submachine gun they stole from a Huk armory. They somewhat timidly told the AFP [Armed Forces of the Philippines] of their love. Everybody loves a lover and the AFP is no different. Red tape was slashed and the wedding with all the trimmings was arranged. After the ceremony, ex-Huks Mr. and Mrs. Diesta walked down the aisle away from communism to a new and peaceful life together.[4]

After the rites "Leonora tearfully embraced [Defense Undersecretary Jose] Crisol," who sponsored the wedding, "and thanked him for giving them a new lease on life." While everybody listened the bride said she "regretted very much" wasting years "in a futile fight against the government" and "right there and then, renounced communism."[5] The couple was promised assistance in their new life, including a job for Diesta, farmland, and a house in one of the government's projects for "rehabilitating ex-rebels." The story in the *Philippines Free Press* was accompanied by a photo of Leonora dressed in military fatigues and a straw peasant hat with her right hand resting on a revolver. The caption read, "Leonora Hipas, a former pistol-packing Amazon, is shown as she and her new husband surrendered to the government. With the Huks she dressed like a man. Like all girls, she wanted a wedding gown for her marriage." The reports revealed the ambivalence of the public toward the Huk Amazons, who, like Leonora, dressed like a man and carried guns but, like most women, were fond of pretty gowns and craved male affection.

Leonora's story highlighted the tensions that surrounded the presence of women in the Huk rebellion, the conundrum they presented to the public and the movement itself, and the seemingly contradictory representations they inspired. Were women like Leonora ruthless malelike warriors or misguided girls who needed love? The reports also revealed how the Philippine state and its military representatives exploited this opportunity to present themselves as "saviors" who "rescued" these women from the communists and reinstalled them in their proper place in society. Most journalists played along completely, portraying communism as the enemy of femininity and domesticity and

Leonora Hipas, in full military gear, is shown with her Huk husband. Pictures of women who looked and dressed like Leonora created and epitomized the public image of the Huk Amazon. (*Manila Times*, October 7, 1954; Courtesy of Rizal Library, Ateneo de Manila University)

Presented side by side with the image of Leonora as Amazon, this photo evoked a contradictory image of the woman as warrior. Here, Leonora is the blushing bride dressed in white who, stripped of her military uniform and revolver, is restored of her femininity. (*Manila Times*, October 7, 1954; Courtesy of Rizal Library, Ateneo de Manila University)

praising women such as Leonora for "giving up the life of the hunted" and becoming dutiful wives. In this narrative of redomestication the Philippine military was portrayed as benevolent and sentimental, facilitating Leonora's transition from rebel to wife and extending its protective care to all Huks, especially women and children. The tone of the reports often seemed to suggest that these women were not really Huks at all but deluded youngsters who, once liberated, would return gratefully to their former homes. In this story line Huk women possessed no agency but were the victims of malevolent communist men whose rescue required the intervention of benevolent military men.

Huk men shared this sense of ambivalence about Huk women, whose presence they believed created serious organizational problems for the movement. While the Huks never prioritized the recruitment of women, they were forced early on to acknowledge their indispensable role in the movement. Although Huk women trained and worked as dedicated revolutionaries, most Huk men hoped their integration into the movement would raise no specific problems related to gender. But women could not separate their political lives from their social, familial, and sexual identities. Even during a revolution women got married, engaged in sexual relations with Huk men, got pregnant, had babies, and raised families—actions that many Huk men believed were a distraction from the revolutionary movement. These issues quickly became a source of contention inside the organization, and the possibility that they would interfere with the revolutionary struggle prompted the Huk leadership to exert control over the personal lives of its guerrillas and supporters, especially women.

From the beginning the Huk organization functioned as an alternative state and society to its most committed members. As a state it had its own elected leadership, an articulated political ideology, and a military equipped with arms and well-conceived strategies and tactics. During the first years of the revolt personal issues were not part of the revolutionary agenda. But as the political struggle intensified and the number of women involved in the organization increased, the Huks were forced to confront issues of sexuality, marriage, and family life directly. As these issues became part of the revolutionary agenda they moved from the private realm to the public, and the party began to actively regulate and determine the personal lives of its members. Just as the Huks sought to promote alternative political ideals to its cadres and supporters, so the Huks rejected the Catholicism, monogamy, and sexual conventionality of mainstream Philippine society. As representatives of an alternative state Huk leaders aimed to control sexual and familial relationships in a way that addressed the unique personal and emotional interests of their members. Consequently, Huk marriages, extramarital relationships, family lives, and children were integrated into the revolutionary culture of the guerrillas, challenging the country's dominant sexual and gender mores. To what extent the party and the movement successfully promoted an alternative sexual and familial culture among its guerrillas is revealed in the choices Huk women made about relationships, marriage, children, and the family. This chapter looks closely at the issues of sexuality, marriage, and family inside the Huk movement through the intimate lives and stories of Huk women.

Courtship and Marriage

In many respects the Huk movement operated like any other political and military organization. While women were largely excluded from certain leadership and military posts, they still assumed important organizational roles. In the committees dealing with propaganda, organization, and education men and women always worked together, although the character of their work and responsibilities often differed. When entering barrios as Huk guerrillas women always accompanied men. And in the Huk camps of the Sierra Madre men and women shared not only working spaces but sleeping spaces as well. Not surprisingly these young men and women, who were in their sexual and emotional prime, grew close to one another and their relationships often became serious. During the course of the rebellion a majority of male and female Huks married within the movement, and women who joined the Huks found their partners in other Huks.

Relationships were common despite the party's insistence that the Huk movement was a political organization, not a social club. Men and women were encouraged to join the struggle to advance political goals not to find suitable partners, and the leadership prioritized the ideological and political development of its cadres without paying much attention to their emotional well-being. Top party intellectual William Pomeroy, who was well placed to know, wrote that "relationships spring up, they cannot be denied."[6] By cultivating an image of brotherhood and sisterhood the movement almost ensured that intimacy would develop among its members. Male and female guerrillas needed each other for inspiration and companionship, as the following letter from a Huk man to a female comrade revealed:

Dearest, . . . I desire to let you know about our travel going to Paho. You know, Ling, when I am departing from you to continue my travel, I felt a great sorrow. I don't know what you feel too, but as for me, though I am already here in Paho, I still picture how you look at us out of the window, the way we exchanged sweet words with each other. I walked but my mind was not in proper mood. The reason why . . . was due to the fact that I am very much in love with you. . . . My sacrifices and turmoil to own you is indeed a great problem . . . [and] whoever came across our path, will cause [*sic*] his life.[7]

In this letter the man (whose alias was Pat) expressed enormous pain about his separation from the female comrade he fondly called Ling (a shortened term for *darling*), promising her that they would be together after he had fulfilled his organizational duty. The letter also revealed a passion, perhaps even an obsession, with the revolutionary lover, warning of violence against anyone who hindered the romance. Such intense relationships between Huk comrades were common, and for many feelings of love and companionship with other guerrillas compensated for the sacrifices that were part of a revolutionary's life.

Such relationships were tolerated because preventing them would have been detrimental to the Huk organization, but the leadership placed some unwritten restrictions on courtship, implicit guidelines that were understood by all. Relationships had to be consensual. Just as they had joined the movement freely, men and women who entered into sexual and intimate relationships should do so of their own free will. Any male guerrilla who forced himself on a woman would be punished, and rape usually merited the punishment of death. The leadership also dealt swiftly with allegations of promiscuity in the camps.[8] But unmarried men were free to court any unmarried women in the camps or barrios as long as their direct supervisors approved and such courtships did not interfere with the performance of their duties. Requests for permission from the leadership were unusual, however, and most Huk men and women were generally given the freedom to negotiate their own personal relations. Grown women rarely asked permission from the party when they accepted a male cadre's proposal, and the party apparently found it impossible to imagine women themselves initiating the rituals of courtship and marriage. Even more interesting, no evidence of homosexual relationships was ever acknowledged in either official or unofficial histories of the Huk rebellion.[9]

While it was relatively easy to enter into these authorized unions conducting a relationship in the Huk movement had its difficulties. Huk men and women lived in highly abnormal circumstances: they belonged to an underground movement relentlessly pursued by government authorities, and their tasks required them to move all the time. Their lives were constantly at risk, and the "normal" experience of wooing and choosing a partner among people of their age was usually carried out under extraordinarily difficult conditions. Women faced even more difficulties than men. For most this was the first time they had left their homes, and even if other family members joined the Huks they were usually separated. Many women missed their families and the security of home. Celia Mariano, for example, cried herself to sleep when she first moved to the forest camps of the Sierra Madre. Zenaida and Luz del Castillo quietly grieved for their dead brother and yearned to be reunited with other members of their family throughout their involvement. The lovelorn Huk Leonora had to keep her feelings for her lover secret. But, despite their need for emotional support, women were usually cautious about initiating relationships with men. Rosenda Torres, who joined the movement during the Japanese Occupation, underscored the specific nature of the conflict for women. "It was taboo," she remarked, "for women to join the Huks." Her mother was worried about her reputation, warning that once she joined she "would not be accepted at home and in the village anymore."[10] As a young, single woman who had joined an organization composed mostly of men, Rosenda was conscious that her commitment to the revolution could be misinterpreted by her family as a youthful desire to be with men.[11] Thus women such as Rosenda did not want to upset or disgrace their families by entering into affairs with men in the movement, and even male Huks understood that other people, especially their barrio supporters, were constantly watching their behavior. But, while Huk women were often mindful of their personal reputations, cultural norms did not impose the same moral constraints on men.

And yet the revolution placed heavy emotional burdens on its cadres, and in many respects the movement became a home away from home, a kind of surrogate family for the revolutionaries, with men acting as both patriarchal authority figures who offered women protection and as lovers and friends who provided companionship. Huk men and women were drawn to each other for a variety of reasons: a need for security, a desire for camaraderie, or plain sexual attraction. Luis Taruc revealed that romances between Huk fighters and the women he referred to as "the girls" grew out of their close interactions in the camps and barrios, and many of these love affairs "survived through the years, ennobled by a common belief in love of country and people."[12] Taruc's views on relationships inside the movement, which played down their emotional content, seem particularly masculine. The "common belief in love of country and people" alluded to by Taruc was certainly present in Huk relationships, but, for women at least, abstract virtue alone did not define their bonds with Huk men.

Men generally made the first move in courting women. "If a single man and a single woman understand each other," confided Elang Santa Ana, "then there was no problem with them being together. The man approaches the woman, and if she did not complain, then they can reach an understanding."[13] When Leonila Sayco first joined the Hukbalahap in 1943 at age seventeen, she was sent to the Forest School, where her instructor, Fidel Gatus, recruited her as his assistant and in quick succession his lover. One of the top instructors in the movement, he was also a widower and eleven years her senior. Leonila was so young, she later recalled, that she "did not quite comprehend these things." But Fidel was kind and protective, and he even encouraged her intellectual advancement; they were wed before the year ended.[14] Courtship was allowed in the Huk movement, admitted both Elang and Leonila, but only with the consent of women.

Courtships often ended in marriage. When a woman accepted a proposal from a man the couple did not have to go through a period of engagement as was common in middle-class civilian life. On agreement couples almost immediately entered into a marriage arrangement. Maxima San Pedro, a Huk woman from Nueva Ecija, insisted that men and women always acted as brothers and sisters but at the same time admitted that courtships were common in the organization. She met her husband, Paco Alcantara, a Huk soldier, in the movement and married him "out of respect and love." Like most Huk women Maxima began her involvement in the movement as a single woman and before long decided to marry.[15] Even though they lived amid war and rebellion, many women dreamed of romance and family life, and they all grew up believing that marriage and family were the most important aspects of a woman's life in the Philippines. Mostly only teenagers when they joined the Hukbalahap, women were in their late twenties or early thirties by the time the HMB revolt ended in the late 1950s, and if they wanted to have a family they had little option but to marry inside the movement. Since family remained a priority for Huk women, marriage inside the movement was almost unavoidable.

Courtship and marriage were therefore an important part of the revolutionary experience, and most Huk women did not believe their commitment to the movement compelled them to compromise their personal needs. Gloria Rivera was a pretty teenager from a peasant family in Pampanga when she joined the Hukbalahap in 1942. Even though she became the political director of Squadron 104, a rank equivalent to that of a commander, men were not intimidated by her and constantly courted her. The wooing did not bother her because, as Gloria put it, "Huk men and women treated one another as comrades and siblings" and no one forced anyone into a relationship other than friendship "even in combat units."[16] In 1943 she met Guillermo Sagum, a fellow squadron commander, and they became intimate while working together, marrying the year before the end of the Japanese Occupation. Since both were equally devoted to the movement they agreed not to let their relationship get in the way of their revolutionary duties.[17] Simeona Punzalan, a strong, big-bodied woman and a commander in the Hukbalahap, found her match in another squadron commander from Bulacan. Masculine in stature, Simeona considered herself lucky when she met her husband, and they married before rejoining the HMB.[18] Pasencia David, who worked as a nurse, was eighteen years old when she met her future husband, who worked in the same Medical Corps, and they continued to work in the movement while living as husband and wife.[19] Similarly, Rosenda Torres worked with Cesario Torres in the education department. Cesario was younger than Rosenda and only became fully involved in the movement after the war, at which point the two were married by the Huks and continued to work full time in the HMB.[20] Ana Sula, a peasant organizer from Pampanga, was only fourteen when she joined the Hukbalahap, and despite several suitors she was too young to accept any of their proposals. Finally, in 1945, at the age of seventeen, she married a young Huk soldier who served in the expansion forces in the Visayas.[21] Loreta Betangkul initially stayed in the barrios as a Huk supporter. Whenever the Huks visited she sheltered them and informed them of enemy activities in the town. When an intelligence officer in Squadron 56 began to notice her Loreta was also attracted to him. Their courtship was short and did not entail the usual rituals, such as constant visits to her home and the formal permission of her parents, and in 1944 they were wed in the movement. Transformed from a Huk barrio sympathizer into a full-fledged member, Loreta joined her husband in the forest camps.[22] Like Loreta, Dominga Adasar, who was from Pampanga and only fourteen when she became a courier, was wooed by a certain young Huk cadre, Centeno, when he came to organize her town. A month before she turned sixteen Dominga married Centeno and joined the Huks in the camps full time. When her husband became a major in the Hukbalahap army, they were constantly separated, seeing each other only once or twice a month, but she accepted this as part of their lives as "revolutionary fighters and lovers."[23]

For women such as Virginia Calma, marriage was never a priority. Virginia was only seventeen but already a dedicated cadre from Pampanga when she met her future husband in the Hukbalahap. The reality of the war made Virginia focus on her work in the resistance. Although Tomas Calma relentlessly pursued her, she was reluctant to get married right away and decided to go back to school immediately after the war. Perhaps feeling pressure from her family and comrades to marry, Virginia finally relented, and in 1946, when Calma, alias Commander Sol, joined the HMB, she followed him as his wife. Unusually, Virginia and her husband had known one another for four years before they married.[24] Narcisa Reyes, a peasant woman from Nueva Ecija, also waited a few years before getting married. She joined the Hukbalahap through her brother and worked in the education division where its chairman, Lino Romero, taught her to read and write and guided her development as a cadre. After a few years Narcisa noticed that Romero's treatment of her had changed. A romantic relationship developed, and they were wed in 1946, four years after they had first met.[25]

The courtship and marriage of Remedios Gomez, the famous Kumander Liwayway, was more complicated. Party leaders and her comrades had long considered Bani Paraiso, the chairman of the Democratic Alliance Party in Central Luzon, an appropriate match for her, and even before they met they were known to one another. A woman commander, her comrades argued, deserved someone with a top-ranking position. Nonetheless, even after they met they waited almost two years before getting married. Remedios explained years later that while she had not chosen her partner she found the perfect husband and comrade in Paraiso, and when he was sent to lead the Huks' expansion efforts in the Visayas Remedios went with him as his wife.[26]

Celia Mariano met William Pomeroy after the war, and, although both held prominent roles in the movement, both believed marriage was an important part of their political lives. After many years of interaction with men in the movement and a number of marriage proposals, Celia was reluctant to marry, believing this would compromise her duties to the party. But with Bill she found both a comrade and a partner.

After working together in the party for more than a year, Bill and Celia married in 1948. Celia later wrote, "In those days of tremendous unrest, upheavals, tension, and turbulence in my country, my marriage to William Pomeroy was to become the most stabilizing and vivifying factor in my life."[27] From the beginning the two saw their commitment to each other as synonymous with their commitment to the country and the Communist Party. This commitment is made clear in Pomeroy's description of their engagement:

> I think of the day when I proposed. We sat on a patch of grass, in front of a house destroyed in the war, on Dewey Boulevard, looking out over a Manila Bay that was crimson at sundown. . . . Do you know what it would mean to marry me? she said. These are not normal times, or, rather, in my country people like us cannot live normal lives. Already I am wanted. You know that. We may have a short time together, of real peace and of the happiness known by others. But sooner or later, there will be decisions to make: I cannot go to your country for I am known as Huk; you could not stay in mine if your sympathies for us are discovered. If we would want to stay together, there would only be the mountains for us. Do you know that? Are you ready for that?[28]

Finding an answer to this question was not hard for Pomeroy. He replied, "I know. I love you. I am ready for it." Celia and Bill found their partners in life and revolution in the Huk movement.

The memories of Huk women about their courtships in the movement were often shaped by a sense of nostalgia for a shared revolutionary past and by affection for partners who remained with them long after the Huk rebellion had ended. It is therefore difficult to ascertain their motives for marrying at a young age or for marrying men who were older and with whom they were not all that intimate. Certainly attraction, and even love, played a role, but sometimes Huk women seem to have exaggerated this motive, forgetting that their courtships occurred during the war or the postwar struggle and therefore their dispositions may have been shaped by a desire for some normalcy in their lives or even for protection from other men inside and outside the movement.

Nonetheless, Huk men and women found nothing wrong with pursuing courtships and marriages in the movement, and Huk women willingly pursued relationships with men who they believed shared their ideals and revolutionary dreams, often overlooking differences in age and political experience. Many Huk couples, like Celia and Bill, lived their married lives in the struggle, and as long as they continued to work for the movement heterosexual companionship and marriage were not viewed as a threat to the revolution. Indeed, such companionship was deemed essential to its very survival.

The Huk Marriage: "In Love and Revolution . . ."

By advocating revolution the Huks sought to build an alternative society and culture in the Philippines, and both leaders and members believed Huk marriages should reflect this aspiration. Marriage was respected as an institution, but it was also revolutionized to fit the movement's radical political vision and agenda. Contemporary Philippine culture places a high value on lifelong monogamy, and, although unofficial unions are tolerated, the Catholic institution of marriage remains strong.[29] While civil marriages are becoming increasingly common in the Philippines, historically they have been considered less meaningful than church marriages. The Huks never directly attacked the Catholic Church, but as communists they saw it as an instrument of the elites and a bastion of conservatism. As a result, most Huk marriages did not take place in Catholic churches.[30] Instead the Huks created their own marriage forms and rituals, and in their alternative society men and women entered into unions that affirmed their devotion not just to each other but also to the revolution.

A marriage of a Huk man and woman was appropriately called a Kasal Huk (Huk marriage). Being Kasal Huk meant going through an elaborate ceremony. Usually the male cadre would seek permission to marry from his direct officer, and upon approval preparations for the wedding could proceed. According to Dominga Centeno, the Huk marriage was officiated not by a priest or a judge but by the highest official of the Huk organization. Leonila Sayco recalled that she and her husband had to participate in counseling with their respective superiors prior to getting married, counseling that was designed to impress on both of them the commitments involved in a Huk marriage not only to one another but to the movement as a whole. Marriage was not conceived as an end to political involvement but as a deepening of revolutionary commitment. According to Pomeroy, Huk marriages were usually performed with the whole camp attending the ceremony and expressed the martial equality of men and women in the movement:

The soldier comrades prefer to swear fidelity with their hands and those of their brides joined upon a pistol, and to take their vows under an arch of rifles held by their comrades. The marrying leader swears them not only to loyalty to each other, but also to loyalty to the movement, above their relationship, and to loyalty to the principle of the equality of men and women, about which he gives a lecture that is the core of the ceremony.[31]

Leonila Sayco offered a similarly martial description of her marriage. The bride and groom, she recalled, "walked together across a row of Huk military men holding their swords up," forming a cross where the couple walked in the middle. In front of superiors and comrades the Huk man and woman pledged their commitment to each other and the revolution. Afterward "they declared that you are already married, and this was reported to the national organization of the Huks."[32] Pomeroy regarded Huk marriage as more legitimate and authoritative than a civil wedding in recounting his marriage to Celia Mariano:

I think of how we were twice-wedded, once by a justice of the peace, and once by the movement to which we belong, in a little ceremony in a small house in Manila, to which the leaders of the movement came and where the principal leader spoke the words that bound us closer than any document of the state, and how we swore in the name of the Philippine national liberation movement to be loyal to each other but never to let our own relationship stand in the way of our loyalty to the cause of the people.[33]

In the Huk marriage ceremony, explained Luis Taruc, the leadership emphasized that "the family must be a bulwark of democracy, and that the devotion of the couple to each other must be matched by the devotion of the couple to their fellow men."[34] The Huk movement thus tried to distinguish its revolutionary culture from the conventions of Philippine society. While the traditional Filipino (Catholic) marriage entailed a commitment to God, the Church, family, and community, in the Huk ceremony couples swore loyalty only to each other and the revolution. The Huk marriage was overtly political, but it was not completely devoid of religious meaning. It also acknowledged the importance of loyalty and fidelity and recognized the essential role of the revolutionary community in supporting the relationship. Since the Huk organization acted as a surrogate family for revolutionaries, taking the oath of commitment in front of other Huks had a potent and important symbolic value.

Indeed, most Huks believed that their marriage in the movement was binding, viewing their pledge as more meaningful than the vows ordinary Filipino couples exchanged in a church. They did not feel it was necessary to marry in a church or court to have a legitimate partnership. Pomeroy believed that Huk marriages were "generally lasting and faithful ones, based upon a mutual service to the people's cause as well as upon mutual affection," and according to him most marriages in the movement were "more enduring than the ordinary 'legal' marriage."[35] Ana Sula agreed, emphasizing that:

> Kasal Huk is a strong marriage. . . . You have to pledge in front of your comrades who raised their guns in salute for you. You were essentially making a pledge in front of the gun. You are putting your life on the line, including all your good virtues. Unlike the priest who just wet you with water and speaks Latin that you cannot understand. When you stand in front of your organization and your comrades, you had no doubts, no regrets . . . you go there because it was your desire to do so.[36]

For Celia Mariano the question of marriage to a person and a cause was not complicated. She had always wanted a balance between her commitment to the struggle and her personal happiness, and with Bill Pomeroy she did not have to prioritize one over the other.

After the marriage ceremony both parties had to sign the Huk marriage contract (see appendix 1). In this contract the Huk couple pledged their union "in the name of the People's Liberation Army, the movement that united them in love and ideals." They also declared themselves "free from their parents' authority," entering into the union as "free adults." By signing this contract the Huk man and woman swore that "the interests of the revolution would come first." In case of misunderstandings in the marriage the couple was required to submit their differences to the organization and to abide by its decision. In revolutionary Huk culture this contract was binding. By performing the marriage ritual and issuing marriage contracts the Huks assumed the same functions as the Philippine state, effectively creating their own society with its own set of matrimonial regulations.

"The Unhappy Problem of Men without Women"

Just as in the world outside the Huk camps not all movement partnerships were storybook romances, and not all marriages endured. And while the practice of marriage was institutionalized in the movement there were no similar guidelines for divorce. The revolutionary movement therefore had the power to sanction the marriage of two comrades but did not have the authority to separate a couple bonded through Huk marriage. It seemed the movement was more concerned with regulating revolutionary unions than revolutionary separations.[37]

Indeed, almost all Huk men and women believed the movement faced one of its biggest challenges when couples entered "undesirable" relationships. The most explosive internal problem faced by the organization was that of "sex opportunism," or the "sex problem," terms that referred to the relationship between married men and single women in the movement.[38] This type of relationship, which Pomeroy described as "the unhappy problem of men without women," was a major issue in the movement and was "not so easily solved."[39] Celia Mariano, the highest-ranking Huk woman, spoke of this problem with passion:

> The particular problem of men-women relationships arose very often. We were leading abnormal lives under abnormal circumstances, and there were times when relationships between men and women contradicted the traditional conservative norms of Filipino customs. Many of our guerrillas were far away from their wives for long periods of time, and loneliness sometimes drove them into amorous relations with some women in the camps. . . . It became a social problem, which we had to solve, because wives whose husbands developed mistresses complained to us from the villages of their mates' unfaithfulness.[40]

These came to be called "*kualingking* cases," occasions when male cadres engaged in extramarital relations with unmarried, mostly young women in the camps while their wives and families remained in the cities and barrios.[41] Often the affairs involved deception—the men hiding the relations from their wives and misleading their new partners and even their comrades. Although the problem first arose during the Japanese Occupation, it became more pronounced during the postwar revolt. While it was possible for male Huk fighters to live in the villages with their wives and children during the war, their participation in the postwar struggle forced them to live in the forest camps and prevented them from visiting their homes. Isolation in the forest and separation from their families in the barrios led many men to seek emotional and sexual intimacy with women guerrillas, and these relations created serious tensions in the movement, as Celia observed, threatening its popularity and support in the barrios and eroding the solidarity and discipline among Huk members.

Kualingking cases were common in the Huk movement.[42] Several Politburo documents mention cases involving "abnormal" sexual relationships between comrades. One unidentified cadre named "Erning" wrote to his comrades clarifying his relationship with a certain "Norma." He acknowledged that he "was in love with Norma, but it is already known to her and her parents" that he was a married man. He explained that he pursued Norma "diplomatically" and not through force. "At present," he wrote, he and Norma "are already together, and nobody is angered by this relationship." He was also aware that "the party did not condemn him," and as far as he knew "the masses did not have any adverse reaction to their relationship."[43] Another case discussed by the Politburo involved one Comrade Nelson, who courted a comrade, Luningning ("sparkle" in English), who was married to another Huk, Comrade Tarzan. Politburo documents reported, "Nel and Lu came together in sexual relation," and after an investigation "both were found guilty." The leadership "decided to break that relation" by sending Nelson on an expansion assignment. Nelson admitted his mistake and "promised to follow the decision." The sexual relationship continued, however, and the case was subsequently reopened and a new decision handed down. The leadership learned that Nelson had refused to go to his assignment, "complaining of sickness of the ear," and that Luningning told her husband Tarzan that she was sick and needed to go to the camp hospital. It became apparent that the two had manipulated Tarzan and their superiors in order to be together. The unfortunate Tarzan, who had "promised that he will do no harm to his wife," then asked the Politburo to send Nelson to another squadron "to avoid any probable trouble that may happen." The Politburo's report concluded that "because of his opportunist tendency and repeated violation of the Politburo's decision, we decided to suspend Nelson's party membership and both of them will be disarmed."[44] At this point the movement still did not have a formally articulated solution to the problem, although it was obvious that movement leaders were getting frustrated with the prevalence of *kualingking* cases. They viewed the problem as disciplinary and therefore subjected the "erring" comrades to military discipline. Huk couples that engaged in extramarital relationships, like Nelson and Luningning, were usually disarmed and expelled from the party.

The best-known *kualingking* cases were those involving high-ranking officers of the Communist Party. When Teofista Valerio first met Casto Alejandrino, she was aware of his position in the movement. She knew he was a former mayor of Pampanga with a remarkable reputation: he had given up everything for the revolution, was a fearless commander, and was one of the most intelligent Politburo members. But, for Teofista, Alejandrino, known affectionately as Gy, was first and foremost her leader and comrade. They met while they were both doing revolutionary work in Nueva Ecija during the war and worked together in the Communist Party—he in the leadership and she as part of the Provincial Committee of Central Luzon. Teofista admired Gy from afar, but she never thought of him as more than a comrade and had a romantic relationship with another Huk soldier.[45] In October 1947, while Teofista was working at the Huk headquarters in the Sierra Madre under Alejandrino, a romantic relationship developed between them. By that time she had broken up with her Huk boyfriend and felt close to Gy, who "never used force" and talked to her "intimately" about his romantic yearnings. After six months, she recalled with a smile, "*sumuko na ako*" (I surrendered to him). But the relationship was complicated from the start. Alejandrino was already married to a woman in the barrio, although he had stopped communicating with her after he joined the Hukbalahap. Before meeting Teofista he had affairs with two different Huk women. But despite his reputation Teofista was attracted to him. She recalled:

> In the beginning . . . I treated him like any of our comrades. But perhaps because I was a woman and he was a man and we were constantly together . . . our feelings developed. We were always together, night and day, we grew close to each other and we understood each other. He then started to tell me what he felt for me. He reassured me that he was no longer with his wife. The entire period that he was in the mountains, his wife never visited him and he never visited her. And so, I believed him. And I had a problem, too. *Mahal ko na rin siya* [I was already in love with him].[46]

Teofista was always reluctant to discuss how much of her attraction to Alejandrino was a result of the power differential between them because as a Huk cadre she believed in the principles of equality— between leaders and members, between men and women—espoused by the organization. But it was clear that Alejandrino's position gave him numerous advantages in the movement, including easy access to women. He chose those he worked with (such as Teofista), paid close attention to potential lovers, and probably removed potential rivals. His numerous relationships inside the movement can be partly explained by the power, authority, and reputation he enjoyed among the Huks. This power was something he constantly used, making it difficult for Teofista to reject his sexual advances.

On May 26, 1948, Teofista Valerio and Casto Alejandrino were married in a simple Huk ceremony. She later admitted that she had no thoughts for the future when they married and never envisioned a time when they would live as a "normal" couple. They never did. While her marriage to Gy lasted, their relationship had to withstand enormous challenges. A short time after their marriage they were separated when Alejandrino contracted a serious illness and was forced to leave the forests of the Sierra Madre to recuperate. Teofista visited him occasionally in Manila and the barrios but returned to the forest camps to continue her revolutionary work. When Gy recovered in early 1949 he returned to the forest headquarters, but a few months later it was Teofista's turn to leave. Pregnant with their first child, she wanted to stay in the forest, but Alejandrino insisted she leave, and in August 1949 she gave birth to their daughter in Manila.

During this period of separation Gy and Teofista exchanged love letters. Their letters reveal a normal, loving couple trying to cope with an abnormal and difficult situation. Soon after her delivery Alejandrino wrote to Teofista approving her choice of a name for their child. "The name you chose for baby was good," he wrote. "I still don't know who should be her godmother. If you want someone, you can go ahead and choose." A few days later he wrote again asking if the baby was already "able to go up to the mountains." In his letters to Teofista, Alejandrino always inquired about the health of mother and child and described his life in the forest. In one letter he asked, "By the way, to whom do you plan to leave Baby when you can already join me in the forest?" Like any couple they addressed each other as "love" or "sweetheart." Yet, there were always words of caution and despair in these letters. Gy wrote constantly that he missed Teofista and asked her to send him necessities such as shoes and pants. He also apologized for not providing for his family and in one letter sent twenty pesos because she needed money. But despite the melancholy of his letters Alejandrino remained focused on his work, excusing himself for neglecting to write because he was doing "work for our people."[47]

Finally, after one year, Teofista felt ready to join Alejandrino in the forest camps. But on September 7, 1950, while awaiting the courier who

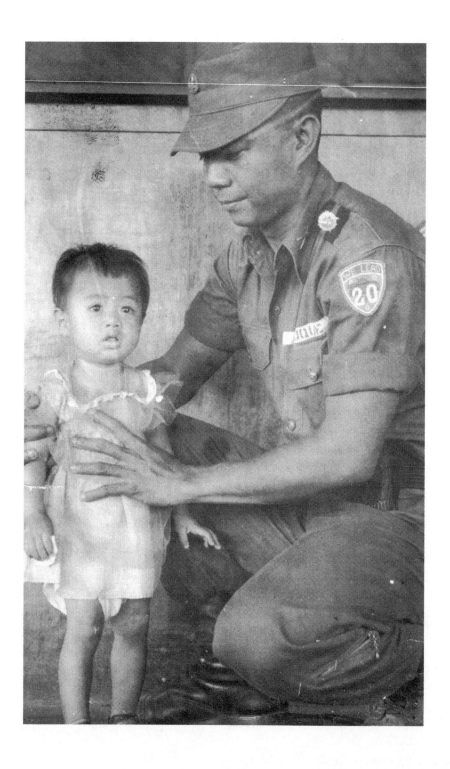

would guide her back to the Huk headquarters in the Sierra Madre, Teofista was arrested by the Philippine army.[48] When they discovered letters from Alejandrino—a wanted communist with a price on his head—Teofista was taken to Camp Murphy and interrogated. When she refused to volunteer any information they stripped her and beat her severely. She would eventually lose the hearing in her left ear as a result of the beatings. But she refused to talk. Teofista spent the next ten years in prison without a single letter from Gy, who was later arrested and remained in prison after Teofista's release. Parted on August 4, 1949, they did not see one another again until August 4, 1970, exactly twenty-one years later. Teofista is still at a loss for words when she attempts to talk about her imprisonment, the loneliest time of her life, when she was separated from her young daughter and yearned for Alejandrino's companionship. Her memories of those days are filled with bitterness.

While Teofista was in prison Alejandrino found a new partner in the forest. The new woman in Alejandrino's life was Belen Bagul-Bagul, a teenage courier from Laguna who joined the HMB in 1948. She first became aware of the Huks during the Japanese Occupation, but she was too young to join the movement. When HMB forces arrived to organize her village in Laguna, however, she quickly embraced their cause and became a member of the Communist Party. Love and romance were far from her mind as she had important tasks to fulfill, including administering first aid as a nurse and working full time as a courier.[49] But Belen's assignments brought her into close contact with top leaders of the Politburo such as Celia Mariano, Jose Lava, Jesus Lava, Ramon Espiritu, and Casto Alejandrino, and in 1950, during a period of disillusionment and uncertainty created by the arrest of Teofista and a number of Politburo members, Belen and Alejandrino grew close. A few months later, on Gy's initiative, Belen began an intimate relationship with him. Like Teofista she admired Alejandrino for his leadership and compassion, but now she began to refer to him endearingly as her "love comrade." Belen believed her relationship with Alejandrino was deeper than

At left: Not only guerrillas were "captured by the military" but also innocent children. Not satisfied with the capture of Teofista, military authorities apprehended Alejandrino's daughter in the hopes of arresting him. The caption that accompanied this photo reported that the "16-month-old Hukling, daughter of No. 2 Huk top brass, Casto Alejandrino, was (also) captured . . . in the residence of her custodian and nurse in Bulacan by the 20th BCT led by Lt. Lazaro Duque (pictured)." (*Manila Times*, February 26, 1952; Courtesy of Rizal Library, Ateneo de Manila University) that of a married couple, and she offered no excuses about her decision to be with him:

> I did not see any problem in our relationship. Even though he was not my husband, I loved him because he was my comrade. It is really different when you are together in principle, or when you believe in the same things. Our bond was stronger than that of siblings or married couples. Of course, if our principles changed, my feelings would have changed. But we were united in principle—we had a cause bigger than ourselves. I knew what our relationship was. It is hard to explain . . . [50]

For Belen, her bond with Alejandrino was a marriage of the minds and signified an equal relationship between two intellectual and political partners. Their shared political commitment became the basis of their emotional bond. But this relationship was not truly one of equals. Belen was only a teenager, had limited education, and was a novice in political life when she joined the Huks, while the much older Alejandrino already had a prominent, uncontested position in the movement. She must have been flattered by his attention and may have conflated her devotion to him with her commitment to the revolution. Alejandrino, in contrast, never felt he needed to justify or explain his relationships in the Huk movement. He respected his partners but not necessarily as political equals. Widely considered to be brilliant but enigmatic, he always talked openly about his relationships, even exhibiting a certain conceit about his amorous conquests. And in his recollections of the Huk rebellion he rarely considered his "forest wives" to be his intellectual partners.[51]

Teofista remembers feeling dejected in prison, although she was philosophical about her relationship with Alejandrino. Harboring no ill feelings toward him or Belen, she viewed the affair in practical terms. Nonetheless, when she heard about the affair, she was

> very hurt, of course. . . . But I accepted it. After feeling my pain, I thought about it seriously. Because Gy was really sickly—he needed someone to take care of him. I also found out that Gy got married to Belen. What can I do? Gy is a man. He was far from me and I would not be able to give him what he wanted.[52]

When she got out of prison Teofista was relieved to discover Gy had not married Belen, although Belen bore him four children, and she was proud to be the only woman he had married inside the movement.

When Alejandrino was imprisoned his romantic relationship with Belen ended, although he saw her and the children periodically. After his release Gy and Teofista lived together briefly as husband and wife in Nueva Ecija. But politics always beckoned him, and for most of his remaining years he lived with the Lavas, his old comrades, in Manila where they continued to work for the PKP. In the end, Teofista remarked poignantly, "Gy was really married to the revolution."

Alejandrino was not the only Politburo leader who had forest wives. Like Belen, Linda Ayala's relationship with Jesus Lava, a top Huk and communist leader, developed out of practical necessity, in this case the personal safety of Lava himself. Linda, who was more commonly known by her alias, Aida, was very young when she joined the HMB. The daughter of tenant farmers in Quezon, her sympathy for the peasants' cause drew her into the Huks, and she eventually became the most important courier of the HMB, working for Mateo del Castillo, Casto Alejandrino, and Jesus Lava. When she met Jesus Lava for the first time in the mid-1950s he was still married to Anita Mayang, who lived in Manila, but had taken up with another Huk woman, Remedios Orejala (alias Zeny) in the forest. Aida, who already had a boyfriend, was at first uninterested in Lava, who was married and more than twice her age. But two events altered her feelings. First, Lava's forest wife Zeny (who was pregnant) was captured by the Philippine military while on an assignment in Manila and Aida's boyfriend decided to surrender to the authorities.[53] Aida decided to stay with the Huks, and by the late 1950s she was working as a courier for Mateo del Castillo, who was then the finance director of the Huk organization.[54] Then one day in 1958, while trekking through the Sierra Madre with del Castillo, Aida was temporarily separated from him. Del Castillo, who was carrying ten thousand pesos in cash, was betrayed by one of his aides and murdered. When news of the murder reached Huk headquarters, Aida, distraught and traumatized, was summoned by Jesus Lava, the top Politburo leader in the forest, and during this period of mutual grief Lava began a relationship with her. Although she was not in love with Lava, he clearly had strong feelings for her and promised to marry her, something he had never done with his other forest wives. In his memoir he praised Aida as a "spoiled brat" and "the target of a lot of criticisms" who was transformed by her experiences in the Huk movement into a woman with "an indomitable will, [and] a persistence and courage not easily found among women comrades."[55] "In this moment of extreme sorrow," he later wrote, he found consolation in Aida's strength of mind and came to regard her as someone who "one could not but trust in this most critical period of struggle." "It was not accidental but rather fortuitous," he observed, "that this same girl was to become my second revolutionary partner in the midst of the rapidly deteriorating situation of the movement."[56] Lava assured Aida that his marriage in the movement was more binding than his church wedding and promised to stay with her rather than return to his wife in Manila, who had refused to join him in the mountains. She accepted his proposal despite the resentment of other suitors, who accused her of choosing Lava because he was a leader in the movement. Aida defended her decision to marry Lava as an act of revolutionary self-sacrifice. "You are all mistaken," she told her comrades. "Do not think that I chose him because he was a top leader. That is not true. I do not love him, but for the sake of the movement, I am willing to be with him. We will not find anyone who will be as intelligent as him; we cannot replace him anymore. So I am giving myself to him."[57] As she explained, her decision reflected the sense of desperation and pessimism that characterized the movement by the late 1950s. She recalled:

> I never thought that I would eventually go down from the mountains to live a normal life. . . . I really believed that we would die in the forest. So I decided to be with him. For me, the most compelling reason was because I wanted to protect him. After what happened to del Castillo, I could not trust our comrades completely. He was our top leader, and I did not want anything to happen to him. I told him the truth—that I married him not because of love but so that I can safeguard him. I never sleep at night because I always watched over him. I only rest during the day. Since we got married, my major assignment was to safeguard him.[58]

Eventually Aida learned to love Lava, especially when she had their first child and they continued to live (and hide) in the forest, producing two more children before the army finally captured Lava in May 1964. While Lava was in jail Aida received marriage proposals from other men, but she rejected them all. As she said, "He will always be the father of my children." On his release Lava rejoined his first wife in Manila, but Aida continued to be part of his life and until the end, Lava considered Aida his wife.

While Jesus Lava considered extramarital affairs to be part of revolutionary culture, the Huk Supremo, Luis Taruc, was more critical. In his autobiography he admitted to joining his "atheist comrades" in their sexual activities:

> I, too, had a loveless sex affair with a Communist girl. . . . Alice agreed that we were compatible and in need of each other. We would "love one another" in the party way, true to the "revolutionary concept" of party policy. But, very soon, in our intimate moments, Alice and I realized that we were Christians more than Communists, more idealistic than materialistic, especially in this most important part of life—this thing we call love. Our deeply rooted Christian upbringing, our conscience and sense of decency compelled us to put an end to our unedifying relationship.[59]

Throughout his life Taruc struggled to reconcile the contradictions between his convictions and actions. As someone who always thought of himself as a romantic revolutionary he was deeply embarrassed by his sexual liaisons with women in the movement, although his wife and the mother of his only child, Gregoria Calma (alias Liza), was herself a Huk cadre. Liza worked as a courier during the Japanese Occupation and as a first-aid instructor in the HMB but was killed by a Philippine army unit in a raid on the Huk headquarters shortly after Taruc left the same camp to lead his forces to Cagayan. He never forgave himself for leaving his wife behind and claimed he never married again. But when he surrendered another woman claimed to be his forest wife. Leonila Dizon was serving as Taruc's secretary when the Philippine army in Quezon captured her, and according to news reports she confessed to investigators that she and Taruc were married under Huk rites.[60] Taruc always refused to acknowledge his relationship with Dizon, and while he spoke lovingly of Liza he hesitated to discuss the other women with whom he was involved.[61] Throughout his life he was disconcerted by the inner conflicts and contradictions that shaped his relationships with women.

Manuel and Belinda Malay also refused to talk about their relationship, but they were quick to offer their judgments about the extramarital relations of their comrades.[62] When she was part of the Huk movement Belinda knew that there were "a lot" of "*kualingking* cases" among Huks, but she felt they were inevitable "because they are far away from their families." In the movement, she explained:

> Men and women were always together. So, their feelings for each other developed. Not only were the two of you always together, but you worked together, you had the same principles, and

shared the same ideology. So the two of you will be drawn to each other—out of principle and ideology. Of course, the one married (usually the man) had to fix his status first. He had to be certain that he is no longer with his family. Both of you had to protect the Huk organization. If it does not hurt the organization that a married man and a woman come together, then the relationship was allowed.[63]

Neither Belinda nor Manuel Malay saw their relationship as a problem. When the rebellion ended, Manuel decided not to return to his first family. He stayed with Belinda, and they lived together as husband and wife.[64]

Felisa Cuyugan, a comrade from the Hukbalahap days and a close friend of Manuel's first wife, was more critical about the relationship between Manuel and Belinda. She believed Manuel had treated his first wife poorly. While his wife had remained in the barrio, sacrificing and working hard to support their family and loyally supporting the Huks, he had deserted them for the Manila-bred and educated Belinda, who was young, beautiful, and middle class. Felisa never understood why Manuel was not censured by the leadership for his actions, but she lost her respect for him.[65]

Although objections like those of Felisa rarely prevented consensual relationships between two comrades, many Huks claimed that the movement was not always tolerant. Federico Maclang and Elang Santa Ana's liaison was an example of a relationship that the movement tried to "correct." Working under Maclang in the organization department of the Hukbalahap, like most young women in the movement, Elang was not initially interested in him for he was older and already had a wife and children living in the barrio. But Elang gradually grew close to Maclang, who trained and patiently educated her and, according to her, was "a great Huk leader with enormous humility."[66] By 1944 Elang and Maclang had become a couple, but Maclang had not left his wife, who was waiting for him in the barrio. Although the relationship between Maclang and Elang was consensual, the leadership decided to punish him by demoting him from a Communist Party leader to the rank and file. This was a harsh punishment, especially for someone like Maclang, who had risen up the party hierarchy after years of working in peasant organizations and the PKP. Maclang felt he was unfairly treated considering that many other Politburo leaders had not even been reprimanded for their sexual liaisons:

In sex . . . it was the erroneous belief of comrades that I had had such problem. In truth, I never had such problem and I was never convinced by the party's decision, not only because I did not really have it, but because I should not have been punished thrice for a single offense.[67]

In a later document Maclang reiterated that he was not convinced that his case was "the same as the common *kualingking* case," and yet he agreed with the party that the movement should not tolerate "double official spouses" as this would prove "harmful to cadres involved and to the entire Party welfare."[68] In the end he accepted his punishment so that he could be with Elang. After the war they lived together and continued their involvement in the HMB, and Maclang once again assumed a leadership position in the organization. Although the couple was never married by the movement or the Church, Elang stated simply, "I was his wife until the day he died."[69]

Maclang's *kualingking* case was well known, but it was the exception rather than the rule, and most men involved in *kualingking* cases went unpunished. Men such as Alejandrino, Lava, and Taruc were never reprimanded for their affairs. Similarly Felicisimo Macapagal (who later became the secretary-general of the PKP) was never censured by the party for his *kualingking* cases, and his affairs did no harm to his revolutionary career. The woman in Macapagal's life was Elena Sawit, a barrio organizer who joined the Hukbalahap. After training in the Forest School she worked under Macapagal in the organization department, and within a few months he had begun to pursue a romantic relationship with her. At first she hesitated because he was a married man with children, but he persuaded her that his relationship with his first wife was over. Macapagal told Elena that he and his first wife had an understanding that they would live separate lives, and to make things more official he went to his superiors in the movement to seek permission for his relationship with Elena. "He was told that he could do what he desired," Elena recalled, and they were soon married in the movement.[70]

During the HMB period Macapagal's relationship with Elena faced another test when they were both assigned to join the expansion forces in Mindanao. Although Elena was pregnant at the time, she had no reservations about moving, and in Mindanao they lived as husband and wife while he worked full time as an HMB organizer and Elena performed occasional tasks for the movement. Since he occupied a top post in the movement's hierarchy, Macapagal was assigned to establish new HMB cells in different areas of Mindanao and Visayas, and during one of these assignments he began a relationship with another Huk woman. When he told Elena about the affair he assured her that the relationship was not serious and promised to stay with her, his "real wife." Instead of condemning him, Elena understood her husband's situation:

> I knew that I could not give him what he needs when we are separated. So, I did not think ill of him. The woman was there with him [in Visayas]. He admitted to me that the woman really wanted to have a child with him. But he did not allow that to happen. He understood that no matter what happens, the child would still be his, and he could not abandon the child. The woman was also young and single and he wanted her to have a better future with somebody. He knew that, in the end, he would be with me and only me.[71]

Despite his infidelity Elena decided to stay with her husband and expressed disgust for Huk men who took advantage of young women in the movement and abandoned the children that resulted from their affairs. But Elena's position was a difficult one. She had moved to Mindanao to be with Macapagal, away from her family and the comrades she knew; she was isolated and poor and had to take care of her family despite her husband's frequent absences. She therefore chose to forgive Macapagal rather than face a harsher fate: abandonment. Elena believed her husband needed a companion, and she accepted that, but she also believed his promise to stay with her. Long after the revolution was over the Macapagals rebuilt their life in Manila, and, although he maintained a relationship with the children of his first wife, he and Elena stayed together for another forty-three years. Like Teofista, Elena's personal struggles had a more lasting impact on her memory, perhaps, than her revolutionary experiences did.

Filomena Tolentino's case was more controversial because it involved an ordinary Huk soldier and a degree of coercion. When Filomena met her future husband in the organization department of the Hukbalahap she was not interested in him at all; he was fifteen years older and already had a family. But soon after meeting her he confessed his love to Filomena. At first she refused him, but he persisted, and one night when Filomena stepped from the house he grabbed her, put a gun to her head, and told her not to scream. With two other men he forced

Filomena to accompany him to his house, where they came face to face with other Huk comrades. Tolentino's comrades warned him that the punishment for taking women by force was immediate execution, but Filomena did not complain because, although Tolentino abducted her, she claimed he did not molest her. Not wanting to be responsible for Tolentino's death, Filomena eventually accepted his proposal. They were married by the Huks and stayed together for the next forty-four years. She also took care of the four children he had with his first wife. While she remained loyal to the Huks, Filomena believed women often found themselves in vulnerable situations inside the movement. Like her, other women were alone and separated from their families and had to rely on either themselves or their male comrades for protection. Although she eventually learned to accept her husband, who proved to be a loyal and hardworking partner, Filomena never quite forgot or forgave their ominous beginning.[72]

Like Filomena, Zenaida, daughter of the PKP leader Mateo del Castillo, was placed in a vulnerable position and forced to accept her Huk husband. Zenaida recalled that even during the war extramarital relationships were common. But the problem, in Zenaida's view, became much worse during the postwar period when the Huks were more isolated from village life and spent much longer periods of time in the forest camps. As a young, single woman, Zenaida felt constantly threatened. Separated from her father and mother, she had to look out for herself. A tall, fair-skinned mestiza born and bred in Manila, her height and posture commanded great attention and admiration from both men and women in the movement, and she had many suitors. But it was her female comrades who persuaded her to marry, arguing that it was better than being preyed upon by the other men in the movement. One close female comrade advised her to marry a single man or she might end up with a married one like many of her female comrades.[73]

But Zenaida wanted to focus on the struggle and did not want to marry. Then one evening while she was fast asleep one of her most persistent suitors slipped into her sleeping space and she woke up next to a man who had his arms around her. She bitterly recalled:

Not only was I dishonored, but I felt that I dishonored my father and my family. . . . Before that incident, he already made advances toward me, but I was able to elude him. But when I woke up and he was next to me, I felt that I did not have any choice.

My other female comrades told me that it was better that I become the wife of a single man; they knew that the other male
comrades would not stop pursuing me until I am married. With
bitterness, I then told him that I agree to marry him.[74]

Although the couple was immediately married in the movement, Zenaida never understood why her Huk husband went unpunished. Perhaps it was because she accepted him in the end. Although the couple
had four children, all born in the forest, the marriage did not last. After
the struggle Zenaida returned to her home in Batangas, left her husband, and eventually married again.

As the experiences of Filomena and Zenaida reveal, not all relationships in the movement were consensual. At the very least Filomena's
"husband" used abduction and emotional blackmail, abusing her sense
of loyalty to the movement, to force her to marry him. And Zenaida's
experience seems a likely case of sexual abuse, perhaps even rape. Both
cases involved young men, but older Huk men were complicit as well.
Indeed, instead of protecting women like Zenaida and Filomena older
Huk men also seemed to prey on them, and it was partly out of fear that
many women married hastily. These marriages were not so much revolutionary partnerships as protective liaisons shaped by a quite abusive,
male-dominated military culture that placed great pressure on young
women guerrillas to select their male protectors quickly. Although Luz
del Castillo, Zenaida's sister, recognized the inevitability of *kualingking*
relationships, she bitterly opposed them, questioning whether the Huks
were really that different in their moral conduct from ordinary people.
As revolutionaries she believed that men and women could have fulfilled their needs for emotional intimacy by becoming comrades rather
than lovers. And she blamed Huk men for this failure. "Men are weak,"
she argued. "I think it is part of their human nature to want sex and they
could not control their urges."[75]

Felisa Cuyugan also said that "*kualingking* cases were very rampant"
and complained with some justice that only the rank-and-file members
were punished for them while the affairs of high-ranking leaders were
ignored. But, like Luz, Felisa thought such unconventional relationships were inevitable. "We were all revolutionaries," she explained, and
"we all needed inspiration. If you are risking your life for a revolution, it
helps to share your life and ideals with someone who is also there with
you."[76] Remedios Gomez, one of the few female Huk military commanders, also saw sexual relationships as a problem for the movement

and opposed them in her own squadron. As the only woman in the squadron for much of the time, she made sure that male soldiers under her command were disciplined and not distracted by women. She also emphasized her care for other women in the movement, insisting that she always "defended the dignity of the Filipino woman." Despite her personal efforts, however, she admitted that sexual relations were common throughout the movement, although she emphasized somewhat defensively that these relationships always required the consent of the woman and did not affect the strength of the Huk movement.[77]

Other female Huks, including Kumander Guerrero, were less sure and more critical of male-female relationships. Guerrero was scornful of the way married men excused their sexual relations with young women as "biological necessity," but she was also critical of women for allowing such infidelities to occur. A firm advocate of discipline and self-control, she believed the leadership was eventually able to regulate these problems both in the squadrons and in the movement as a whole.[78] Celia Mariano also detested the way married men were able to conduct relationships with unmarried women without official reproach or punishment. Years later the issue still puzzled and angered her:

> Men have to fulfill their sexual instincts. They need sex. How could they have sex unless they got it from a woman? And of course they got the consent of the woman first. They seduced the women first. There were a few women in the camps and in the party, and because these men were charming and attractive, so the women fell for them. . . . There was a need for them—that is what they told me. They could not get along for a month without sexual intercourse. When the urge came, they had to fulfill it. It was not because they wanted to oppress a woman; it was because they wanted to answer the urges in their body.[79]

Celia refused to accept such excuses, insisting that it was possible to control sexual instincts as she and Bill had done.

Some men in the movement agreed with Celia and condemned an interest in women as a form of revolutionary weakness. This attitude comes through strongly in the movement's discussion of the *kualingking* cases, which were usually based on the confessions or self-appraisals of men about their affairs. One cadre named Abra, for example, expressed regret that "the incident with the girl was not kept a secret," adding, with a sense of relief, "I believe she will not bear, and it will have no political implication. I will try not to do this weakness again."[80] Self-appraisals by leading Politburo members betrayed a similar sense of weakness and guilt regarding sex.[81] Party secretary-general Jose Lava, who used the alias Gregorio Santayana, wrote revealingly:

> On the question of sex, against which I have consciously struggled to set an example within the party, I must admit that I still have a weakness. I cannot positively say that separated from my family for long stretches of time, I would not feel its nonfulfillment very badly, to the point of deterioration in my health and affecting my efficiency in work.[82]

Sexual and extramarital relations thus posed a moral and political dilemma for the Huks. Politburo members, who were supposed to set a moral example within the movement, engaged in sexual relations and became targets of criticism while their "mistresses" were regarded with disdain, sometimes even by the womanizers themselves.[83] The situation created tensions within the movement, weakening solidarity and discipline in the ranks. An unsigned Politburo document dated November 11, 1949, for example, raised the issue of whether a certain commander "Cap" would do well in his expansion assignment. The party raised some doubts about assigning Cap, stating that the "main problem" was "Cap's security" in his new place of assignment where he was already "well known." But a "subsidiary problem" was "the objection of Cap's wife to such assignment because of *kualingking* with a woman there." The party decided that as long as "the main problem can be solved" the "subsidiary problem should not stand in the way of assigning Cap in a place where he can give most service to the revolution."[84] Most *kualingking* cases were not so easily resolved.

Moreover, Huk commanders and leaders, whose prominence in the movement made them more desirable to the women, were often those most guilty of *kualingking* offenses. Politburo leaders had unlimited access to women and did not have to seek permission to enter into extramarital affairs, and, while most women seem to have entered willingly into relationships with Huk leaders, differences in status and age further complicated matters. Most Huk leaders were married with children while many Huk women were still in their teens, and while it was true that women often married young in peasant societies at this time the age gap between the men and the women was often considerable. Young and impressionable, these young women—whose initial relationship with their more powerful male comrades was that of a subordinate to a leader—may have entered into these affairs out of a sense of obligation without fully understanding its consequences.

At the same time one cannot ignore the agency of the women who developed relationships with their more powerful and experienced male comrades. While they were often young, they were not necessarily naive. Joining the Huks had already helped to transform many of these women into politically mature individuals who were often keenly aware of power dynamics inside the movement, and their decision to enter into a relationship with a married comrade, especially if he was a party leader, could be interpreted as political calculation, even savvy. These women were very much aware that a relationship with a leader meant an increase in their own status and prestige within the movement, and for some this was as close as they could get to the reins of power in the Huk movement.[85]

Nevertheless, there was a general feeling among Huk members that extramarital relationships compromised the growth and solidarity of the movement. The leadership's access to women consequently aroused great resentment among rank-and-file soldiers. Linda Ayala's relationship with Jesus Lava, for example, was questioned by her fellow comrades, who believed she chose him because of his leadership position. Because women were few, when Huk leaders took a forest wife it directly diminished opportunities available to rank-and-file male soldiers, who also resented the fact that Politburo and Communist Party leaders almost always went unpunished when caught in extramarital affairs while people such as themselves suffered the harshest consequences of *kualingking* offenses. This practice replicated norms in the larger society, where higher status ensured preferential access to women, but it weakened guerrilla solidarity and undermined the movement's claim to be promoting social reform and equality of the sexes among both the soldiers and their peasant supporters. Taruc later wrote in his memoir that the "sex problem" reflected the immorality and "transient sex relationships common among the Communist leadership."[86]

Women such as Rosenda Torres also noticed the discrepancy between male leaders and soldiers. She believed the *kualingking* cases were really about personalities and that the problems they created became more acute when popular Huk leaders who "recklessly entered into these affairs" denied the same opportunities to ordinary soldiers. Naturally those who did not have easy access to women harbored feelings of envy and jealousy, and Rosenda noticed that such relationships made her comrades uneasy. She believed that "most of the leaders are not conservative, and so they did not think that because they are already married, then they could not have other partners in the forest." Women, she explained, were "attracted to leaders because of their intelligence and

214   *Love and Sex in the Time of Revolution*

power, and they willingly and knowingly engaged in these affairs."[87] When the leadership finally acknowledged that the sex problem had to be addressed Rosenda was pleased. For her it was a sign of the movement's maturity that its members were willing to acknowledge and debate the problem and try to change their ways.

What most concerned the Huks about these liaisons was the threat they posed to the movement's popular support among conservative, Catholic villagers, who resented not only the seemingly immoral behavior of its members but also the abandonment of barrio wives. Both the press and the local society kept a close watch on the political, and sexual, activities of the guerrillas, and most articles about captured Huk Amazons were accompanied by stories of women's intimate relations with men in the movement. Most of these women were "married" to Huk men and were usually arrested when they went to Manila or returned to their villages to give birth. Even after the rebellion the Huks' "immoral relationships in the forest" continued to fascinate the press as a major article in the *Philippines Free Press* demonstrates:

> Men living in the mountains, so close to women, with no other form of relaxation but the pleasurable company of the opposite sex, made use of their companions in a manner contrary to decent living. They were always tense, always on the alert before the ever-present danger of death—and the tension found release in prohibited sexual relationships.[88]

According to the reporter, the leaders who used their positions to take advantage of the women under their care were the most culpable. "With lectures on party policy and a little flattery, coupled with these women's childlike simplicity and their hero worship of their leaders," argued the author, "high-ranking Huks had no trouble winning them over and conquering all resistance. The walls of modesty crumbled; illicit relationships blossomed and became one of the great scandals of the Huk movement." The article concluded that "communism apparently leads to fornication in the forest, promiscuity in the party," and "with no moral or religious principles to keep them away from evil, the Huks fell headlong into the precipitous abyss of sex and grave moral disorder."[89] Communist guerrillas were portrayed not only as dangerous rebels but also as immoral and irreligious human beings and the male leaders of the Huk rebellion as sexual predators who led their female victims astray by polluting their minds with ideological rubbish and their hearts with false promises of love and protection. The Huks therefore threatened not only Philippine democracy but also its culture of sexual decency and Catholic morality. These issues plagued the movement at the height of the Huk rebellion, and as the sex question became a threat to the movement's solidarity and its reputation in Philippine society the leadership felt that its resolution was urgent.

The Revolutionary Solution of the Sex Problem

In 1950, for the first time in its history, the PKP began to confront gender and sex issues in the movement and particularly the problems raised by the *kualingking* cases. The leadership appointed a committee composed of five people, including Celia and William Pomeroy, to study and solve the sex problem. Celia was the only woman on the committee. After long and sometimes acrimonious debates the committee drafted a remarkable document titled "The Revolutionary Solution of the Sex Problem" (hereafter RSSP; see appendix 2).[90]

Because the sex problem was considered a political not a moral issue the committee offered a policy to guide its cadres. The first part of the document provided a context for understanding the problem and why it occurred; the second part outlined a solution and set forth a series of regulations to govern extramarital relationships. The document began by providing a brief history of the sex problem, noting that it first "projected itself" during the Japanese Occupation. "For lack of a revolutionary orientation on this problem," the document stated, "the party lost some valuable cadres who were ordered liquidated" even in "flimsy cases" that involved nothing more than married men flirting with female cadres. Party members were also expelled "simply because they justifiably no longer find happiness with their spouse and preferred the company of more revolutionary mates." In these cases party discipline had been too harsh and arbitrary. But in other cases party discipline had been too lax, and at the "other extreme," wrote the committee, "some cadres were talented in sustaining all forms of abnormal sex relationships on the flimsy ground of 'biological necessity.'" After the war the problem "again projected itself until it has now developed into a political question of importance."[91]

Acknowledging the inevitable coupling of sex and revolution, the document then provides a rationale for (hetero)sexual relationships between guerrillas. "Men and women [revolutionaries and nonrevolutionaries]," it argued, "are born with sex and emotional necessities," and when these needs are frustrated they can lead to failing health and other "abnormalities."[92] "While it cannot be denied that sex desires can be sublimated," it continued, such desires could not be completely eliminated "short of actual removal of the organs from which the desire is generated."[93] Although it seems hard to believe the committee considered such a drastic solution to the sex problem, it did feel compelled to acknowledge that "the removal of such organs" or prolonged periods of celibacy produced "abnormal results not conducive to the full development of one's faculties" and prolonged sexual frustration could undermine the efficiency of the movement.[94] The document then presented a "scientific" analysis of abnormal sexual relations: "It must be recognized that the urge to enter into abnormal sex relations is motivated by varying considerations, foremost among which are the satisfaction of biological necessity and the satisfaction of emotional hunger."[95] Since "biological necessity" compelled such behavior in men—though not apparently in married women—extramarital relationships were deemed permissible by the party.

In arriving at a solution to the sex problem the committee emphasized that the decisive criterion "should be none other than the overall interest of the revolution." The document, however, failed to present a set of criteria to determine exactly what the interests of the revolution were except to argue that they were "a composite of many factors that can be determined only by actual knowledge of all the facts surrounding each individual case." In the end the body responsible for determining the "overall interest of the revolution" was "none other than the organ to which the frustrated cadre belongs, subject only to review by the next higher organ." According to the RSSP, the party would allow a man to take a forest wife only if he observed strict regulations. Before entering into an extramarital relationship the "frustrated cadre" was required to present his problem to his regional command (RECO) and to convince its members that either his health or his work was being adversely affected by the absence of his wife.[96] The "higher organ" would then examine all the facts surrounding the cadre's case and might even call for an investigation to determine the truth of his claims. According to the RSSP, this investigation should include the following:

1. The effect of sex or emotional frustration on the health and efficiency of the cadre
2. Possibilities of sublimating sex or emotional desire, which will make unnecessary the entering into abnormal sex relationships, without adversely affecting his health and efficiency

3. Possibilities of malingering by the frustrated cadre to convince the members of the organ of the adverse effects of sexual or emotional frustration
4. Possibilities of keeping the abnormal relationship within a limited circle
5. In case the abnormal relationship cannot avoid affecting wider circles, the probable effect of such knowledge on them as far as the participation in the revolution is concerned
6. Possibilities of the couple living together in cases where the spouse of the cadre concerned is also a party member or even not a party member.[97]

After a detailed examination of the facts the investigating committee would hand down its decision, and if it approved the "abnormal sex relation" the cadre was required to inform both his prospective forest wife and his legal wife of his intentions. He also had to agree to settle down with only one woman at the end of the struggle. William Pomeroy outlined the sex regulations adopted by the party in a much clearer fashion:

Firstly, a married man cannot take a forest wife unless he can convince the leading committee in the Reco to which he belongs that either his health or his work are being adversely affected by absence from his wife. Secondly, he must write to or otherwise communicate with his wife in the lowland and inform her of his intention and need to take a forest wife. He must, at the same time, under the principle of equality, give his wife the freedom to enter into a similar relationship in the barrio or city if she, too, finds herself unable to withstand the frustration. Thirdly, the forest wife must be clearly informed that the man is already married and that their relationship will terminate when he is able to return to his regular wife. In other words, there must be no deception of the regular wife and no deception of the forest wife. If, at the end of the struggle, a man should decide that he prefers a permanent relation with the forest wife, he must completely separate from the previous wife.[98]

Celia Mariano elaborated on the final requirements:

1. A married man entering a relationship with a woman comrade in a camp must inform her of his married state and let her know whether their relationship would be temporary or permanent

2. The man must inform his wife of his relationship with another woman, explaining the circumstances, and let her know whether his relationship with the other woman would be temporary or permanent.[99]

Although the recommendations of the Politburo committee were adopted, they generated an acrimonious debate. While many agreed with the party's general approach, some believed the new policy was too strict while others believed it was too lenient. Troubled by the party's authorization of extramarital relationships, some party members insisted that barrio wives should not only be informed of but also consent to their husband's affair.[100] The view of party leaders, however, was clearly articulated by Federico Maclang, alias O. Beria, who agreed that the report provided a convincing analysis of the problem and proposed a convincing solution. In a letter dated October 1950 he stated that the party "cannot forcefully expel cadres for the reason alone of the sex problem," and, although he agreed that the most "acceptable way" to solve the "sex problem" was to practice monogamy, he acknowledged that "every human being has biological urges."[101]

But for Celia Mariano the sex problem was only one manifestation of the larger issue of the relationship between men and women in the Philippines. In an article published in *Ang Komunista* (The Communist), the official organ of the Communist Party of the Philippines, Celia, who wrote under the name Rene Raquiza, pondered the problems of sexual morality as they affected the Huk movement. For her the root cause of the sex question lay in the "feudalist and capitalist mentality carried over from a semi-feudal, capitalist society" that still shaped the attitudes of Huk cadres.[102] Unfortunately, she lamented, cadres suffered from the moral double standard of bourgeois society, where "a man is lauded for his successful amatory ventures with many women," while a "woman, single or married, is frowned upon when she has affairs with men."[103] In the movement male comrades did not hesitate to initiate relationships, extramarital or otherwise, with women. Celia believed this attitude prevailed because of Huk cadres' lack of understanding of the "woman question":

Sex[ual] morality problems are tied up with the woman question. . . . The woman question is mainly concerned with the problem of advancing the woman to her rightful and permanent place—that of equality with man in all aspects of life. When

certain men look to women only for the satisfaction of their comfort and pleasures, only as romantic toys or playthings, only as
amusements to pass time with, in the party this may wind up as a
sex case.[104]

She concluded that her Huk comrades had not yet been emancipated
from this point of view and that this mentality led them to engage in
"un-Communist-like sex relationships."[105]

Celia Mariano's views reflected similar debates in other communist
parties, especially the Russian party and the Comintern, which had
strong links with the Communist Party of the Philippines. As early as
the 1920s, Soviet communists had debated the "woman question," and
women's issues, most notably the problem of women's exploitation and
oppression under capitalism, were an important part of official Soviet
policy. To communist intellectuals such as Alexandra Kollantai, Clara
Zetkin, and Lenin himself, the subordination of women and conventional notions of sex and marriage were the product of capitalism and a
bourgeois social order.[106] Bourgeois society was marked by false sexual
morality, unhealthy sexual relations, and a system of marriage that, according to Lenin, was characterized by "decay, putrescence and filth"
and amounted to little more than a "license for the husband for bondage
for the wife."[107] Only through an exposition of the real distortions and
hypocrisy of bourgeois morality could the revolutionary (working)
classes arrive at a program for women's emancipation. These communist intellectuals believed in the transformation of the family and political life to allow for more equality of the sexes. They therefore urged
their fellow revolutionaries to regard themselves as a group, not as individuals or as couples, and practice a form of collective solidarity in
which men and women could work for the benefit of the movement not
only for themselves. Communist morality meant that "the needs and
interests of the individual must be subordinated to the interests and
aims of the collective."[108]

But, although the Huk leadership promoted the ideas advanced by
international communism, the policies they pursued were also shaped
by their own understanding of Philippine culture.[109] Filipino communists initially wanted to separate the personal from the political, but the
presence of women made this impossible, leaving the leadership with
little choice but to address issues of gender, sexuality, family, and morality in the Huk movement. Consistent with ideas of communist morality, the Huk cadres condemned bourgeois notions of love and morality

as oppressive to both men and women, arguing that "capitalist relations of production do not permit the full flowering of relationships."[110] They believed that relationships should be based on mutual inclination, love, and trust rather than the coercive sanction of religion or the state. And yet, as the RSSP showed, the Huks still considered extramarital affairs to be abnormal relationships, implicitly accepting the primacy and "normality" of conventional bourgeois marriage. "In the Philippines," the document explained, "the religious, moral and social convictions of the majority of the masses consider monogamy as the correct man-woman relationship," beliefs reinforced by the entrenched power of the Catholic Church.[111] But even though they recognized the influence and importance of Philippine cultural norms by drafting a "revolutionary solution" to the sex problem communist leaders attempted to alter conventional culture. While referring to extramarital relations as abnormal reflected official Catholic dogma and Philippine law, the party was well aware that many Filipino families were complex and men in the larger society often supported mistresses or even "second" wives and families in part because divorce was illegal in the Philippines.[112] By legitimizing *kualingking* cases, the Huks both acknowledged and attempted to distinguish themselves from the evasions and hypocrisy of mainstream society, especially in matters of sex and family life.

The Sex Problem and Solution Revisited

The revolutionary solution of the sex problem (RSSP) offers important insights into male-female relations and the internal dynamics of the Huk movement. More significant, the document revealed a rift between men and women in the movement. Although Celia Mariano was part of the group that drafted the solution, the document clearly addressed itself, explicitly and implicitly, to the problems of male cadres. Celia believed, as did many other Huk women, that the RSSP was the best the party could produce, even though it clearly did not empower women. The solution gave men control, allowing them to practice a kind of temporary, revolutionary polygamy. The document cited "biological necessity" as the justification for this policy and argued that "being in the firing line intensifies sex appetites."[113] Since men were engaged in combat and women were rarely in the front lines, the document addressed only the issues raised by male sexual appetites, which even under normal circumstances were viewed as largely uncontrollable. This argument was a common one in discussions of the sex problem.[114]

Party policy ignored not only the possibility that female cadres might have needs similar to those of men but more seriously the status and specific needs of women in the movement. In fact women's views about the sex problem were neither solicited nor considered, and for the most part the RSSP treated women simply as the objects, and occasional victims, of male desire.

The document itself hinted at this contempt for women. Besides treating women as "objects of desire" for men, the document implied that women were part of the problem. As the document and its accompanying personal testimony indicated, male cadres could sublimate their sexual needs if they were alone, but the presence of women made this more difficult. It made the repression of their sexual desires seem unnecessary and even foolish. Comrade Alunan, for example, confessed that his greatest weakness as a revolutionary was women and he constantly craved their attention and company.[115] But women guerrillas were not the only female threat to male revolutionary commitment. The RSSP also outlined the "justifiable grounds" on which a male guerrilla could seek a permanent separation from his former or barrio wife: her hostility to the revolution, her hindrance to his activities as a cadre, her refusal to join the cadre in the movement, and her marital disloyalty."[116] Male guerrillas who wanted to enter into a *kualingking* affair could justify their behavior by denouncing the counterrevolutionary views of their wives, women who often stayed in the village to take care of the man's home and children. Indeed, a wife's very absence from the forest camps could be interpreted as an indication of her hostility toward the revolution, justifying her replacement. Succumbing to the demands of women, in other words, whether they were revolutionaries or opponents of the revolution, was a form of male weakness. And the RSSP was clear in its call for stronger, more virile men who were able to both engage and control their "natural" sexual urges.

In these respects the use of the word *organ* in the sex document had several interesting implications. Throughout the document, *organ* was used interchangeably to refer to both the authoritative body in the party that would grant approval of the abnormal sexual relation and to the part of the man's body that generated the sexual desire. Were these organs somehow connected? The party aimed to treat the sex problem both "scientifically" and "objectively," and this might explain the connection between the two definitions. Since the body's organ generated the sexual desire (the scientific reason) and the higher organ determined the cadre's claim (the objective condition), then not only were extramarital sexual relations natural but they should be allowed. The party understood sex anatomically and scientifically as being generated by actual organs, not sensually or socially, and thus the solution called for the sublimation, not the complete elimination, of sexual desires. Male cadres who acknowledged the problem were given a solution that recognized rather than repressed their biological needs. The term *organ* referred to both the source of and the solution to the sex problem. Implicitly the leadership was attempting to concentrate the power of male sexuality in the upper echelons of the party. Only the higher organs of the party could determine the validity of a cadre's sexual problem and legitimize a solution. Significantly, the party leadership was almost exclusively male, and those who elaborated on and drafted the new sex policy were the same people who had engaged in multiple sexual liaisons with young girls. With a few exceptions, including Celia and William Pomeroy, most Politburo leaders were part of the sex problem, and they now became a central part of its solution. Almost inevitably their solution was in harmony with their own interests, giving them the freedom to initiate sexual relationships with Huk women and greater control over the sexual economy of the Huk camps by enhancing official regulation of the rank and file. Indeed, it is clear that the RSSP was written not only to regulate future sexual relationships but also to legitimize existing extramarital relationships.

The case of Illuminada Calonje illustrates some of the problems and tensions created by the new policy on sexual relations and marriage. Calonje, also known as Luming, was chairman of the National Communications Division (NCD, also known as courier division).[117] Active in both the Hukbalahap and the HMB, she rose through the hierarchy because of her dedication and performance, although she never became a member of the Central Committee. After she became involved with the married Politburo leader Ramon Espiritu, alias Johnny, her case was discussed by the Huk leadership and the party reprimanded her several times for her liaison. In a meeting held on July 31, 1950, the party reported the following findings:

> Com[rade] Luming is guilty of maneuvering not for purposes of careerism, but because of her love for Com. Johnny (Johnny dissenting); no final finding yet whether or not Com. Johnny is in turn in love with Luming.[118]

In a subsequent report in September the party made the "final analysis and decision about the relationship," handing down its decision and imposing disciplinary action on Luming:

Majority of SEC [Secretariat] believes that there is at least a love relationship between the two, but Com[rade] Johnny denies same. Com. Johnny admits that Com. Luming is in love with him, but Com. Johnny denies that he reciprocates her love, although he reciprocates her kindness. Because of Com. Johnny's denial of his love, and in accordance with previous decisions re: Luming, she will cease to work in NCD, and will be assigned to take care of sick comrades coming from the provinces.[119]

This was a demotion for the lovelorn Luming, but needless to say the unenamored Espiritu was left unpunished. As a subsequent Politburo report demonstrated, the leadership was relentless in imposing its will:

Give Com. Luming last warning to execute decision of SEC completely, by staying in the hospital and not frequently visiting Com. Johnny, and if she fails to execute decision, she will be given field assignment. Ask Com. Johnny to have showdown with Luming to tell the party the truth about her suspected love for Johnny.[120]

In the last document regarding this matter the party proudly stated that it had "settled Coms. Johnny-Luming case under the 'Revolutionary Solution of Sex Problem.'" It then instructed all Politburo members to keep this decision strictly confidential. The principal victim of this "solution" was clearly Luming, who, aside from the humiliation of confessing her apparently unrequited love for Espiritu, was made to relinquish her responsibilities and was marginalized within the movement. This widely documented case demonstrated the sexual double standard that shaped the party's implementation of the RSSP.

As Celia Mariano recalled, the RSSP created quite a stir in the movement. But, like her male comrades, she was quick to defend the policy as rigid but "fair," especially for the women—both the wife and the "mistress."[121] According to her, "the man who is the *kualingking* originator will not be satisfied" because it is "difficult to tell one's wife about an affair and the mistress that she is only temporary or that they will only live together while he cannot live with his wife." Ultimately, in Celia's opinion, the real solution to the sex problem would be greater honesty and a change in male attitudes toward women. Men "must look at women as human beings" she explained, "and not as sex objects, because women have feelings . . . they have sentiments, they can be hurt and can feel oppressed."[122] William Pomeroy insisted that the regulations were strictly followed.[123] In reality, however, the party had no way of measuring the success of the RSSP.

From the perspective of women the RSSP was clearly flawed. Although the policy facilitated extramarital liaisons, it placed no limit on these types of relationships and provided no space for women to express their views and needs. Not only did it fail to address the coercion of women but the policy also did nothing to protect them from men. Of all the cases discussed by the Politburo only Federico Maclang was removed from his position of leadership and reduced to the rank and file for his *kualingking* case, and in the case of Luming Calonje it was the woman who was punished for her extramarital relationship with Politburo leader Ramon Espiritu. The majority of men suffered no political consequences as a result of their affairs. In the end not everyone was pleased with the party's "revolutionary solution to the sex problem." Luis Taruc was one of its biggest critics:

> Despite our favorite claim that "Communists are people of a different mold" . . . we were no different from our "class enemy." Indeed, in a sense, we were worse; we exploited our own class sisters and comrades, taking advantage of their hero-worshipping loyalty, their trusting simplicity and credulity.[124]

Indeed, the party's valiant efforts to address issues concerning sexuality, together with its failure to understand women's issues, may have further alienated its male and female members and intensified divisions in the movement.

Married Life and the Huklings

One important provision in the RSSP directly addressed the issue of guerrillas engaging in temporary relationships. The document warned married cadres who entered into a temporary, "abnormal relationship with the opposite sex," that "it is incumbent upon the new mates to see to it that their abnormal relationship does not bear any fruit, which will only further complicate the problem. For this purpose, it is their duty to master the techniques of birth control." As this statement suggests, providing official sanction to abnormal relationships did not resolve the sex problem. Indeed, in some ways it marked only the beginning. Relationships between Huk men and women introduced new issues to the movement, as family life and particularly children created complications and difficulties.

Among the Huks it was a common mantra that the revolution should always come first, and for Huk women this pledge was put to the test when they married or had children. Despite their unconventional lifestyle, the views of Huk men and women with regard to family life did not significantly differ from those of their counterparts in the villages and cities. Like "normal" Filipino couples Huk men and women also placed great importance on family life. And, although Huk women may have used basic methods of birth control, there is no evidence that they practiced abortion or infanticide. In fact, as the frequent press stories about captured "Huklings" (Huk babies) revealed, family life and children coexisted in the revolutionary struggle and the challenges of reconciling the two could be heartbreakingly difficult.[125]

Once they joined the revolution women faced incredibly hard choices. Celia and Bill Pomeroy, for example, chose what most Huks regarded as the most extreme option: not having children. In his memoir Bill wrote that he and Celia decided "to postpone the having of children" until the struggle was over. Feeling that "so many women in this country were drawn to the movement and have had their contribution ended by marriage and by the having of children too soon," both Bill and Celia believed they had a duty to set the opposite example.[126] Celia, however, was more torn than Bill. Unlike other Huk women, she never considered leaving her children with relatives, a common practice among those who decided to remain in the forest. But the struggle proved a lengthy one for Celia and Bill. In the forest and subsequently in prison, the couple endured years of separation, and by the time their situation normalized it was too late for Celia to bear a child. Forty years later she still pined for the child she and Bill never had, consoling herself with the idea that she was able to dedicate herself exclusively to the revolutionary struggle. "A child would have meant compromise," she rationalized, and that would have created conflict between two people who were "totally dedicated to the movement." If she had children, Celia explained, she would probably have devoted more time to her child than to the movement, "so it is better that we did not have any children."[127]

But other women rejected such self-sacrifice, and despite their increasingly difficult situations many Huk women refused to let their revolutionary lives constrain their family lives. When Gloria Aquino joined the Hukbalahap in 1942 she quickly married Peregrino "Reg" Taruc, already a high-ranking Huk leader and ten years her senior. Since Gloria was only fifteen when she became a Huk, Reg sought permission from her father to marry her. When she married Taruc, Gloria recalled, "I just became a wife." After a year she had her first child, Linda, and while her husband worked full time for the movement and moved around constantly she stayed behind in the forest camps of the Sierra Madre, doing housekeeping chores and caring for her daughter. During the HMB period, as government counterinsurgency operations became more frequent, Gloria made the painful decision to send Linda to her mother in the barrio, but Gloria never wanted to be separated from Taruc. She gave birth three more times in the forest and sent all her children to the barrio to be cared for by their grandmother. Only when the Huk rebellion was over was she reunited with her children.[128]

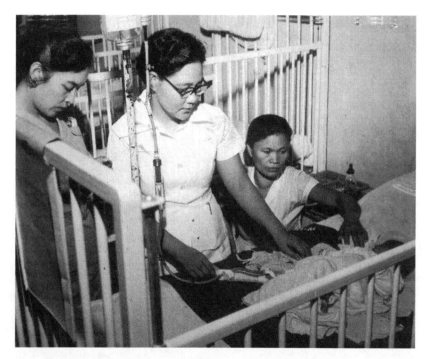

The decision of Gloria Aquino, wife of Huk leader Peregrino Taruc, to have children and stay in the revolution almost had fatal consequences. The state and the press capitalized on her heartbreaking story to further delegitimize the Huks and criticize its women. According to a newspaper cover story, "The daughter of Taruc and Aquino, born in the hills . . . is fighting for her life at the Philippine General Hospital. The baby is suffering from acute anemia and malnutrition. Photo shows the child, while receiving a blood transfusion." (*Manila Times*, September 3, 1954; Courtesy of Rizal Library, Ateneo de Manila University)

Gloria's experience was common. Silvestre Liwanag, a Huk commander, married Rosita Manuel in 1942. During the Hukbalahap and HMB periods, Rosita followed Liwanag on his assignments for the movement, conceiving three times in the forest and returning each time to her barrio in Pampanga to give birth. Although she tried to keep her children with her, the leadership ordered them sent to the barrios where they would be safe. "At first, our children stayed with us," she recalled, "but it became increasingly difficult to have them with you since the children constantly cried and the enemies can hear them."[129] Forced to leave her children with three different families, two of whom were relatives and the other an ordinary peasant supporter, each had a different surname. Nonetheless she and Liwanag spent time with them in the village, and on several occasions the children were able to spend time with their parents in the forest camps. But the dangers were real, and

The capture of "erstwhile" no. 3 Huk leader Silvestre Liwanag and his wife, Rosita Manuel, was considered "one of the most outstanding accomplishments of the Philippine Constabulary." Even though the couple already had children during this time, their capture without them demonstrates Rosita's decisions to distribute their children to relatives and friends so she could constantly stay with her Huk husband. (*Manila Times*, n.d. [late 1950s]; Courtesy of Rizal Library, Ateneo de Manila University)

228 ~ *Love and Sex in the Time of Revolution*

on one such occasion at the end of 1949 the result was fatal. In a surprise encounter with the Philippine military in a forest clearing near the camp, one of the children was shot in the head while being held by her father. Rosita silently mourned her child while consoling herself with the belief that "there was nothing left to do but to accept what happened."[130]

Belen Bagul-Bagul's family life was equally turbulent. Belen joined the HMB during its most critical period and was one of the last to leave the forest and the struggle. At first she did not fully understand the kind of personal sacrifices required of a revolutionary who was also a mother. She had four children with the Politburo leader Casto Alejandrino, and during the HMB period, relentlessly pursued by the government, she was separated from her children, who were raised by different peasant families. Two children were left with peasant supporters in Bulacan, a third was raised by relatives in Pampanga, and her only son was left with relatives in Bataan. Despite the pain caused by these separations, she later recalled, "I understood that this was part of the struggle and our movement. This was part of our life. I knew that my priority then was to fulfill everything that was required of us." At the time Belen hoped her children would understand her decisions, but when she finally limited her political activities toward the end of the Huk rebellion she was able to raise only her youngest child. The others grew up without her.[131]

Like Belen, Zenaida del Castillo gave birth four times in the forest during the HMB period, each time sending her one-month-old child to the barrio to be cared for by peasant supporters. Although they did not spend their early years with their mother, unlike Belen, Zenaida was reunited with her children when she came down from the mountains in 1958. Despite the pain of giving up her children during her revolutionary years, she believes the choice she made was the right one for her, her children, and the revolution. She recalled:

> It was very painful to give them up. . . . But I was doing it because I was convinced with our cause. If I insisted to take care of my children [in the forest], many comrades would be placed in danger. If the child cries, the PC would surely find out. If they did, then they will attack the entire camp. If that happens, it would be my fault. In fact, the decision then was to abort the child. I did not want that. I felt that they resented me. I said that my marriage is legitimate, so I want to have my children. If I die here, who will follow me?[132]

Zenaida considered herself lucky to have found people she trusted to take care of her children. Linda Ayala, also known as Aida, was less fortunate. During her years in the HMB she had three children, all born in the forest, with the Politburo leader Jesus Lava. Because both Lava and Aida were heavily involved in the struggle, she had to give up her first two children to be raised by a close family friend. Afraid of losing another child, she decided to leave the camps and conduct underground work for the movement in the village where she had her third baby. She also tried to locate her other two children, only to find that her first child had died and her second had run away from home. She never found her second child. "That is why there was something in me that decided not to give up my third child," she later explained, although many people tried to persuade her to leave her child in the barrio and return to Lava. "But I refused. I want to take responsibility for my third child. I did not give him up—I raised him." Aida never regretted her decision: "It turned out that he would be the only child that I will ever know."[133]

Almost all the Huk women wanted to be both revolutionaries and mothers, although many realized that they could not be both and many made the painful decision to leave their children in the care of others in the hope that they would be reunited later. But the majority of women in the Hukbalahap chose to leave the movement to raise their children. While they remained committed to the struggle, women such as Narcisa Reyes, for example, found it impossible to reconcile marriage, pregnancy, and children with their continued involvement in the Huk rebellion. A peasant woman from Nueva Ecija, Reyes was recruited by the Huks during the war and immediately began to work as a teacher in the education department even though she did not know how to read or write. When she married a fellow Huk in 1944 and became pregnant, she left the movement. "I became dizzy and weak when I got pregnant," she explained, "and at first, I just wanted a short break from the movement, but in the end my husband himself decided that I should leave the movement."[134] While her husband continued to play an active role in the HMB, Narcisa settled back into barrio life and began to build a home for herself and her baby.

Narcisa's experience became increasingly common among Huk women, especially after World War II. The Huks believed in the importance of family and kinship ties and used them to recruit women into the movement, but the same personal networks that encouraged women to join the Hukbalahap encouraged their demobilization in the HMB. Marriage and the establishment of a family were the most important reasons for the diminished role of women in the movement.[135] As the women stated themselves, this was not an easy decision. They still sympathized with the Huks and believed the revolutionary struggle was necessary, but their priorities had changed, and their families, especially their children, now came first. Thus, Simeona Punzalan, the brave Kumander Guerrero, who married a Huk soldier and was widowed in 1948 while she was pregnant, left the movement to raise her only child. Filomena Tolentino, who married a Huk soldier who already had children, also returned to her village to look after them. Although she continued to support the HMB indirectly, her days as a full-time revolutionary came to an end.[136] Luz del Castillo wanted to rejoin her father, mother, brothers, and youngest sister in the struggle, but she decided against it when she gave birth to three children in close succession. After the birth of her first child she remembered thinking, "How can I possibly leave her when no one else can take care of her?"[137] Elang Santa Ana believed that her most important contribution to the revolution was maintaining her household, raising her children, and earning a living so that her Huk husband could carry out his duties as a high-ranking party member. Gloria Rivera, who was a Huk military leader, also relinquished her arms after 1945 and the birth of her first child. "When I already have my child," she recalled, "it was just natural that I raise him and I do not want people to say that the reason why I joined the movement was because I could not afford to feed my child." Like other Huk women she wanted to prove to others that she could take care of her family.[138] The famous Kumander Liwayway's experience reflects many of these women's emotional conflicts. She lost her husband in 1948 and was left alone to care for her only child. She did not marry again, and, despite her subsequent successes and hardships, her biggest regret about being a Huk was having only one child. As she admitted, "I always dreamed about having a big family," but she soon realized this dream would remain unfulfilled. While these women's decisions reflected a move toward domesticity, their revolutionary experiences remained with them, and many of them continued to challenge conventional norms by becoming the main breadwinner for their families and being both mother and father of their children who were left by their revolutionary fathers.

The loss of so many valuable female cadres posed an enormous dilemma for the Huks, and in addition to the sex problem the so-called family problem became another source of bitter conflict in the movement. The problem was two-fold: marriage and children often forced

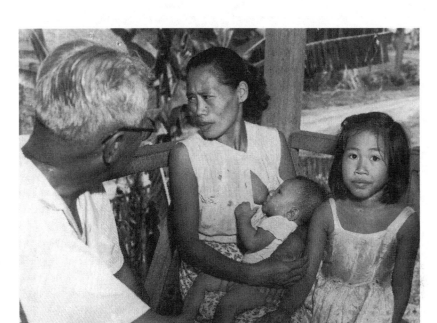

A government chief interviews captured Huk Amazon Luciana Capindian, alias Commander Lawin, who was apparently arrested when she went home to take care of her newborn child. A picture of a captured Amazon, suckling a child, with another child nearby, was an irresistible one for the press during the Huk rebellion. (*Manila Times*, July 1955; Courtesy of Rizal Library, Ateneo de Manila University)

women to abandon the revolution, and it weakened the commitment of both male and female cadres, who were often reluctant to become more active in the rebellion and to join the "expansion teams," which tried to spread the insurgency beyond its traditional stronghold in Central Luzon, because this forced them to neglect their spouses and children.[139] Politburo leaders rightly worried that cadres were torn between their revolutionary duties and their family lives. One unidentified comrade, for example, was judged "hopeless" by the Politburo. He slept day and night, refused to take meals, and avoided work due to "sickness," all because "his going home is hindered."[140] The case of one Comrade Leo clearly illustrates the leadership's response to the family problem. When Leo refused to accept an expansion assignment because of poor health the Politburo investigated the "real reasons" for his refusal:

Discussed problem of Leo . . . and analyzed real reasons for Leo's [refusal of the expansion assignment] . . . unanimous in following

Another wonderful photo of "Amazon and child" shows a captured teenage Amazon, Petra Dadap, holding her newborn baby while being interrogated by a military official. Petra gave birth to a daughter just a week earlier, and her husband, Commander Vida, was killed the month before. (*Manila Times*, July 24, 1954; Courtesy of Rizal Library, Ateneo de Manila University)

conclusions: a) For security reasons, Leo feels safer in the city than any other place; b) Leo is not prepared to leave his family, knowing how little the party is in a position to help families of cadres.[141]

Although Leo was reluctant to leave his family without economic support, the Politburo, ignoring the issue altogether, unanimously decided that the state of Leo's health was "not sufficient ground" for him to refuse his expansion assignment. When he continued to refuse, the party expelled him from the Politburo and the Central Committee, reminding members that the movement would not tolerate "unpreparedness for full sacrifice," including the sacrifice of self and family. A Huk soldier named del Valle, who also refused an expansion assignment because of his family, was assigned only light tasks "such as typing" and fed on "roots and grasses." His superiors agreed that the punishment was extreme but necessary because of del Valle's "commissions against the masses and the organization."[142] In almost all their deliberations the Huk leaders arrived at the same conclusion: "the revolution must come first."[143] In his memoir Bill Pomeroy told the story of "Ete," a popular soldier who married a young Huk woman and was court-martialed in July 1950 for "desertion in the face of the enemy." Serving as part of an ambush team, Ete left the firing line, telling his comrades that he had a headache. But according to Pomeroy he was actually concerned about the safety of his wife, Anita. Ete was sentenced to death by firing squad, and Pomeroy offered the following justification for his execution:

> The natural impulse of a man and a wife is to protect each other. But . . . in this movement it is not the individual that counts, but the cause of all. . . . If one cadre is wounded or captured, shall we risk the lives of two for a personal attachment, and thereby injure the whole?[144]

In 1950, the same year in which the RSSP was issued, the Politburo, under the leadership of Jose Lava, alias Gregorio Santayana, released another policy document entitled "Struggle against Awaitism," which analyzed the relationship between family and revolution.[145] Awaitism, which Lava called the "most important practical political problem" confronting the movement, referred to the phenomena "whereby people already convinced that there is no other way left except the armed struggle for national liberation, either do not participate at all, or else participate haphazardly." This disease manifested itself in a spectrum of engage-ment that ran "from total non-participation to non-total participation" among both the "unorganized masses" and the Huks themselves. Ac-cording to Lava, many Huks were guilty of waiting passively for the rev-olution to triumph rather than committing themselves to the struggle in a disciplined way.[146] Within the party, the problem of awaitism mani-fested itself in the avoidance of a sharp and decisive struggle against the enemy, in "individual self-preservation," and in a refusal "to abandon everything, employment, family and comforts, in order to devote full time to the revolution." With the same sense of impatience and dismis-siveness the party leadership often displayed toward the sex problem, Lava denounced awaitism as a "noncommunist, nonproletarian ideol-ogy having its roots in petty bourgoise [sic] individualism, selfishness, wavering, and indecisiveness."[147]

Lava's argument linked the problem of awaitism to the family lives of Huk cadres. As party leaders often complained, they faced difficulties in "counteracting awaitism" because of the "screens" employed by cadres to hide the true reasons for their vacillation. The most common screen was the so-called family problem, which made it difficult for the party to recruit new guerrillas or force existing members to accept expansion as-signments because this meant abandoning their families. "In the course of our drive to send out expansion cadres to undeveloped areas," the Po-litburo stated, "the most common excuse we encountered that delayed the implementation of our expansion plans is the family problem."[148] Another screen that the leadership believed was used by cadres to justify their inertia was the belief that "the masses were not yet ready" and to force them into militant struggles would only drive them away from the Huks. Party leaders believed this was just another excuse for inaction inspired by rank-and-file members' fears for their own and their fami-lies' personal safety.[149] But, despite its view of the family as a source of revolutionary weakness, the party could not easily ignore its impor-tance. Communist Party leader Casto Alejandrino believed the family issue influenced many of the decisions taken by rank-and-file Huks and limited the potential of the movement. During the Japanese Occupation it was a challenge to sustain a "prolonged armed struggle" because many soldiers wanted "to see the fighting war over and return to their fami-lies."[150] Taruc agreed, stating that "even during the wartime period, the majority of cadres were reluctant, even in the face of extreme hardship, to leave the vicinity of their homes in Central Luzon."[151]

Related to the family problem was the baby problem. When women gave birth they often found it difficult to fulfill their duties in the movement, and party leaders and male cadres were not particularly sympathetic. When Comrade Elsie, for example, asked to be relieved of her duties as chief of communications "on the ground of the baby problem," her request was summarily rejected by the Secretariat.[152] Comrade Paes expressed his frustration at not being able to use Comrade Zeny as a courier because she "was on the family way."[153] This issue had a serious impact on most Huk women, including Liwayway, Guerrero, Elang, Filomena, and Luz, all of whom, the party believed, had "turned their backs to the revolution to become mothers."[154]

The party's solution to the family and baby problems was to demand the integration of spouses (especially wives) and older children into the movement and to insist on the distribution of younger children to friends or relatives who were not directly involved in the rebellion. Men were directed to encourage their wives to join them in the forest camps where, according to Celia Mariano, those without clear assignments washed clothes and cooked for the guerrillas. But party policy was ambivalent and unclear. The presence of wives who were not dedicated to the movement, were merely "decorations," and stayed just to be near their husbands was also an annoyance to party leaders, and most of these women eventually left the camps. Women who bore children but refused to part with them were sent home as young children in the camps threatened the security of everyone. In fact, far from resolving the family problem, integration increased its impact on the Huk camps.

According to the Huk leadership, marriage and family life created a further problem: financial opportunism, the embezzlement or misuse of the movement's funds by Huk soldiers and party cadres. Taruc told the story of Kumander Bakal of Bulacan who "received from an aunt 100 pesos as a contribution to the Huk and 20 pesos for himself" and "spent the combined sum on himself and his bride-to-be." According to Taruc, he "had been a loyal soldier of the Huk since 1942 and had reached the rank of a battalion commander with a clean record," but now he was charged with "financial opportunism" and shot.[155] The party leadership rarely expressed sympathy when it felt that the revolution was at stake. Although it was well aware of the hardships imposed on poor peasant families by involvement in the movement, Huk leaders feared that activists would be tempted to embezzle resources in order to improve the situation of their families and kin. This problem was addressed head-on in another Politburo report (also completed in 1950) titled "Finance Opportunism: Its Basic Causes and Remedies."[156] "Because of the difficulties of underground activities, which prevented close supervision and frequent check-up," the report stated, "finance opportunism" had become rampant within the party and the HMB.[157] Examples of this problem listed in the report included that of a cadre who used movement funds to purchase jewelry for his family and male cadres of the armed forces who "sought to dazzle young girls with gifts." The party believed some cadres saw the "display of jewelry" or "fine clothes" as an "effective means of commanding the respect of others, both within the party and outside." Most significant, party leaders concluded that some cadres had the "perverted concept that it is disgraceful for a comrade working full time in the revolution to have his family standard of living not improved or even lowered." While it insisted on revolutionary sacrifice, the party clearly believed that familial and sexual relationships encouraged petit -bourgeois self-indulgence and financial corruption among the Huk rank and file.[158]

Occasionally the party contributed funds to help the families of its most dedicated cadres. The family of Comrade Timan, who, despite receiving "inhumane treatment" when captured by the enemy, did not betray the movement, was given some money because her family incurred debts to save her.[159] Comrades "LT" and "Johnny" were also given an allowance to help their families.[160] But, although the party occasionally recognized the importance of the family to the revolutionary lives of its cadres, its general attitude toward family life was antagonistic. The party believed that the best way to solve the problems created by family ties was to break up the nuclear families of party cadres, integrate their productive members into the revolutionary movement, and entrust the care of dependents to kin or others who were not directly involved in the movement.[161] To mitigate the temptation of finance opportunism the party tried to find "ways and means of distributing to their relatives and friends the small children of party cadres, while making the wives and older children of our cadres, particularly those without visible means of livelihood, work for the revolution." But even this was not an ideal solution. In the end, the report concluded, a more heroic solution was required. Huks, it declared, "should by example and education project the communist virtues of selflessness, self-sacrifice (including sacrifice of families), and frugality in living."[162]

While party leaders generally interpreted all familial problems as a source of weakness, what these problems demonstrated clearly was the very embeddedness of the Huks in the social and familial networks of Central and Southern Luzon. This embeddedness, which was a source of strength and support in the Huk movement, inadvertently limited the success of the Huks in other areas. Most Huks were indeed reluctant to take up expansion assignments, not because of awaitism, as party leaders believed, but because they did not want to be alienated from the very source of their strength and support. For ideologues in the movement, however, devotion to the revolution, not the family, was the movement's greatest strength.

Feminism and the Woman Question

Women were at the center of party debates about marriage, sex, and family, and yet their opinions were almost completely ignored. The leadership never gave serious consideration to women's perspectives in formulating its policies, even though it was clear that the presence and involvement of women introduced personal issues that deeply affected the internal dynamics of the Huk movement. The solutions outlined by the party were explicitly addressed to men rather than women, and the leaders clearly had different expectations of its male and female cadres. Women were more or less expected to accept extramarital liaisons proposed by male cadres, and, while the movement valued men's participation in the struggle, women who placed too much importance on family responsibilities were usually encouraged to leave. Women received less support than their male counterparts, and their concerns and issues were consistently treated as problems that required political and strategic solutions. These solutions subjected women to male political and sexual control, and with increasing frequency men blamed them for the failings of the movement as a whole.

While some party leaders believed that the "problems" created by women's participation could be prevented by integrating them more fully into the movement, this was not the dominant point of view. Both Celia and Bill Pomeroy insisted that some of the blame lay in the men and "many men could have no problem if they had overcome their feudal outlooks and had involved their wives in the struggle beside them."[163] But in the Hukbalahap and the HMB, most leaders and Huk men refused to address women's issues on women's terms despite the loyalty of their female comrades to the movement. Ultimately women had to look out for their own needs, and it is no coincidence that the woman who worked hardest to promote a woman's agenda among the Huks was

Celia Mariano. Her struggle against the casual and sometimes coercive sexism of her male comrades allows us to see deeper into the highly gendered political culture of the Huk movement.

Celia's growth as a feminist took years. While her male comrades readily and successfully introduced her to dialectical materialism, political economy, revolutionary politics, and the state, no one ever discussed the "woman question" with her. At first, guided only by her own experience, Celia learned how different women's issues and concerns were from those of men. When she attended her first party school she had an experience she never forgot:

> In the party school, we were about twelve who were studying there, only two women, the others men. One thing that happened was that the men built a toilet outside the house. But when you squat in the toilet, your body could be seen down to the chest. I thought, My God, how could we women go in there? So, what we did was to go a little way out to a stream. You had to cross a log so that you could hide among the bushes. One day, when we were having classes, I felt that I had to respond to the call of nature, so I left the room and went there. And when I crossed the log, I fell into the water. Of course, I shouted. So all the comrades came out and fished me out of the water. . . . After I changed my clothes, I began to criticize these comrades. I said, "You people, you only think of yourselves as men, you do not think of our situation as women. You expect us to use that toilet. You did not even think of building a toilet for us. You just think of yourselves as men. You don't think of the women. You don't bother with the needs of women."[164]

After Celia complained, her male comrades admitted that they had not been sensitive enough to the needs of the women, and after the school session finished that day all her male comrades built a toilet for the women. Celia believed the incident served as a lesson to the men, but it was not the only lesson she taught them. She explained:

> One evening, when we are already sleeping, . . . we could hear them telling sex jokes. It was lurid, they made me sick. The next day, we had our lessons first, but always at the end there was a part called "Criticism–Self-Criticism." I told the comrades, "I don't want to be rude or abominable to you, but your conduct last night was to me outrageous. You were talking and telling sex

jokes. I don't understand how you communists can behave in that manner. You should know by this time what is wrong, what is good, and what is bad. For you to talk in that way in the presence of your comrades who are women shows no sensitivity at all as to how we feel about these jokes. Do you want your wives to listen to these jokes? Or your sisters? Or your mothers? And if you behave this way in the future, we will not think of you as comrades. You are not worthy to be communists."[165]

Once again, Celia's male comrades bowed their heads in embarrassment, accepting her criticism. But while Celia was already sensitive to the issues that separated her from her male comrades she did not pursue the question of women's rights further until the postwar period.

Celia's growing awareness of the woman question was shaped by two works that had a profound influence on her views. The first was a pamphlet called "The Woman Question," by Clara Zetkin, a leading figure in German socialism, which discussed the problems of women in general and explained that women were considered inferior to and exploited by men in many societies. Celia also read Lenin's "The Emancipation of the Working Woman," which she said stirred her imagination.[166] She recalled:

> It brought me a new outlook—I began to see how we women in general have been exploited and oppressed. And I also saw how the Communist Party and all the parties allowed this to happen and even went along with this custom. Women must fight for equal rights with men because you cannot generally say that men are more intelligent than women. That's why from the time I read these two books I became a feminist. I was always trying to see how women were treated in the party and elsewhere. I became very sensitive to the question of the treatment of women.[167]

These works helped Celia formulate her own feminist ideology. From the beginning she understood that there was a disparity between men's and women's roles in the movement, and, although she did not pay particular attention to the recruiting and educating of women, she noticed that they were usually relegated to support roles as cooks, laundresses, nurses, first-aid workers, and couriers. Keeping such thoughts largely to herself and spending most of her time at leadership meetings with men, she managed to avoid domestic tasks but continued to fraternize with women in the camps. She never discussed political issues with them. During the postwar period, however, she formed a women's division, which was responsible for recruiting and educating women. Despite the indifference of the party, and even the women themselves, to her proposal, she persisted:

> The first thing I did was to look around for the women I knew in the party who would be willing to form with me a Women's Committee—Ka Sophia, Rosenda Torres, Nene Mallari, and Isabel. We met once a week in my house, and I discussed [political] questions with them to politicize them, to open their minds to the oppression of women. It did not take just a week or a month; it had taken a long time for me, too. They understood it, but it did not excite them. They did not become dynamic about it.[168]

But Celia refused to give up and with her urging and leadership this core of women decided to create a Women's Forum, a venue where women could come together and discuss issues that affected them, including issues of international political significance. Eventually, under Celia's leadership, the Women's Forum became a women's organization with a professional and intellectual membership that lobbied Congress for price controls and campaigned for more job opportunities and child care facilities.[169]

By the late 1940s Celia had become a strong advocate for women's issues inside the party, but she had still not developed a coherent feminist ideology that the party could or would embrace. For a long time she remained silent about the attitude of the party leadership toward women, but her frustration intensified as the sex problem among the Huks became a more prominent issue. Finally she saw a chance to express her point of view in a way that would compel her male comrades to listen, and her decision to do so marked a turning point in her life:

> In February 1950 the HMB held a big, two-week conference in the Laguna forest of leaders and the most dedicated cadres of our movement, forty men with me as the only woman. We discussed the problems of the movement and decided on our tasks for the immediate future. On the last day of our meeting, comrades who wanted to raise any question not covered were given ten minutes each to talk. I asked to be given half an hour to speak on the woman question. Somebody in the crowd asked, "What is the woman question?" I turned to the questioner and

said, "I am asking the chair to give me half an hour to speak so that I can explain to all of you the importance of understanding the woman question." But the chairman conceded only fifteen minutes to me. . . . I spoke about the woman question—the problem of women's inequality with men, about women being considered inferior to men in all aspects of living. I pointed to examples of capable women, active in our movement, who after being married to our men comrades became mere housekeepers. I cited cases of many women in our camps that were looked upon as just sex objects, not treated with [the] respect and dignity that they deserved. I said I was not proud of the fact that I was the only woman in that conference. It was no indication that women couldn't play an important role in the movement. It showed the failure of the movement's leaders to recognize that women deserved the same rights and opportunities as men.[170]

Although Celia did not expect the party to change overnight, she made her mark that day, the first time in the history of the Huk movement that the woman question had been formally presented and discussed. Seizing the opportunity, she followed up her speech by writing a series of articles on women's issues for the party's official paper, *Titis*, in which she tried to educate party leaders and the Huk rank and file about the problems women confronted in the movement and how to address them.

By 1950 Celia was not only a committed communist but was also becoming a feminist. Her views were not widely shared in the movement. During her entire revolutionary career Zenaida del Castillo remembered only two or three times when the cadres discussed the exploitation of women in society. As an active and well-connected party member, she mingled with male leaders who discussed such issues as imperialism, national liberation, and communism with her but not the women's issues she deemed important. As much as she loved the camaraderie among men and women in the movement, she was well aware that women did not have the same opportunities as men.[171] Even before World War II, Elang Santa Ana was aware that women in Philippine society were waging a battle for suffrage, and, although she was only a young, peasant woman in the barrio, she understood that women needed to demand political rights. When she became a guerrilla Elang saw a similar struggle for equality taking place within the Huk movement, although, like most Huk women, she kept her views to herself.[172] Like Celia, Rosenda Torres was also educated, and she finished her college degree while she was active in the HMB. She also wondered why so few women attended important meetings in the movement and questioned the prevailing view that women's organization was divisive and "women were not supposed to meet as women." Among the leaders, she recalled, only Celia insisted on giving women more responsibility. But, although she attended some of the women's meetings organized by Celia, she did not take them seriously and later regretted not pushing a women's agenda more aggressively.[173]

Celia blamed the movement, and especially the sexist attitudes of male cadres, for the subordination of Huk women and defended her views uncompromisingly. In his description of one debate about the woman question, Bill Pomeroy captured Celia's determination and the opposition she confronted:

> After a long discussion that gets heated it is decided that the older men, who are peasants, suffer from a feudal outlook that makes them less ready to accept youth and women as equals. Celia has to point out the role of women in the struggle, and that a woman who can stand on her own and argue should be encouraged rather than repressed. One old peasant is stubborn about accepting his weakness; he wants to study the matter.[174]

Despite her deeply held belief in women's equality, Celia understood and on occasion even excused the patriarchal political culture of the Communist Party. Like other Huk women she realized that men and women in the movement were not only communists but also the products of Philippine society and that it was not easy for them to break with the traditions and ideas that had guided them throughout their lives. Women were supposed to wed, give birth, raise children, and support their husbands in the home. Men were supposed to make all the decisions, especially in public and political life. Women in the Philippines are brought up to believe that they are inferior to men, Celia explained,

> and that their chief work is to become a housewife and to take care of children. Women are not trained or made conscious of the fact that they can be useful as citizens who can work outside the home. So there are very few women who are interested in working outside the home; instead most think that their work is inside the home — that they must be good housewives, train their children, and always follow the wishes of their husbands.[175]

Regretfully, Celia admitted that this same mentality was reproduced in the party and the Huk movement. Like other Filipino men, Huk men expected the women in their families to stay at home, cook and wash, and take care of their children. Although the party did not discourage the involvement of women, this involvement was limited by highly conventional assumptions about women and gender, and these assumptions were rarely questioned. Celia believed women themselves were partly to blame, although ultimately she regarded them as victims of their conventional upbringing:

> I don't think the men would stop any woman from using her abilities; it is just that the women are backward. They are brought up that way. From the time you are a child, you are given dolls; you are not even taught how to ride a bicycle. . . . [Y]ou are brought up to be a woman—to learn only embroidery and prayers. And you are taught how to cook, how to keep your house clean, all the housework. That's all women are taught.[176]

Although she understood the social basis of the problem, Celia worked tirelessly "to change this situation of the inequality between men and women" within the Huk movement.[177] Celia's feminist ideas were not fully formed in the 1940s and 1950s and grew with her subsequent political experience and education, but she nevertheless played a critical role as an advocate for women's issues. But her success was limited. Even as women became more aware of their own interests and more critical of the party, they encountered indifference from their male comrades who generally failed to fully recognize their talents and achievements. But they also confronted the indifference of other women. From peasant backgrounds and with little formal education, most Huk women were unfamiliar with the woman question and most believed that Huk men treated women in the movement with respect and decency. According to Gloria Aquino, Huk men were very protective of Huk women and their reputations, and it was rare for a man to "force himself on a woman" because "the punishment was the firing squad."[178] The amicable relationships between men and women were one of the main reasons Araceli Mallari stayed in the organization, and she later remarked that "it was the only time in my life when I felt united to people who shared the same thoughts, ideologies, and fought the same battles."[179] Understandably, most women who served in the Huk movement did not think men controlled or dominated them, and they generally had

little sense of possessing interests apart from those of their male comrades. Even in their later recollections about the Huks women talked
easily about national liberation, land reform, and political rights but sel-
dom mentioned women's issues.

Women rarely invoked their gender to explain their role in the
movement or even to explain their failure to rise through the ranks.
Teofista Valerio, for example, was involved in both the Hukbalahap and
the HMB movements, but despite her experience she "did not advance
in the organization," perhaps because she was not able to fully express
her views and ideas to the leadership. "Maybe [this was] because I was
shy," she explained, or "because I was not very educated." Because she
had only finished fourth grade, Teofista did not believe that she was fit
to play a leadership role, although she knew that men who were just
as uneducated had managed to rise in the party hierarchy. Although
she believed she had given "100 percent to the movement," she did not
connect her place in it to the woman question.[180] She was not unusual.
Hesitant to push their own political claims, most Huk women remained
loyal followers and supporters rather than leaders, embodiments of the
sacrificial virtues that many Huk men believed comprised the ideal
revolutionary.

Love, Sex, and Revolution

The Huk revolutionary movement was more than just a political and
military organization. It was a complex microcosm of society composed
of male and female cadres who struggled to balance their revolutionary
and personal lives. To fully understand a movement as complex as this,
it is necessary to examine not only the political aspects of the organization but also the intimate lives of its male and female members. Issues of
sexuality, gender, and family shaped their lives, which were not experienced as separate from the revolutionary struggle but as closely entwined. Such issues have always shaped revolutionary movements. Like
the Huks, women in other revolutionary struggles have attempted to
balance their personal and revolutionary lives, but the leaders of these
movements, who were also predominantly male, adopted varying ratio-
nales and methods to address the personal and familial issues they faced.

In the Chinese and Vietnamese revolutions, for example, party leaders formulated no clear policy on sexual and personal relationships inside
the movements. In the Chinese Communist Party relationships were
tolerated but not incorporated into the revolutionary agenda. Indeed,

Helen Young describes vividly how pregnant women and their newborn children were left behind by Chinese guerrillas during the rigors of the Long March.[181] And those women who became leaders in the Chinese Communist party, according to Christina Gilmartin, acquired their status through their sexual relationships with powerful men in the party.[182] In Vietnam sexual or romantic relationships were neither explicitly nor implicitly tolerated. Karen Turner emphasizes how North Vietnamese women had to forgo romantic and sexual desires until after the revolution, which often resulted in unhealthy relationships with men who regarded former women rebels as past their reproductive prime and possessed of scarred, unattractive, and infertile bodies.[183] In her memoir of the Vietnamese revolution, Dang Thuy Tram describes how she constantly repressed her romantic love for fellow comrades because of her fear of being reprimanded and her belief that those feelings had no place in the revolution.[184] Dora Maria Tellez, a female military commander in the Nicaraguan revolutionary movement of the 1980s, also recalled how prevalent "the problem of male chauvinism" was among her male comrades, who believed women were only fit for domestic tasks and only good "for screwing."[185] In the Greek resistance of the 1940s romantic entanglements between men and women were expressly prohibited because, according to one female activist, "our goal was not only to kick out the enemy but to serve as guide for the people." Men and women therefore treated each other "platonically and comradely," and the "built-in" cultural sanction of "respect women or die" ensured that they were not abused by men in the movement. One attractive and "hot-blooded" girl, for example, was expelled from the movement by her female comrades who feared she would seduce men.[186] Perhaps, as Jeff Goodwin has argued, the sexual and familial ties of Huk cadres "hardly made them the best candidates for a high-risk insurgency" and a "male-dominated movement" would have been "more solidaristic had more of its leading cadres been libidinally unattached."[187]

But the Huks belonged not only to a military organization. From early on in the struggle they recognized the crucial role that the family and the community played in the revolutionary organization. Familial and personal networks brought men and women into the movement, and the Huks realized these ties had to be encouraged if they wished to preserve the loyalty and commitment of cadres and the communities from which they came. In their acknowledgment and regulation of personal, sexual, and familial issues in the movement, the Huks were both more tolerant of the needs of their male cadres and more receptive to the problems of women, creating a space for them in an otherwise male-dominated military organization. Their approach could be interpreted as ideological weakness, and yet their practices reflected the more tolerant cultural attitudes about gender in Philippine society. But they also challenged cultural norms. Huk leaders were aware, for example, that marriage created divided loyalties for its cadres, so they encouraged and authorized special Huk marriages that recast the traditional marriage ceremony "into a ritual affirmation not only of the couple's loyalty to one another, but also their joint commitment to the struggle."[188] The movement also recognized that the revolution made demands on its cadres that were at odds with Catholic practices of courtship and marriage in Philippine society. In terms of sexual relations a culture of "monogamy" still prevailed but party policy toward the "sex problem" provided room for flexibility. The movement clearly wanted to challenge the assumptions of the mainstream culture and to adapt this culture to revolutionary circumstances. The revolution therefore legitimized the violation of traditional Catholic ideas about gender, sexuality, and family and directly challenged the institutional power of the Philippine church and state.

And yet, although the Huks sought to transform the overall society's sexual and gender relations to accommodate revolutionary interests, their ideas were still framed within a conventional discourse about gender and sexuality. In their revolutionary solutions to the sex, family, and baby problems, male Huk leaders not only failed to address the interests of Huk women but also often blamed them for the failings of the movement. Their response to the "problems" created by the presence of women implicitly demonstrated the movement's belief that affectual relationships, unless they were regulated and controlled by male leaders, eroded the solidarity of the movement and undermined the collective identity and discipline of communist cadres.[189] Yet they never fully recognized that the struggle itself would have been impossible without the support and participation of hundreds of women and that the difficulties created by their presence paled in comparison with the difficulties that would have been created by their absence. Ultimately, party leaders were incapable of seeing the issues of sex, gender, and family as anything but peripheral and harmful to the revolution.

Despite its revolutionary nature, the Huk movement's approach to sexuality reinforced its militarized and masculinized culture. Like other military organizations, including the Philippine Armed Forces and constabulary units, the Huk movement was shaped by a polarized sexual culture that perceived women as "models of servitude, subordination and sexual availability in stark contrast to masculine military domination, competition and sexual prowess."[190] According to Anne-Marie Hilsdon, when women join military organizations they are immediately subjected to different sexual expectations and regulatory mechanisms. She argues:

> Any notion of controlling male sexuality, specifically sexual behavior and parenthood, is dismissed . . . Women are more closely watched. . . . "Impeccable behaviour" is expected of military and police women, who are courted by both married and unmarried male officers and personnel. For example, police women were expected to resist the sexual advances of men while alone in offices on duty with them, but male desire and sexual practice remained unquestioned. Women must have "courage, moral fiber, and upbringing to resist all this," and must have preserved their "good" [girl] image. Men were more lenient on other men and women who committed such "immoralities." Yet there seemed to be little comparable scrutiny of male sexual behavior.[191]

For Hilsdon femininity in militarized organizations is "epitomized by obedience, 'forcefulness' (including circumspection, sexual abstinence and chastity) and control—the opposite of masculine authority and aggression."[192] By prioritizing military and revolutionary duty over familial duty, the Huks to some extent replicated the discourses and practices of sexuality in the Philippine military.[193] At the same time they confronted the sexual aggression that had always characterized the Philippine military. Their efforts to regulate issues of love, sex, marriage, and children demonstrated both an awareness of sexual discrimination and an eagerness to protect women from the predatory instincts of men.

The focus of Huk leaders on the problematic nature of women's participation also represented a failure to analyze the strengths and weaknesses of the movement and to appreciate the needs and aspirations of its male and female cadres. Most of the discussions about sex and family problems in the movement occurred in the early 1950s when the rebellion was in decline and Huk squadrons faced almost daily attacks from constabulary forces. Huk leaders believed the conflicts created by the presence of women accounted for the weakness of the movement. But when the government declared an all-out war against the Huks the movement was pushed farther into the mountains and farther into isolation and despair. This isolation led to a decline in the movement's morale and exacerbated the problems of family life, weakening the guerrillas' resolve and their capacity to fight. It was not the presence of women that led to the weakness and isolation of the movement. Personal relationships within the movement did become more intense, sometimes compromising the commitment of particular cadres, but this was a natural response to the prospect of death and defeat. What eroded morale was the failure of the male Huk leaders to deal properly with the place of women in the movement and their tendency to respond to the problems the presence of women created by regulating sexual behavior, a policy that ignored the complexity of personal relationships and created a system of control that was often opposed to the interests and desires of their members. It was not sex and passion that undermined the Huk movement but the failure of the movement to tolerate and integrate the personal passions of its members.

Women in particular suffered from these contradictory policies concerning gender and sexuality. By recruiting women and then relegating them to support roles, by advancing a few to positions of command and allowing others to serve the sexual needs of powerful males, the party fostered serious tensions within its ranks. Despite the party's formal commitment to women's equality, leaders made little effort to treat this issue seriously. Although the woman question was an important issue in communist movements all over the world after the 1920s, the Philippine Communist Party only discussed this issue, and then reluctantly, toward the end of the rebellion in the 1950s.[194] Women's issues were taken seriously only when they appeared to hamper male military capabilities. Celia Mariano, the lone female member of the Politburo, was constantly frustrated with her "sexist comrades," who "looked at women as sex objects or domestic helpers." Although she pushed women's issues during her tenure in the Politburo, she was largely silenced by male leaders, who "considered these issues as secondary."[195] Indeed, while the Huks sought to change the social and gender order in Philippine society, most of its members acted according to highly conventional notions about gender and sexuality. By promoting patriarchal assumptions and failing to consider the way in which participation in the movement transformed the experiences and attitudes of men and women, the Huk leaders allowed an organizational strength to become an organizational liability.

Nonetheless, the Huks did try to make the emotional and sexual lives of their male and female members part of their revolutionary agenda, and their efforts moved issues of sex and family life from the private to the public realm as Huk leaders weighed the "private" interests and desires of individual cadres against the collective interests of the revolutionary movement. As a result personal issues of family, sex, and morality became integral to the movement's culture, and personal matters, formerly negotiated by individual men and women, were discussed and addressed by the movement as a whole. In this respect, at least, the Huk movement was truly revolutionary.

5

Amazons in
the Unfinished Revolution

In early 1952, while Celia Mariano and William Pomeroy were preparing notes for their next educational session, their forest camp came
under surprise attack from the Philippine military. They were nearly
killed and were temporarily separated while fleeing the camp. But they
recovered and established another forest camp in an even more secluded
area of the Sierra Madre. A few months later, however, in April 1952,
they sustained another attack, and this time they did not escape.
"Around noontime," Celia recalled, "a volley of gunfire descended on
our huts and sent us dashing down a hillside. Some of our comrades, including women, were killed."[1] Bill Pomeroy detailed these dramatic
events in his memoir:

> When the rapid fire begins we are for one moment stunned,
> heads jerked to each other. Then we are on our bared feet, racing
> for the edge of the drop beyond the hut. The enemy has come
> over the top of the mountain and has descended behind us, into
> the middle of the camp, and is firing upon us from among the
> empty huts. The noise is deafening. The ground is churned at
> our feet and bits of twig and bark fly about our heads.[2]

A bullet grazed Bill's ankle, and he tripped down a steep descent. With
his "glasses smashed and head cut," he lay "senseless behind a large
tree." Injured and virtually blind without his glasses, Pomeroy was unable to go any further. He recalled Celia saying, "I have to leave you."
Then they "exchanged a look of love, pity and terror," touched hands,

and separated.[3] The next thing he knew he was surrounded by cursing men who were threatening him with their rifles. This "strange, blind struggle in the forest" was the end of the line for Bill Pomeroy.

With a handful of comrades Celia was able to escape and find a hiding place in the dense forest. But the soldiers were everywhere and clearly determined to continue their search for the fugitive Huks. Once, as a group of soldiers were eating in a clearing, Celia and her fellow guerrillas watched silently from the trees. When the soldiers left the Huks ran into the clearing to scavenge scraps of food, licking the insides of empty cans. Celia remembered that the inside of an empty can of lard "tasted like butter to me."[4] Trying to elude the pursuing soldiers they "scurried like rabbits all over the mountains," but after six days of running Celia and her comrades were captured, "exhausted, starving, feeble, and frightened."[5] Celia and Bill were reunited at the headquarters of the Philippine army.

All the major Manila newspapers hailed their capture as a triumph for the Armed Forces of the Philippines (AFP). The assault on the forest camp was part of a larger plan, code-named Operations Four Roses, whose intent was to capture the four highest-ranking leaders of the HMB: Luis Taruc, Jesus Lava, Alfredo Saulo, and Jose de Leon (known as Kumander Dimasalang). The "prize catch," the "Yank Huk" William Pomeroy, after a mere two days of operations was treated by the Manila press as a victory for the AFP, and the headlines were accompanied by photos of Pomeroy dressed in military fatigues, looking "pale and haggard, unkempt . . . badly needing a haircut . . . [and] scared as he was helped out of a jeep."[6] "I am delighted to hear of Pomeroy's capture," declared Philippine president Elpidio Quirino in a telegram conveying his "warmest congratulations and the people's gratitude to the gallant officers and men" of the AFP.[7] The U.S. embassy was equally quick to disown Pomeroy, assuring the Philippine government that it would not intervene in his case despite the fact that he was an American citizen. He "should be tried by a Philippine court," declared the embassy, "for his association with the Huks and the local communists."[8] His capture, according to a reporter for the *Philippines Free Press,* was the "sorry ending of the sad story of former American GI turned Huk, William Pomeroy."[9]

When newspapers covered the capture of Celia Mariano several days later, the press coverage was more restrained and Celia was invariably referred to as the "wife of Pomeroy," undermining her prominent position in the Huk organization. Found with three other Amazons "sitting dejectedly under a tree," according to the *Manila Times*, when Celia saw a soldier's rifle pointing at her she stood up and said, "Don't shoot, I'll give up." The article continued as if she were a contestant in a revolutionary beauty contest or fashion show:

> Mrs. Pomeroy appeared haggard . . . but still looked charming even in her ragged grey blouse and faded blue skirt. She was very thankful for the kind treatment accorded her by the army . . . and the first thing she asked for upon her arrival was food and fresh clothes . . . [for] she had not eaten for five days.[10]

Major Manila newspapers and magazines published several photos of the arrests of Celia Mariano and Bill Pomeroy in April 1952. The caption printed with this photo read: "Sporting a newly-pressed, olive-drab uniform, Mrs. Pomeroy is shown having coffee with Major General Calixto Duque, AFP chief of staff, at the command post of the 12th BCT in Nueva Ecija . . . before enplaning for the IMA headquarters, on the first leg of her journey to Camp Murphy." Her calm appearance and blank gaze masked the pain, trepidation, and defeat that came with her arrest. (*Manila Times*, April 18, 1952; Courtesy of Rizal Library, Ateneo de Manila University)

Like Bill, Celia was seen as a prize catch for Operations Four Roses.[11] The Philippine government wasted no time charging the Pomeroys with the crimes of rebellion, murder, robbery, and arson.[12]

The capture of Celia and Bill Pomeroy came at the height of the offensive against the Huk guerrillas, and their arrests symbolized the government's increasingly successful battle against the rebels and the impact of American military aid, which had helped to transform the Philippine army into a counterinsurgency force. But the challenge to the Huks was not just external; internally the movement was also coming under pressure, and while the government launched mock agricultural reform programs and intensified military repression Huk leaders remained divided over policy issues and military strategy. Peasant support in the towns and barrios was wavering. By 1952 the Huk rebellion was in decline, and

Accompanying this rare, intimate photo was the following caption: "After the wild freedom on the Huklands in the Sierra Madres, and a brief separation following her husband's earlier capture, Celia Pomeroy is shown above embracing her husband, William Pomeroy, as they were reunited yesterday afternoon in captivity." The highest-ranking couple in the Huk movement had fallen, were briefly reunited, and would be separated again for the next ten years. (*Manila Times*, April 18, 1952; Courtesy of Rizal Library, Ateneo de Manila University)

a year later "the movement's remaining leaders were powerless to prevent even larger numbers of armed peasants from leaving."[13] By the mid-1950s only a handful of desperate rebels were scattered around Central and Southern Luzon, and the surrender of the last Huk leaders and followers in 1956 marked the end of the largest peasant revolution the country has ever known.

Most personal memoirs and general histories of the rebellion attribute the defeat of the Huks to the Philippine government's counterinsurgency program.[14] While recognizing the importance of counterinsurgency operations—and in particular the role of U.S. military intervention—this book offers a different perspective on the development and decline of the Huk rebellion, one that pays much more attention to the movement's internal dynamics. Incorporating women's stories and placing issues of gender, sexuality, and family at the center of the Huk rebellion not only provides an alternative and complementary interpretation of its decline but also offers a new perspective on the functioning of this revolutionary movement as a whole.

Starting in World War II women were recruited into the Huk movement through social networks shaped by patterns of kinship, community, and political organization, and the nature of these relations shaped female participation in the movement. Once they had joined, however, the Huks attempted to alter women's traditional roles by training them to be effective guerrillas and even advancing a few to positions of leadership and command. The movement also challenged conventional gender relations by instituting its own marriage ceremony and allowing married men to enter into liaisons with single women, effectively placing the sexual relationships and married lives of male and female cadres on the revolutionary agenda. Nonetheless most Huk women reproduced their traditional roles in the forest camps, assuming a subordinate position to men in the movement and rarely advancing up the organizational ladder. The privileged position of male leaders was clearly highlighted by their sexual liaisons with young and subordinate female guerrillas, which was justified by a largely spurious sexual egalitarianism and a pseudo-scientific discourse about male sexuality. This deep double standard, which is best grasped through gender analysis but is not limited to gender relations, had important consequences for the strength of the revolutionary movement. Despite its egalitarian ideology, the male-dominated Huk movement was undercut by a conventional discourse about appropriate gender roles and sexuality, a discourse that diminished the potential contribution of women, blamed them for organizational "weakness," and failed to address the needs and deep-seated aspirations of both male and female members.

The Decline of the Huk Movement

As an ardent supporter of the HMB, Araceli Mallari allowed leaders of the Politburo to use her house in Manila as a meeting place whenever they were in the capital, and by observing their dispositions during these meetings she was able to assess the strength of the Huk movement. She recalled that early on members of the Politburo were very optimistic. Although they argued at times, they displayed "great camaraderie."[15] Araceli remembered how they used to part with the exclamation, "See you in Malacanang!"[16] But by the early 1950s such optimism had vanished, and as "the leaders became increasingly disheartened" the hardships involved in the struggle "became evident in their weary faces." For Araceli their increasingly somber mood indicated that "the rebellion was drawing to a close."[17]

In the early months of 1950 the Central Committee of the PKP, believing that a "revolutionary situation" existed in the country, called for the overthrow of the Philippine government, the first time it had done so in its revolutionary history. At this time the movement claimed around 15,000 armed guerrillas and more than 50,000 barrio supporters, and Huk leaders believed victory was within reach.[18] A plan for expansion of the HMB from Central to Southern Luzon, for example, predicted that these areas would soon become "stable mass bases of [the] Liberation Movement" and would be "stronger than the four Central Luzon provinces." National economic and political crises, and the people's "exposure to the Huks' progressive principles," believed party leaders, was creating mass discontent with the government and widespread sympathy for the Huk movement.[19] Indeed, when the HMB celebrated its eighth anniversary in 1950, the secretary-general of the Communist Party was overjoyed that the popular response was so favorable despite the negative character of government propaganda. "Newspapers," according to one Politburo report, "cannot summon enough moral indignation to arouse [the] hostility of the people" and "government officials and men of wealth are very jittery."[20] The party predicted that HMB membership would increase from 10,800 in July 1950 to 173,000 by September 1951.[21] Supremo Luis Taruc believed the Huks had at least a million supporters in Central and Southern Luzon.[22] During 1950 Politburo documents constantly emphasized "expansion" and "hastening the tempo" of the revolutionary struggle in order to speed up the "eventual overthrow of the present government."[23] To expand the movement more rapidly the party required each member to recruit at least three new persons every three months.[24]

But within a few months signs of the Huks' decline were already apparent. Much of this can be attributed to the changing face of the Philippine government. In August 1950 President Elpidio Quirino appointed a congressman from Zambales, Ramon Magsaysay, as his new secretary of national defense. A former guerrilla in World War II, Magsaysay had a definite plan for defeating the Huks, which entailed not only strengthening the Philippine military but also developing a political program that encouraged Huks to surrender and peasants to relinquish their support for the rebels. Magsaysay's first step was to increase the number of well-trained soldiers stationed in Central Luzon, a measure he claimed was intended to protect innocent villagers from both Huk violence and landlord lawlessness.[25] Under his leadership control of the Philippine Constabulary and the Armed Forces of the Philippines was consolidated in the Department of National Defense, and eleven new battalion combat teams (BCTs) were created and trained in antiguerrilla warfare. By focusing their military attacks on the Huks and pursuing a policy of coercion and conciliation in the barrios, these BCTs forced the Huks to retreat to their mountain bases, successfully cutting them off from their peasant supporters. Supporting the rebellion had placed a serious strain on people in the barrios, who were exhausted after years of warfare. As food became increasingly scarce, peasant support for the guerillas ebbed.[26] In response the Huks became more desperate and more willing to use coercive methods to extract aid from the villagers, alienating the very people they had sworn to protect.

The election of Ramon Magsaysay as president of the Philippines in 1954 further undercut the Huk movement and its support in Central and Southern Luzon. A self-styled populist who prided himself on his ability to connect with ordinary Filipinos, Magsaysay transformed the military into a more effective and less abusive institution, proclaiming the AFP and PC protectors of barrio people. He also made the rebellion much more costly to the Huk movement. Between 1950 and 1955 the military claimed that it killed over 6,000 Huks, wounded nearly 2,000, captured 4,700, and forced almost 9,500 to surrender and accept an official amnesty.[27] Magsaysay's program of reform, which included improved infrastructure, the construction of health clinics, the creation of agrarian courts, and the provision of credit to small farmers, also appealed to Central Luzon peasants despite its often propagandist goals.[28] All of these projects, as well as Magsaysay's personal touch and the image of reform he projected first as secretary of defense and then as president, played on the peasantry's hope that revolt was no longer necessary.[29]

But perhaps the most important turning point in the history of the Huk rebellion occurred on October 18, 1950, with the wholesale arrest of Politburo leaders in Manila. Acting on information from a former Huk cadre, military intelligence agents and Manila police detectives simultaneously raided twenty-two homes and apartments in Metro Manila, capturing "the big six" officers in the HMB and PKP's national leadership, including the PKP secretary-general and finance chief Jose Lava, Angel Baking (propaganda chief), Federico Maclang (organization bureau chief), Ramon Espiritu (education department chief), Federico Bautista (military department chief), and one woman, Illuminada Calonje, also known as Salome Cruz, the chief of the communications center.[30] Government soldiers also rounded up hundreds of other Huks and Huk sympathizers and seized thousands of pages of Politburo documents.[31] Huk leaders in the forest headquarters, who read about the arrests in the press, felt immediately isolated and paralyzed by the arrest of the entire urban leadership.[32] As the BCTs intensified their operations in Central and Southern Luzon, Huk leaders and cadres found it impossible to rebuild their political organization. They were too busy trying to survive.[33] By 1952 it was becoming impossible for the Huks to stay for more than a week in one place, and in April of that year Celia and Bill Pomeroy were captured. That October a military intelligence unit, aided by a Huk defector, infiltrated the Huk regional headquarters in Panay, killing Kumander Guillermo Capadocia and his top aides, an operation that put an end to Huk expansion plans in the Visayas.[34] Finally, in May 1954, Supremo Luis Taruc surrendered. Huk leaders such as Casto Alejandrino and Jesus Lava remained at large until the 1960s, but it was apparent by the mid-1950s that the popular insurgency in Luzon was at an end and only a handful of desperate, hungry guerrillas now roamed the Sierra Madre. In 1956 the Philippine government declared that peace and order had finally been restored in Central Luzon.

Challenges from Within

A few months after the mass Politburo arrests, Bill Pomeroy was unable to hide his frustration and disillusionment:

A storm was shaking in the forest . . . and the leaves are falling. In the forest there are always falling leaves, and new ones that grow to replace them. But in the HMB there are fewer recruits now, too, and no arms for the new ones. It is a bad season, . . . We had thought that the people moved at our pace, to the rapid click of the mimeograph machine. We had thought that by the leaders' setting a high tempo, we could set up the tempo of the revolution. . . . We have been living in a fool's paradise![35]

Pomeroy believed the revolution had been compromised not only by the government's counterinsurgency programs but also by the rebels themselves. "When the tide of the struggle is running our way," he wrote, "individual weaknesses are submerged in the flood of high spirits; when the enemy is strong and the tide is not our way, those weaknesses emerge and turn men into the slimy things that scuttle for safety on the exposed shoreline."[36] Questioning his own comrades' commitment to the revolution, Pomeroy felt powerless to prevent them from leaving, and he lashed out at the Huks and their peasant supporters, who lacked the "class consciousness" to make a victorious revolution possible.

But other party leaders blamed themselves. Jesus Lava, for example, believed the party had underestimated American influence in Asia and in hindsight believed that the party's decision to launch an armed struggle against the government was premature and failed to take into consideration the strength of the U.S.-backed Philippine army.[37] Another party leader, Alfredo Saulo, agreed, remarking that the Huks "did not know when to advance and when to retreat," and Luis Taruc similarly attributed the decline of the rebellion to the party leadership.[38] In his view, by insisting that the communist revolution was at hand, by converting the Huk organization from a guerrilla force into a regular army, by levying revolutionary taxes on people who were impoverished and "broken in body and spirit," party leaders had demonstrated an "arrogant disregard to the peasantry's needs," precipitating the collapse of the movement and the erosion of its popular support.[39]

All of these arguments (which reflect male perspectives) have some validity, but they ignore or evade issues of gender and sexuality. And yet, as Taruc's comments reveal, such issues were critical to the fate of the movement. Indeed, as he suggests, when the PKP began to call for an intensification of the revolutionary struggle in the early 1950s and for creation of a "regular army," it also began to restrict the space that women occupied in the guerrilla movement and consequently to sever the complex ties of community and kinship that supported the Huks in the peasant villages of Central Luzon. These ties, mediated and preserved by Huk women, were the lifelines of the movement, and as they frayed the movement faltered and fell.[40]

The Personal Is Political: The Politics of Gender, Sexuality, and Family

From the start, the Huks knew that waging a revolutionary struggle against the Philippine state was going to be difficult. And yet, while it seemed inconceivable that a band of peasant guerrillas could defy both the Philippine state and the government of the United States, the Huks posed a formidable threat. Even more unexpectedly, this resistance movement mobilized an unprecedented number of women, mostly from peasant backgrounds and with limited formal education. These women enthusiastically joined the Hukbalahap in the nationalist struggle against the Japanese during World War II, and, although many returned to civilian life after 1945, many supported the more explicitly revolutionary program of the HMB and continued to serve in the guerrilla army during the postwar rebellion. For the first time in Philippine history a significant number of women participated in a major revolutionary movement. For these women, joining the guerrilla struggle marked a radical departure from their usual lives, transforming their political ideas and their sense of personal identity. But, despite their significant collective role in the movement and the ascent of a few women to positions of leadership and authority, most Huk women remained subordinate to men and were expected to perform conventional tasks such as cooking, washing, housekeeping, and child care in the forest camps and barrios. Perhaps Felisa Cuyugan encapsulated women's view of themselves as Huks when she emphatically remarked that she "was first and foremost a wife before a revolutionary."[41]

The presence of women in the movement also created problems, and in order to address them the party placed issues of personal relations on the revolutionary agenda. Sexual and family issues only placed additional burdens on guerrillas, who party leaders believed not only "lacked class consciousness" and "devotion to the revolution" but were also "undisciplined, . . . untrained and uneducated in military and political matters."[42] The Huk leadership therefore embarked on a strict program of political education and military training that prioritized the aims of the revolution and promoted upright "moral qualities" among the guerrillas. The party also formulated policies and created documents specifically to address "problems" related to women, gender, sexuality, and family in the Huk movement, including "The Revolutionary Solution of the Sex Problem" (RSSP), "The Struggle against Awaitism," "Solutions to the Baby and Family Problems," and "Iron Discipline." But the efforts of the leadership to regulate personal relationships in policies such as those laid out in the RSSP often reproduced the same sexual double standard that had given rise to problems in the first place, alienating both leaders and members and highlighting the inequalities and contradictions within the Huk organization.

Women in the Huk movement were often subjected to abuse and harbored feelings of helplessness. Some were coerced to serve the sexual needs of male cadres, while others were forced to marry to protect themselves from predatory fellow guerrillas. The revolutionary sexual policy failed to alleviate this situation by not taking into consideration women's needs and feelings about entering into extramarital liaisons. A Huk man was allowed to unilaterally discontinue his relationship with his wife—just by informing her of his decision—and enter into another sexual relationship, usually with a young, single Huk woman. The male cadre was also given sole power to choose which woman he would stay with after the struggle. Despite the existence of the policy sexual problems persisted, leading to the common and publicized view of male Huks as sexual predators. Following the capture of Bill Pomeroy, for example, one newspaper report indicated that "discipline was deteriorating among the Huks" because of "sexual problems" brought about by the "the indulgence of immorality among party leaders."[43] A cadre in one confidential party document appealed to the leadership to do everything it could "to stop the spread of 'abnormal' opportunism of women."[44]

The party imposed harsh penalties on members found guilty of the "family problem." A certain Lieutenant Mabine was disarmed because he failed to report to his superiors when he left the camp to stay with his seriously ill wife. "I asked her permission to leave her to report to you," he wrote, "but she answered that even though she will die she will be happy as long as I am with her." Mabine pleaded, "Major, I have always followed your orders if not for some important circumstances. . . . [P]lease forgive me for all shortcomings." His letter ended with the request that his pistol be returned to him for if "something will happen, I will have nothing to use."[45] Pomeroy related a similar incident in *The Forest*:

A man volunteers to speak. When he rises we see he is unarmed. He is one who has "committed a weakness" and has been disarmed, and it is part of his punishment to stand before gatherings like this and to criticize himself. He recounts shamefacedly his failing: he has mishandled money of the movement. There is complete silence while he speaks and, when he sits down at last, no applause.[46]

Financial opportunism was always associated with the desires of the individual cadres to provide for their families. While the party sometimes tried to be sensitive to their needs, its policies regarding families were often rigid, and those believed to have placed their families before the revolution usually received harsh punishments.

Indeed, when the PKP intensified its commitment to a revolutionary confrontation with the Philippine state, and the government intensified its military operations against the Huks, women's position in the movement became even more difficult and contentious. As military discipline became harsher, the party began to use expulsion to maintain it. "Under the present revolutionary situation," the minutes of a Central Committee meeting held on July 22, 1950, declared, "all Party members, including rank and file, should obey party decisions and assignments, including abandoning their employment and transferring to other territories. . . . [T]hose who refuse to accept the assignment shall be expelled."[47] One party member who was found to have "low political maturity" was subjected to hard labor to reform his "incorrect ideology," and those who disobeyed party rules or committed grave offenses were removed from their positions or disarmed.[48] Repeated offenses resulted in severe punishment, sometimes even death.

According to Luis Taruc the leadership ordered several executions in the movement "in order to give teeth to Party discipline, create a precedent, and strike fear" in the hearts of its already suffering guerrillas.[49] It even imposed the death penalty on cadres who committed "minor errors," which were usually the result of family issues. Because of increased government counterinsurgency operations in the 1950s many parents and wives of Huks tried to persuade their loved ones to surrender. Some Huks in the movement, "toughened by Communist tactics and by years of fighting," instituted a test: those Huks asked by their relatives to surrender should prove their loyalty to the revolution by liquidating their relatives. Taruc himself testified to three cases in which this order was implemented. But according to Taruc there were other brutal executions:

> A young nurse named Lita asked permission to go home, to rest and recuperate and to get a new supply of clothes. She was suspected of planning to surrender and was "liquidated" on the orders of leaders. . . . A Huk women's organizer who was known as a nagger was liquidated by a fellow Huk, allegedly for suggesting that her husband surrender. But it seems that he had grown tired of her nagging and was then living with another woman. Her brother, a Huk commander, turned against the movement when he learned of the murder. . . . A minor error of an eighteen-year-old girl who was the number two of a cadre caused her death. She had committed her "crime" when she had fallen into the hands of government troops and was interrogated [and] she revealed the address where she slept when she visited a nearby *barrio*. The storeowner was not killed and there were no official repercussions of any sort. But still, she was shot without trial. . . . Executed with her was a platoon commander of the GHQ [General Headquarters] security force named Etti. He had fell ill one day and left his post, after appointing his assistant to take over. He was court-martialed, charged with dereliction of duty, and executed by a firing squad. . . . Half a dozen young boys were executed for similar "offenses."[50]

What is revealing about this list is the number of women who are doubly dismissed by both the movement and Taruc himself, described in disparaging terms such as "nagger" and "number two," who were executed for exhibiting such personal "weaknesses" as attempting to surrender, failing to withstand interrogation, or trying to protect their ties to husbands, families, and communities, the latter a form of disloyalty that was understood and condemned as distinctly feminine.

But what is most striking about these examples is the climate of misogyny and suspicion toward women that they reveal in a movement that, despite its difficulties integrating women in the past, had always accepted them. Taruc later attacked the party for heartless and unnecessary violence. Even veteran commanders who had served in the movement for years were executed on suspicion of spending paltry sums from party funds on their personal and familial needs.[51] But others disagreed. Bill Pomeroy, for example, disputed the idea that the Huk movement was a "movement of blood purges" and argued that leaders generally practiced restraint in imposing party discipline.[52] He supported the party's use of execution to punish violations such as theft and agreed with Casto Alejandrino, the vice commander of the Huks, who insisted that the leadership only did what was best for the movement. "We were under a battle situation," Alejandrino explained, "and you cannot have an army without military discipline. . . . [I]t is just like wanting to have an omelet without breaking the eggs. A group of men, armed men without discipline, is not an army; it is a mob."[53]

The imposition of military discipline, primarily for cases involving the personal and emotional lives of Huk members, had serious implications for the strength and solidarity of the movement and for women in particular. Not only did the movement lose many valuable cadres because of its strict adherence to military discipline, but it also inevitably alienated many of its male and female members and barrio supporters. Torn between devotion to the movement and their families, most guerrillas found it increasingly difficult to balance their personal and revolutionary lives. And the leadership, believing it alone could determine what was best for the movement, was unrelenting in both forcing its cadres to subordinate their personal desires and familial responsibilities and making sure that their failures did not go unpunished. Jeff Goodwin argues that the contradiction between the personal relations, or "libidinal ties," of Huk cadres and the high level of discipline expected of them created problems of solidarity in the movement, and he suggests, in agreement with party leaders, that perhaps the "male-dominated movement would have been more solidaristic had more of its cadres been libidinally unattached."[54] According to him, the high-risk nature of the Huk insurgency required libidinal withdrawal, a separation from friends and family, to ensure uncompromising devotion to the movement and, presumably, strategic success.

Goodwin's argument assumes a relatively static understanding of the movement and the process of Huk mobilization. As we have seen, during the early years of the Huk struggle—first against the Japanese and subsequently against the Philippine state—such a libidinally detached, male-dominated strategy would have been a recipe for disaster. The Huk resistance drew its greatest strength, as do most guerrilla armies, from its close relationship with barrio life in Central and Southern Luzon. Its success was a function of embeddedness, not detachment. By 1950-51 this situation had changed as the BCTs pursued an increasingly successful strategy of counterinsurgency in the barrios and the mountains. But it is not clear that even in this context a policy of militarized masculine solidarity made sense. Indeed, this was precisely the path the Huk leadership chose, and it led to failure.

The policy was profoundly unrealistic and at odds with the distinctive culture that had developed within the Huk movement. Separating the personal and political lives of the revolutionaries was an impossible task, especially given the central role that women and kinship relations had played in the development of the movement. The policy of detaching the guerrillas from friends and family and even pitting them against one another was not likely to succeed in a society in which the family was and remains the primary and most critical source of social relationships and personal identity. Huks were willing to sacrifice much for the movement, but few were able or willing to completely abandon their familial and personal loyalties. Forcing them to do so, and subjecting them to severe military discipline when they failed to acquiesce, undermined morale, destroyed the solidarity of the movement, and ultimately led to its permanent decline.

What the party leaders failed to grasp was that the personal and affective ties that they believed weakened the Huks were in fact a source of strength, literally rooting the movement in the peasant communities of the Luzon countryside. Indeed, it was the subsequent isolation of its members, and their growing separation from their family and community, that placed the movement on the defensive, and when the government declared all-out war on the Huks the movement was pushed deeper into its mountain retreats. Separation from families (and especially wives) in the villages created an embattled atmosphere in the Huk camps and fueled a sense of suspicion and distrust at just the moment when Huk cadres had nobody else to depend on but one another. And geographical and social isolation led to ever more intense personal relationships between men and women at just the moment when the male-dominated Huk leadership sought to regulate such relationships and subject them to more punitive party discipline. Such regulatory and disciplinary efforts proved detrimental to the well-being of the guerrillas and to the Huk movement as a whole.

The party and the predominantly male Huk membership also failed to recognize the importance of women and to fully integrate them into its ranks, especially the wives of party cadres and soldiers.[55] Advancing them to positions of political and military leadership would have greatly benefited the movement, but instead most Huk women remained in the camps, providing household support and sex or, to quote Sofia Logarta, to "make the [movement] more joyful."[56] Even after years of revolutionary work, many women still regarded themselves as the "weaker sex."[57] But women, and the issues of gender, sexuality, and family life their presence raised, were central to the revolutionary experience. Despite the expressly political goals propagated by the Huks, and their insistence on waging a primarily military and ideological struggle against the Philippine state and society, the participation of women forced them to take personal issues seriously. Revolutionary movements are not shaped purely by conventional political ideology but by the personal relationships and culture of their members, and it was the presence of women that forced the Huk leadership to confront personal and "women's" issues and issues of gender, sexuality, marriage, and family life. Their perception of these "problems" was often flawed, and so were their solutions. But nonetheless they grappled with them, and their efforts played an important role in the success and failure of the Huk movement. Putting women at the center of the story, in other words, not only enhances our understanding of this revolutionary movement but also alters the way we think about the history of the Huk rebellion.

The Unfinished Revolution

The Huk rebellion not only represented a political challenge to the Philippine government but it also attempted to alter the dominant social and gender culture of Philippine society. The Huks initially did this through the recruitment of female cadres. The whole process of mobilizing women for political involvement was unprecedented in Philippine history, especially since women, while they dominated the domestic sphere, usually assumed subordinate status to men in public and political life.[58] Although peasant women were central to the rural economy, they were often considered conservative, traditional, and deferential in their relationships with men. The Huk movement gave these peasant women an opportunity to engage in politics directly, giving them confidence in their ability to change their communities and society as a whole and to venture beyond their traditional social roles. The prominence of these so-called Amazons in newspapers and the public imagination helped shape the national debate about the proper role of the Filipina in society, challenging society's conventional views about what women should and should not do. However limited and compromised its efforts may have been, the Huk movement was determined to address the gender issue, perhaps for the first time in Philippine revolutionary history.

Five former Amazons leave the Pampanga provincial jail with their children. These women were freed "just a mere 15 minutes after they pleaded guilty and were convicted of illegal association." Their freedom, whose sweet taste was seen on the big smiles of these women, demonstrates how society can just as easily embrace (as well as repudiate) former guerrillas, especially repentant women and mothers, back to its fold. (*Manila Times*, mid-1950s; Courtesy of Rizal Library, Ateneo de Manila University)

In many ways the Huk movement subverted the existing social and gender inequities in Philippine society. The Huks promoted a social revolution, bringing together members of the middle class, professionals, intellectuals, peasants, and workers in support of causes such as land reform, equal rights, and social justice. The Huk organization also created a classless structure in which everyone in principle had an opportunity to influence the movement's decisions and actions. Male peasants, even those without a formal education, were able to assume leadership positions. Leaders and the rank and file were also equal in theory and enjoyed the same privileges and responsibilities.[59] Together Huk cadres promoted the virtues of brotherhood, equality, and compassion, setting themselves apart from ordinary Filipinos.[60] The Huk organization also attempted to promote a new morality and a new sexual and gender culture for its communist cadres, one that was flexible and eschewed bourgeois and Catholic values. Traditional marriages were altered, and while the Huks upheld the practice of monogamy they allowed for some flex-ibility within it. In marriage a man and woman swore loyalty to each other and the revolution in front of their comrades while married men were permitted to have relationships with female comrades. The for-mulation of party policies regarding sex, families, and children took into consideration a new morality and equality between the sexes.[61] "The Huk must be morally superior to his oppressors," Pomeroy stressed. "[A]n act of protest against corruption or tyranny is not enough . . . [for] all the rotten values of the old society must be repudiated and re-placed by living examples of the values of the new society."[62] The Huk movement attempted to institute such a revolution and bring about cul-tural as well as economic and political change in Philippine society.

But the process of "molding and producing new people" was often difficult, and it presented the Huk organization with enormous chal-lenges. In the course of the rebellion the Huks realized how difficult it was to realize these new ideals, and they often failed in their goals of transforming society's sexual and cultural norms. Although they advo-cated radical policies, the individual and collective experience of Huk women revealed how ingrained gender inequities and sexual divisions were in Philippine society and how they shaped the Huk movement. Luis Taruc often praised the "faithful" women in the barrios, who sup-plied "soldiers with cooked food, wrapped in banana leaves," yet he also expressed disappointment with his male comrades for expecting women to do traditional tasks. "Indicative of the attitude of our men was the fact that the women's organizations in the barrios insisted on washing and ironing their dirty clothes," he wrote, and "women set up special committees for this purpose."[63] Jesus Lava blamed such failings on the "feudal relations" that prevailed in the countryside and society in gen-eral. Women were simply not considered equal to men, and such atti-tudes were also commonplace among the Huk cadres themselves.[64] The treatment of women and the movement's approach to issues of gender, sexuality, and family indicated that the Huks in many ways failed to lib-erate themselves from the very cultural traditionalism that they were fighting against.

As a result, the movement's attempts to institute a new kind of mo-rality for its cadres fell short of expectations. Problems related to sex, family life, and the children of Huk guerrillas were treated as political issues, and the solutions they proposed often reinforced rather than rev-olutionized existing social norms. The party's revolutionary sexual pol-icy, for example, aimed to restrict unhealthy relations between men and women but also placed women at a disadvantage. The Huk wedding ceremonies also performed a function similar to that of marriages in the larger society—to legitimize the relationship between a man and a woman—and were intended to be big celebratory occasions where people meet to revivify the commitment of all celebrants.[65] Despite its stated aims, the Huk movement remained largely conventional in its morality and firmly male dominated. Celia Mariano was frustrated with the party's inability to transform the attitudes of its cadres:

> There is a tendency on the part of cadres to separate their Party life from their private lives. . . . This is essentially a carry-over from the conditions of bourgeois society, in which "working and living" are separate entities. That is why in the matter of sex morality, we have the spectacle of intellectually advanced cadres still clinging to feudal forms of relationships even if there is intellectual acceptance of the Marxist concept of equality between the sexes. More so is the feudal attitude toward the opposite sex prevalent among the rank and file.[66]

Celia constantly challenged the tendency of men within the Huk movement to subordinate social ties and personal issues to the economic and political goals of the revolution, and the tendency of the party to treat the emancipation of women as secondary to the larger struggle for national liberation and social justice.[67]

The internal social dynamics of the Huk movement, and especially the relationships between men and women, profoundly affected the outcome of the revolutionary struggle. While Huk women struggled to reconcile their personal desires for intimacy and family life with the impersonal aims of the revolution, Huk men navigated uneasily between the demands of matrimonial responsibility and what they referred to as "biological necessity." In practice, however, both sexes tended to default to more traditional gender roles and in so doing missed a unique chance to transform their revolutionary rhetoric into an even more revolutionary reality. Certainly there were important factors other than gender that weakened the movement: the imperial policies of the United States, the strength of the Philippine Armed Forces, class differences within the Huk movement, and the gradual alienation of rural and peasant supporters from the more urban and intellectual leadership of the movement. But none of these explanations pays sufficient attention to the problems created by the critical role that women played in the male-dominated Huk movement.

Looking back years later members of the movement wondered whether the party's relatively progressive approach to gender contributed to its eventual decline. Rather than making sex and kinship so key to recruitment and mobilization, they argued, might it not have been wiser to ignore or suppress the issues raised by women's involvement in the movement altogether, insisting on more puritanical relations between male and female cadres or even insisting on the traditional standard of an all-male military force? But, while the inclusion of women in the Huk Rebellion introduced unanticipated strains, within those very challenges lay latent opportunities. Although many women in the movement never really abandoned their traditional roles, others were transformed through the demands placed on them in the movement, finding within themselves wellsprings of political activism and creativity only partially tapped by the revolution's leadership. And collectively the role played by Huk women was vital, grounding the insurgency in the culture and community of its peasant supporters. When these ties were frayed by the further masculinization and militarization of the PKP and the Huk movement after 1950, the rebellion lost its popular basis of support and in some respects its rationale. At the broadest level the explication of the underutilized potential of women within this resistance movement suggests the importance, militarily and socially, of rising to and transcending the challenges posed by gender.

Incorporating gender—a concept that is fluid and constantly altered and negotiated—certainly complicates and deepens the history of the Huk rebellion. And if nothing else it retrieves the experiences of these remarkable women from historical neglect. Many of these women suffered greatly because of their involvement in the Huk struggle, losing their homes and livelihoods and in some cases losing their husbands and even their children. Afterward these women attempted to rebuild their lives, often by themselves or as single mothers. Yet it was hard to find a Huk woman who harbored regret.[68] Teofista Valerio, for example, spent ten years and a day in prison, where she learned to read and write (taught by Celia Mariano) and earned small sums doing laundry for soldiers and fellow inmates. When she was released her husband, Casto Alejandrino, remained in prison, incarcerated for another ten years, leaving Teofista to raise their only daughter alone. But she insisted many years later, "My consciousness, my views in life expanded because of my experiences." And, although she abandoned her political activism and declined when asked to become "the national president of the women's sector of the Communist Party" in order to raise her daughter, she never stopped being political. She explained:

> Until now, my thoughts are about society. . . . Until now, our way of life is still down. It's hard to govern [a country] that's in debt. All of us Filipinos, even our grandchildren, would have debts. I am seventy-one years old but what hasn't changed is how I think of our country. Our demand is, even if we can't have equality, then to alleviate the ones who are in a dire state — but that hasn't been realized.[69]

Like Teofista, Filomena Tolentino retained a clear political vision of Philippine society. Widowed early and left to raise her children by herself, she did not abandon politics and became a prominent feminist leader in the 1970s and 1980s, helping organize the Samahan ng Progresibong Kababaihan sa Pilipinas (Association of Progressive Women in the Philippines), or SPKP, even during the years of Martial Law.[70] She also helped establish a new women's organization, the Kapisanan ng Bagong Pilipina (Association of the New Filipina), or KaBaPa, which recruited former female veterans of the Hukbalahap. As its president she successfully raised the profile of women and women's issues in the PKP.[71]

Other women got involved in mainstream politics. In 1955 Elang Santa Ana ran as a Nacionalista Party (NP) candidate for the Municipal Council in her town of Talavera, Nueva Ecija, winning the election despite the fact that she had no campaign money and was closely identified with her husband, Federico Maclang, who was still in prison for his involvement with the Huks and the PKP.[72] Elang not only garnered the largest number of votes but also "became the first woman ever elected to a municipal office in Talavera's history."[73] In many ways the election served as the culmination of her lifetime involvement in local politics. Remedios Gomez, the famous Kumander Liwayway, became a leader among her former Huk comrades, serving with Luis Taruc on the Executive Committee of the Huk Veterans Organization. Although she temporarily left politics after her imprisonment and the death of her husband to care for her only son, when former comrades approached her to help them in the late 1980s she did not hesitate. Even in her seventies, Remedios frequently traveled between Manila and Pampanga to help former war veterans (and Huk rebels) lobby for pensions from the Philippine government. For more than twenty years she met with these veterans, filled out the necessary official forms for them, submitted them to the appropriate government agency, and followed up without receiving any type of remuneration.[74] She constantly laments the current state of the former Huk movement and its members—former leaders and comrades who stopped talking to each other and remained divided over issues in the past and the present and former guerrillas who despite their past sacrifices continued to be miserably poor and neglected. For Remedios helping her former comrades get their pensions was a logical continuation of her responsibilities as a Hukbalahap commander.[75]

Like Remedios, Rosenda Torres was often asked to speak to women in the nascent Philippine feminist movement of the 1970s and 1980s. The two women usually talked to female activists about their experiences as Huk guerrillas and addressed their concerns about the role of political, revolutionary women in Philippine society, belatedly receiving from these young feminists the recognition they never received from their contemporaries. Rosenda, who was one of the few highly educated women in the Huk movement, eventually became a professor at the Polytechnic University of the Philippines (PUP) but still considers having been a Huk her primary achievement. Like most prominent women in the movement, she was captured and imprisoned and even after her release suffered the stigma of being a former communist. Nonetheless she returned to school and became an academic, a writer and poet, establishing a literary group at PUP with her husband, the former Huk intellectual Cesario Torres, and publishing a journal, *Panday Lipi*. Rosenda credits most of her accomplishments to her experience and education in the Huk movement.[76]

For Celia Mariano, her years in the Huk struggle were the most memorable and difficult of her life. After spending ten years in prison separated from her husband, William Pomeroy, she went into exile in the United Kingdom.[77] Living in London gave her a sense of peace and freedom she never knew in the Philippines, and she used this to immerse herself in the international struggle for women's rights. In 1978 she joined the National Assembly of Women (NAW), a British women's organization that advocates full equality for women in all areas of public and private life. Echoing her days in the Huk movement, Celia also worked as an editor for NAW's journal, *SISTERS* (Sisters in Solidarity to End Racism and Sexism), and wrote about women's issues and struggles around the world. In the late 1970s she was invited to join the KaBaPa, priding herself on being part of a movement that by the 1990s claimed about twenty thousand members, including many of her former friends in the Hukbalahap and HMB. She always believed that the

KaBaPa was the "strongest, biggest and the most progressive women's organization in the Philippines" and saw its establishment and her own membership as bringing her involvement in women's issues full circle.[78]

Whatever its inadequacies, for women like Celia the Huk movement redefined their sense of place in Philippine society and history. In recruiting women to the revolutionary movement the Huks broke new ground, challenging the division between the personal and the political and making sexual and familial relationships a central part of the political and social debate inside the organization. While women sometimes felt ignored or undervalued, the experience and the political education they acquired transformed their sense of identity and their vision of transforming Philippine society. Haltingly and imperfectly, the Huks instituted what was just the beginning of a sexual and gender revolution that remains unfinished to this day.

Appendix 1

Politburo Exhibit I-38: "Marriage Contract"

TO WHOM IT MAY CONCERN:

That We, _____ and _____ of right ages, and the first a resident of barrio _____ municipality of _____ Province of _____, Philippines, agreed to all and everybody now present of the following:

That we swear the truth that we are the only very persons stated in this contract;

That it is deep in our mind, close in our heart, in our free will and a heartfelt happiness will be ours when we are married. No person can obstruct our marriage and that this is sworn by us that our parents have permitted us for this marriage;

That in the name of the People's Liberation Army and the rise of the Democratic People, we swear that we are not threatened, intimidated or forced to be married only to live as husband and wife and during our living we will not involve or prejudice anybody;

That during our living as husband and wife we will continue to be members of our organization and be with the rise of the Democratic People. We also swear that all will cooperate and our rise will continue up to the end as we know that this revolution has a purpose of liberating [and] giving progress to the tenants, laborers and the poor mass[es] and we as a part of the poor;

That we swear and promise during our livelihood, even if problems and misunderstanding may arise, we will arrange it with the organization [and] if that problem or misunderstanding cannot be settled by us or our parents we will always respect the decision of our organization of those problems and misunderstandings;

We swear that we will live together peacefully and avoid deceiving each other and we will try to make ourselves a model couple in our humble place and will show others that we are a family who can guide our children, who in the future will be citizen[s] of our land; and

That we aknowledge [*sic*] and respect the decision and rules in our present situation and will always respect that decision because we know it is democratic and for the people.

As a truth of our statements in this document, we sign this voluntarily and through our own free will and nobody has threatened us this _____ of _____, at barrio of _____, municipality of _____ Province of _____, Philippines.

_____

Signature of Husband   Signature of Wife
Age ____ years old.   Age ____ years old.

_____

Witness for Husband

_____

Witness for Wife

Translated into English from Visayan.

Appendix 2

Politburo Exhibit I-15: "The Revolutionary Solution of the Sex Problem"

I. Presentation of the Problem:

One of the difficult problems which has confronted the Party is the problem of formulating a revolutionary solution to the sex problem, which, because of its continueing [*sic*] recurrence, has already developed into a political question.

Before the last war, there was no sex problem within the Party, and although there were some cases involving abnormal sex relationships, such cases were isolated. The sex problem first projected itself during the Japanese fascist occupation of our country, when, for the first time, the Party had to engage in an armed struggle involving the abandonment of normal family lives by most of its cadres. For lack of a revolutionary orientation on this problem, the Party lost some valuable cadres who were ordered liquidated even for such flimsy cases of married men flirting with female cadres. On the other extremes [*sic*], some cadres were talented in sustaining all forms of abnormal sex relationships on the flimsy ground of "biological necessity." There were also cases where members were expelled from the Party simply because they justifiably no longer find happiness with their spouse and preferred the company of more revolutionary mates.

With the return of American imperialist peace and the resulting return of some modicum of normalcy in family life, the sex problem subsided. However, with the resumption of the armed struggle after the coming to power of the puppet Liberal Party in 1946, the sex problem again projected itself, until now it has developed into a political question of importance.

In order to present the problem correctly to permit a revolutionary solution, it is necessary to divorce it from individual pre-conceived notions of morality (feudal and capitalist), and view the problem from a completely dialectical materialism standpoint, with the interest of the revolution as the sole criterion, and with a view to laying the foundations of future communist sex morality.

It cannot be questioned that man and woman (revolutionaries or non-revolutionaries) are born with sex and emotional necessities lead to failing health and other form of abnormalities which affects adversely the efficiency and behaviour of those frustrated sexually or emotionally. However, it cannot be denied that sex desires can be sublimated, although it cannot be completely eliminated short of actual removal of the organs from which the desire is generated. It is also demonstrated scientifically that removal of such organs produce abnormal results not conducive to the full development of one's faculties. Finally, it must be observed that the excitement produced by being in the firing line intensifies sex appetites.

The above are undisputed facts of natural science. How, [to come to] the actual facts of social life and social attitudes. Because of the double standard of feudal and capitalist morality which is still dominant in our country, abnormal sex relationships of married man [*sic*] while frowned upon, are not as much condemned as abnormal sex relationships of married women. The religious, moral and social convictions of the majority of the masses consider monogamy as the correct man-woman relationship, although the capitalist relations of production do not permit full flowering of such relationship. Needless to say, it is only under a communist society of complete equality of men and women (politically, economically and socially) can real and complete monogamy exist and be observed without the necessity of sanctions other than communist ethics.

Who are the parties to an abnormal relationship which complicates the problem of sex? Aside from the married spouse who finds necessity for satisfaction of his or her biological and emotional necessities, there is his or her living spouse living apart, and the new mate entering into abnormal relations.

Finally, it must be recognized that the urge to enter into abnormal sex relations is motivated by varying considerations, foremost among which are the satisfaction of biological necessity and the satisfaction of emotional hunger. In all cases, it will be found that these two motivations co-exist but in varying proportions, with one dominant over the other.

II. Revolutionary Solution of the Problem:

Before we can arrive at a revolutionary solution to the problem as presented above it is first necessary to arrive at the correct criterion by which to judge cases of such abnormal sex relationships. While we must consider individual justice to all parties concerned in the relationships and the attitudes of surrounding masses, the decisive criterion should be none other than the over-all interest of the revolution.

The question [brings with] itself: who and how is the over-all interest of the revolution to be determined?

This brings us to the correct organizational procedure in such determination. It must at once be recognized that circumstances will vary in each individual case, that it is impossible in any single document, however comprehensive, to anticipate all situations and thereby provide a revolutionary solution to each individual case. The over-all interest of the revolution is a composite of many factors which can be determined only by actual knowledge of all the facts surrounding each individual case. Consequently, the correct organ to determine the over-all interest of the revolution involved in cases of abnormal sex relationships is none other than the organ to which the frustrated cadre belongs, subject only to review by the next higher organ to avoid possibilities of personal friendships and resentment from being decisive in the determination of the over-all interest of the revolution.

In view of the above, the SEC promulgates the following rules of procedure in the determination of the over-all interest of the revolution, which sanctions married (male and female) to enter into abnormal sex relationships with members of the opposite sex:

1. The frustrated cadre should present his or her problem to the organ to which he/she belongs for a complete examination of all the surrounding facts. The burden of the presentation of facts is on the cadre presenting the problem. The other members of the organ should question the cadre concerned on the facts which he presented to convince themselves that lies, rationalizations and exaggerations should not pass for facts. If necessary, the other members of the organ can make their own investigations outside of the organ. Investigation from his or her spouse in order to enter into a new normal relationship. All facts presented and findings of facts by the organ concerned should be reduced to writing and transmitted to the next higher organ.

2. The following facts should be inquired into: effect of sex or emotional frustration on the health and efficiency of the cadre; possibilities of sublimating sex or emotional desire which will make unnecessary the entering into abnormal sex relationships, without adversely affecting his/her health and efficiency; possibilities of malingering by the frustrated cadre to convince the members of the organ of the adverse effects of sex or emotional frustration; possibilities of keeping the abnormal relationship within a limited circle; in case the abnormal relationship cannot avoid looking to wider circles, the probable effects of such knowledge on them as far as the participation in the revolution is concerned, and as far as their own sex behaviour in cases where the spouse of the cadre concerned is also a Party member or even not a Party member, possibilities of their living together.

3. The organ concerned shall make its own findings of fact, summarize the advantages and disadvantages to the revolution of permitting the frustrated cadre to enter into abnormal sex relationship, and formulate its concrete recommendations to the next higher organ.

4. The next higher organ shall make its own investigation if it is not satisfied with the findings of facts by the lower organ. Even if it is satisfied with the lower organ's findings of facts, it shall review the summary of advantages and disadvantages to the revolution of granting such permission as well as the concrete recommendations.

5. Only after the higher organ has given final approval to the permission to enter into abnormal sex relationship can the cadre concerned be justified to begin the implementation of such permission.

Any overt act implementing abnormal sex relationships before final approval is granted by the higher organ should be criticized and punished, based on the gravity of the offenses.

6. After approval of the higher organ is obtained, the cadre and organ concerned should see to it that the whole truth about the civil status of the frustrated cadre is known to the proposed new mate; and where the frustrated cadre has no intention to separate from his or her spouse, such fact must be told to the proposed new mate. Where the frustrated cadre does not propose to separate from his or her spouse, the Party shall not consider the new relationship as one of husband and wife and the parties to the new relationship shall have no right to claim such relationship of husband and wife.

7. Where the frustrated cadre requests separation from his or her spouse in order to enter into a new normal relationship of husband and wife, both the organ concerned and the higher organ shall investigate the spouse to determine the truth of the statements of the frustrated cadre. The following shall be considered justifiable grounds for separations: positive hostility to the revolution; positive hindrance to the activities of the cadre concerned; unjustifiable refusal of the spouse to join the cadre concerned so they can live together; and marital disloyalty of spouse to the cadre concerned.

8. In cases where permission has been granted to a married cadre to enter into abnormal relationship with the opposite sex, without separation from the spouse, it is incumbent upon the new mates to see to it that their abnormal relationship does not bear any fruit which will only further complicate the problem. For this purpose, it is their duty to master the techniques of birth control.

9. In no case shall permission be granted to any cadre to enter into more than one abnormal sex relationship, at any single time.

SEC [Secretariat]

9/12/50

Notes

Introduction

1. Teodosio Lansang, "Exclusive Interview with 'Liwayway' Huk Commander," *Truth Magazine*, August 1 and August 14, 1947.

2. Ibid., 11.

3. Ibid., 14.

4. Ibid., 15.

5. "Woman Huk Commander Facing Trial for Sedition, Rebellion," *Manila Times*, August 7, 1947; "Habeas Corpus Writ for Huk Girl," *Manila Times*, October 27, 1947.

6. Lansang, "Exclusive Interview," 12.

7. "Huk Leader's Top Contact Is Arrested," *Manila Times*, September 9, 1950.

8. Ibid., 6.

9. "Alejandrino Wife to Face Charges," *Daily Mirror*, September 9, 1950.

10. See Eduardo Lachica, *Huk: Philippine Agrarian Society in Revolt*; and Alfred Saulo, *Communism in the Philippines: An Introduction*.

11. For an authoritative treatment of the rise and fall of the Huks, see Benedict Kerkvliet, *The Huk Rebellion: A Study of Peasant Revolt in the Philippines*.

12. Ibid., 174–78; see also Politburo Exhibit O-180-253, "Milestones in the History of the Communist Party of the Philippines," by Gregorio Santayana [Jose Lava], n.d.

13. For more information on the success of U.S. counterinsurgency measures against the Huks, see Daniel B. Schirmer and Stephen Shalom, *The Philippines Reader: A History of Colonialism, Neocolonialism, Dictatorship, and Resistance*, 105–23.

14. Jesus Lava, interview with the author, Mandaluyong City, Manila, November 1993. Unfortunately there is no official record of the actual number of women directly involved in the Hukbalahap and HMB movements. But based on my interviews and conversations with former Huk men and women, the massive amount of coverage of "Amazon" captures in newspapers, and the considerable attention the Huk leadership paid to issues related to gender and family, I think 10 percent is the lowest possible estimate of the female composition of the Huk movement.

15. For feminist historical works, see, for example, Joan Scott, *Gender and the Politics of History*; Jane Atkinson and Shelly Errington, eds., *Power and Difference: Gender in Island Southeast Asia*; Louise Tilly and Joan Scott, *Women, Work, and Family*; Micaela di Leonardo, ed., *Gender at the Crossroads of Knowledge: Feminist Anthropology in the Postmodern Era*; Guida West and Rhoda Lois Blumberg, eds., *Women and Social Protest*; and Cynthia Enloe, *Does Khaki Become You? The Militarization of Women's Lives*.

16. Barbara Watson Andaya, "Studying Women and Gender in Southeast Asia."

17. Doug McAdam, "Gender as Mediator of the Activist Experience: The Case of Freedom Summer."

18. Since women in most societies face structural and cultural constraints in political participation, it is a puzzle how they are recruited to high-risk social movements. In his study of the students who participated in the Mississippi Freedom Summer project, Doug McAdam explains that gender—the elaborate belief system about maleness and femaleness that is encoded in social structures—affected the level of involvement of men and women. Women faced much greater opposition to their participation than males did, and many were intimidated during their recruitment interviews. Those who did make it to Mississippi experienced varied forms of discrimination (ibid., 1212–25).

19. Christina Kelley Gilmartin, *Engendering the Chinese Revolution: Radical Women, Communist Politics, and Mass Movements in the 1920s*.

20. McAdam, "Gender as Mediator of the Activist Experience," 1213.

21. Gilmartin, *Engendering the Chinese Revolution*, 2.

22. Joan Scott, "Gender: A Useful Category of Historical Analysis," 50.

23. Scott, *Gender and the Politics of History*, 2–3.

24. Recent works on women and revolution include Karen Kampwirth, *Women and Guerrilla Movements*; Christina K. Gilmartin, *Engendering the Chinese Revolution*; Helen P. Young, *Choosing Revolution: Chinese Women Soldiers on the Long March*; Mary Ann Tetrault, ed., *Women and Revolution in Africa, Asia, and the New World*; Sandra Taylor, *Vietnamese Women at War*; and Karen Turner with Phan Thanh Hao, *Even the Women Must Fight: Memories of War from North Vietnam*.

25. See, for example, West and Blumberg, *Women and Social Protest*; Ruth Howe and Michael Stevenson, *Women and the Use of Military Force*; Sonia Kruks, Rayna Rapp, and Marilyn Young, eds., *Promissory Notes: Women in the Transition to Socialism*; Enloe, *Does Khaki Become You?*; and Eva Isaksson, *Women and the Military System*.

26. Recent volumes on collective action, including Sidney Tarrow, *Power in Movement: Social Movements, Collective Action, and Politics,* and Doug McAdam, Charles Tilly, and Sidney Tarrow, *Dynamics of Contention,* still reflect the political-structural bias in social movement research but recognize the influential role of cultural forces, including gender, in collective action. Other recent works, including Ronald Aminzade et al., *Silence and Voice in the Study of*

Contentious Politics, and Jeff Goodwin, James Jasper, and Francesca Poletta, eds., *Passionate Politics: Emotions and Social Movements*, seek to bring back "emotion" in social movements to address earlier gaps in collective action research.

27. See especially Kerkvliet, *Huk Rebellion*; Lachica, *Huk*; Saulo, *Communism in the Philippines*; and Alvin Scaff, *The Philippine Answer to Communism*. More recent works include Teresita Maceda, *Mga Tinig Mula Sa Ibaba: Kasaysayan ng Partido Komunista ng Pilipinas at Partido Sosialista ng Pilipinas sa Awit, 1930-1955* (*Voices from Below: A History of the Communist Party and Socialist Party through Song, 1930-1955*); Jose Dalisay Jr., "The Lava Brothers: Blood and Politics"; and Jose Dalisay Jr., *The Lavas: A Filipino Family*. Jeff Goodwin explores issues of sexuality and solidarity in a more recent article, "The Libidinal Constitution of a High-Risk Social Movement: Affectual Ties and Solidarity in the Huk Rebellion, 1946-1954."

28. The peasantry in various historical and cultural contexts has been the focus of Western historiography on revolutions since the 1960s. Many scholars have explored how and why peasants became participants in major revolutions and rebellions in the twentieth century. They were the victims of the modernization process when their traditional roles and relations in society were radically altered. They had the most to lose when the extension of market relationships was carried out to replace subsistence farming. And they were the least protected when the state—colonial and national—decided to engage in technological innovation and effective administration. Historians and social scientists have explored the kinds of social structures and historical situations that produced peasant rebellions, such as the Huk rebellion, in the twentieth century. But none of these works gave particular consideration to the issues of gender and sexuality in peasant revolutionary movements. For more in-depth studies on peasant rebellions, including the Huk movement, see Harry J. Benda, "Peasant Movements in Colonial Southeast Asia"; Michael Adas, *Prophets of Rebellion: Millenarian Protest against the European Colonial Order*; Michael Adas, "Bandits, Monks, and Pretender Kings: Patterns of Peasant Resistance and Protest in Colonial Burma, 1826-1941"; Theda Skocpol, "What Makes Peasants Revolutionary?"; Eric Hobsbawm, *Primitive Rebels: Studies in Archaic Forms of Social Movements in the 19th and 20th Centuries*; Benedict Kerkvliet and James C. Scott, eds., *Everyday Forms of Peasant Resistance in Southeast Asia*; Barrington Moore, *Social Origins of Democracy and Dictatorship*; Jeffrey Paige, *Agrarian Revolution: Social Movements and Export Agriculture in the Underdeveloped World*; James C. Scott, *The Moral Economy of the Peasant: Rebellion and Subsistence in Southeast Asia*; James C. Scott, *Weapons of the Weak: Everyday Forms of Peasant Resistance*; Eric Wolf, *Peasant Wars of the Twentieth Century*; John Walton, *Reluctant Rebels: Comparative Studies of Revolution and Underdevelopment*; and Hue-Tam Ho Tai, *Millenarianism and Peasant Politics in Vietnam*.

29. And yet several studies on women in revolutionary movements, especially in the so-called Third World, have demonstrated the overwhelming

participation of peasant women. In her study of women involved in guerrilla struggles in Latin America, *Women and Guerrilla Movements,* Karen Kampwirth made similar observations about both the conservatism of peasant women and their willingness to join revolutionary struggles.

30. Mina Roces, "Is the Suffragist an American Colonial Construct? Defining 'the Filipino Woman' in Colonial Philippines."

31. See Joan Landes, "Marxism and the 'Woman Question.'"

32. Politburo Exhibit I-15, "The Revolutionary Solution of the Sex Problem," September 12, 1950.

33. Politburo Exhibit O-757, "Finance Opportunism: Its Basic Causes and Remedies," October 10, 1950.

34. William Pomeroy, *The Forest: A Personal Record of the Huk Guerrilla Struggle in the Philippines*; Luis Taruc, *Born of the People*; Luis Taruc, *He Who Rides the Tiger*; Dalisay, *The Lavas*; Jesus Lava, *Memoirs of a Communist.* Taruc's first book was probably largely written by William Pomeroy, but Taruc always claimed it as his own autobiography, and a faithful reflection of his own views and experiences.

35. Although it is limited, there has been some significant scholarship on women in the postwar Philippines in recent years. Most of these works discuss Filipina women during the Martial Law and post–Martial Law period from the 1970s onward. There are few full-length studies of women in the Philippines in the immediate postwar period. See for example the works of Mina Roces, especially *Women, Power, and Kinship Politics: Female Power in Post-war Philippines.*

36. Shulamit Reinharz, with assistance from Lynn Davidman, *Feminist Methods in Social Research.*

37. Janet Hart, *New Voices in the Nation: Women and the Greek Resistance, 1941–1964.*

38. Alessandro Portelli, *The Death of Luigi Trastulli and Other Stories: Form and Meaning in Oral History,* 50. See also Barbara Allen and William Lynwood Montell, *From Memory to History: Using Oral Sources in Local Historical Research*; and Paul Thompson, *The Voice of the Past: Oral History.*

39. Agnes Khoo, *Life as the River Flows: Women in the Malayan Anticolonial Struggle.*

40. Sheila Rowbotham, *Hidden from History: Rediscovering Women in History from the 17th Century to the Present.*

41. I conducted interviews mostly in Manila and the province of Pampanga in Central Luzon. Since I wanted to compile a comprehensive account of the revolt, I also covered different areas in the region, including Tarlac, Bulacan, Nueva Ecija, Laguna, Batangas, and Quezon (formerly Tayabas).

42. Although the interviews were conducted in Tagalog, I use my own English translations of them when I quote the women in this book. It is difficult to convey in English the exact meanings of the words used by the women, but I have tried to be faithful to them, and some of the translations are literal.

43. Portelli, *Death of Luigi Trastulli*, 52.

44. I focused on major newspapers in the postwar Philippines, including the *Manila Times, Philippines Free Press, Daily Mirror,* and *Manila Chronicle.* These newspapers are readily available in Manila at the Rizal Library of Ateneo de Manila University and at the Lopez Library and Museum.

Chapter 1. Women at War

1. Filomena Tolentino, interview with the author, Floridablanca, Pampanga, October 1993.

2. Elang Santa Ana-Maclang, interview with the author, San Ricardo, Talavera, Nueva Ecija, January 1994 and March 1997. See also Benedict Kerkvliet, "Manuela Santa Ana vda. de Maclang and Philippine Politics."

3. Central Luzon is comprised of the provinces of Pampanga, Bulacan, Tarlac, Nueva Ecija, Bataan, and Zambales. Southern Luzon includes the provinces of Cavite, Laguna, Batangas, Rizal, and Quezon (formerly Tayabas).

4. According to Marshall McLennan, the first decades of the twentieth century produced significant transformations in the Central Luzon region, which included the construction of elaborate roads and irrigation systems to develop agriculture. But by the end of the nineteenth century, with the closing of the frontier, land became a valuable and limited resource and Central Luzon's villages began to suffer from a surplus of labor. While the amount of arable land remained constant, the population increased from 717,000 to over 1.3 million between 1903 and 1939. Both the landowners and the peasants became desperate for land. See Marshall S. McLennan, "Changing Human Ecology on the Central Luzon Plain: Nueva Ecija, 1705–1939."

5. Ibid., 79.

6. See ibid.; and Benedict Kerkvliet, *The Huk Rebellion: A Study of Peasant Revolt in the Philippines.*

7. Elena Sawit-Macapagal, interview with the author, Novaliches, Quezon City, September 1993.

8. Kerkvliet, *Huk Rebellion.*

9. Brian Fegan, "The Social History of a Central Luzon Barrio," 102.

10. Generoso Rivera and Robert McMillan, *An Economic and Social Survey of Rural Households in Central Luzon,* 58.

11. Marshall S. McLennan, "Land and Tenancy in Central Luzon Plain," 680. The discrepancy in land arrangements was also reflected in the *Census of the Philippine Islands,* 1939, vol. 2.

12. Obtaining land by fraudulent means includes producing false titles and forging the signatures of illiterate farmers in loan documents. See Fegan, "Social History of a Central Luzon Barrio," 102.

13. Peasants became increasingly alienated under this system. Even though it was they who grew, harvested, and milled the rice and cane, they did not

have enough rice to sell and had to borrow money for food. Kerkvliet, *Huk Rebellion*, 20.

14. Rivera and McMillan, *Economic and Social Survey*, 62.

15. According to Kerkvliet, landlords also "extracted more from the peasantry, gave less in return, and passed down to their tenants and laborers losses they encountered." Kerkvliet, *Huk Rebellion*, 21–25.

16. Rivera and McMillan conclude that the family is the strongest and most important social institution in the Philippines; it is the center of society, "with economic life, religion, government, education, health, recreation, and other major life activities largely dependent upon, and subordinate to, its strengths and weaknesses." Rivera and McMillan, *Economic and Social Survey*, 125.

17. Donn Hart, *Compradinazgo: Ritual Kinship in the Philippines*; Robert J. Morais, *Social Relations in a Philippine Town*.

18. Jeff Goodwin, "The Libidinal Constitution of a High-Risk Social Movement: Affectual Ties and Solidarity in the Huk Rebellion, 1946–1954."

19. These values shape the relationships within real and ritual kinship groups. Mina Roces explains that "a Filipino is expected to be aware of his or her *utang na loob* obligations and although repayment cannot be measured, he or she should always attempt to repay it. Failure to fulfill one's *utang na loob* . . . brings *hiya* . . . on the side of the guilty party. . . . Violation of social norms elicits a deep sense of shame, and to call a Filipino *walang hiya* (or shameless) is to wound him deeply." Mina Roces, *Women, Power, and Kinship Politics: Female Power in Post-war Philippines*, 11. Along with *pakikisama*, these values promote smooth relations within kin groups.

20. "Denying assistance to a kinsman," in a context of hardship, was viewed as "an offense against the moral standards of group relations—an insult to one's parents and a token of disrespect for the entire kin group." F. Landa Jocano, "Elements of Filipino Social Organization," 22; and Goodwin, "The Libidinal Constitution of a High-Risk Social Movement," 58. The claims of parents on their children were particularly formidable, and children were expected to care for their parents in old age. See Donn Hart, *Compradinazgo*; Morais, *Social Relations in a Philippine Town*; Jocano, "Elements of Filipino Social Organization"; Akira Takahashi, *Land and Peasants in Central Luzon: Socioeconomic Structure of a Philippine Village*; and Leela Dube, *Women and Kinship: Comparative Perspectives on Gender in South and Southeast Asia*.

21. Morais, *Social Relations in a Philippine Town*, 22.

22. Families related by kinship are closely interdependent in every aspect of social and economic life, including cooperative work in the form of plowing and harrowing fields, lending farm implements, giving food, offering land for use as seedbeds, and providing support in election campaigns. Families shared not only economic activities such as harvesting crops, building houses, constructing schools, and cleaning irrigation ditches but social activities such as caring for the sick, burying the dead, engaging in recreational activities, and

solving everyday problems. The family and community acted as a "bank, an insurance agency and a welfare organization," as all members engaged in a high degree of cooperation and mutual aid. Rivera and McMillan, *Economic and Social Survey*, 133.Girls and women in Central Luzon had strong ties not only to their parents but also to their siblings, grandparents, aunts, uncles, cousins, neighbors, and wider circles of kin, real and ritualistic. See Takahashi, *Land and Peasants*, 112; Rivera and McMillan, *Economic and Social Survey*, 133; and Goodwin, "The Libidinal Constitution of a High-Risk Social Movement," 58–59.

23. John Larkin, *The Pampangans: Colonial Society in a Philippine Province*, 306.

24. Fegan, "Social History of a Central Luzon Barrio," 102.

25. See Peter Stanley, *A Nation in the Making: The Philippines and the United States*; Norman Owen, ed., *Compadre Colonialism: Studies on the Philippines under American Rule*; and Ruby Paredes, ed., *Philippine Colonial Democracy*.

26. American government authorities leaned on the very Filipino "oligarchs" and "caciques" to meet the exigencies of colonial control and in the process restricted suffrage to the wealthy and educated while cultivating patron-client relations with them. Julian Go observes that "instead of imparting democratic values to the Filipinos, the Americans kept the existing Filipino elite in control, unwittingly taught them 'tactics of guile and manipulation [over the colonial apparatus],' and, in the end, perpetuated pre-existing sociopolitical hierarchies." Julian Go, "Introduction: Global Perspectives on the U.S. Colonial State in the Philippines," 14.

27. Since 1902 the presence of hundreds of workers in Manila had provided an opportunity for mobilization by competing labor organizations in the Philippines, and each one attempted to attract hundreds of militant workers. See Daniel Doeppers, *Manila, 1900–1941: Social Change in a Late Colonial Metropolis*. By the 1920s socialist ideas dominated the organized labor movement in Manila. See Alfredo Saulo, *Communism in the Philippines: An Introduction*, for an exhaustive treatment of the rise of the Communist Party of the Philippines.

28. The establishment of the KAP came after a struggle with other workers' groups in Manila. Crisanto Evangelista's leadership was threatened when conservative elements of the COF, led by Ruperto Cristobal and Isabelo Tejada, ousted him as secretary in 1928. He did not leave the COF but made plans to gain control of the federation and called for new radical measures, such as the establishment of a workers' party, to advocate for class struggle and "to wrest leadership of the 'masses' from the bourgeois, U.S. supported political parties." The showdown between the Evangelista faction and the conservatives at the May 1, 1929, convention resulted in what Saulo calls the "most serious and far-reaching split in the history of Philippine labor." At the convention Evangelista and his supporters walked out after unauthorized delegates were sent by Tejada's group to undermine Evangelista's agenda and leadership. Evangelista's new group then launched the KAP. Saulo, *Communism in the Philippines*, 16.

29. The Cry of the Balintawak was the first public call for independence from the Spanish regime by Filipino revolutionaries. In August 1896 leaders and members of the revolutionary movement Katipunan (Brotherhood) gathered in Balintawak, a suburb of Manila, where they wielded their weapons, tore up their *cedulas*, or residence certificates, and openly defied the Spanish.

30. Politburo Exhibit O-180-253, "Milestones in the History of the Communist Party of the Philippines," by Gregorio Santayana [Jose Lava], n.d.

31. Luis Taruc, *Born of the People*, 36; and Teresita Maceda, *Mga Tinig Mula Sa Ibaba: Kasaysayan ng Partido Komunista ng Pilipinas at Partido Sosialista ng Pilipinas sa Awit, 1930–1955* (Voices from Below: A History of the Communist Party and Socialist Party through Song, 1930–1955), 34.

32. Filomena Tolentino, interview with the author, October 1993.

33. Marcosa de la Rosa-Timban, interview with the author, Tondo, Manila, October 1993.

34. Ibid.

35. Taruc, *Born of the People*, 46.

36. This was the first public gathering of Communists after the increased repression experienced by the party since 1931. During that year permits for the public meetings and demonstrations were refused or canceled at the last minute and Communist leaders were placed under arrest for holding meetings. In 1933, during the annual convention of the KAP, the labor organization of the PKP, government agents intervened, arresting everybody and charging the leaders with illegal association. The courts in Manila declared both the PKP and KAP illegal and sentenced twenty Communist leaders, including Crisanto Evangelista, Jacinto Manahan, Guillermo Capadocia, and Mariano Balgos, to eight years and one day of *destierro* (banishment) to the provinces. In 1935 President Quezon enlisted the support of labor to respond to the international call for a united front against fascism. Through the intervention of James S. Allen, a high official of the Communist Party of the United States, the president pardoned and released Evangelista and other Communist leaders on December 31, 1936. Both Quezon's government and the Communists agreed, at least in principle, to combat the growing menace of fascism. The PKP continued to hold public meetings and demonstrations with the primary purpose of forming a real united front. See James Allen, *The Philippine Left on the Eve of World War II*; and Saulo, *Communism in the Philippines*, 5–15.

37. Kerkvliet states that the AMT claimed seventy thousand members and the KPMP sixty thousand. Kerkvliet, *Huk Rebellion*, 45.

38. Marcosa de la Rosa-Timban, interview with the author, October 1993.

39. Harry J. Benda, "The Japanese Interregnum in Southeast Asia," 65–79.

40. Ibid., 70–72.

41. Teodoro Agoncillo, *The Fateful Years: Japan's Adventure in the Philippines, 1941–45*, 66–67.

42. Ikehata Setsuho, "The Japanese Occupation Period in Philippine History," 1–5.

43. Agoncillo, *Fateful Years*, 67.

44. Ibid., 67–78.

45. President Quezon and his vice president, Sergio Osmeña, established a Commonwealth government in exile with headquarters in Washington, DC. Quezon hoped to take the reins of an independent Philippine Republic when the war was over. Tragically, he suffered from tuberculosis and died in New York before the war's end. See ibid.; and Ikehata Setsuho and Ricardo Jose, eds., *The Philippines under Japan: Occupation Policy and Reaction*.

46. Agoncillo, *Fateful Years*, chaps. 7–8. For a brief background discussion and dramatic photographs of the beginning of the Japanese Occupation, see Ricardo Jose and Lydia Yu-Jose, *The Japanese Occupation of the Philippines: A Pictorial History*.

47. The Japanese military government established control in almost all the colonial territories in Southeast Asia, paralyzing the British in Malaya, Burma, and Thailand and the Dutch in present-day Indonesia. It granted limited powers to the Vichy-controlled regime in French Indochina. See Alfred W. McCoy, ed., *Southeast Asia under Japanese Occupation*; Milton Osborne, *Region of Revolt: Focus on Southeast Asia*; and Milton Osborne, *Southeast Asia: An Introductory History*.

48. Ma. Felisa A. Syjuco, *The Kempei Tai in the Philippines, 1941–1945*.

49. Ikehata and Jose, *Philippines under Japan*, 39 and 277.

50. Syjuco, *Kempai Tai*, 24

51. Motoe Terami-Wada, "The Filipino Volunteer Armies," in Ikehata and Jose, *Philippines under Japan*, 59–98; Kerkvliet, *Huk Rebellion*, 65.

52. Ikehata, "Japanese Occupation Period," 1–2.

53. Agoncillo, *Fateful Years*, 67.

54. Kerkvliet, *Huk Rebellion*, 62.

55. The infamous Bataan Death March occurred soon after the Japanese occupied Manila. With the surrender of the American and Filipino troops Japan completed its occupation of the Philippines. Accounts of the occupation always include a description of the march. See Teodoro Agoncillo's works, including *Fateful Years* and "Bataan and Corregidor Revisited." Many personal accounts, mostly by American soldiers, have been published in recent years. See William E. Dyess, *Bataan Death March: A Survivor's Account*; Lester Tenney, *My Hitch in Hell: the Bataan Death March*; Donald Knox, *Death March: The Survivors of Bataan*; and Corban K. Alabado, *Bataan, Death March, Capas: A Tale of Japanese Cruelty and American Injustice*.

56. The water cure torture was a common and effective form of punishment that was also used by the Americans against rebel Filipinos during the Philippine American War. See Paul Kramer's recent investigation of this form

of torture in "Water Cure: Debating Torture and Counter-insurgency a Century Ago."

57. Rosenda Torres, interview with the author, Santa Mesa, Manila, December 1993 and June 1997.

58. Filomena Tolentino, interview with the author, October 1993.

59. Felisa Cuyugan, interview with the author, San Fernando, Pampanga, November 1993.

60. During the interview Puring Bulatao described these events and her experiences during the war. She expressed a strong desire to have her account published. By using her account, which she wrote in almost perfect English, I am in a way giving her a space, however small, in the historical rendering of the occupation. Fort Santiago, referred to by Puring, was built during the Spanish colonial period and was used by the Japanese as a military prison where they tortured and imprisoned Filipinos. Puring Bulatao, interview with the author, Paco, Manila, October 1993.

61. Vicente Rafael examines the prominent role that rumor played in ordinary peoples' resistance and nationalism during World War II. According to him, ordinary Filipinos expressed their anticipation of liberation and nationhood by spreading rumors or gossip in Tagalog, the vernacular language, which provided them space within their discourse about the nation, empowered them, and effectively reversed societal hierarchy. See Vicente Rafael, "Anticipating Nationhood: Identification, Collaboration, and Rumor in Filipino Responses to Japan."

62. Ibid., 118.

63. Agoncillo, *Fateful Years*, 312.

64. See Rafael, "Anticipating Nationhood," 120.

65. Nakano Satoshi, "Appeasement and Coercion," 22.

66. This was an administrative policy that the Japanese promoted in most of its occupied territories in Southeast Asia. For the most part, Southeast Asians in countries such as Malaya and present-day Indonesia embraced this move. And because the Japanese administration exercised a looser rein than its Western predecessors had done the terms of reference left much of local society relatively uncontrolled. This fostered improvisation and vitality in contrast to the routinized, mechanized, highly controlled Western administrations. See Harry Benda, *The Crescent and the Rising Sun: Indonesian Islam under the Japanese Occupation*, chap. 1; Benda, "Japanese Interregnum in Southeast Asia," 65–79; Theodore Friend, *Blue Eyed Enemy: Japan against the West in Java and Luzon, 1942–1945*; and Grant Goodman, *Imperial Japan and Asia: A Reassessment*.

67. Such organizations were popular throughout Southeast Asia. The Japanese, in stark contrast to the Western powers' disregard of Southeast Asian religions, often brought rural and urban religious leaders together in mass meetings that took place under military control. Benda, "Japanese Interregnum in Southeast Asia," 69.

68. For works on the cultural propaganda activities of the Japanese in the Philippines, see Rafaelita Hilario-Soriano's dissertation "The Japanese Occupation of the Philippines with Special Reference to Japanese Propaganda, 1941–1945"; Marcelino Foronda Jr., *Cultural Life in the Philippines during the Japanese Occupation, 1942–1945*; and Motoe Terami-Wada's master's thesis, "The Cultural Front in the Philippines, 1942–1945: Japanese Propaganda and Filipino Resistance in Mass Media."

69. Felisa Cuyugan, interview with the author, November 1993.

70. Maxima San Pedro-Alcantara, interview with the author, San Ricardo, Talavera, Nueva Ecija, January 1994.

71. Luz del Castillo, interview with the author, Tandang Sora, Quezon City, December 1993.

72. And yet most of these stories proved to be real. The truth of Japanese soldiers raping women and forcing them into sexual slavery, for example, is already part of the narrative of World War II in the Pacific. Personal accounts of women who were raped or forced into prostitution by Japanese soldiers and became "sexual slaves" or "comfort women" have surfaced in the Philippines. An autobiography by Maria Rosa Henson, *Comfort Woman: Slave of Destiny*, is the moving account of a girl who at age fifteen was abducted by the Japanese, raped, and later forced to become a comfort woman. Several testimonies are compiled in *War Crimes on Asian Women: Military Sexual Slavery by Japan during World War II—The Case of the Filipino Comfort Women*. These experiences were not unique to Filipinas. See George Hicks, *The Comfort Women: Japan's Brutal Regime of Enforced Prostitution in the Second World War*; Yuki Tanaka, *Japan's Comfort Women: Sexual Slavery and Prostitution during World War II and the U.S. Occupation*; Yoshimi Yoshiaki, *Comfort Women: Sexual Slavery in the Japanese Military during World War II*; Sangmie Choi Schellstede, ed., *Comfort Women Speak: Testimony by Sex Slaves of the Japanese Military*; Margaret Stetz and Bonnie B. C. Oh, eds., *Legacies of the Comfort Women of World War II*; and Chungmoo Choi, ed., *The Comfort Women: Colonialism, War, and Sex*.

73. Taruc, *Born of the People*, 65.

74. Kerkvliet, *Huk Rebellion*, 78.

75. Saulo, *Communism in the Philippines*, 30.

76. Other Communist leaders, including Guillermo Capadocia and Agapito del Rosario, were also arrested and suffered under the Japanese. See Eduardo Lachica, *Huk: Philippine Agrarian Society in Revolt*, 105; and Saulo, *Communism in the Philippines*, 177.

77. Taruc, *Born of the People*, 66.

78. According to Kerkvliet nearly all villagers in San Ricardo, Talavera, Nueva Ecija, agreed with this observation. Kerkvliet, *Huk Rebellion*, 65.

79. See, for example, ibid.; and Taruc, *Born of the People*.

80. Kerkvliet, *Huk Rebellion*, 98.

81. Saulo, *Communism in the Philippines*, 31; Kerkvliet, *Huk Rebellion*, 97.

82. Maceda, *Mga Tinig Mula sa Ibaba*, 120.

83. Saulo, *Communism in the Philippines*, 31; Maceda, *Mga Tinig Mula sa Ibaba*, 118.

84. While many PKP leaders, including Luis Taruc, Casto Alejandrino, Juan Feleo, and Mateo del Castillo, devoted themselves to the Hukbalahap, the party did not assume the leadership of the resistance in Central Luzon. Kerkvliet states, "Undoubtedly, some of them helped the Hukbalahap to become what it did. But it would be incorrect to say that these persons controlled the resistance in Central Luzon, as so much of its origins can be traced to local organizations and far more numerous were leaders who were not in the PKP." Kerkvliet, *Huk Rebellion*, 104.

85. Ibid., 67.

86. Ibid., 75, 94–95.

87. Ibid., 87.

88. William Pomeroy, letter to the author, March 15, 1999; William Pomeroy, *The Forest: A Personal Record of the Huk Guerilla Struggle in the Philippines*, 26.

89. Pomeroy, letter to the author, March 15, 1999.

90. Politburo documents reveal that there were no systematic plans to enlist women and train them as Huk soldiers.

91. Unfortunately, the number of women who formally joined the Hukbalahap was never officially recorded. In Central Luzon, especially, the majority of women residents were assumed to have been part of the support base.

92. Kerkvliet, *Huk Rebellion*, 94–95.

93. Maxima San Pedro-Alcantara, interview with the author, January 1994.

94. Teofista Valerio-Alejandrino, interview with the author, Santa Rita, Cabiao, Nueva Ecija, November 1993 and July 1997.

95. Avelina Santos, interview with the author, Mexico, Pampanga, October 1993.

96. Maria and Felicidad Angeles, interview with the author, Santa Rosa, Nueva Ecija, November 1993.

97. Candelaria Pangan, interview with the author, Santa Ana, Pampanga, October 1993.

98. Ibid.

99. Elang Santa Ana-Maclang, interview with the author, January 1994 and March 1997.

100. Ibid.

101. Puring Bulatao, interview with the author, October 1993.

102. Juana Fajardo, interview with the author, Santo Cristo, Gapan, Nueva Ecija, November 1993.

103. Cion Amorao, interview with the author, Cabiao, Nueva Ecija, July 1997.

104. Vicenta Lacanilao, interview with the author, San Miguel, Bulacan, May 1997.

105. Teofista Valerio-Alejandrino, interview with the author, November 1993 and July 1997.

106. Taruc, *Born of the People*, 67; Kerkvliet, *Huk Rebellion*, 86.

107. Much of the information about Mateo del Castillo was derived from Kerkvliet, *Huk Rebellion*, 50, 142.

108. Zenaida del Castillo, interview with the author, Laurel, Batangas, January 1994.

109. Ibid.

110. Ibid.

111. Luz del Castillo, interview with the author, December 1993.

112. Ibid.

113. Ibid.

114. Marcosa de la Rosa-Timban, interview with the author, October 1993; Kerkvliet, *Huk Rebellion*, 37.

115. Ibid.

116. Bella Simpauco, interview with the author, Project 4, Quezon City, October 1993.

117. Maria Manalang, interview with the author, San Simon, Pampanga, April 1997.

118. Vicenta Soliman, interview with the author, San Miguel, Bulacan, May 1997; Anita Laban-Laban, interview with the author, Kalayaan, Laguna, April 1997.

119. Araceli Mallari, interview with the author, Caloocan City, Manila, October 1993.

120. In her brief study of the role of women in the Huk movement, Sofia Logarta writes that none of the women she interviewed "joined the movement because of the influence of a husband." But this is a misleading statement as many women testified that they joined the Huks to be close to their husbands. Sofia Logarta, "The Participation of Women in the Huk Movement," 131.

121. Pasencia David, interview with the author, San Fernando, Pampanga, November 1993.

122. Felisa Cuyugan, interview with the author, November 1993.

123. Elena Gonzales, interview with the author, Mexico, Pampanga, October 1993.

124. Rosita Manuel-Liwanag, interview with the author, San Fernando, Pampanga, December 1993.

125. Ibid.

126. Leonila Sayco Gatus-Palo, interview with the author, San Fernando, Pampanga, October 1993.

127. Elena Sawit-Macapagal, interview with the author, September 1993.

128. Amparo and Belen Valerio, interview with the author, Santa Rita, Cabiao, Nueva Ecija, November 1993.

129. Ana Sula, interview with the author, Santa Ana, Pampanga, October 1993.

130. In Pampanga, ordinary members such as Filomena Tolentino not only knew Huk leaders such as Casto Alejandrino, Silvestre Liwanag, and Remedios Gomez but also neighbors such as Felisa Cuyugan, Viring Sese-Guas, Alejandra Silverio, and Pasencia David, who were Huk supporters. Elang Santa Ana, Maxima San Pedro, Marcela Simbulan, Servando Kaisip, and Rosalino Bacani were all from the village of San Ricardo, Talavera, Nueva Ecija, and all were members of the Hukbalahap. Teofista Valerio-Alejandrino knew not only her sisters but also her neighbors in Santa Rita, Cabiao, former Huk comrades such as Celia Reyes, Romana Sigwa, and Pablo Santos. In the nearby city of Cabanatuan, Teofista also knew Dominga Centeno, Felisa Pineda, Ruperta Risio, and Marcosa Cenan, who also joined the Huks. In Bulacan, Apolinario Lacanilao, Federico Cava, Maximino Gamboa, Vicenta Soliman, and Catalina Hernandez still see each other to talk about their Huk days.

131. Araceli Mallari, interview with the author, October 1993.

132. Taruc, *Born of the People*, 67.

133. Quoted in ibid., 68–69.

134. Women such as Luz del Castillo, Araceli Mallari, Narcisa Reyes, Ruperta Risio, Ana Sula, and Elang Santa Ana all attended the Forest School and were impressed with the seriousness of the Huk organization.

135. Araceli Mallari, interview with the author, October 1993.

136. Quoted in Taruc, *Born of the People*, 69–70.

137. Filomena Tolentino, interview with the author, October 1993.

138. Virginia Calma, interview with the author, Diliman, Quezon City, November 1993 and June 1997.

139. Women eventually engaged in combat. For a more thorough discussion of this see chapter 3.

140. Kapampangan is the most commonly spoken language in the province of Pampanga and Central Luzon, although almost everyone also spoke Tagalog. It is the language that forms the foundation of Filipino, the national language of the Philippines.

141. Rosenda Torres, interview with the author, December 1993 and June 1997.

142. Ibid.

143. Leonila Sayco Gatus-Palo, interview with the author, October 1993.

144. Virginia Calma, interview with the author, November 1993 and June 1997.

145. According to Kerkvliet, the newspaper *Katubusan*, which was only one or two pages in length, "praised the Hukbalahap's victories, lambasted fascism, the Japanese regime, and its Filipino 'puppets'; and hailed the approaching

American forces." But it remains unclear exactly how many articles reached Hukbalahap squadrons and Central Luzon villages. Unfortunately, most, if not all, issues of *Katubusan* have been destroyed. Kerkvliet, *Huk Rebellion*, 96.

146. Taruc, *Born of the People*, 119.

147. Godofredo Mallari, interview with the author, Caloocan City, Manila, October 1993.

148. Teofista Valerio-Alejandrino, interview with the author, November 1993 and July 1997.

149. Elang Santa Ana-Maclang, interview with the author, January 1994 and March 1997.

150. Taruc, *Born of the People*, 118.

151. Godofredo Mallari, interview with the author, October 1993.

152. Luz del Castillo, interview with the author, December 1993.

153. The lyrics I reproduce in this book were taken from Teresita Maceda's seminal work on the songs of the Communist and Socialist parties in the Philippines, *Mga Tinig Mula sa Ibaba*. Thanks to her we now have written versions of all of them in the original Tagalog and Kapampangan. Sheila Zamar and I translated the lyrics that appear in this book.

154. Ibid. The songs here appear in ibid., 114, 136, and 128.

155. Zenaida del Castillo, interview with the author, January 1994.

156. The zarzuela was brought to the Philippines by friars and settlers during Spanish colonization. Usually containing religious themes, the *sarswela* was adapted to Filipino cultural preferences and is considered an integral part of the nation's music. During the war the battle between good and evil, represented by Spanish Christians and Muslims during the Spanish period, was portrayed as a battle between the Japanese and the Huks.

157. Filomena Tolentino, interview with the author, October 1993.

158. Zenaida del Castillo, interview with the author, January 1994.

159. Taruc, *Born of the People*, 121.

160. Ibid.; Pomeroy, *The Forest*.

161. Leonila Monteverde, interview with the author, Mauban, Quezon, July 1997.

162. Lutgarda Gana, interview with the author, Anao, Mexico, Pampanga, November 1993.

163. Belen Valerio, interview with the author, November 1993.

164. Marcosa de la Rosa-Timban, interview with the author, October 1993.

165. Elena Sawit-Macapagal interview.

166. Belen Valerio, interview with the author, November 1993.

167. Amparo Valerio, interview with the author, November 1993.

168. Taruc, *Born of the People*, 121.

169. See ibid.; and Jesus Lava, interview with the author, Mandaluyong City, Manila, November 1993.

170. See Taruc, *Born of the People*; and Luis Taruc, *He Who Rides the Tiger: The Story of an Asian Guerrilla Leader*.

171. Prima Sobrevinas, interview with the author, Santa Cruz, Laguna, November 1993.

172. Maxima San Pedro-Alcantara, interview with the author, January 1994.

173. Rosita Manuel-Liwanag, interview with the author, December 1993.

174. Avelina Santos, interview with the author, October 1993.

175. Araceli Mallari, interview with the author, October 1993.

176. Jesus B. Lava, *Memoirs of a Communist*, 14.

177. Kerkvliet, *Huk Rebellion*, 104.

178. Jose and Jose, *Japanese Occupation of the Philippines*, 167.

179. Ikehata and Jose, *Philippines under Japan*, 18.

180. As early as 1942 the Japanese military established the Bureau of Constabulary as a way to arm the local population, and in 1943 it armed Neighborhood Association members with bamboo spears to be used exclusively for self-defense. But by the end of 1944 members of the BC and the associations were joining the guerrillas in significant numbers, forcing the Japanese authorities to disarm 80 percent of them. Throughout the war the Japanese treated the Huks with disdain, holding them responsible for their military failures and the barrios' lackluster support for the Japanese war effort. See Terami-Wada, "The Filipino Volunteer Armies," 73.

181. Kerkvliet, *Huk Rebellion*, 104.

182. Pomeroy, *The Forest*, 147.

183. Ibid., 147.

184. And yet, even in his praise for the Huk woman, Pomeroy's statement, "For the chance to contribute to her country more than just the act of giving it *sons*," could not mask the patriarchal notions he shared with other men in Philippine and Huk society. Like other men he seemed to think that producing "sons" who would become "citizens" was a more heroic task than producing daughters.

185. Filomena Tolentino, interview with the author, October 1993.

186. See David A. Snow, Louis A. Zurcher Jr., and Sheldon Ekland-Olson, "Social Networks and Social Movements: A Microstructural Approach to Differential Recruitment"; Doug McAdam, "Recruitment to High Risk Activism: The Case of Freedom Summer"; and, more recently, Mario Diani and Doug McAdam, eds., *Social Movements and Networks: Relational Approaches to Collective Action*.

187. McAdam, "Recruitment to High Risk Activism," 65.

188. I am using the term *high-risk social movement* after ibid., 64–90; and Goodwin, "The Libidinal Constitution of a High-Risk Social Movement," 54. Anne-Marie Hilsdon uses the term *low-intensity warfare* to refer to guerrilla movements such as that of the Huks and, more recently, the New People's

Army. See Anne-Marie Hilsdon, *Madonnas and Martyrs: Militarism and Violence in the Philippines,* 15.

189. Jacqueline Siapno defines *agency* as the "complex interplay of militancy, activism and piety," looking at the place of the sacred within the political and the political within the sacred. In other words, female agency is not necessarily limited to resistance, opposition, and militancy. It can also be found in activities that are not purely political such as participation in religious or kinship networks. See Jacqueline Siapno, *Gender, Islam, Nationalism, and the State in Aceh: The Paradox of Power, Co-optation, and Resistance.*

190. Logarta, "Participation of Women," 132.

191. Historical accounts of major revolutions in which women were major actors—such as the Chinese, Vietnamese, Nicaraguan, Mexican, and Kenyan revolutions—similarly point out the discrepancy between the roles of men and women guerrillas. In these movements female tasks were performed exclusively by women and distinguished from those of men. While these revolutionary movements recognized how crucial women were to the struggle, they still assigned them tasks such as cooking and washing and roles as couriers and secretaries. Rarely did women advance to leadership posts. For works on the role of women in other revolutionary movements, see Cora Ann Presley, *Kikuyu Women, the Mau Mau Rebellion, and Social Change in Kenya*; Luise White, "Separating Men from the Boys: Constructions of Gender, Sexuality, and Terrorism in Central Kenya, 1939–1959"; Margaret Randall, *Sandino's Daughters: Testimonies of Nicaraguan Women in Struggle*; Margaret Randall, *Sandino's Daughters Revisited: Feminism in Nicaragua*; and Judith Stacey, *Patriarchy and Socialist Revolution in China.*

192. Linda Reif, "Women in Latin American Guerilla Movements: A Comparative Perspective," 148.

193. Cynthia Enloe, *Does Khaki Become You? The Militarization of Women's Lives,* 11; Cynthia Enloe, *Maneuvers: The International Politics of Militarizing Women's Lives.*

194. Enloe, *Does Khaki Become You?* 160–61.

195. Reif, "Women in Latin American Guerilla Movements," 151.

196. Anne-Marie Hilsdon makes similar observations about women in the Philippine military and the New People's Army, the armed guerrilla movement under the new Communist Party of the Philippines (CPP) established in 1969. There were systematic efforts to exclude women from the Philippine military and relegate them to noncombatant roles in the NPA. See Hilsdon, *Madonnas and Martyrs.*

197. See Alfred W. McCoy, *Closer Than Brothers: Manhood at the Philippine Military Academy*; and Alfred W. McCoy, "'Same Banana': Hazing and Honor at the Philippine Military Academy."

198. Florencia Mallon, *Peasant and Nation: The Making of Postcolonial Mexico and Peru.*

199. Hilsdon, *Madonnas and Martyrs*, 79.
200. Enloe, *Does Khaki Become You?* 13.
201. Nancy Gallagher, "The Gender Gap in Popular Attitudes toward the Use of Force," 34.
202. See, for example, Micaela di Leonardo, *Gender at the Crossroads of Knowledge: Feminist Anthropology in the Postmodern Era*; and Guida West and Rhoda Lois Blumberg, eds., *Women and Social Protest*.
203. See Elizabeth Eviota, *The Political Economy of Gender: Women and the Sexual Division of Labour in the Philippines*.
204. Hilsdon, *Madonnas and Martyrs*, 41.
205. Enloe, *Does Khaki Become You?* 160.
206. Ibid., 123.
207. Eileen Findlay, *Breaking Bounds: The Brigadas Femeninas of the Cristero Rebellion*.
208. Jeanne Frances Illo calls for a redefinition of the term *maybahay* (housewife), especially in reference to rural women. She argues that in the Philippine rural economy women engage in activities, often referred to as noneconomic or nonproductive, that do not earn a wage or directly yield a profit. Her research in a fishing village in Luzon, however, demonstrates that for rural women economic and noneconomic work are inseparable and being a *maybahay* means being a total worker, producing both goods and labor. Jeanne Frances Illo, "Redefining the *Maybahay* or Housewife: Reflections on the Nature of Women's Work in the Philippines."
209. Karen Gottschang Turner, with Phan Thanh Hao, *Even the Women Must Fight*, 137.
210. Ibid.
211. Ibid.
212. See Daniel B. Schirmer and Stephen Rosskamm Shalom, eds., *The Philippines Reader: A History of Colonialism, Neocolonialism, Dictatorship, and Resistance*, 69–70.
213. Marcosa de la Rosa-Timban, interview with the author, October 1993.
214. Luz del Castillo, interview with the author, December 1993.

Chapter 2. Comrades in Arms

1. This song is reproduced from Teresita Maceda's wonderful work on the songs of the Left in the Philippines, *Mga Tinig Mula sa Ibaba*, 153.
2. Most accounts of the Huks acknowledge the leadership role played by the Communist Party in the rebellion. Benedict Kerkvliet, however, argues that the party "did not cause the [peasant] unrest and rebellion. . . . They helped to shape it." I tend to agree with Kerkvliet that neither the party nor communism instigated the rebellion, but I believe it played a major role in the Huk struggle and that most, if not all, HMB leaders were also leaders of the

PKP. See Benedict Kerkvliet, *The Huk Rebellion: A Study of Peasant Revolt in the Philippines,* 262.

3. Ikehata Setsuho, "The Japanese Occupation Period in Philippine History," 18.

4. Ricardo Jose and Lydia Jose, *Japanese Occupation of the Philippines,* 221.

5. Ikehata, "Japanese Occupation Period," 18.

6. David Joel Steinberg, *The Philippines: A Singular and a Plural Place,* 103.

7. Filipino elite collaboration with the Japanese is probably one of the most important issues in postwar Philippine society and historiography. See Hernando Abaya, *Betrayal in the Philippines;* David Joel Steinberg, *Philippine Collaboration in World War II;* Teodoro A. Agoncillo, *The Burden of Proof: The Vargas-Laurel Collaboration Case;* and Mauro Garcia, ed., *Documents on the Japanese Occupation of the Philippines.*

8. See Steinberg, *Philippine Collaboration;* and Steinberg, *The Philippines.*

9. See Julian Go and Anne Foster, eds., *The American Colonial State in the Philippines.*

10. In order to receive postwar aid for rehabilitation the Filipino Congress approved the Bell Trade Act, which granted U.S. residents rights and privileges equal to those of Filipino citizens in exploiting natural resources and owning and operating public utility projects. Ikehata, "Japanese Occupation Period," 19.

11. See Kerkvliet, *Huk Rebellion,* 143–59; and Eduardo Lachica, *Huk: Philippine Agrarian Society in Revolt,* 121–25.

12. The real reasons for refusing to seat these representatives were apparently two. First, the Roxas administration and most congressmen and senators simply wanted DA representatives out of the way so they could secure majority support in Congress and disable the opposition. Second, these representatives strongly opposed the controversial Bell Trade Act. See Lachica, *Huk,* 120; and Kerkvliet, *Huk Rebellion,* 133–43.

13. Kerkvliet, *Huk Rebellion,* 153–54.

14. Alvin Scaff, *The Philippine Answer to Communism,* 28.

15. Recent works on the cold war focus on its role in the politics of postwar Southeast Asia, particularly the conflict in Vietnam and the third world in general. There is still no comprehensive book on the influence of cold war politics in Philippine postwar society, although recent books on Philippine politics contain treatments of the cold war period, including Patricio Abinales and Donna Amoroso, *State and Society in the Philippines;* and Eva-Lotta Hedman and John Sidel, *Philippine Politics and Society in the Twentieth Century: Colonial Legacies, Post-colonial Trajectories.*

16. Beginning in the 1920s several delegates from prominent labor organizations, including the future PKP secretary-general Crisanto Evangelista, had met with top-ranking communist leaders in Moscow and attended Lenin University, establishing a relationship with the international communist leadership in Russia. In succeeding years the PKP worked to gain admission to the

Communist International (Comintern) by advancing the role of the working-class party in the fight against American imperialism in the Philippines. In Moscow in 1935, during the launch of the worldwide United Front struggle against fascism, the Seventh World Congress approved the membership of the PKP in the Comintern. Ironically, the PKP was admitted on the recommendation of the Communist Party of the United States of America (CPUSA). See Alfredo Saulo, *Communism in the Philippines: An Introduction.*

17. Ibid., 51.

18. Department of National Defense, *Handbook on the Communist Party of the Philippines,* 74.

19. Mariano Balgos and Lazaro Cruz were the other members of the Politburo. Lachica, *Huk,* 123.

20. Ibid., 130.

21. Historical Commission, Partido Komunista ng Pilipinas, *Communism in the Philippines: The P.K.P., Book 1.* Benedict Kerkvliet states that the Huk rebellion was actually "another phase in the Central Luzon peasantry's prolonged struggle" to undermine the central role of the Communist Party in leading the revolution. He claims that the communist leaders did not cause the revolt nor did they inspire or control the peasant movement during the struggle. "True, some important peasant leaders were party members," he writes, "but they joined the rebellion and acted on behalf of the peasants in spite of the PKP, not because of it." Kerkvliet, *Huk Rebellion,* 167, 262.

22. See William Pomeroy, *The Forest: A Personal Record of the Huk Guerilla Struggle in the Philippines*; and Jesus Lava, *Memoirs of a Communist.*

23. Politburo Exhibit O-1035, "Military Discipline within the Party as a Supplement to Democratic Centralism," September 13, 1950; and Politburo Exhibit F-41, "Ang demokratikong centralismo," n.d. Laid down by Lenin, democratic centralism purportedly called for the election of leading party committees by the membership of the given party organization, regular reports by elected committees to the membership, execution of the decisions of higher committees by lower committees, rigid discipline within the party, subordination of the majority to the minority, and full initiative for lower organs as long as the courses of action taken conform to the policy decisions of the party. See also Department of National Defense, *Handbook on the Communist Party of the Philippines.*

24. Party discipline required members' total submission and obedience and was based on a belief that collectively the party always acted in the best interests of the movement. Freedom of discussion and criticism gave all party members the right to discuss and criticize vital issues and matters of policy in accordance with democratic procedures. Although it was probably less widely practiced, self-criticism was the process whereby party members revealed their shortcomings and defects in order to become better cadres. Through these rituals the party aimed to develop cadres who would support the Huk movement (and the party) in its efforts to lead the "masses" toward building a communist society.

Department of National Defense, *Handbook on the Communist Party,* 69; Politburo Exhibit A-90, "The Development of the Communist Party," Panay Organization Committee, n.d.

25. Politburo Exhibit G-3, "Huk Principles," n.d.

26. Since peasants tilled the land for the landlords' profit they were seeking what they believed was their due, not necessarily their own land, as Kerkvliet asserts, but a share of the profits and access to loans through improved relations with the landlords. See Kerkvliet, *Huk Rebellion,* 250–52.

27. Special Committee on Un-Filipino Activities, House of Representatives of the Republic of the Philippines, *Report on "Communism in the Philippines."*

28. Civil Affairs Office, Department of National Defense, *Report on Communism and the Serviceman.*

29. This sentiment is expressed in several sources, including Politburo documents of the PKP; personal accounts of and treatments by Politburo leaders themselves, particularly Luis Taruc, Jose Lava, and William Pomeroy; and government materials on communism in the Philippines.

30. Politburo Exhibit M-190, "Additional Political-Military Strategic Conceptions: Clarification of the Enlarged PB Conference Resolution," n.d. The party admitted that it failed to "clearly project to the masses the war aims of U.S. imperialism, so that when the Americans came [after World War II], they were hailed as liberators by the people, including even our own masses, instead of being considered as conquerors which they really were." Politburo Exhibit O-180-253, "Milestones in the History of the Communist Party of the Philippines," by Gregorio Santayana [Jose Lava], n.d.

31. William Pomeroy came to the Philippines in October 1944 with General Douglas MacArthur's forces in the Leyte invasion, moving in the course of the campaign from Leyte to Mindoro and then to Fort Stotsenberg, Clark Field, in Pampanga. Before reaching Pampanga, he became aware of the Hukbalahap. By then he was a member of a U.S. Army historical writing team, and therefore he had access to military intelligence reports that mentioned the Hukbalahap. As he was a member of the Communist Party of the United States, he closely identified with the Hukbalahap soldiers he met in the town of Arayat, which led to the idea of writing a book about conditions in Central Luzon. Pomeroy fell in love with the country and with a Huk guerrilla, Celia Mariano, whom he eventually married. He returned to the Philippines in 1947 to work as a freelance journalist, writing for American magazines and the *Philippines Free Press.* William Pomeroy, letter to the author, March 15, 1999. See also William Pomeroy, *The Forest.*

32. Pomeroy, *The Forest,* 21.

33. Ibid.

34. Ibid., 69.

35. Ibid., 70.

36. Like his followers, Luis Taruc was a farmer who did not complete his education and eventually became involved with the growing peasant radicalism in Pampanga. From 1936 on he worked full time for the peasant movement, attending meetings all over the province, participating in demonstrations and marches, and, most important, developing close relationships with other peasants. Pedro Abad Santos, founder of the Philippine Socialist Party, was the most influential figure in his political life, and it was because of him that Taruc joined the party. After the war, according to Taruc, the Huk veterans once again took to the hills together with disgruntled peasants to fight for justice for the poor, for a democratic government, and for greater freedom for the Philippines. See Luis Taruc, *Born of the People*; and Luis Taruc, *He Who Rides the Tiger*.

37. Jesus Lava, interview with the author, Mandaluyong City, Manila, November 1993. See also Lava, *Memoirs of a Communist*.

38. Kerkvliet wrote: "Many who in April had expected things to improve were rebelling by the next September, Why? The reason . . . was repression. Repression by itself did not cause the rebellion, but it pushed many people to believe they had no choice but to fight back with guns." Kerkvliet, *Huk Rebellion*, 143.

39. For personal memoirs of Huk leaders see Taruc, *Born of the People*; Taruc, *He Who Rides the Tiger*; and Pomeroy, *The Forest*. For more recent accounts see Lava, *Memoirs of a Communist*; and Jose Dalisay, *The Lavas: A Filipino Family*.

40. See especially Kerkvliet, *Huk Rebellion*; Saulo, *Communism in the Philippines*; Lachica, *Huk*; and Scaff, *Philippine Answer to Communism*.

41. Unfortunately, there is no existing record of exactly how many men and women were mobilized during the HMB period. Newspaper accounts of "Huk Amazons," however, contradict the notion that only a handful of women joined the HMB. While women did not join it as overwhelmingly as they had joined the Hukbalahap, many continued to support the movement indirectly in the villages of Central Luzon.

42. Araceli Mallari, interview with the author, Caloocan City, Manila, October 1993.

43. Avelina Santos, interview with the author, Mexico, Pampanga, October 1993.

44. Purificacion Bulatao, interview with the author, Quezon City, October 1993.

45. Amparo and Belen Valerio, interview with the author, Santa Rita, Cabiao, Nueva Ecija, November 1993.

46. Felisa Cuyugan, interview with the author, San Fernando, Pampanga, November 1993.

47. Ana Sula, interview with the author, Santa Ana, Pampanga, October 1993.

48. Leonila Sayco Gatus-Palo, interview with the author, San Fernando, Pampanga, October 1993.

49. Filomena Tolentino, interview with the author, Floridablanca, Pampanga, October 1993.

50. Elang Santa Ana-Maclang, interview with the author, San Ricardo, Talavera, Nueva Ecija, January 1994 and March 1997. According to Kerkvliet, Elang never joined the PKP "in part because she could not see herself living the regimented, single-purpose life that was expected of party members" but she allowed Federico to go about his revolutionary work. It would seem that this comment was made with the benefit of hindsight as Elang herself reiterated that during most of their young lives together she was unaware of Federico's party activities. See Benedict Kerkvliet, "Manuela Santa Ana vda. de Maclang and Philippine Politics."

51. Marcosa de la Rosa-Timban, interview with the author, Tondo, Manila, October 1993.

52. Ibid.

53. Luz del Castillo, interview with the author, Tandang Sora, Quezon City, December 1993.

54. Rosenda Torres, interview with the author, Santa Mesa, Manila, December 1993 and June 1997.

55. Virginia Calma, interview with the author, Diliman, Quezon City, December 1993 and August 1997.

56. Teofista Valerio-Alejandrino, interview with the author, Santa Rita, Cabiao, Nueva Ecija, November 1993 and July 1997.

57. Ibid.

58. Ibid.

59. Ibid.

60. Ibid. Teofista's articulate rendering of her motivations and those of the Huks set her apart from many former Hukbalahap women. Not only did she completely embrace the "official" story of HMB origins, as espoused by the PKP and the Huk leadership, but she also personalized and expressed them eloquently. Did she have complete trust in the Huks even then or did she have doubts? We may never have answers to these questions. Teofista may have chosen to believe in the genuineness of their motivations, especially after suffering defeat as an HMB guerrilla, including a ten-year imprisonment.

61. Zenaida del Castillo, interview with the author, Laurel, Batangas, January 1994.

62. Linda Ayala, interview with the author, Makati City, Manila, January 1994, and Mauban, Quezon, July 1997.

63. Belen Bagul-Bagul, interview with the author, Bulacan, November 1993.

64. Elena Sawit-Macapagal, interview with the author, Novaliches, Quezon City, September 1993. Her husband would eventually become the Communist Party's secretary-general in the 1980s.

65. Ibid.

66. Rosita Manuel-Liwanag, interview with the author, San Fernando, Pampanga, December 1993.

67. Gloria Aquino-Taruc, interview with the author, Diliman, Quezon City, July 1997.

68. Dominga Centeno, interview with the author, Cabanatuan, Nueva Ecija, November 1993.

69. For a more detailed discussion of the issue of married life and family, see chapter 4.

70. Luz del Castillo, interview with the author, December 1993.

71. Filomena Tolentino, interview with the author, October 1993.

72. Leonila Sayco Gatus-Palo, interview with the author, October 1993.

73. Janet Hart, *New Voices in the Nation: Women in the Greek Resistance, 1941–1964*, 242–44.

74. Kerkvliet, *Huk Rebellion*, 166–67.

75. Department of National Defense, *Handbook on the Communist Party*, 69–71.

76. "I, Tomasa Arnao," a Politburo document, stated, "In my own understanding and belief in the determination and purpose of the National Liberation Movement now existing in the Philippines and . . . the People's Liberation Army, that could give liberty, happiness, progress, and democratic peace to the true and loving Filipino people and mother Philippines, that is why in my own free will and without intimidation and threat, I am giving the possession to FC [Field Command] 2, RECO [Regional Command] 6 & 7 of HMB my one lot of land, situated in Barrio Bulay, as my donation and help to the National Liberation Movement." Politburo Exhibit I-40, "Contract between Tomasa Arnao and Santiago Apostol That Piece of Land Is Given as Donation and Help to the National Liberation Movement," September 1, 1950. The authenticity of this document is obviously in question. It is unusual for peasant women to write as fluently as Tomasa. It is also doubtful that written contracts such as this were ever produced during the rebellion. While I was unable to locate similar documents among the Politburo exhibits I examined, this contract seems indicative of the kind of support the Huks enjoyed, although mostly unwritten and unarticulated.

77. Leon Ty, "Nervous Peace in Nueva Ecija," *Philippines Free Press*, October 29, 1949.

78. Politburo Exhibit B, "Ang Partido Komunista (The Communist Party)," n.d., emphasis mine. It's quite interesting that "women" were included as one of the vices guerrillas should avoid. It demonstrates both the patriarchal and chivalrous values that guided Huk men. On the one hand, women are seen as a form of vice, and on the other hand, men are advised not to take advantage of women, but to respect them.

79. Felisa Cuyugan, interview with the author, November 1993.

80. Araceli Mallari, interview with the author, October 1993.

81. Marcosa de la Rosa-Timban, interview with the author, October 1993.

82. Rosenda Torres, interview with the author, December 1993 and June 1997.

83. Sofia Logarta, "The Participation of Women in the Huk Movement," 138.

84. Pomeroy, *The Forest*, 15–16.

85. Ibid., 15.

86. Rosita Manuel-Liwanag, interview with the author, December 1993.

87. Dominga Centeno, interview with the author, November 1993.

88. Belen Bagul-Bagul, interview with the author, November 1993.

89. Department of National Defense, *Handbook on the Communist Party*, 165.

90. See, especially, Anne-Marie Hilsdon, *Madonnas and Martyrs: Militarism and Violence in the Philippines*.

91. Department of National Defense, *Handbook on the Communist Party*, 167.

92. Linda Ayala, interview with the author, January 1994 and July 1997.

93. Ibid.

94. Unfortunately, I was not able to interview Illuminada Calonje, and thus, I am unable to provide more background information about her.

95. Politburo Exhibit M-1320–1321, "Letter to Luming from Enteng," June 8, 1949.

96. Politburo Exhibit M-171, "Letter to Ka Beria from Leo" (in Tagalog), April 6, 1950.

97. Department of National Defense, *Handbook on the Communist Party*, 165, emphasis mine. This language is revealing. The courier referred to in the English translation of the handbook is male even though women made up the majority of the couriers.

98. I have found no further information about these women. See ibid., 167, quoting a 1950 government report.

99. Rosita Manuel-Liwanag, interview with the author, December 1993.

100. Teofista Valerio-Alejandrino, interview with the author, November 1993 and July 1997.

101. The issue of identity has rarely been explored in the literature on the Huk rebellion, and yet identity construction is essential to understanding why men and women stay in social and revolutionary movements. Charles Tilly adds that collective identity represents shared meanings and experiences among socially embedded actors. This is especially true for people who join social and revolutionary movements in which participants articulate specific political identities and yet their individual identities are not erased. Identities, as Craig Calhoun reiterates, are "not static, preexisting conditions that can be seen as exerting causal influence on collective action; at both personal and collective labels" they are "changeable products of collective action." Craig Calhoun,

"The Problem of Identity in Collective Action." See also Charles Tilly, *Stories, Identities, and Political Change*; Charles Tilly, *Identities, Boundaries, and Social Ties*; and Charles Tilly, "Contentious Action."

102. In his seminal *Pasyon and Revolution: Popular Movements in the Philippines, 1840–1910*, Reynaldo Ileto looks at the popular ritual of the singing of the Passion of Christ to explore the revolutionary ideas of the "inarticulate masses." Teresita Maceda builds on this historiographical tradition in *Mga Tinig Mula sa Ibaba*. As mentioned in chapter 1, Maceda published the songs in their original languages, mostly Tagalog and Kapampangan. Sheila Zamar and I provided the English translations of the songs and quotations from the book that appear here.

103. Quoted and translated from Maceda, *Mga Tinig Mula sa Ibaba*, 126.

104. Ibid.

105. Ibid., 10.

106. Ibid., 138–41, 344–45.

107. "Babaeng Walang Kibo" also became a popular theme song for women in other leftist/feminist groups associated with the new Communist Party of the Philippines and the New People's Army. Ibid., 50, 261.

108. Ibid.

109. Communist Party of the Philippines, "Constitution of the Communist Party of the Philippines," art. II, sec. 1. See also Saulo, *Communism in the Philippines*, appendix 1, 151.

110. See, for example, Sofia Logarta, "The Participation of Women in the Huk Movement"; Taruc, *Born of the People*; Taruc, *He Who Rides the Tiger*; Pomeroy, *The Forest*; and Lava, *Memoirs of a Communist*.

111. Most works on the Huk rebellion contain the implicit assumption that men belonged at the head of the movement without expressing any need to explain why women did not assume leadership positions. Interviews with Politburo leaders, including Jesus and Jose Lava, Casto Alejandrino, Luis Taruc, and Celia and Bill Pomeroy, frequently included statements about women's inability to understand the complexities of communist dogma. Celia Mariano-Pomeroy was always mentioned as the exception to the rule.

112. Felisa Cuyugan, interview with the author, November 1993.

113. Teofista Valerio-Alejandrino, interview with the author, November 1993 and July 1997.

114. Ibid.

115. According to most male Huk leaders, it is likely that very few Huk men understood the formal teachings of communism. They insisted on their own knowledge of the ideology, and, while they promoted its teaching in the movement, they certainly did not discriminate against peasant members who had limited education and did not understand communism the way they did. See Lava, *Memoirs of a Communist*; Taruc, *Born of the People*; Taruc, *He Who Rides the Tiger*; and Pomeroy, *The Forest*.

116. Luz del Castillo, interview with the author, December 1993.

117. Rosenda Torres, interview with the author, December 1993 and June 1997.

118. Belen Bagul-Bagul, interview with the author, November 1993.

119. Zenaida del Castillo, interview with the author, January 1994.

120. Ibid.

121. Elang Santa Ana-Maclang, interview with the author, January 1994 and March 1997.

122. Dominga Centeno, interview with the author, November 1993.

123. Rosenda Torres, interview with the author, December 1993 and June 1997.

124. Maceda, *Mga Tinig Mula sa Ibaba,* 199–200.

125. Ibid., 202.

126. See Margaret Randall, *Sandino's Daughters: Testimonies of Nicaraguan Women in Struggle*; Margaret Randall, *Sandino's Daughters Revisited: Feminism in Nicaragua*; Sandra Taylor, *Vietnamese Women at War*; and Karen Turner, with Phan Thanh Hao, *Even the Women Must Fight: Memories of War from North Vietnam.* On the Chinese revolution, see Christina K. Gilmartin, *Engendering the Chinese Revolution*; and Helen P. Young, *Choosing Revolution: Chinese Women Soldiers on the Long March.*

127. Politburo Exhibit M-204-211, "Coordinate Revolutionary Activities in the Cities and Towns and the Armed Struggle in the Field," n.d.

128. These statements were made by Jesus Lava, Carto Alejandrino, Rosita Manuel-Liwanag, Gloria Aquino, and Prima Sobrevinas in their interviews with the author.

129. See Logarta, "Participation of Women," 131.

Chapter 3. Women on Top

1. This famous battle led by Felipa Culala appears in several accounts. See Eduardo Lachica, *Huk: Philippine Agrarian Society in Revolt,* 107; Benedict Kerkvliet, *The Huk Rebellion: A Study of Peasant Revolt in the Philippines,* 63; and Luis Taruc, *Born of the People,* 63–65.

2. Taruc, *Born of the People,* 65.

3. Alfred W. McCoy supports this assertion. According to him the Philippine military only welcomed its first female soldiers in 1963 while the Philippine Military Academy admitted its first female cadets in 1993. The stature gained by Dayang-Dayang as a combat commander was therefore unprecedented in the military history of the Philippines. See Alfred W. McCoy, *Closer Than Brothers: Manhood at the Philippine Military Academy,* 20.

4. Taruc, *Born of the People,* 129.

5. Celia Mariano-Pomeroy, letter to Jeff Goodwin, February 26, 1993 (used with permission); Taruc, *Born of the People,* 128–30.

6. As discussed in chapter 2 the realities of postwar reconstruction also shaped this debate, as the state prolonged its reliance on its colonial relationship

with the United States, giving Americans continued access to military bases and the country's natural resources. Works on the United States' influence on Philippine politics in the postwar period emphasize the persistence of patronage relations between Americans and their former elite collaborators. As the country rebuilt itself issues such as collaboration, economic dislocation, and the collapse of peace and order played a key role in shaping an independent Philippines. See chapter 2 for prominent works on the issues of U.S. intervention and elite wartime collaboration in the postwar Philippines.

7. When the Americans occupied the Philippines in 1898 the female literacy rate was only 10 percent in contrast to a male literacy rate of nearly 30 percent. American colonial policy promoted universal education, and for the first time a large proportion of Filipinas attended public schools. In 1908 the Philippine Legislature founded the University of the Philippines, opening up the study of medicine, dentistry, nursing, pharmacy, fine arts, agriculture, and engineering to both men and women. In just a few years the number of women attending schools and universities more than tripled, and by the 1940s the number of females in the professional sector was significant. More and more women were employed in teaching and health-related occupations, benefiting from the colonial government's efforts to address the high incidence of illiteracy, disease, and malnutrition. A place in the government bureaucracy became a much sought after occupation for female graduates of high school and college. See Carolyn Sobritchea, "American Colonial Education and Its Impact on the Status of Filipino Women."

8. While ultimately beneficial, educational expansion was a direct imposition of the colonial government on the native population. Although more and more men and women acquired an education, the pattern whereby women were "institutionally segregated and occupationally restricted" was perpetuated for years to come. Mary Grace Ampil Tirona, "*Panuelo* Activism," 114.

9. Ibid., 118–20.

10. Tirona calls this movement *panuelo* activism to distinguish these women from contemporary female activists and feminists. According to her these women, who belonged to the upper and middle classes, were reticent individuals and not very political. She writes, "Dressed in their *panueloed ternos,* they looked too dainty and too fragile for activism." "Panuelo" refers to the stiff kerchief worn over the shoulder as part of the formal, traditional dress, or *terno,* with butterfly sleeves. Ibid., 118.

11. Georgina Reyes Encanto, *Constructing the Filipina: A History of Women's Magazines (1891–2002),* 41.

12. These women's organizations included the Asociacion Feminista Ilonga (1906), founded by Pura Villanueva Kalaw, the Liga Nacional de Damas Filipinas (1922), and the Women's Citizen's League (1928), the latter two organized by Maria Ventura. Tirona states that the early efforts of individual women, though "lacking in force and conviction," can be considered "feminist waves of thought." Tirona, "*Panuelo* Activism," 120. Pura Villanueva-Kalaw,

herself a suffragist, chronicles the long process of getting women the right to vote in *How Women Got the Vote.*

13. Pilar Hidalgo Lim, "Josefa Llanes Escoda."

14. Quoted in Tirona, "*Panuelo* Activism," 121–22.

15. Mina Roces, "Is the Suffragist an American Colonial Construct? Defining 'the Filipino Woman' in Colonial Philippines," 29.

16. Louise Edwards and Mina Roces, "Orienting the Global Women's Suffrage Movement."

17. Tirona, "*Panuelo* Activism," 126.

18. Ibid.

19. These organizations included the Catholic Women's League, the Philippine Association of University Women, and the Women's Writers. Ibid., 118–23.

20. Ibid., 123–28.

21. Roces, "Is the Suffragist an American Colonial Construct?" 29.

22. This "retreat to the home" phenomenon reflects postwar developments in the United States. See Elaine Tyler May, *Homeward Bound: American Families in the Cold War Era.*

23. Quoted in Carmelita Corpuz, *Mula Noon Hanggang Gabriela: Ang Kababaihan sa Kasaysayan ng Pilipinas hanggang mga, 1980* (From the Past to Gabriela: Women in the History of the Philippines up to 1980), 68.

24. Ibid.

25. Amaryllis T. Torres, *The Filipina Looks at Herself: A Review of Women's Studies in the Philippines,* 10.

26. Encanto, *Constructing the Filipina,* 59. This perception is mirrored in May, *Homeward Bound,* chap. 1.

27. Encanto, *Constructing the Filipina,* 61.

28. McCoy states that from the 1920s on the idea of "the woman behind the man behind the gun" seemed to be an accepted reality. See McCoy, *Closer Than Brothers,* 44.

29. Anne-Marie Hilsdon, *Madonnas and Martyrs: Militarism and Violence in the Philippines,* 21.

30. McCoy, *Closer Than Brothers,* 69.

31. See also the works of Cynthia Enloe, including *Does Khaki Become You? The Militarization of Women's Lives*; and *Maneuvers: The International Politics of Militarizing Women's Lives.*

32. Elizabeth Uy Eviota, *The Political Economy of Gender: Women and the Sexual Division of Labour in the Philippines,* 79, 99.

33. Carolyn I. Sobritchea, "Gender Ideology and the Status of Women in a Philippine Rural Community," 100.

34. Maria Paz Mendoza-Guazon, *The Development and Progress of the Filipino Woman,* 65.

35. Mina Roces, "Negotiating Modernities: Filipino Women, 1970–2000," 122.

36. Roces, *Women, Power, and Kinship Politics*, 8.

37. Aida Santos-Maranan argues that these women's groups were used to propagate the legitimacy of the newly installed Philippine government, which had the full blessing of American colonial authorities. Aida Santos-Maranan, "Do Women Really Hold Up Half the Sky? Notes on the Women's Movement in the Philippines," 47.

38. Roces, *Women, Power, and Kinship Politics*, 48–49.

39. Hilsdon, *Madonnas and Martyrs*, 29.

40. According to Mina Roces, it was after 1983 that the tenor changed and women began to organize themselves for reasons other than supporting their male kin. Roces, "Negotiating Modernities," 22. Leonora Angeles also states that women's organizations in the 1950s acted as appendages or auxiliaries to all-male organizations, which were responsible for creating these auxiliaries in the first place. But, unlike Roces, Angeles saw the emergence of feminist organizations as having occurred much earlier, in the late 1960s. Leonora Angeles, *Feminism and Nationalism: The Discourse on the Woman Question and Politics of the Women's Movement in the Philippines*.

41. Roces, "Negotiating Modernities," 123–24.

42. Most of the revolts recorded during the Spanish period recognized the participation of *babaylans* and described how stripping them of their power had led them to revolution. Although most of the leaders of these movements were male, many of the *babaylan* participants were women whose traditional power was similarly crushed by the Spanish. For studies on the participation of *babaylans* in millenarian revolutionary movements see David Sturtevant, *Popular Uprisings in the Philippines, 1840–1940*; and Reynaldo Ileto, *Pasyon and Revolution: Popular Movements in the Philippines, 1840–1910*. For an in-depth study of the *babaylans* see the recent impressive work of Carolyn Brewer, *Shamanism, Catholicism, and Gender Relations in Colonial Philippines, 1521–1685*; and also Alfred W. McCoy's "*Baylan:* Animist Religion and Philippine Peasant Ideology," 338–423.

43. Gabriela Silang is still considered by many to be the ultimate Amazon in Philippine revolutionary history, and her legend lives on among feminists in the Philippines. In fact the biggest women's organization in the country is called Gabriela. See Tirona, "*Panuelo* Activism." And yet there is still no comprehensive account of the life and legend of Gabriela Silang.

44. Founded by Andres Bonifacio, the Katipunan (Brotherhood) is considered the largest and most prominent movement against Spain, essentially launching a revolution in 1896. The Filipino woman, according to Andres Bonifacio and Emilio Jacinto, both leaders of the Katipunan, deserved to be part of the new nation. They stated that, although "women are weak and must be protected by men," they would be men's partners and supporters. Another intellectual, Apolinario Mabini, wrote in the movement's newspaper, *Kartilya* (Doctrine), a section dedicated to women in his Programa Political de la Republica Filipina (Political Program of the Philippine Republic). In his vision of

the new Philippine Republic women would have the right to vote, to be elected, to study in any university, and to practice a profession. See Romeo Cruz, "Ang Pilipina sa Panahon ng Himagsikan at Digmaang Pilipino-Amerikano" (The Filipina in the Period of Revolution and the Philippine-American War), 75.

45. Women have been incorporated into the history of the Philippine Revolution against Spain, although not much is known about them individually. Current scholarship contains only brief, sketchy biographical information. See Thelma Kintanar, ed., "Women in History and Revolution"; Rafaelita H. Soriano, *Women in the Philippine Revolution*; Luis Camara Dery, *Remember the Ladies and Other Historical Essays on the 1896 Philippine Revolution*; and brief treatments in Hilsdon, *Madonnas and Martyrs*; Mary John Mananzan, Asuncion Azcuna, and Fe Mangahas, eds., *Sarilaya: Women in Arts and Media*; and Corpuz, *Mula Noon Hanggang Gabriela*.

46. David Sturtevant, *Popular Uprisings in the Philippines*, 287.

47. Ibid., 277–85.

48. These and similar headlines and cover stories appeared in the *Philippines Free Press*, *Manila Times*, and *Manila Chronicle* between 1946 and 1959.

49. For an in-depth discussion of the term *Amazon* see my "Capturing the Huk Amazons: Representing Women Warriors in the Philippines, 1940s–1950s."

50. See, for example, "Amazon Captured," *Philippines Free Press*, March 21, 1948; "Wife of Huk Regional Area Supervisor Captured by PC," *Manila Times*, March 21, 1948; and "Pretty Girl Denies Any Huk Connection," *Manila Times*, October 20, 1948.

51. "Huk Amazon Unit Encountered by PC," *Manila Times*, September 15, 1948.

52. "183 Huks Slain in Pampanga, Five Amazons among Fatalities," *Manila Times*, September 25, 1948.

53. For further exploration of the historical and cultural significance of Amazons or warrior women in different contexts, see Sharon W. Tiffany and Kathleen J. Adams, *The Wild Woman: An Inquiry into the Anthropology of an Idea*; Shirley Castelnuovo and Sharon R. Guthrie, *Feminism and the Female Body: Liberating the Amazon Within*; Abby Kleinbaum, *The War against the Amazons*; Josine Blok, *The Early Amazons: Modern and Ancient Perspectives on a Persistent Myth*; and Lyn W. Wilde, *On the Trail of the Women Warriors: The Amazons in Myth and History*.

54. Wilde, *On The Trail of the Women Warriors*, 1.

55. "Pretty Girl Denies Any Huk Connection," *Manila Times*, October 20, 1948.

56. "Hunger Taking Lives of Huks," *Manila Times*, October 9, 1948.

57. "4 Amazons, Huk Held, One Slain," *Daily Mirror*, August 31, 1953.

58. "Amazon Finance Officer Nabbed," *Daily Mirror*, October 31, 1953.

59. "Huk Message Unit Broken, 3 Amazons Arrested," *Manila Times,* October 2, 1953.

60. Leon Ty, "Guerrilleras," *Philippines Free Press,* October 12, 1946.

61. Ibid.

62. Elieser M. Chavez, "Women in War," *Philippines Free Press,* December 10, 1949.

63. Ibid.

64. Beauty pageants occupy an important and fascinating place in studies about Philippine culture and society. See the works of Mina Roces; and Fenella Cannell, *Power and Intimacy in the Christian Philippines.*

65. "Waling Waling Nabbed," *Manila Times,* May 1, 1952.

66. "Woman Huk Found Dying," *Manila Times,* September 17, 1948.

67. "Catapatan, 4 Others Slain," *Manila Times,* April 4, 1952.

68. "Top Woman Huk Dies," *Manila Times,* April 29, 1948.

69. "Huks Led by Woman Clash with PC," *Manila Times,* March 25, 1950.

70. "Woman Huk Fights and Flees," *Manila Times,* April 20, 1950.

71. Filemon V. Tutay, "Poor Babies!" *Philippines Free Press,* June 28, 1952.

72. The depictions of Huk Amazons and their relationships with their children are consistent with the representations of Amazon women in Greek mythology. In this myth, Amazon warriors exclusively live among themselves, but they do not completely abandon their desires or sexuality. Most reject marriage but have sexual intercourse with men in neighboring villages at least once a year. After the men have made them pregnant they send them away. The females that are born are retained by the Amazons, but males are adopted by the men or in some versions mutilated or killed by the female warriors. See Francois Hartog, *The Mirror of Herodotus: The Representation of the Other in the Writing of History.*

73. There were literally hundreds of articles on the captured Huklings. While some were devoted exclusively to them, most information on these children appeared alongside treatments of Huk Amazons who fled and abandoned their children or were killed with them. For longer treatments of Huklings see Filemon V. Tutay, "Poor Babies!" *Philippines Free Press,* June 28, 1952; Jose A. Quirino, "The Seven Huklings of EDCOR," *Philippines Free Press,* July 2, 1955; and "Huk Baby," *Philippines Free Press,* March 1, 1952.

74. Most of the material for Celia Mariano-Pomeroy's biography was obtained through a series of interviews I conducted with her in Twickenham, England, in October and November 1998. Since my interviews were conducted in English, I am using her words directly unless stated otherwise.

75. Celia Mariano-Pomeroy, interview with the author, Twickenham, England, October and November 1998. I visited Celia several times after our initial meetings, and we always talked about her days in the Huk movement.

76. Celia Mariano-Pomeroy, interview with the author, October and November 1998.

77. See Diana Reed, "WWII Forgotten Heroine" (interview with Celia Pomeroy), 11.

78. Jesus B. Lava, *Memoirs of a Communist,* 78.

79. Celia Mariano-Pomeroy, speech delivered at the Malibongwe Conference for South African Women, Amsterdam, January 11, 1990.

80. Reed, "WWII Forgotten Heroine," 12.

81. Ibid., 13.

82. Celia Mariano-Pomeroy, interview with the author, October and November 1998.

83. Reed, "WWII Forgotten Heroine," 13.

84. Most of the information on the life of Remedios Gomez is derived from my interviews with her. Remedios Gomez, interview with the author, Project 4, Quezon City, and Anao, Mexico, Pampanga, October and November 1993 and July 1997.

85. Teodosio Lansang, "Exclusive Interview with 'Liwayway' Huk Commander," *Truth Magazine,* August 1 and 14, 1947.

86. Ibid., 10.

87. Ibid., 12.

88. Remedios Gomez, interview with the author, October and November 1993 and July 1997.

89. Ibid.

90. Taruc, *Born of the People,* 103.

91. Luis Taruc, *He Who Rides the Tiger,* 112.

92. Taruc, *Born of the People,* 103.

93. Lansang, "Exclusive Interview," 13.

94. Remedios Gomez, interview with the author, October and November 1993 and July 1997.

95. Simeona Punzalan-Tapang, interview with the author, San Simon, Pampanga, January 1994 and April 1997.

96. Ibid.

97. Ibid.

98. Taruc, *Born of the People,* 103.

99. Ibid.

100. Gloria Rivera-Sagum, interview with the author, San Luis, Pampanga, January 1994.

101. Luzviminda is a contraction of the three main geographical areas of the Philippines: Luzon, Visayas, and Mindanao.

102. Gloria Rivera-Sagum, interview with the author, January 1994.

103. Newspaper stories that covered her arrest included "Amazon Captured," *Philippines Free Press,* March 21, 1948; "Wife of Huk Regional Area Supervisor Captured by PC," *Manila Times,* March 21, 1948; and "Pretty Girl Denies Any Huk Connection," *Manila Times,* October 20, 1948.

104. Leonila Monteverde, interview with the author, Quezon, June 1997.

105. Pasencia David, interview with the author, San Fernando, Pampanga, November 1993.

106. Clark S. Carter, "Revolt in the Philippines," 9–12. As a freelance writer Pomeroy used the pseudonym Clark S. Carter to conceal his identity as a Huk cadre and supporter.

107. Ibid., 10–12.

108. Celia Mariano-Pomeroy, interview with the author, October and November 1998.

109. Celia Mariano-Pomeroy, "Experiences as a Guerrilla in the Philippines."

110. Ibid.

111. Celia Mariano-Pomeroy, interview with the author, October and November 1998.

112. Ibid.

113. William Pomeroy, letter to the author, March 15, 1999; William Pomeroy, interview with the author, Twickenham, England, October 1998; Candy Gourlay, "Happy Birthday Celia and Thanks."

114. Mariano-Pomeroy, "Experiences as a Guerrilla."

115. William Pomeroy, *The Forest: A Personal Record of the Huk Guerrilla Struggle in the Philippines*, 82–83.

116. Ibid., 204.

117. Ibid.

118. Simeona Punzalan-Tapang, interview with the author, January 1994 and April 1997.

119. Remedios Gomez, interview with the author, October and November 1993 and July 1997.

120. Several newspaper stories covered the arrest and trial of Liwayway, including "Woman Huk Commander Facing Trial for Sedition, Rebellion," *Manila Times*, August 7, 1947; "Habeas Corpus Writ for Huk Girl," *Manila Times*, October 27, 1947; and Lansang, "Exclusive Interview."

121. Remedios Gomez, interview with the author, October and November 1993 and July 1997.

122. Liwayway's lawyer also claimed that she won her case because her detention was deemed illegal since the warrant for her arrest was issued without a preliminary investigation. "Habeas Corpus Writ for Huk Girl," *Manila Times*, October 27, 1947; "Huk Woman Wins Freedom from MP," *Manila Times*, November 5, 1947.

123. Simeona Punzalan-Tapang, interview with the author, January 1994 and April 1997.

124. Celia Mariano-Pomeroy, interview with the author, October and November 1998.

125. See Taruc, *He Who Rides the Tiger*; Lava, *Memoirs of a Communist*; and Pomeroy, *The Forest*. Her rise to the Politburo is also mentioned in Alfredo

Saulo, *Communism in the Philippines*, 48; and Nick Joaquin [Quijano de Manila], "The Huk from Rochester, N.Y.," 131.

126. Celia Mariano-Pomeroy, interview with the author, October and November 1998.

127. Ibid.

128. Celia Mariano-Pomeroy, letter to Jeff Goodwin, February 26, 1993 (used with permission); Taruc, *Born of the People*, 63.

129. Taruc, *Born of the People*, 63.

130. Celia Mariano-Pomeroy, letter to Jeff Goodwin, June 21, 1993 (used with permission).

131. Taruc, *Born of the People*, 103.

132. Lansang, "Exclusive Interview," 10.

133. Celia Mariano-Pomeroy, letter to Jeff Goodwin, June 21, 1993.

134. Taruc, *Born of the People*, 102.

135. Remedios Gomez, interview with the author, October and November 1993 and July 1997.

136. Lansang, "Exclusive Interview," 12.

137. Three major perspectives dominate discussions of the making of the Philippine nation and identity. The first is what most scholars call "elite nationalism," the emergence of a Filipino consciousness in the second half of the nineteenth century among the *ilustrados*, the educated elites. Reiterating Benedict Anderson's idea of the "imagined community," historians argue that nationalism in the Philippines emerged from the shared experiences and ideals of Filipinos living in Spain who found unity and solidarity outside their home country. They sought to realize their common desire for independence for their Motherland. See Benedict Anderson, *Imagined Communities: Reflections on the Origin and Spread of Nationalism*; John Schumacher, *The Propaganda Movement: The Creation of a Filipino Consciousness, the Making of the Revolution*; John Schumacher, *The Making of a Nation: Essays on Nineteenth-Century Filipino Nationalism*; and Onofre D. Corpuz, *The Roots of the Filipino Nation*. The second perspective examines the more popular forms of nationalism, emphasizing mobilization of the masses (the peasants and the working classes) and their popular aspirations for independence, which culminated in the revolution against Spain in 1896. See especially Teodoro Agoncillo, *The Revolt of the Masses: The Story of Bonifacio and the Katipunan*; and Ileto, *Pasyon and Revolution*. More recent Philippine scholars credit both the elites and the masses and critique the determining role of the 1896 anticolonial revolution in the articulation of Filipino nationalism, but they remain vague about the processes that led to the emergence of a united Filipino identity. See Vicente Rafael, *White Love and Other Events in Philippine History*; and Floro C. Quibuyen, *A Nation Aborted: Rizal, American Hegemony, and Philippine Nationalism*.

138. Partha Chatterjee, *The Nation and Its Fragments: Colonial and Postcolonial Histories*, 117–19.

139. Janet Hart, *New Voices in the Nation: Women in the Greek Resistance, 1941–1964*, 272.

140. Ibid.

141. See May, *Homeward Bound*.

142. Saskia Wieringa explains that "women had been both vocal actors in the political arena and 'good' mothers and wives. These two roles had merged, in fact, as women needed to play their political role *in order to be* good mothers of the Indonesian people and the nation and wives as helpmates of the men in struggle." Saskia Wieringa, *Sexual Politics in Indonesia*, 99, emphasis in original.

143. Ibid., 7, 130; see also 34–36.

144. According to Blackburn, state gender ideology refers to the assumptions about gender on which the state acts and the way it attempts to influence the construction of gender in society. In Indonesia male leaders of the young independent state curbed women's activities and controlled the construction of womanhood and femininity, which aimed to, like the Greek government, put "women in their place." The notion of *kodrat* (natural destiny), in which men are the breadwinners and women the homemakers, remained intact despite the reality that poor, especially peasant women in Indonesia equally contribute to household income. Even though this ideology is contested, regimes in postcolonial Indonesia (from independence to the Old Order and New Order) consistently emphasized the maternal role of the woman in society. Susan Blackburn, *Women and the State in Modern Indonesia*, 9, 11.

145. Wieringa, *Sexual Politics*, 34–35. During President Suharto's New Order regime (1967–1998), this state gender ideology and the concomitant construction of womanhood became militarized, resulting in the definition of masculinity as a model of discipline and repression and emphasizing "the need for mothers to maintain vigilance over family morality and for the state to monitor family life." Blackburn adds that "official speeches and state-controlled media continually stressed the ideal wife and mother, aware of her *kodrat*, maintaining approved Indonesia traditions, carrying out her assigned development tasks and raising her children as good citizens." Blackburn, *Women and the State*, 26.

146. I should point out that women themselves, especially those belonging to the women's movements, have continually contested and challenged male gender constructions and their own subordination. The Gerakan Wanita Indonesia (Indonesian Women's Movement or Gerwani) mobilized women in various periods to protect and advance women's political and social rights. See Wieringa, *Sexual Politics*, for an in-depth treatment of this movement.

147. Barbara Watson Andaya, "Gender, Warfare, and Patriotism in Southeast Asia and in the Philippine Revolution."

148. Ibid., 10–11.

149. Christina Kelley Gilmartin, *Engendering the Chinese Revolution: Radical Women, Communist Politics, and Mass Movements in the 1920s*.

150. Other communist and revolutionary organizations in countries such as Russia, Cuba, and Mexico had similar practices. See the collection of essays in Mary Ann Tetrault, ed., *Women and Revolution in Africa, Asia, and the New World*; and Lois Smith, *Sex in Revolution: Gender, Politics, and Power in Modern Mexico.*

151. Gilmartin, *Engendering the Chinese Revolution,* 108–9.

152. Anne-Marie Hilsdon notes the use of the imagery of the *"amasona"* to refer to the female guerrillas of the New People's Army, the armed wing of the new Communist Party of the Philippines established in 1969. Like the Huk Amazons, these *amasonas* earned their label because of their fighting and horsemanship skills, which were equal to those of men. But she writes that "underlying the use of such iconography is often a fear of female sexuality," and the term becomes derogatory, justifying the discipline and punishment of women warriors. Hilsdon, *Madonnas and Martyrs,* 34.

153. See Enloe, *Does Khaki Become You?*; and Hilsdon, *Madonnas and Martyrs.*

154. Several recent books about the New People's Army highlight its remarkable female guerrillas, who often called themselves Amazons in part as a tribute to the Huk women. See *Pulang Mandirigma: Images of the New People's Army* (Red Rebel: Images of the New People's Army); *Kasama: A Collection of Photographs of the New People's Army of the Philippines*; and Hilsdon, *Madonnas and Martyrs.*

Chapter 4. Love and Sex in the Time of Revolution

1. The capture of Leonora and Oscar was featured in several stories, including Emiliano D. Reynante, "Lovelorn Huks Marry," *Philippines Free Press,* October 16, 1954; David Baquirin, "Cupid, Alias J. Crisol, Writes Happy Chapter in Huk Romance," *Manila Times,* October 7, 1954; "Huk Sweethearts to Wed Tomorrow," *Daily Mirror,* October 5, 1954; and "2 Surrendered Huk Lovers Wed," *Manila Chronicle,* October 6, 1954.

2. "Huk Sweethearts to Wed Tomorrow," *Daily Mirror,* October 5, 1954.

3. Emiliano D. Reynante, "Lovelorn Huks Marry," *Philippines Free Press,* October 16, 1954, 1.

4. Ibid.

5. David Baquirin, "Cupid, Alias J. Crisol, Writes Happy Chapter in Huk Romance," *Manila Times,* October 7, 1954.

6. William Pomeroy, *The Forest: A Personal Record of the Huk Guerilla Struggle in the Philippines,* 142.

7. Politburo Exhibit A-69, "Letter from Pat" (in Hiligaynon, with English translation), March 23, 1950.

8. Pomeroy related an incident in his memoir in which a girl was sent home for promiscuous behavior. Pomeroy, *The Forest,* 142.

9. Can communists be homosexuals? Unfortunately, this question was not explored anywhere in the official and unofficial histories of the Huk rebellion. My initial foray into this topic was met with both shock and nervous laughter by my interviewees. It was a topic that wasn't encouraged further.

10. Rosenda Torres, interview with the author, Santa Mesa, Manila, December 1993 and June 1997.

11. In a predominantly Catholic society like that of the Philippines, a woman's virginity is highly valued; it is something that needs to be protected, and that is why parents usually prevent daughters from going out with men unchaperoned. Losing one's virginity before marriage tarnishes not only a woman's reputation but also that of her whole family. See Fenella Cannell, *Power and Intimacy in the Christian Philippines.*

12. Luis Taruc, *He Who Rides the Tiger*, 44. Throughout his book Taruc calls the women who joined and supported the Huks "girls" and the male members "men," displaying a paternalistic attitude toward women.

13. Elang Santa Ana-Maclang, interview with the author, San Ricardo, Talavera, Nueva Ecija, January 1994 and March 1997.

14. Leonila Sayco Gatus-Palo, interview with the author, San Fernando, Pampanga, October 1993.

15. Maxima San Pedro-Alcantara, interview with the author, San Ricardo, Talavera, Nueva Ecija, January 1994.

16. Gloria Rivera-Sagum, interview with the author, San Luis, Pampanga, January 1994.

17. Ibid.

18. Simeona Punzalan-Tapang, interview with the author, San Simon, Pampanga, January 1994 and April 1997.

19. Pasencia David, interview with the author, San Fernando, Pampanga, November 1993.

20. Rosenda Torres, interview with the author, December 1993 and June 1997.

21. Ana Sula, interview with the author, Santa Ana, Pampanga, October 1993.

22. Loreta Betangkul, interview with the author, Anao, Mexico, Pampanga, October 1993.

23. Dominga Adasar-Centeno, interview with the author, Cabanatuan, Nueva Ecija, November 1993.

24. Virginia Calma, interview with the author, Diliman, Quezon City, November 1993 and June 1997.

25. Narcisa Reyes-Romero, interview with the author, Cabiao, Nueva Ecija, November 1993.

26. Remedios Gomez, interview with the author, Project 4, Quezon City, and Anao, Mexico, Pampanga, October and November 1993 and July 1997.

27. Celia Mariano-Pomeroy, "Experiences as a Guerrilla in the Philippines."

28. Pomeroy, *The Forest*, 31.

29. See Cannell, *Power and Intimacy,* especially part 1, chaps. 1 and 2, on marriage.

30. It is interesting to note that despite the central and contested role marriage plays in Philippine society there is no historical and systematic study on this institution available. In *Power and Intimacy* Fanella Cannell looks at the importance of kinship and rituals in marriage customs in the Bicol region. She similarly comments on the dearth of materials on marriage in the Philippines and had to rely on works about marriage in Southeast Asia in general.

31. Pomeroy, *The Forest*, 143.

32. Leonila Sayco Gatus-Palo, interview with the author, October 1993.

33. Pomeroy, *The Forest*, 31.

34. Taruc, *He Who Rides the Tiger*, 124.

35. Pomeroy, *The Forest*, 143.

36. Ana Sula, interview with the author, October 1993.

37. This practice was "rectified" by the new Communist Party of the Philippines, established in 1968. The CCP, in a landmark document entitled "On the Relation of the Sexes," also regulated divorces among comrades. And yet, as Anne-Marie Hilsdon states, women's desires for family, home, and children were held "sacrosanct by revolutionaries" and continued to shape their lives. See especially Anne-Marie Hilsdon, *Madonnas and Martyrs: Militarism and Violence in the Philippines*, 39; and Patricio N. Abinales, *Love, Sex, and the Filipino Communist or Hinggil sa Pagpipigil ng Panggigigil.*

38. See, for example, Politburo Exhibit O-180-253, "Milestones in the History of the Communist Party of the Philippines," by Gregorio Santayana [Jose Lava], n.d.; and Jeff Goodwin, "The Libidinal Constitution of a High-Risk Social Movement: Affectual Ties and Solidarity in the Huk Rebellion, 1946–1954."

39. Pomeroy, *The Forest*, 142.

40. Mariano-Pomeroy, "Experiences as a Guerrilla in the Philippines."

41. Although most of the Huk men and women knew about the *kualingking* cases, no one seems to know the origin of the term. It is not a Tagalog or Kapampangan word but probably developed among the Huks themselves. Despite its obscure origins, almost everyone in the movement understood what *kualingking* meant.

42. Interviews with Huk women reveal that such sexual liaisons were common, even rampant, in the movement. Many women were even willing to name names, though most refused to elaborate. Many claimed that both Politburo leaders and rank-and-file members engaged in these relations. Since the sex problem continues to be a sensitive issue, especially for women, not everyone I interviewed was willing to tell me their stories.

43. Politburo Exhibit H-36, "Letter to Ka Sulo from Erning," May 8, 1950.
44. Politburo Exhibit O-282-284, "Letter to Com[rade]s. Gaston and Beria re: Reports and Information from Plaridel," April 29, 1950.
45. Teofista Valerio-Alejandrino, interview with the author, Santa Rita, Nueva Ecija, November 1993 and July 1997.
46. Ibid.
47. The love letters, part of the captured documents of the Politburo, are housed in the archives of the University of the Philippines Library.
48. Teofista's arrest was covered in major newspapers. She was considered a "prize catch" by the military, but perhaps that was due more to her association with Alejandrino than to her role in the Huk movement. See "Huk Leader's Top Contact Is Arrested," *Manila Times,* September 9, 1950; and "Alejandrino Wife to Face Charges," *Daily Mirror,* September 9, 1950. Details of her capture appear in the introduction to this volume.
49. Belen Bagul-Bagul, interview with the author, Santa Cruz, Laguna, November 1993.
50. Ibid.
51. In my numerous encounters with Casto Alejandrino I saw a truly brilliant and interesting yet enigmatic character. He was always spoke openly about his relationships, and I'll always be indebted to him for enthusiastically introducing me to his forest wives. It is easy to see that women found him charismatic, but I think he can also be a bit of a sexist who never really gave the women their due recognition in the movement. I don't believe he even recognized how much pain he may have caused his partners.
52. Teofista Valerio-Alejandrino, interview with the author, November 1993 and July 1997.
53. The arrest of Remedios Orejala, Jesus Lava's Huk wife, was headline news in many newspapers. See "Lava's Alleged Wife Captured," *Manila Chronicle,* July 15, 1956; "Lava Wife Refuses to Talk at Probe," *Daily Mirror,* July 16, 1956; "Lava's Wife Faces Rebellion Charges," *Manila Chronicle,* July 22, 1956; and "Lava Is No Commie, Says Wife," *Manila Times,* July 22, 1956. I do not know why Lava failed to mention her during our numerous encounters. While Lava did mention Zeny in his memoir he did not provide many details. See Jesus Lava, *Memoirs of a Communist,* 204-6.
54. Linda Ayala, interview with the author, Makati City, Manila, January 1994, and Santo Niño, Quezon, June 1997.
55. Lava, *Memoirs of a Communist,* 217.
56. Lava always acknowledged Linda Ayala as his wife. But, although he included a picture of her in his memoir, the things he said about her barely fit a page of his book, which runs to four hundred pages. Ibid., 217-18.
57. Linda Ayala, interview with the author, January 1994 and June 1997.
58. Ibid.
59. Taruc, *He Who Rides the Tiger,* 64-65.

60. Among other stories, Leonila Dizon's capture is described in "Taruc's Girl Secretary Is Captured," *Manila Times,* October 12, 1948; "Pretty Girl Denies Any Huk Connection," *Manila Times,* October 20, 1948; and "Late Flashes from the Huk Front: Taruc Wife Revealed," *Philippines Free Press,* November 6, 1948.

61. Luis Taruc, interview with the author, Quezon, November 1993 and July 1997.

62. Manuel and Belinda Malay, interview with the author, Manila, October 1993. I have used pseudonyms for this couple on the request of the woman.

63. Ibid.

64. Ibid.

65. Felisa Cuyugan, interview with the author, San Fernando, Pampanga, November 1993.

66. Elang Santa Ana-Maclang, interview with the author, January 1994 and March 1997.

67. Politburo Exhibit N-67-76, "Self-Appraisal by O. Beria," n.d.

68. Politburo Exhibit N-170-171, "Letter to Com[rade] Bonifacio from O. Beria," October 4, 1950.

69. Elang Santa Ana-Maclang, interview with the author, January 1994 and March 1997.

70. Elena Sawit-Macapagal, interview with the author, Novaliches, Quezon, September 1993.

71. Ibid.

72. Filomena's situation draws attention to the issue of rape and coercion inside the Huk movement. The question of how many women shared her experience will probably remain uncertain. But it is easy to see why these women, who exhibited great courage and bravery as Huks, still felt incredibly vulnerable inside and outside the movement and believed they needed men for protection and security. Very few women, in fact, left their Huk husbands after the struggle. Filomena Tolentino, interview with the author, Floridablanca, Pampanga, October 1993.

73. Zenaida del Castillo, interview with the author, Laurel, Batangas, January 1994.

74. Ibid.

75. Luz del Castillo, interview with the author, Tandang Sora, Quezon City, December 1993.

76. Felisa Cuyugan, interview with the author, November 1993.

77. Remedios Gomez, interview with the author, October and November 1993 and July 1997.

78. Simeona Punzalan-Tapang, interview with the author, January 1994 and April 1997.

79. Celia Mariano-Pomeroy, interview with the author, Twickenham, England, October and November 1998.

80. Politburo Exhibit I-1t, "Minutes of the Meeting by All Members of the Staff of FC-62," October 11, 1950.

81. Self-appraisals were a common practice within communist circles and a way for Party leaders and members to reveal personal weaknesses that hampered the movement. See Politburo Exhibit O-1043, "Self-appraisal and Appraisal as a Weapon to Strengthen the Party," n.d.

82. Politburo Exhibit N-9-11, "Self-Appraisal by Gregorio Santayana," n.d.

83. Celia Mariano-Pomeroy, interview with the author, October and November 1998.

84. Politburo Exhibit O-310-311, "Letter to the Com[rade]s. of the PB," unsigned, November 11, 1949.

85. Christina Gilmartin makes similar observations about prominent women in the Chinese Communist Party who attributed their advance within the leadership hierarchy to the rank of their partners. See Christina Kelley Gilmartin, *Engendering the Chinese Revolution: Radical Women, Communist Politics, and Mass Movements in the 1920s.*

86. Taruc, *He Who Rides the Tiger,* 64.

87. Rosenda Torres, interview with the author, December 1993 and June 1997.

88. "What the Huks Think of Sex," *Philippines Free Press,* July 29, 1967. The article was published after the military released to the media the crucial "sex document" written by the Huk leadership in 1950. Politburo Exhibit I-15, "The Revolutionary Solution of the Sex Problem," September 12, 1950; hereafter RSSP.

89. "What the Huks Think of Sex."

90. RSSP. Another version is found in Politburo Exhibit I-16, "Revolutionary Resolution Pertaining to the Problem in the Relation between Man and Woman," [1950].

91. RSSP, 1.

92. The consistent use of the term *abnormalities,* while not explicitly explained in the document, may refer to several types of unconventional relationships. The most obvious, of course, was the abnormality of married men engaging in sex with women other than their wives. But the term might also suggest a fear of homosexual sex, something that no Huk or communist member would dare to even acknowledge.

93. RSSP, 1.

94. Pomeroy, *The Forest,* 143.

95. RSSP, 2.

96. Ibid.; Pomeroy, *The Forest,* 144.

97. RSSP, 3.

98. Pomeroy, *The Forest,* 144.

99. Celia Mariano-Pomeroy, interview with the author, October and November 1998.

100. Pomeroy, *The Forest,* 145; Goodwin, "The Libidinal Constitution of a High-Risk Social Movement," 61.

101. Politburo Exhibit N-170-171, "Letter to Com[rade] Bonifacio from O. Beria," October 4, 1950.

102. Rene Raquiza [Celia Mariano-Pomeroy], "Problems of Sex Morality in Our Party Today," 42-52.

103. Ibid., 42.

104. Ibid., 44.

105. Ibid.

106. Alexandra Kollantai, Clara Zetkin, and Vladimir Lenin wrote numerous articles about women's oppression and the struggle for equality. See Alix Holt, ed., *Selected Writings of Alexandra Kollantai*; Clara Zetkin, *Clara Zetkin: Selected Writings*; and Vladimir Lenin, *The Emancipation of Women: From the Writings of V. I. Lenin.*

107. Quoted by Clara Zetkin, "Lenin on the Woman Question," in *Emancipation of Women,* 102, 105.

108. Holt, *Selected Writings of Alexandra Kollantai,* 230.

109. The Politburo leaders I interviewed, including Celia and Bill Pomeroy, informed me that the solution they drafted was not based on any single book or article. Both of them were involved in the formulation of the policy, but it was Jose Lava, then secretary-general of the PKP, who eventually wrote the RSSP. In a 1998 interview Celia revealed that many of her ideas about women's issues and morality were derived from the writings of Zetkin and Lenin.

110. Raquiza, "Problems of Sex Morality," 44.

111. The practice of monogamy is entrenched in Catholicism, the official religion of the Philippines, and advocated by the powerful Catholic Church. Bigamy, the act of having two wives, is illegal and considered a crime in the Philippines. The exception, of course, is when the man is a Muslim, who by religious law is allowed to have more than one wife. Under Philippine law, only one marriage is sanctioned.

112. See Goodwin, "The Libidinal Constitution of a High-Risk Social Movement," 59.

113. RSSP, 4.

114. Goodwin, "The Libidinal Constitution of a High-Risk Social Movement," 61.

115. Politburo Exhibit N-380-384, "Communist Party of the Philippines, Seventh Regional Committee, Third Meeting," June 18, 1950.

116. RSSP, 3.

117. Unfortunately, I was not able to interview Luming Calonje. She had a major falling out with party members in the 1950s, and few people know of her whereabouts. My efforts to locate her were unsuccessful.

118. Politburo Exhibit O-328-330, "Letter to the Com[rade]s. of the PB," unsigned, July 31, 1950.

119. Politburo Exhibit O-643, "Letter to Com[rade]s. of PB," unsigned, September 2, 1950.

120. Politburo Exhibit M-42, "Letter to Com[rade]s. of the PB from Greg re: SEC Decisions in Meet Dated October 13," September 30, 1950. It's interesting that the RSSP was completed on September 12, 1950, and only a few weeks later it was used to "solve" the problem between Luming and Johnny. One cannot help but wonder whether the drafting of the RSSP was specifically prompted by this case, but it is instructive to know that the RSSP was implemented in the movement, at least in this case. Other documents pertaining to Luming include Politburo Exhibits M-12, M-20, M-22-23, and M-25-26.

121. Celia's constant use of the word *mistress* reflects her conservative attitudes toward these women, who were themselves cadres and communists like her, but had relationships with married men. By calling them mistresses Celia seems closer to a bourgeois moralist than a revolutionary feminist.

122. Celia Mariano-Pomeroy, interview with the author, October and November 1998.

123. Pomeroy, *The Forest,* 144.

124. Taruc, *He Who Rides the Tiger,* 64. See also Goodwin, "The Libidinal Constitution of a High-Risk Social Movement," 62.

125. See chapter 3 for a discussion of the Amazons and captured Huklings.

126. Pomeroy, *The Forest,* 142.

127. Celia Mariano-Pomeroy, interview with the author, October and November 1998.

128. Gloria Aquino-Taruc, interview with the author, Diliman, Quezon, July 1997.

129. Rosita Manuel-Liwanag, interview with the author, San Fernando, Pampanga, December 1993.

130. Ibid.

131. Belen Bagul-Bagul, interview with the author, November 1993. One relevant issue connected to having children was the birth control options for Huk women. Why did dedicated cadres such as Belen or Gloria have multiple children under increasingly difficult circumstances? No woman ever discussed birth control during the interviews I conducted. I suspect this was a reflection of the dominant culture during the Huk rebellion when birth control was not a conscious or available option for women.

132. Zenaida del Castillo, interview with the author, January 1994. It was very rare for a Huk woman to discuss the option of abortion during the Huk struggle.

133. Linda Ayala, interview with the author, January 1994 and June 1997.

134. Narcisa Reyes-Romero, interview with the author, November 1993.

135. An in-depth discussion of the demobilization of women in the HMB is found in chapter 2.

136. Filomena Tolentino, interview with the author, October 1993.

137. Luz del Castillo, interview with the author, December 1993.

138. Gloria Rivera-Sagum, interview with the author, January 1994.

139. Goodwin, "The Libidinal Constitution of a High-Risk Social Movement," 63–64; Politburo Exhibit O-321, "Letter to PB (Out) from SEC," May 27, 1950.

140. Politburo Exhibit O-282–284, "Letter to Com[rade]s. Gaston and Beria re: Reports and Information from Plaridel," April 29, 1950.

141. Politburo Exhibit O-13–14, "Letter to Com[rade]s. of PB from Gaston Silayan," October 22, 1949.

142. Politburo Exhibit M-379, "Letter to Com[rade] Plaridel from O. Beria," October 8, 1950.

143. See Pomeroy, *The Forest*; Taruc, *Born of the People*; Taruc, *He Who Rides the Tiger*; and Lava, *Memoirs of a Communist*.

144. Pomeroy, *The Forest*, 62. See also Goodwin, "The Libidinal Constitution of a High-Risk Social Movement," 60.

145. Politburo Exhibit N-1022–1026, "Struggle against Awaitism," by Gregorio Santayana [Jose Lava], 1950.

146. Ibid. This weakness is often referred to as the "free-rider problem" in many communist organizations. See also Goodwin, "The Libidinal Constitution of a High-Risk Social Movement," 63.

147. Politburo Exhibit N-1022–1026, "Struggle against Awaitism."

148. The document reveals the unsympathetic attitude of the leadership toward its members. After further investigation the party decided that many of these cadres were unemployed and an economic burden rather than a means of support to their families, which in most cases were no longer financially dependent on them. But instead of understanding this situation, the party concluded that the main problem afflicting these cadres was awaitism and family problems were secondary.

149. According to the Politburo, cadres were also reluctant to become more involved in the movement because of their "alleged discontent with the party leadership, due either to alleged incorrect cadre policy or alleged disagreement with the political line of the party." The "most subtle screen" was laziness or irresponsibility in performing tasks for the movement. For the "masses," the most common screen was their "alleged belief that . . . [they had] not yet exhausted all legal, parliamentary methods of struggle." Some barrio folks who refused to join the organization employed the screen of their "alleged disagreement with the policy of armed struggle." The party believed that all these issues were merely excuses for awaitism. What they really show is how significant the issue of the family was in the Huk movement. Politburo Exhibit N-1022–1026, "Struggle against Awaitism." See also Politburo Exhibit P-14, "Complete Measures to Struggle Awaitism," [1950].

150. Goodwin, "The Libidinal Constitution of a High-Risk Social Movement," 64.

151. Taruc, *He Who Rides the Tiger*, 248; Goodwin, "The Libidinal Constitution of a High-Risk Social Movement," 63.

152. Politburo Exhibit O-321–323, "Letter to the Com[rade]s. of the PB," unsigned, May 27, 1950.
153. Politburo Exhibit M-444, "Letter to O. Beria from Paes," April 11, 1950.
154. This was a common assertion by many Politburo leaders. Jesus Lava, Jose Lava, and Casto Alejandrino, interview with the author, Mandaluyong City, Manila, November 1993.
155. Taruc, *He Who Rides the Tiger*, 152.
156. Politburo Exhibit O-757, "Finance Opportunism: Its Basic Causes and Remedies," October 10, 1950. See also Politburo Exhibit N-272–279, "Ang ating suliranin sa pananalapi" (Our Problem in Finances), January 1950.
157. Politburo Exhibit O-757, "Finance Opportunism: Its Basic Causes and Remedies," October 10, 1950.
158. See Goodwin, "The Libidinal Constitution of a High-Risk Social Movement," for a brief discussion of the problem of finance opportunism.
159. Politburo Exhibit N-331, "Letter to Ober from Enteng," June 29, 1950.
160. Politburo Exhibit O-319–320, "Letter to the Com[rade]s. of the PB," unsigned, April 29, 1950.
161. Goodwin, "The Libidinal Constitution of a High-Risk Social Movement," 63.
162. Politburo Exhibit O-757, "Finance Opportunism: Its Basic Causes and Remedies." See also Politburo Exhibit N-284–286, "Suliranin sa kadre, tulong na pananalapi at suliranin ng mga pamilya" (Problem of Cadres, Financial Assistance, and Family Problem), March 1950.
163. Pomeroy, *The Forest*, 144.
164. Celia Mariano-Pomeroy, interview with the author, October and November 1998.
165. Ibid.
166. For these works, see Zetkin, *Clara Zetkin*; and Lenin, *The Emancipation of Women*.
167. Celia Mariano-Pomeroy, interview with the author, October and November 1998.
168. Ibid.
169. Celia remained in the Women's Forum from 1947 to 1950. While the forum was a public organization that aimed to recruit women on a broad base, it also served as a front for recruiting women into the HMB and communist movements. For her the most important result of the formation of the women's division was the increasing involvement of women in party work and their eventual rise to responsible posts in the HMB and the PKP.
170. Mariano-Pomeroy, "Experiences as a Guerrilla in the Philippines."
171. Zenaida del Castillo, interview with the author, January 1994.
172. Elang Santa Ana-Maclang, interview with the author, January 1994 and March 1997.

173. Rosenda Torres, interview with the author, December 1993 and June 1997.

174. Pomeroy, *The Forest*, 34.

175. Celia Mariano-Pomeroy, interview with the author, October and November 1998.

176. Ibid.

177. It is undeniable that Celia was and continues to be a staunch feminist, but it is clear that her assessments of the party's failures regarding women's issues grew out of her political activism in the years after her involvement in the Huk rebellion. While she understands that male chauvinism and female passivity in the movement reflected the general culture of Philippine society then, she seems to be unforgiving of her comrades' weaknesses, though she admits that her own growth as a feminist took years.

178. Gloria Aquino-Taruc, interview with the author, July 1997.

179. Araceli Mallari, interview with the author, Caloocan City, Manila, October 1993.

180. Teofista Valerio-Alejandrino, interview with the author, November 1993 and July 1997.

181. See Helen P. Young, *Choosing Revolution: Chinese Women Soldiers on the Long March.*

182. See Gilmartin, *Engendering the Chinese Revolution.*

183. See Karen Turner, with Phan Thanh Hao, *Even the Women Must Fight: Memories of War from North Vietnam.*

184. See Dang Thuy Tram's moving memoir *Last Night I Dreamed of Peace: The Diary of Dang Thuy Tram.*

185. Cynthia Enloe, *Does Khaki Become You? The Militarization of Women's Lives*, 171.

186. Janet Hart, *New Voices in the Nation: Women and the Greek Resistance, 1941–1964*, 168.

187. Goodwin, "The Libidinal Constitution of a High-Risk Social Movement," 66.

188. Ibid., 60.

189. Through a sociological and psychological analysis of the sexual problems of the Huk movement, or what he terms its "libidinal constitution," Jeff Goodwin similarly argues that affectual relationships eroded the solidarity of this exclusive and high-risk social movement. Affectual ties among the movement's predominantly male members undermined their collective identity and discipline. Goodwin writes that the "libidinal opportunity structure" created by these activists' affectual and sexual ties allowed emotional or "libidinal withdrawal" from, and weakened identification with, the insurgency, thereby contributing to its eventual disintegration. See Goodwin, "The Libidinal Constitution of a High-Risk Social Movement," 60–66.

190. Hilsdon, *Madonnas and Martyrs*, 66.

191. Ibid., 69.
192. Ibid., 66. See also works by Cynthia Enloe, including *Does Khaki Become You?*; *Maneuvers: The International Politics of Militarizing Women's Lives*; and, more recently, *The Curious Feminist: Searching for Women in a New Age of Empire.*
193. Hilsdon made similar observations in the sexual culture of the New People's Army. See Hilsdon, *Madonnas and Martyrs,* 72–76.
194. See Joan Landes, "Marxism and the 'Woman Question.'"
195. Celia Mariano-Pomeroy, interview with the author, October and November 1998.

Chapter 5. Amazons in the Unfinished Revolution

1. Celia Mariano-Pomeroy, "Experiences as a Guerrilla in the Philippines."
2. William Pomeroy, *The Forest: A Personal Record of the Huk Guerrilla Struggle in the Philippines,* 212.
3. Ibid., 213.
4. Nick Joaquin [Quijano de Manila], "The Huk from Rochester, N.Y.," 134.
5. Mariano-Pomeroy, "Experiences as a Guerrilla in the Philippines."
6. Filemon Tutay, "Pomeroy Is Captured," *Philippines Free Press,* April 19, 1952. Other stories included "Yank Huk Captured in Battle," *Manila Times,* April 12, 1952; Joseph Majul, "Wm. Pomeroy First to Fall in New Drive," *Manila Times,* April 12, 1952; "Operations Four Roses," *Philippines Free Press,* April 27, 1952; "Pomeroy Confesses to Army" and "Nervous Grin in Pomeroy, Feature on Surrender," *Manila Times,* April 14, 1952; and "Escape Routes Sealed as Area Is Bottled Up: Pomeroy Disclosures Assembled," *Manila Times,* April 15, 1952.
7. Majul, "Wm. Pomeroy First to Fall in New Drive," *Manila Times,* April 12, 1952.
8. "Huk Chieftain Talks: Ex-GI Due Here Today," *Manila Times,* April 13, 1952.
9. Tutay, "Pomeroy Is Captured," *Philippines Free Press,* April 19, 1952.
10. "Celia Pomeroy, UP Graduate Turned Huk," *Manila Times,* April 15, 1952.
11. "Pomeroy's Wife Is Captured," *Manila Times,* April 16, 1952; "7th BCT Seizes Woman in NE Huk Hideout," *Manila Times,* April 16, 1952; "Rebel Couple Are Reunited in Army Camp," *Manila Times,* April 17, 1952.
12. Newspapers continued their coverage of the Pomeroys' arrests. See "Pomeroys Communists, Says AFP Intelligence," *Manila Times,* April 15, 1952; "Pomeroys Face Charges," *Manila Times,* April 22, 1952; and "Pomeroy Listed as AFP Readies Accusations," *Manila Times,* April 27, 1952.
13. Benedict Kerkvliet, *The Huk Rebellion: A Study of Peasant Revolt in*

the Philippines, 234. Kerkvliet gives an authoritative account of the decline of the rebellion, which looked at both the external forces, including increased counterinsurgency operations by the Philippine government and weakened peasant support, as well as the internal divisions within the movement.

14. See especially Pomeroy, *The Forest*; Luis Taruc, *He Who Rides the Tiger*; and Jesus B. Lava, *Memoirs of a Communist.*

15. Araceli Mallari, interview with the author, Caloocan City, Manila, October 1993.

16. Malacanang is the presidential palace. The greeting indicated the Politburo's confidence that eventually the Huks would take the official reins of power in the Philippines.

17. Araceli Mallari, interview with the author, October 1993.

18. Benedict Kerkvliet writes that "in both size and organizational strength, the peasant rebellion grew between 1946 and late 1948." Kerkvliet, *Huk Rebellion,* 174. See also Victor Lieberman, "Why the Hukbalahap Movement Failed."

19. Politburo Exhibit N-1061-1062, "Letter to OB [Organizational Bureau] from Narding," March 31, 1950.

20. Politburo Exhibit O-315, "Letter to the Com[rade]s. of the PB," unsigned, April 6, 1950.

21. Politburo Exhibit O-271-272, "Overall Plan of Expansion and Development of the Party, HMB, and Mass Organizations," n.d.

22. Luis Taruc, interview with the author, Quezon, November 1993 and July 1997. See also Taruc, *He Who Rides the Tiger.*

23. These documents include Politburo Exhibits M-190, O-315, and M-33.

24. Politburo Exhibit O-1029, "Hasten the Tempo of Our Recruiting Work," July 12, 1950. See also Politburo Exhibit N-524-528, "Decisions at the Enlarged ED[ucation] Conference," April 2, 1950.

25. For biographies of Ramon Magsaysay, see Carlos P. Romulo and Marvin M. Gray, *The Magsaysay Story*; Jose Abueva, *Ramon Magsaysay: A Political Biography*; and the most recent, Manuel F. Martinez, *Magsaysay: The People's President.* Most works on Magsaysay are hagiographic presentations of what many believed to be the "most popular president" of the Philippines. They rarely criticized his close relationship with the U.S. government.

26. Kerkvliet, *Huk Rebellion,* 244.

27. Ibid., 245.

28. The best example of Magsaysay's rural reform program is the Economic Development Corps (EDCOR) program, which spent several million pesos and resettled 950 peasant families on land they were given in Mindanao. And yet it is still unclear that EDCOR was successful.

29. See Alvin Scaff, *The Philippine Answer to Communism*; Lieberman "Why the Hukbalahap Movement Failed"; and Eduardo Lachica, *Huk: Philippine Agrarian Society in Revolt.*

30. The arrest of the Politburo members was headline news for several days. See "105 Red Suspects, Including 'Big 6,' Arrested," *Manila Times,* October 20, 1950; "15 Top Red Suspects Locked Up in Muntinlupa," *Manila Times,* October 21, 1950; and Filemon Tutay, "The BIG ROUNDUP," *Philippines Free Press,* October 28, 1950.

31. Lachica, *Huk,* 131; Kerkvliet, *Huk Rebellion,* 220.

32. See "105 Red Suspects, Including 'Big 6,' Arrested," *Manila Times,* October 20, 1950; "15 Top Red Suspects Locked Up in Muntinlupa," *Manila Times,* October 21, 1950; "Red Suspects Held in Jail, Await Charges," *Manila Times,* October 22, 1950; Tutay, "The BIG ROUNDUP," *Philippines Free Press,* October 28, 1950; and Filemon Tutay, "Big Catch," *Philippines Free Press,* October 28, 1950.

33. Kerkvliet, *Huk Rebellion,* 245.

34. Lachica, *Huk,* 131–32.

35. Pomeroy, *The Forest,* 157.

36. Ibid.

37. F. Sionil Jose, ed., "The Huks in Retrospect: A Failed Bid of Power."

38. Ibid., 85.

39. Taruc, *He Who Rides the Tiger.*

40. Sofia Logarta similarly argues that women's primary role was to facilitate "life within the movement" and form a "strong link between the guerrillas and their mass support." When it restrained women's work the movement seriously weakened its ties to the villages. See Sofia Logarta, "The Participation of Women in the Huk Movement," 138.

41. Felisa Cuyugan, interview with the author, San Fernando, Pampanga, November 1993.

42. Kerkvliet, *Huk Rebellion,* 219.

43. Tutay, "Pomeroy Is Captured," *Philippines Free Press,* April 19, 1952; "Escape Routes Sealed as Area Is Bottled Up: Pomeroy Disclosures Assembled," *Manila Times,* April 15, 1952.

44. Politburo Exhibit N-169, "Letter to SEC [Kalihiman Secretariat] c/o Ka Beria from Bonifacio," September 30, 1950.

45. Politburo Exhibit A-84, "Letter to Major Kulafu from Lt. Mabine" (in Hiligaynon, with English translation), May 19, 1950.

46. Pomeroy, *The Forest,* 17.

47. Politburo Exhibit O-326-327, "Letter to the Com[rade]s. of the PB," unsigned, July 22, 1950.

48. Pomeroy, *The Forest,* 140.

49. Taruc, *He Who Rides the Tiger,* 148. Documents on "military discipline" include Politburo Exhibit A-59, "Military Discipline," n.d.; Politburo Exhibit F-35, "Disiplina militar para sa HMB" (Military Discipline for the HMB), n.d.; and Politburo Exhibit F-38, "Analysis of the Developing Situation and Our Tasks," n.d.

50. Taruc, *He Who Rides the Tiger*, 149–53.

51. Many Huk leaders would argue that all of Taruc's revelations were mere justifications for his surrender, but they agreed with him that discipline was imposed harshly during the latter part of the revolt. Jose and Jesus Lava and Casto Alejandrino, interviews with the author, Mandaluyong City, Manila, November 1993.

52. Pomeroy, *The Forest*, 71.

53. Ibid., 140; quoted in Jose, "Huks in Retrospect," 88.

54. Jeff Goodwin, "The Libidinal Constitution of a High-Risk Social Movement: Affectual Ties and Solidarity in the Huk Rebellion, 1946–1954," 65–66.

55. The Huk movement might have attained increased solidarity if it had attracted more women. But, beyond recruiting them, Huk women needed to be trained as cadres who identified strongly with the struggle. Unlike the Huk leaders, the revered leader of the Vietnamese revolution, Ho Chi Minh, believed in the central role women could play in Vietnam's struggle for independence. From the beginning he called on women, who, he remarked, comprised half the population, to join the struggle. Since 1930 Communist Party doctrine had encouraged women to believe there was a place in the hierarchy for them and that they would not be tied to the home and the demands of a husband and oppressive mother-in-law. By the 1940s the party was advocating "universal suffrage, democratic liberties, equality among all ethnic groups and between men and women." "Uncle Ho" had also called informally for an end to arranged marriages and increased opportunities for women to learn to read, study, participate in politics, and be truly men's equals. Because of the importance he accorded to women—in discourse and practice—they responded enthusiastically to his call. See Karen Gottschang Turner, with Phan Thanh Hao, *Even the Women Must Fight: Memories of War from North Vietnam*; Sandra Taylor, *Vietnamese Women at War*; and Sophie Quinn-Judge, "Women in the Early Vietnamese Communist Movement: Sex, Lies, and Liberation."

56. Logarta, "Participation of Women," 139.

57. Politburo Exhibit I-22, "Why I Joined the Huk/Leyte, Betty and Rita" (in Hiligaynon), n.d. In this testimony the female cadre constantly refers to herself as the "weaker sex." This term was also commonly used by my female Huk informants.

58. Cristina Montiel and Mary Racelis Hollnsteiner, *The Filipino Woman: Her Role and Status in Philippine Society*, 15.

59. Bill Pomeroy believed that the Huk movement was a model of an egalitarian society in which there was no division between leaders and members. "Not only must a leader have the fewest weaknesses," he observed, "but he gets no rewards for his position, only the reward of additional responsibility. . . . [A] leader eats the same food, the same amount of it, at the same table, as does the merest rank-and-file member, he wears the same weathered and frayed clothes,

332 ❧ Notes to pages 266–270

he has the same articles of equipment in his pack. . . . He must exhibit complete equality in his relations with all Huks, the highest comradeship, without favoritism, without arrogance, with patience, with fairness. He must be personally unambitious and self-sacrificing . . . the only type of person that can truly look after the interests of the people." Pomeroy, *The Forest*, 140–42.

60. Indeed, party leaders believed that the rationale behind the Huks' strict military discipline was not only to protect the interests of the revolution but also to set its cadres apart from the mainstream culture. Any person found guilty of abusing women or mishandling money was severely punished. Finance opportunism, for example, was described by Pomeroy as "the counterpart of graft or the embezzlement of public funds in the government" against which the Huks fought. A sense of responsibility was therefore a highly lauded virtue. In Huk society, Pomeroy believed, there was "no place for corruption. Every corrupting influence is banned in the camps. Gambling is strictly forbidden. Drinking is completely prohibited. Abuse of the *barrio* people, looting, rape, are punishable by death." Ibid., 146.

61. See Rene Raquiza [Celia Mariano-Pomeroy], "Problems of Sex Morality in Our Party Today," 43. Luis Taruc reiterated that a communist, by nature, is a "sensitive man" who denounces and rejects any type of violence against women. Taruc, *He Who Rides the Tiger*, 150.

62. Pomeroy, *The Forest*, 141.

63. Taruc, *He Who Rides the Tiger*, 44–48.

64. Jesus Lava, interview with the author, November 1993.

65. Goodwin, "The Libidinal Constitution of a High-Risk Social Movement," 65.

66. Raquiza, "Problems of Sex Morality," 46.

67. This conflict of nationalism versus feminism has characterized most revolutionary movements with significant numbers of female members. It remained the central conflict for women in the New People's Army of the new Communist Party of the Philippines. In an important study Leonora Angeles probed this conflict in the various women's movements in Philippine history. See Leonora Angeles, *Feminism and Nationalism: The Discourse on the Woman Question and Politics of the Women's Movement in the Philippines*. See also Mary John Mananzan, *The Woman Question in the Philippines*.

68. While this could be explained by nostalgia and the romance of the revolution, having sacrificed the prime years of their lives to the cause, most women refused to believe that the Huk movement had failed.

69. Teofista Valerio-Alejandrino, interview with the author, Santa Rita, Cabiao, Nueva Ecija, November 1993 and July 1997.

70. Declared by President Ferdinand Marcos, the Martial Law period in the Philippines formally lasted from 1972 to 1981, although Marcos's tenure lasted until 1986. See David Steinberg, *The Philippines: A Singular and a Plural Place*, chap. 7.

71. Filomena Tolentino, interview with the author, Floridablanca, Pampanga, October 1993.

72. Benedict Kerkvliet, "Manuela Santa Ana vda. de Maclang and Philippine Politics."

73. Ibid., 401.

74. During the 1980s, former Hukbalahap guerrillas were recognized for their role in the anti-Japanese resistance and acknowledged as World War II veterans, which entitled them to government pensions. They therefore needed to prove that they belonged to a Hukbalahap squadron during the war and were advised not to reveal (or ignore) their postwar HMB involvement.

75. Remedios Gomez, interview with the author, Project 4, Quezon City, and Anao, Mexico, Pampanga, October and November 1993 and July 1997.

76. Rosenda Torres, interview with the author, Santa Mesa, Manila, December 1993 and June 1997. *Panday Lipi*, roughly translated as "Forging the race, family" is also the name of their literary group.

77. On his release Bill Pomeroy was deported to the United States. When the American government refused to grant Celia a visa to live in the United States the two decided to make England their home. See Vina A. Lanzona, "Romancing a Revolutionary: The Life of Celia Mariano-Pomeroy."

78. Celia's assessment is somewhat overstated. There are other prominent social movements in the Philippines, in particular Gabriela, the country's largest women's organization, which is affiliated with the Communist Party of the Philippines. Although KaBaPa does have a considerable following, Gabriela has far more members and has been much more influential in advancing women's rights. See ibid., 267, 277.

Bibliography

Primary Sources

Politburo Exhibits and Other Documents

Note on the Sources: Most of the primary sources used in this book are documents issued by the Political Bureau (Politburo) of the Partido Komunista ng Pilipinas (Communist Party of the Philippines), or PKP. The collections of documents have two names: Captured Documents of the Politburo (most of which were acquired by the Philippine military during the wholesale arrests of Politburo leaders in 1950) and Politburo Exhibits (which were used as evidence during the trials of the captured leaders). In my citations I use the latter term. The documents are identified by the letter and the page(s) under which they appear in the collections. Most of the documents kept at Camp Crame, the headquarters of the Armed Forces of the Philippines, have been declassified but remain inaccessible to the public. Others are housed in the Special Collections of the Main Library of the University of the Philippines. The documents listed here are housed at the library unless otherwise specified.

Communist Party of the Philippines. "Constitution of the Communist Party of the Philippines." 1946.
Politburo Exhibit A-47. "Principles of Hukbong Mapagpalaya ng Bayan [HUK]" (in Visayan, with English translation), n.d.
Politburo Exhibit A-59. "Military Discipline" (English and Tagalog), n.d.
Politburo Exhibit A-69. "Letter from Pat" (in Hiligaynon, with English translation), March 23, 1950.
Politburo Exhibit A-71. "Letter from the People's Liberation Army," n.d.
Politburo Exhibit A-84. "Letter to Major Kulafu from Lt. Mabine" (in Hiligaynon, with English translation), May 19, 1950.
Politburo Exhibit A-90. "The Development of the Communist Party," Panay Organization Committee, n.d.
Politburo Exhibit B. "Ang Partido Komunista" (The Communist Party), unsigned, n.d.
Politburo Exhibit CC-46. "Affidavit of Teofista Valerio," Camp Murphy, Quezon City, September 10, 1950.
Politburo Exhibit F-7-23. "Dialectical Materialism," n.d.

335

Politburo Exhibit F-35. "Disiplina militar para sa HMB" (Military Discipline for the HMB), n.d.

Politburo Exhibit F-38. "Analysis of the Developing Situation and Our Tasks," n.d.

Politburo Exhibit F-41. "Ang demokratikong centralismo" (The Democratic Centralism), n.d.

Politburo Exhibit G-3. "Huk Principles," unsigned, n.d.

Politburo Exhibit G-6. "Organizational Structure of the Huk" (document captured during the operation against the dissidents of Mt. Diladila, Calinog, Iloilo), September 1950.

Politburo Exhibit GG. "Organizational Chart of the PKP," n.d.

Politburo Exhibit H-36. "Letter to Ka Sulo from Erning," May 8, 1950.

Politburo Exhibit I-1t. "Minutes of the Meeting by All Members of the Staff of FC-62," October 11, 1950.

Politburo Exhibit I-11. "Report to FC-2 from S. Golez," July 30, 1950.

Politburo Exhibit I-15. "The Revolutionary Solution of the Sex Problem," September 12, 1950.

Politburo Exhibit I-16. "Revolutionary Resolution Pertaining to the Problem in the Relation between Man and Woman" (in Hiligaynon, with English translation), [1950].

Politburo Exhibit I-22. "Why I Joined the Huk/Leyte, Betty and Rita" (in Hiligaynon, with English translation), n.d.

Politburo Exhibit I-38. "Marriage contract," n.d.

Politburo Exhibit I-40. "Contract between Tomasa Arnao and Santiago Apostol That Piece of Land Is Given as Donation and Help to the National Liberation Movement," September 1, 1950.

Politburo Exhibit I-56. "Graduation Program, National School, Regional Command 6 & 7, FC-62."

Politburo Exhibit M-12. "Letter to Ka Luming from Leo," July 11, 1950.

Politburo Exhibit M-20. "Letter to Ka Luming from Gaston," n.d.

Politburo Exhibit M-22–23. "Letter to Johnny from Gaston," July 31, 1950.

Politburo Exhibit M-25–26. "Letter to Ka Luming from Gaston," December 26, 1949.

Politburo Exhibit M-33. "Letter to the Com[rade]s. of the PB from Gavino re: Intelligence Information," n.d.

Politburo Exhibit M-42. "Letter to Com[rade]s. of the PB from Greg re: SEC Decisions in Meet Dated October 13," October 15, 1950.

Politburo Exhibit M-171. "Letter to Ka Beria from Leo" (in Tagalog), April 6, 1950.

Politburo Exhibit M-190. "Additional Political-Military Strategic Conceptions: Clarification of the Enlarged PB Conference Resolution," n.d.

Politburo Exhibit M-204–211. "Coordinate Revolutionary Activities in the Cities and Towns and the Armed Struggle in the Field," n.d.

Politburo Exhibit M-379. "Letter to Com[rade] Plaridel from O. Beria," October 8, 1950.

Politburo Exhibit M-444. "Letter to O. Beria from Paes," April 11, 1950.

Politburo Exhibit M-1320-1321. "Letter to Luming from Enteng," June 8, 1949.

Politburo Exhibit N. "State of the Nation and Call to Action by the Central Committee," March 29, 1950.

Politburo Exhibit N-9-11. "Self-Appraisal by Gregorio Santayana," n.d.

Politburo Exhibit N-62-63. "Letter to Com[rade] Enteng from O. Beria," September 21, 1950.

Politburo Exhibit N-67-76. "Self-Appraisal by O. Beria," n.d.

Politburo Exhibit N-169. "Letter to SEC [Kalihiman-Secretariat] c/o Ka Beria from Bonifacio," September 30, 1950.

Politburo Exhibit N-170-171. "Letter to Com[rade] Bonifacio from O. Beria," October 4, 1950.

Politburo Exhibit N-272-279. "Ang ating suliranin sa pananalapi" (Our Problem in Finances), January 1950.

Politburo Exhibit N-280-283. "Impiltrasyon" (Infiltration), February 1950.

Politburo Exhibit N-284-286. "Suliranin sa kadre, tulong na pananalapi at suliranin ng mga pamilya" (Problem of Cadres, Financial Assistance, and Family Problem), March 1950.

Politburo Exhibit N-331. "Letter to Ober from Enteng," June 29, 1950.

Politburo Exhibit N-380-384. "Communist Party of the Philippines, Seventh Regional Committee, Third Meeting," June 18, 1950.

Politburo Exhibit N-524-528. "Decisions at the Enlarged ED[ucation] Conference," April 2, 1950.

Politburo Exhibit N-1022-1026. "Struggle against Awaitism," by Gregorio Santayana [Jose Lava], 1950.

Politburo Exhibit N-1061-1062. "Letter to OB [Organizational Bureau] from Narding," March 31, 1950.

Politburo Exhibit O-13-14. "Letter to Com[rade]s. of PB from Gaston Silayan," October 22, 1949.

Politburo Exhibit O-17-35. "Twenty Years of Struggle of the CPP," by Gregorio Santayana [Jose Lava], n.d.

Politburo Exhibit O-36-74. "Strategy and Tactics," n.d.

Politburo Exhibit. O-180-253. "Milestones in the History of the Communist Party of the Philippines," by Gregorio Santayana [Jose Lava], n.d.

Politburo Exhibit O-271-272. "Overall Plan of Expansion and Development of the Party, HMB, and Mass Organizations," n.d.

Politburo Exhibit O-282-284. "Letter to Com[rade]s. Gaston and Beria re: Reports and Information from Plaridel," April 29, 1950.

Politburo Exhibit O-310-311. "Letter to the Com[rade]s. of the PB," unsigned, November 11, 1949.

Politburo Exhibit O-315. "Letter to the Com[rade]s. of the PB," unsigned, April 6, 1950.

Politburo Exhibit O-319-320. "Letter to the Com[rade]s. of the PB," unsigned, April 29, 1950.

Politburo Exhibit O-321. "Letter to PB (Out) from SEC," May 27, 1950.

Politburo Exhibit O-321-323. "Letter to the Com[rade]s. of the PB," unsigned, May 27, 1950.

Politburo Exhibit O-326-327. "Letter to the Com[rade]s. of the PB," unsigned, July 22, 1950.

Politburo Exhibit O-328-330. "Letter to the Com[rade]s. of the PB," unsigned, July 31, 1950.

Politburo Exhibit O-503-504. "Cardinal Rules for Obtaining Information," n.d.

Politburo Exhibit O-643. "Letter to Com[rade]s. of PB," unsigned, September 2, 1950.

Politburo Exhibit O-662. "Twenty Years of Struggle of the CPP," by Gregorio Santayana [Jose Lava], n.d.

Politburo Exhibit O-749-753. "Accounting for the People's Funds Received and Spent to Finance the Revolution," [1950].

Politburo Exhibit O-757. "Finance Opportunism: Its Basic Causes and Remedies," October 10, 1950.

Politburo Exhibit O-1029. "Hasten the Tempo of Our Recruiting Work," July 12, 1950.

Politburo Exhibit O-1035. "Military Discipline within the Party as a Supplement to Democratic Centralism," September 13, 1950.

Politburo Exhibit O-1043. "Self-appraisal and Appraisal as a Weapon to Strengthen the Party," n.d.

Politburo Exhibit P-14, "Complete Measures to Struggle Awaitism," [1950].

U.S. and Philippine Government Publications

Census of the Philippine Islands, 1918, taken under the direction of the Philippine Legislature. Washington, DC: U.S. Bureau of Census; Manila: Bureau of Printing, 1921.

Census of the Philippine Islands, 1939, taken under the direction of the Philippine Legislature. Washington, DC: U.S. Bureau of Census; Manila: Bureau of Printing, 1940.

Civil Affairs Office, Department of National Defense. *Report on "Communism and the Serviceman."* Manila: Civil Affairs Office, 1951.

Department of National Defense. *Handbook on the Communist Party of the Philippines.* Manila: Armed Forces of the Philippines, 1961.

Philippine Islands. *Board of Educational Survey.* Manila: Bureau of Printing, 1925.

Philippine Republic. *Bureau of Census and Statistics.* Manila: Bureau of Printing, 1960.

Republic of the Philippines. *Report of the President's Action Committee on Social Amelioration to the People of the Philippines.* Manila: Bureau of Printing, October 1949.

Special Committee on Un-Filipino Activities, House of Representatives of the Republic of the Philippines. *Report on "Communism in the Philippines."* Manila: Bureau of Printing, May 1952.

———. *Report on the Illegality of the Communist Party of the Philippines.* Manila: Bureau of Printing, 1951.

———. *General Report on Communism and the Communist Party.* Manila: Bureau of Printing, 1949.

U.S. Department of State, Foreign Relations of the United States. "A Report to the President by the National Security Council on the Position of the United States with Respect to the Philippines," Washington, DC: U.S. Government Printing Office, November 1950.

Newspaper and Magazine Articles

"Alejandrino Wife to Face Charges." *Daily Mirror,* September 9, 1950.

"Amazon Captured." *Philippines Free Press,* March 21, 1948.

"Amazon Finance Officer Nabbed." *Daily Mirror,* October 31, 1953.

Baquirin, David. "Cupid, Alias J. Crisol, Writes Happy Chapter in Huk Romance." *Manila Times,* October 7, 1954.

"Bulacan Judge Frees Woman Huk." *Manila Times,* April 29, 1948.

Carter, Clark S. [William Pomeroy]. "Revolt in the Philippines." *Salute: The Picture Magazine for Men* 2, no. 10 (October 1947): 9-12. Produced by former editors and writers of *Yank* and *Stars and Stripes.*

"Catapatan, 4 Others Slain." *Manila Times,* April 4, 1952.

"Celia Pomeroy, UP Graduate Turned Huk." *Manila Times,* April 15, 1952.

Chavez, Elieser M. "Women in War." *Philippines Free Press,* December 10, 1949.

"Escape Routes Sealed as Area Is Bottled Up: Pomeroy Disclosures Assembled." *Manila Times,* April 15, 1952.

"15 Top Red Suspects Locked Up in Muntinlupa." *Manila Times,* October 21, 1950.

"4 Amazons, Huk Held, One Slain." *Daily Mirror,* August 31, 1953.

Gourlay, Candy. "Happy Birthday Celia and Thanks." *Filipinos in Europe,* summer 1995.

"Habeas Corpus Writ for Huk Girl." *Manila Times,* October 27, 1947.

"Huk Amazon Captured." *Manila Times,* February 17, 1959.

"Huk Amazon Unit Encountered by PC." *Manila Times,* September 15, 1948.

"Huk Baby." *Philippines Free Press,* March 1, 1952.

"Huk Chieftain Talks: Ex-GI Due Here Today." *Manila Times,* April 13, 1952.
"Huk Leader's Top Contact Is Arrested." *Manila Times,* September 9, 1950.
"Huk Message Unit Broken, 3 Amazons Arrested." *Manila Times,* October 2, 1953.
"Huks Led by Woman Clash with PC." *Manila Times,* March 25, 1950.
"Huk Sweethearts to Wed Tomorrow." *Daily Mirror,* October 5, 1954.
"Huk Woman Wins Freedom from MP." *Manila Times,* November 5, 1947.
"Hunger Taking Lives of Huks." *Manila Times,* October 9, 1948.
Lansang, Teodosio. "Exclusive Interview with 'Liwayway' Huk Commander." *Truth Magazine,* August 1 and 14, 1947.
"Late Flashes from the Huk Front, Taruc Wife Revealed." *Philippines Free Press,* November 6, 1948.
"Lava Is No Commie, Says Wife." *Manila Times,* July 22, 1956.
"Lava's Alleged Wife Captured." *Manila Chronicle,* July 15, 1956.
"Lava's Wife Faces Rebellion Charges." *Manila Chronicle,* July 22, 1956.
"Lava Wife Refuses to Talk at Probe." *Daily Mirror,* July 16, 1956.
Majul, Joseph. "Wm. Pomeroy First to Fall in New Drive." *Manila Times,* April 12, 1952.
"Nervous Grin In Pomeroy, Feature on Surrender." *Manila Times,* April 14, 1952.
"183 Huks Slain in Pampanga, Five Amazons among Fatalities." *Manila Times,* September 25, 1948.
"105 Red Suspects, Including 'Big 6,' Arrested." *Manila Times,* October 20, 1950.
"Operations Four Roses." *Philippines Free Press,* April 27, 1952.
"Pomeroy Confesses to Army." *Manila Times,* April 14, 1952.
"Pomeroy Listed as AFP Readies Accusations." *Manila Times,* April 27, 1952.
"Pomeroys Communists, Says AFP Intelligence." *Manila Times,* April 15, 1952.
"Pomeroys Face Charges." *Manila Times,* April 22, 1952.
"Pomeroy's Wife Is Captured." *Manila Times,* April 16, 1952.
"Pretty Girl Denies Any Huk Connection." *Manila Times,* October 20, 1948.
Quirino, Jose A. "The Seven Huklings of EDCOR." *Philippines Free Press,* July 2, 1955.
Raquiza, Rene [Celia Mariano-Pomeroy]. "Problems of Sex Morality in Our Party Today." *Ang Komunista* (The Communist) 1, no. 1 (August 1950): 42–52.
"Rebel Couple Are Reunited in Army Camp." *Manila Times,* April 17, 1952.
"Red Suspects Held in jail, Await Charges." *Manila Times,* October 22, 1950.
Reed, Diana. "WWII Forgotten Heroine" (interview with Celia Pomeroy). *Kamusta,* no. 2 (1995): 11–13.
Reynante, Emiliano D. "Lovelorn Huks Marry." *Philippines Free Press,* October 16, 1954.
"7th BCT Seizes Woman in N[ueva] E[cija] Huk Hideout." *Manila Times,* April 16, 1952.

"Taruc's Girl Secretary Is Captured." *Manila Times,* October 12, 1948.
"Top Woman Huk Dies." *Manila Times,* April 29, 1948.
Tutay, Filemon. "Big Catch." *Philippines Free Press,* October 28, 1950.
———. "The BIG ROUNDUP." *Philippines Free Press,* October 28, 1950.
———. "Pomeroy Is Captured." *Philippines Free Press,* April 19, 1952.
———. "Poor Babies!" *Philippines Free Press,* June 28, 1952.
"2 Surrendered Huk Lovers Wed." *Manila Chronicle,* October 6, 1954.
Ty, Leon. "Guerrilleras." *Philippines Free Press,* October 12, 1946.
———. "Nervous Peace in Nueva Ecija." *Philippines Free Press,* October 29, 1949.
"Waling Waling Nabbed." *Manila Times,* May 1, 1952.
"What the Huks Think of Sex." *Philippines Free Press,* July 29, 1967.
"Wife of Huk Regional Area Supervisor Captured by PC." *Manila Times,* March 21, 1948,
"Woman Huk Commander Facing Trial for Sedition, Rebellion." *Manila Times,* August 7, 1947.
"Woman Huk Fights and Flees." *Manila Times,* April 20, 1950.
"Woman Huk Found Dying." *Manila Times,* September 17, 1948.
"Yank Huk Captured in Battle." *Manila Times,* April 12, 1952

Speeches, Letters, and Correspondence

Mariano-Pomeroy, Celia. "Experiences as a Guerrilla in the Philippines." Lecture delivered at the Centre of Southeast Asian Studies, University of Kent, May 17, 1991.
———. Letter to Jeff Goodwin, February 26, 1993 (used with permission).
———. Letter to Jeff Goodwin, June 21, 1993 (used with permission).
———. Speech delivered at the Malibongwe Conference for South African Women, Amsterdam, January 11, 1990.
Pomeroy, William. Letter to the author, March 15, 1999.

Interviews

Crisanta Abejero, Luisinia, Laguna, April 1997.
Dominga Adasar-Centeno, Cabanatuan, Nueva Ecija, November 1993.
Casto Alejandrino, Mandaluyong City, Manila, November 1993.
Briccio Almiranez, Mauban, Quezon, June 1997.
Cion Amorao, Cabiao, Nueva Ecija, July 1997.
Felicidad Angeles, Santa Rosa, Nueva Ecija, November 1993.
Maria Angeles, Santa Rosa, Nueva Ecija, November 1993.
Gloria Aquino-Taruc, Diliman, Quezon City, July 1997.
Felisa Armia, Santa Cruz, Laguna, April 1997.
Linda Ayala, Makati City, Manila, January 1994, and Santo Niño, Quezon, June 1997.
Rosalina Bacani, San Ricardo, Talavera, Nueva Ecija, March 1997.

Belen Bagul-Bagul, Santa Cruz, Laguna, November 1993.
Gonzalo Beltran, Aliaga, Nueva Ecija, March 1997.
Pacita Beltran, Aliaga, Nueva Ecija, March 1997.
Loreta Betangkul, Anao, Mexico, Pampanga, October 1993.
Cecilia Bianzon-Pineda, Cabanatuan, Nueva Ecija, July 1997.
Hilario Bulaon, San Miguel, Bulacan, May 1997.
Puring Bulatao, Paco, Manila, October 1993.
Cenon Bungay, San Simon, Pampanga, April 1997.
Agustin Calma, Anao, Mexico, Pampanga, July 1997.
Virginia Calma, Diliman, Quezon City, November 1993 and June 1997.
Bonifacio Carriaga, Tarlac, Tarlac, July 1997.
Zenaida del Castillo, Laurel, Batangas, January 1994.
Luz del Castillo-Valerio, Tandang Sora, Quezon City, December 1993.
Federico Cava, San Miguel, Bulacan, May 1997.
Marcosa Cenan, Cabanatuan, Nueva Ecija, July 1997.
Felisa Cuyugan, San Fernando, Pampanga, November 1993.
Pasencia David, San Fernando, Pampanga, November 1993.
Apolinaria Domingo, Polilio, Cabanatuan, Nueva Ecija, July 1997.
Ramon Espiritu, Quezon City, October 1993.
Filemon Esteban, Camiling, Tarlac, July 1997.
Juana Fajardo, Santo Cristo, Gapan, Nueva Ecija, November 1993.
Eligio Gamboa, San Miguel, Bulacan, May 1997.
Maximino Gamboa, Malolos, Bulacan, August 1997.
Lutgarda Gana, Anao, Mexico, Pampanga, November 1993.
Leonila Sayco Gatus-Palo, San Fernando, Pampanga, October 1993.
Remedios Gomez, Project 4, Quezon City, and Anao, Mexico, Pampanga,
    October and November 1993 and July 1997.
Agripina Gomez-Briones, San Simon, Pampanga, April 1997.
Elena Gonzales, Mexico, Pampanga, October 1993.
Catalina Hernandez, Malolos, Bulacan, August 1997.
Ligaya Kabayan-Ordanez, Aliaga, Nueva Ecija, November 1993.
Africano Kabigting, Santa Lucia, Santa Ana, Pampanga, October 1993.
Servando Kaisip, San Ricardo, Talavera, Nueva Ecija, March 1997.
Anita Laban-Laban, Kalayaan, Laguna, April 1997.
Apolinario Lacanilao, Malolos, Bulacan, August 1997.
Marcelino Lacanilao, Anao, Mexico, Pampanga, November 1993.
Vicenta Lacanilao, San Miguel Bulacan, May 1997.
Diosdado Lagman, Victoria, Tarlac, July 1997.
Maria Lapuz, Cabanatuan, Nueva Ecija, July 1997.
Abner Layola, Luisiana, Laguna, April 1997.
Felomino Laurel, Mauban, Quezon, June 1997.
Romulo Laurente, Santo Rosario, Bulacan, May 1997.
Jesus Lava, Mandaluyong City, Manila, November 1993.

Jose Lava, Mandaluyong City, Manila, November 1993.
Silvestre Liwanag, San Fernando, Pampanga, December 1993.
Flora Maglaqui-Domingo, Polilio, Cabanatuan, Nueva Ecija, July 1997.
Araceli Mallari, Caloocan City, Manila, October 1993.
Godofredo Mallari, Caloocan City, Manilla, October 1993.
Iladia Mallari, Cabanatuan, Nueva Ecija, July 1997.
Maria Manalang-Pangan, San Simon, Pampanga, April 1997.
Lucia Manlutac, Tondo, Manila, August 1997.
Rosita Manuel-Liwanag, San Fernando, Pampanga, December 1993.
Celia Mariano-Pomeroy, Twickenham, England, October and November 1998.
Trinidad Mendoza-Bugnot, Paradise, Tarlac, July 1997.
Leonila Monteverde, Mauban, Quezon, June 1997.
Loreto Palentinos, Santa Cruz, Laguna, April 1997.
Candelaria Pangan, Santa Ana, Pampanga, October 1993.
Sotera Perez-Inocencio, Tarlac, Tarlac, July 1997.
Felisa Pineda, Cabanatuan, Nueva Ecija, July 1997.
Tomas Policarpio, Capas, Tarlac, July 1997.
William Pomeroy, Twickenham, England, October 1998.
Petras Punzalan-Santos, San Simon, Pampanga, April 1997.
Simeona Punzalan-Tapang, San Simon, Pampanga, January 1994 and April 1997.
Consolacion Relucio-Tiangko, Cabiao, Nueva Ecija, July 1997.
Celia Reyes, Santa Rita, Cabiao, Nueva Ecija, July 1997.
Narcisa Reyes-Romero, Cabiao, Nueva Ecija, November 1993.
Ruperta Risio, Cabanatuan, Nueva Ecija, July 1997.
Gloria Rivera-Sagum, San Luis, Pampanga, January 1994.
Juliano del Rosario, San Miguel, Bulacan, May 1997.
Epifania del Rosario-Flores, Tondo, Manila, August 1997.
Marcosa de la Rosa-Timban, Tondo, Manila, October 1993.
Gemiliano Sagun, San Emiliano, Cabanatuan, Nueva Ecija, July 1997.
Maria Sagun, Aliaga, Cabanatuan, Nueva Ecija, July 1997.
Felicidad Sagun-Alcantara, Aliaga, Cabanatuan, Nueva Ecija, July 1997.
Maxima San Pedro-Alcantara, San Ricardo, Talavera, Nueva Ecija, January 1994.
Elang Santa Ana-Maclang, San Ricardo, Talavera, Nueva Ecija, January 1994 and March 1997.
Avelina Santos, Mexico, Pampanga, October 1993.
Pablo Santos, Santa Rita, Cabiao, Nueva Ecija, July 1997.
Elena Sawit-Macapagal, Novaliches, Quezon City, September 1993.
Viring Sese-Guas, San Fernando, Pampanga, December 1993.
Romana Sigwa, San Jose, Nueva Ecija, July 1997.
Alberta Silverio, Floridablanca, Pampanga, December 1993.

Alejandra Silverio, San Fernando, Pampanga, December 1993.
Marcela Simbulan-Agustin, Talavera, Nueva Ecija, January 1994.
Bella Simpauco, Project 4, Quezon City, October 1993.
Prima Sobrevinas, Santa Cruz, Laguna, November 1993.
Vicenta Soliman, San Miguel, Bulacan, May 1997.
Ana Sula, Santa Ana, Pampanga, October 1993.
Carmen Sunga-Torres, Tondo, Manila, August 1997.
Luis Taruc, Diliman, Quezon City, December 1993 and July 1997.
Peregrino Taruc, Diliman, Quezon City, July 1997.
Filomena Tolentino, Floridablanca, Pampanga, October 1993.
Cesario Torres, Santa Mesa, Manila, December 1993 and June 1997.
Rosenda Torres, Santa Mesa, Manila, December 1993 and June 1997.
Erasto Trinidad, Kalayaan, Laguna, April 1997.
Amparo Valerio, Santa Rita, Cabiao, Nueva Ecija, November 1993.
Belen Valerio, Santa Rita, Cabiao, Nueva Ecija, November 1993.
Teofista Valerio-Alejandrino, Santa Rita, Cabiao, Nueva Ecija, November 1993
and July 1997.
Consolacion Villafuerte, Victoria, Tarlac, July 1997.
Dominga Villamin, Santa Cruz, Laguna, April 1997.

Secondary Sources

Abaya, Hernando. *Betrayal in the Philippines.* With a new introduction by Renato Constantino. Quezon City: Malaya Books, 1970.
Abinales, Patricio N. *Love, Sex, and the Filipino Communist or Hinggil sa Pagpipigil ng Panggigigil.* Pasig City: Anvil Press, 2004.
Abinales, Patricio, and Donna Amoroso. *State and Society in the Philippines.* Lanham, MD: Rowman and Littlefield, 2005.
Abueva, Jose. *Ramon Magsaysay: A Political Biography.* Manila: Solidaridad Publishing House, 1971.
Adas, Michael. "Bandits, Monks, and Pretender Kings: Patterns of Peasant Resistance and Protest in Colonial Burma, 1826-1941." In *Power and Protest in the Countryside,* ed. Robert P. Weller and Scott E. Guggenheim, 75-105. Durham, NC: Duke University Press, 1982.
———. *Prophets of Rebellion: Millenarian Protest against the European Colonial Order.* Chapel Hill: University of North Carolina Press, 1979.
Agoncillo, Teodoro A. "Bataan and Corregidor Revisited." In *History and Culture, Language and Literature: Selected Essays of Teodoro A. Agoncillo,* ed. Bernadita Reyes Churchill, 380-81. Diliman: University of the Philippines Press, 2003.
———. *The Burden of Proof: The Vargas-Laurel Collaboration Case.* Diliman: University of the Philippines Press, 1984.

———. *The Fateful Years: Japan's Adventure in the Philippines, 1941–45.* 1965. Quezon City: University of the Philippines Press, 2001.

———. *The Revolt of the Masses: The Story of Bonifacio and the Katipunan.* 1956. Diliman: University of the Philippines Press, 1996.

Alabado, Corban K. *Bataan, Death March, Capas: A Tale of Japanese Cruelty and American Injustice.* San Francisco: Sulu Books, 1995.

Allen, Barbara, and William Lynwood Montell. *From Memory to History: Using Oral Sources in Local Historical Research.* Nashville: American Association for State and Local History, 1981.

Allen, James. *The Philippine Left on the Eve of World War II.* Minneapolis: MEP Publications, 1993.

———. *The Radical Left on the Eve of War: A Political Memoir.* Quezon City: Foundation for Nationalist Studies, 1985.

Alzona, Encarnacion. *Social and Economic Status of Filipino Women, 1565–1932.* Manila: University of the Philippines Press, 1933.

Aminzade, Ronald, et al. *Silence and Voice in the Study of Contentious Politics.* New York: Cambridge University Press, 2001.

Andaya, Barbara Watson. *The Flaming Womb: Repositioning Women in Early Modern Southeast Asia.* Honolulu: University of Hawaii Press, 2008.

———. "Studying Women and Gender in Southeast Asia." *International Journal of Asian Studies* 4, no. 1 (2007): 113–36.

———. "Gender, Warfare, and Patriotism in Southeast Asia and the Philippine Revolution." In *The Philippine Revolution of 1896: Ordinary Lives in Extraordinary Times,* ed. Florentino Rodao and Felice Noelle Rodriguez, 1–30. Quezon City: Ateneo de Manila University Press, 2001.

Andaya, Leonard. "Ethnicity in the Philippine Revolution." In *The Philippine Revolution of 1896: Ordinary Lives in Extraordinary Times,* ed. Florentino Rodao and Felice Noelle Rodriguez, 49–82. Quezon City: Ateneo de Manila University Press, 2001.

Anderson, Benedict. *Imagined Communities: Reflections on the Origin and Spread of Nationalism.* Rev. ed. New York: Verso, 1991.

———. *Java in a Time of Revolution: Occupation and Resistance, 1944–1946.* Ithaca, NY: Cornell University Press, 1972.

Angeles, Leonora. "Feminism and Nationalism: The Discourse on the Woman Question and Politics of the Women's Movement in the Philippines." M.A. thesis, University of the Philippines, 1989.

Ariola, Fe Capellan. *Si Maria, Nena, Gabriela, atbp.: Kuwentong Kasaysayan ng Kababaihan* (Maria, Nena, Gabriela, etc.: Historical Stories of Women). Manila: Gabriela and Institute of Women's Studies, Saint Scholastica College, 1989.

Atkinson, Jane, and Shelly Errington, eds. *Power and Difference: Gender in Island Southeast Asia.* Stanford: Stanford University Press, 1990.

Azarcon, Pennie S., ed. *Kamalayan: Feminist Writings in the Philippines.* Quezon City: Pilipina, 1987.

Baclagon, Uldarico S. *Lessons from the Huk Campaign in the Philippines.* Manila: M. Colcol, 1960.

Benda, Harry J. *Continuity and Change in Southeast Asia: Collected Journal Articles of Harry J. Benda.* New Haven, CT: Council on Southeast Asia Studies, Yale University, 1972.

———. *The Crescent and the Rising Sun: Indonesian Islam under the Japanese Occupation, 1942-1945.* The Hague: W. van Hoeve, 1958.

———. "The Japanese Interregnum in Southeast Asia." In *Imperial Japan and Asia: A Reassessment,* ed. Grant Goodman, 65-79. New York: East Asian Institute, Columbia University, 1967.

———. "Peasant Movements in Colonial Southeast Asia." *Asian Studies* 3 (1965): 420-34.

Binh, Tran Tu. *The Red Earth: A Vietnamese Memoir of a Life on a Colonial Rubber Plantation.* Athens: Center for International Studies, Center for Southeast Asian Studies, Ohio University, 1985.

Blackburn, Susan. *Women and the State in Modern Indonesia.* Cambridge: Cambridge University Press, 2004.

Blok, Josine. *The Early Amazons: Modern and Ancient Perspectives on a Persistent Myth.* New York: Brill, 1995.

Bradley, Harriet. *Men's Work, Women's Work: A Sociological History of the Sexual Division of Labor in Employment.* Minneapolis: University of Minnesota Press, 1989.

Brewer, Carolyn. *Shamanism, Catholicism, and Gender Relations in Colonial Philippines, 1521-1685.* Burlington, VT: Ashgate, 2004.

Butler, Thomas, ed. *Memory, History, Culture, and the Mind.* Oxford: Blackwell, 1989.

Calhoun, Craig. "The Problem of Identity in Collective Action." In *Macro-Micro Linkages in Sociology,* ed. Joan Huber, 51-75. Newbury Park, CA: Sage, 1991.

Camagay, Maria Luisa. *Working Women of Manila in the Nineteenth Century.* Quezon City: University of the Philippines Press and the University Center for Women Studies, 1995.

Cannell, Fenella. *Power and Intimacy in the Christian Philippines.* New York: Cambridge University Press, 1999.

Castelnuovo, Shirley, and Sharon R. Guthrie. *Feminism and the Female Body: Liberating the Amazon Within.* Boulder: Rienner, 1998.

Chatterjee, Partha. *The Nation and Its Fragments: Colonial and Postcolonial Histories.* Princeton, NJ: Princeton University Press, 1993.

Chungmoo Choi, ed. *The Comfort Women: Colonialism, War, and Sex.* Durham, NC: Duke University Press, 1997.

Constantino, Renato. *The Philippines: A Past Revisited.* Manila: Renato Constantino, 1975.

Constantino, Renato, and Letizia Constantino. *The Philippines: The Continuing Past.* Quezon City: Foundation for Nationalist Studies, 1978.

Corpuz, Carmelita. *Mula Noon Hanggang Gabriela: Ang Kababaihan sa Kasaysayan ng Pilipinas hanggang mga 1980* (From the Past to Gabriela: Women in the History of the Philippines up to 1980). Manila: De La Salle University Press, 2003.

Corpuz, Onofre D. *The Roots of the Filipino Nation.* Quezon City: Aklahi Foundation, 1989.

Crippen, Harlan. "Philippine Agrarian Unrest: Historical Backgrounds." *Science and Society* 10 (1946): 337–60.

Crisol, Jose M. "Communist Propaganda in the Philippines—1950–1953." *Philippine Studies* 1 (December 1953): 207–22.

Croll, Elisabeth. *Feminism and Socialism in China.* New York: Schocken, 1978.

Cruz, Romeo. "Ang Pilipina sa Panahon ng Himagsikan at Digmaang Pilipino-Amerikano" (The Filipina in the Period of Revolution and the Philippine-American War). In *Women's Role in Philippine History: Selected Essays,* 59–62. 2nd ed. Quezon City: Center for Women's Studies, University of the Philippines, 1996.

Dalisay, Jose, Jr. "The Lava Brothers: Blood and Politics." *Public Policy* (University of the Philippines) 2, no. 3 (July–September 1998): 87–112.

———. *The Lavas: A Filipino Family.* Pasig City: Anvil, 1999.

Dang Thuy Tram. *Last Night I Dreamed of Peace: The Diary of Dang Thuy Tram.* Trans. Andrew Pham. New York: Harmony, 2007.

Davis, Miranda, ed. *Third World, Second Sex: Women's Struggles and National Liberation—Third World Women Speak Out.* London: Zed, 1983.

de Guzman, Odine, ed. *Body Politics: Essays on Cultural Representations of Women's Bodies.* Diliman: University Center for Women's Studies, University of the Philippines, 2002.

De Mel, Neloufer. *Women and the Nation's Narrative: Gender and Nationalism in Twentieth-Century Sri Lanka.* Lanham, MD: Rowman and Littlefield, 2001.

Dery, Luis Camara. *Remember the Ladies and Other Historical Essays on the 1896 Philippine Revolution.* Manila: M and L Enterprises, 2000.

Diani, Mario, and Doug McAdam, eds. *Social Movements and Networks: Relational Approaches to Collective Action.* New York: Oxford University Press, 2003.

di Leonardo, Micaela, ed. *Gender at the Crossroads of Knowledge: Feminist Anthropology in the Postmodern Era.* Berkeley: University of California Press, 1991.

Doeppers, Daniel. *Manila, 1900–1941: Social Change in a Late Colonial Metropolis.* Quezon City: Ateneo de Manila University Press, 1984.

Dube, Leela. *Women and Kinship: Comparative Perspectives on Gender in South and Southeast Asia.* Tokyo: United Nations University Press, 1997.

Duiker, William. *The Communist Road to Power in Vietnam.* Boulder, CO: Westview Press, 1981.

Dyess, William E. *Bataan Death March: A Survivor's Account.* Lincoln, NE: Bison Books, 2002.

Edwards, Louise, and Mina Roces. "Orienting the Global Women's Suffrage Movement." In *Women's Suffrage in Asia: Gender, Nationalism, and Democracy,* ed. Louise Edwards and Mina Roces, 1–23. New York: Routledge-Curzon, 2004.

Eisen, Arlene. *Women and Revolution in Vietnam.* London: Zed, 1984.

Encanto, Georgina Reyes. *Constructing the Filipina: A History of Women's Magazines (1891–2002).* Diliman: University of the Philippines Press, 2004.

Enloe, Cynthia. *The Curious Feminist: Searching for Women in a New Age of Empire.* Berkeley: University of California Press, 2004.

———. *Does Khaki Become You? The Militarization of Women's Lives.* London: South End, 1983.

———. *Maneuvers: The International Politics of Militarizing Women's Lives.* Berkeley: University of California Press, 2000.

———. *The Morning After: Sexual Politics at the End of the Cold War.* Berkeley: University of California Press, 1993.

Entenberg, B. "Agrarian Reform and the Hukbalahap." *Far Eastern Survey* 15 (14 August 1946): 245–48.

Estrada-Claudio, Sylvia. *Rape, Love, and Sexuality: The Construction of Women in Discourse.* Diliman: University of the Philippines Press, 2002.

Eviota, Elizabeth. *The Political Economy of Gender: Women and the Sexual Division of Labor in the Philippines.* London: Zed, 1992.

Eviota, Elizabeth, ed. *Sex and Gender in Philippine Society: A Discussion of Issues on the Relations between Women and Men.* Manila: National Commission on the Role of Filipino Women, 1994.

Fegan, Brian. "The Social History of a Central Luzon Barrio." In *Philippine Social History: Global Trade and Local Transformations,* ed. Alfred W. McCoy and Edilberto C. de Jesus, 91–130. Quezon City: Ateneo de Manila University Press, 1982.

Feliciano, Myrna. "The Filipina: A Historical Legal Perspective." In *Women's Role in Philippine History: Selected Essays,* 9–33. 2nd ed. Quezon City: Center for Women's Studies, University of the Philippines, 1996.

Fifield, Russell H. "The Hukbalahap Today." *Far Eastern Survey* 20 (January 1951): 13–18.

Findlay, Eileen. "Breaking Bounds: The Brigadas Femeninas of the Cristero Rebellion." M.A. thesis, University of Wisconsin-Madison, 1988.

Foronda, Marcelino, Jr. *Cultural Life in the Philippines during the Japanese Occupation, 1942–1945.* Manila: Philippine National Historical Society, 1975.

Friend, Theodore. *Blue Eyed Enemy: Japan against the West in Java and Luzon, 1942–1945.* Princeton, NJ: Princeton University Press, 1988.

Gallagher, Nancy. "The Gender Gap in Popular Attitudes toward the Use of Force." In *Women and the Use of Military Force,* ed. Ruth H. Howes and Michael R. Stevenson, 23–37. Boulder: Rienner, 1993.

Garcia, Mauro, ed. *Documents on the Japanese Occupation of the Philippines.* Manila: Philippine Historical Association, 1965.

Gilmartin, Christina Kelley. *Engendering the Chinese Revolution: Radical Women, Communist Politics, and Mass Movements in the 1920s.* Berkeley: University of California Press, 1995.

Go, Julian. "Introduction: Global Perspectives on the U.S. Colonial State in the Philippines." In *The American Colonial State in the Philippines: Global Perspectives,* ed. Julian Go and Anne Foster, 1–42. Durham, NC: Duke University Press, 2003.

Goldstone, Jack. *Revolution and Rebellion in the Early Modern World.* Berkeley: University of California Press, 1991.

Goodman, Grant. *Imperial Japan and Asia: A Reassessment.* New York: East Asian Institute, Columbia University, 1967.

Goodwin, Jeff. "The Libidinal Constitution of a High-Risk Social Movement: Affectual Ties and Solidarity in the Huk Rebellion, 1946–1954." *American Sociological Review* 62 (February 1997): 53–69.

———. *No Other Way Out: States and Social Revolutionary Movements, 1945–1991.* New York: Cambridge University Press, 2001.

Goodwin, Jeff, James Jasper, and Francesca Poletta, eds. *Passionate Politics: Emotions and Social Movements.* Chicago: University of Chicago Press, 2001.

Goodwin, Jeff, and Theda Skocpol. "Explaining Revolutions in the Contemporary Third World." *Politics and Society* 17 (1989): 489–507.

Guerrero, Amado. *Philippine Society and Revolution.* Manila: Pulang Tala Publications, 1971.

Hart, Donn. *Compradinazgo: Ritual Kinship in the Philippines.* Quezon City: Ateneo de Manila University Press, 1977.

Hart, Janet. *New Voices in the Nation: Women and the Greek Resistance, 1941–1964.* Ithaca, NY: Cornell University Press, 1996.

Hartog, Francois. *The Mirror of Herodotus: The Representation of the Other in the Writing of History.* Trans. Janet Lloyd. Berkeley: University of California Press, 1988.

Hedman, Eva-Lotta, and John Sidel. *Philippine Politics and Society in the Twentieth Century: Colonial Legacies, Post-colonial Trajectories.* New York: Routledge, 2000.

Henson, Maria Rosa. *Comfort Woman, Slave of Destiny.* Pasig City: Philippine Center for Investigative Journalism, 1996.

Hicks, George. *The Comfort Women: Japan's Brutal Regime of Enforced Prostitution in the Second World War.* New York: Norton, 1995.

Hidalgo Lim, Pilar. "Josefa Llanes Escoda." In *Ruby Jubilee Yearbook, 1921–1961,* 8–9, 108–10. Manila: National Federation of Women's Clubs of the Philippines, 1961.

Hilario-Soriano, Rafaelita. "The Japanese Occupation of the Philippines with Special Reference to Japanese Propaganda, 1941–1945." Ph.D. diss., University of Michigan, 1948.

Hilsdon, Anne-Marie. *Madonnas and Martyrs: Militarism and Violence in the Philippines.* Quezon City: Ateneo de Manila University Press, 1995.

Historical Commission, Partido Komunista ng Pilipinas. *Communism in the Philippines: The P.K.P., Book 1.* Manila: Communist Party of the Philippines, 1996.

Hobsbawm, Eric. *Primitive Rebels: Studies in Archaic Forms of Social Movements in the 19th and 20th Centuries.* New York: Norton, 1965.

————. *Revolutionaries.* New York: Pantheon, 1973.

Hoeksema, Renze L. "Communism in the Philippines: A Historical and Analytical Study of Communism and the Communist Party in the Philippines and Its Relations to Communist Movements Abroad." Ph.D. diss., Harvard University, 1956.

Holt, Alix, ed. *Selected Writings of Alexandra Kollantai.* New York: Norton, 1977.

Howe, Ruth, and Michael Stevenson. *Women and the Use of Military Force.* Boulder: Rienner, 1993.

Huen, P. Lim Pui, James Morrison, and Kwa Chong Guan, eds. *Oral History in Southeast Asia: Theory and Method.* Singapore: Institute of Southeast Asian Studies, 1998.

Hunt, Lynn. *Politics, Culture, and Class in the French Revolution.* Berkeley: University of California Press, 1984.

Ikehata Setsuho. "The Japanese Occupation Period in Philippine History." In *The Philippines under Japan: Occupation Policy and Reaction,* ed. Ikehata Setsuho and Ricardo Jose, 1–20. Quezon City: Ateneo de Manila University Press, 1999.

Ikehata Setsuho, and Ricardo Jose, eds. *The Philippines under Japan: Occupation Policy and Reaction.* Quezon City: Ateneo de Manila University Press, 1999.

Ileto, Reynaldo. *Pasyon and Revolution: Popular Movements in the Philippines, 1840–1910.* Quezon City: Ateneo de Manila University Press, 1979.

Illo, Jeanne Frances. "Redefining the *Maybahay* or Housewife: Reflections on the Nature of Women's Work in the Philippines." In *Women and Gender Relations in the Philippines,* ed. Jeanne Frances Illo, 165–80. Quezon City: Women's Studies Association of the Philippines, University of the Philippines, 1999.

Illo, Jeanne Frances, ed. *Women and Gender Relations in the Philippines.* Quezon City: Women's Studies Association of the Philippines, University of the Philippines, 1999.

Isaksson, Eva, ed. *Women and the Military System.* New York: St. Martin's, 1988.

Jacoby, Erich H. *Agrarian Unrest in Southeast Asia.* Bombay: Asia Publishing House, 1961.

Joaquin, Nick [Quijano de Manila]. "Fall of Dr. Lava." In *Amalia Fuentes and Other Etchings,* 93–110. Manila: National Book Store, 1977.

———. "The Huk from Rochester, N.Y." In *Nora Aunor and Other Profiles,* 120–38. Manila: National Book Store, 1977.

———. "Taruc: Tiger in a Tank." In *Ronnie Poe and Other Silhouettes,* 109–28. Manila: National Book Store, 1977.

Jocano, F. Landa. "Elements of Filipino Social Organization." In *Philippine Kinship and Society,* ed. Y. Kikuchi, 1–26. Quezon City: New Day, 1989.

Johnson, Kay Ann. *Women, the Family, and Peasant Revolution in China.* Chicago: University of Chicago Press, 1983.

Jones, David E. *Women Warriors: A History.* Washington, DC: Brassey's, 1997.

Jose, F. Sionil, ed. "The Huks in Retrospect: A Failed Bid of Power" (interview with Casto Alejandrino, Jesus Lava, Alfredo Saulo and Luis Taruc). *Solidarity,* no. 102 (1985): 64–103.

Jose, Ricardo, and Lydia Jose. *The Japanese Occupation of the Philippines: A Pictorial History.* Manila: Ayala Foundation, 1997.

Kampwirth, Karen. *Women and Guerrilla Movements.* University Park: Pennsylvania State University Press, 2002.

Kasama: A Collection of Photographs of the New People's Army of the Philippines. Makati: International Concerns for Philippine Struggles, 1987.

Kaut, Charles R. "Endogamy and Exogamy in Tagalog Society: Adjustment to a Changing Resource Base." In *Social Change in Modern Philippines: Perspectives, Problems, and Prospects,* ed. Mario Zamora, Donald Baxter, and Robert Lawless, 161–65. Norman: Department of Anthropology, University of Oklahoma, 1978.

Kerkvliet, Benedict. *Everyday Politics in the Philippines: Class and Status Relations in a Central Luzon Village.* Berkeley: University of California Press, 1990.

———. *The Huk Rebellion: A Study of Peasant Revolt in the Philippines.* 1977. Boston: Rowman & Littlefield, 2002.

———. "Manuela Santa Ana vda. de Maclang and Philippine Politics." In *Lives at the Margin: Biography of Filipinos Obscure, Ordinary, and Heroic,* ed. Alfred W. McCoy, 389–421. Madison: Center for Southeast Asian Studies, University of Wisconsin, 2000.

——— "Peasant Rebellion in the Philippines: The Origins and Growth of the HMB." Ph.D. diss., University of Wisconsin–Madison, 1972.

———. "Peasant Society and Unrest Prior to the Huk Revolution." *Asian Studies* 9 (August 1971): 164–213.

Kerkvliet, Benedict, and James Scott, eds. *Everyday Forms of Peasant Resistance in Southeast Asia.* London: Frank Cass, 1986.

Khoo, Agnes. *Life as the River Flows: Women in the Malayan Anti-colonial Struggle.* Petaling Jaya, Malaysia: SIRD Press, 2004.

Kintanar, Thelma, ed. "Women in History and Revolution." Special issue of *Review of Women's Studies* 5, no. 2 and 6, no. 1 (1996).

Kleinbaum, Abby. *The War against the Amazons.* New York: New Press, 1983.

Knox, Donald. *Death March: The Survivors of Bataan.* New York: Harvest, 1981.

Kramer, Paul. "Water Cure: Debating Torture and Counter-insurgency a Century Ago." *New Yorker,* February 25, 2008.

Kruks, Sonia, Rayna Rapp, and Marilyn Young, eds. *Promissory Notes: Women in the Transition to Socialism.* New York: Monthly Review Press, 1989.

Lachica, Eduardo. *Huk: Philippine Agrarian Society in Revolt.* Manila: Solidaridad, 1971.

Landes, Joan. "Marxism and the 'Woman Question.'" In *Promissory Notes: Women in the Transition to Socialism,* ed. Sonia Kruks, Rayna Rapp, and Marilyn Young, 15-28. New York: Monthly Review Press, 1989.

Lanzona, Vina A. "Capturing the Huk Amazons: Representing Women Warriors in the Philippines, 1940s-1950s." *South East Asia Research* 17, no. 2 (forthcoming).

———. "Romancing a Revolutionary: The Life of Celia Mariano-Pomeroy." In *Lives at the Margin: Biographies of Filipinos Obscure, Ordinary, and Heroic,* ed. Alfred W. McCoy, 279-336. Madison: Center for Southeast Asian Studies, University of Wisconsin, 2000.

Larkin, John. *The Pampangans: Colonial Society in a Philippine Province.* Berkeley: University of California Press, 1972.

Lava, Jesus. "The Huk Rebellion." *Journal of Contemporary Asia* 9 (1979): 75-81.

———. *Memoirs of a Communist.* Pasig City: Anvil, 2002.

Leighton, Richard M., Ralph Sanders, and José N. Tinio. *The Huk Rebellion: A Case Study in the Social Dynamics of Insurrection.* Washington, D.C.: Industrial College of the Armed Forces, 1964.

Lenin, Vladimir. *The Emancipation of Women: From the Writings of V. I. Lenin.* New York: International Publishers, 1966.

Lewis, John Wilson, ed. *Peasant Rebellion and Communist Revolution in Asia.* Stanford: Stanford University Press, 1974.

Lieberman, Victor. "Why the Hukbalahap Movement Failed." *Solidarity* 4 (October-December 1966): 22-30.

Lindio-McGovern, Ligaya. *Filipino Peasant Women.* Philadelphia: University of Pennsylvania Press, 1997.

Logarta, Sofia. "The Participation of Women in the Huk Movement." In *Women's Role in Philippine History: Selected Essays,* 131-40. 2nd ed. Quezon City: Center for Women's Studies, University of the Philippines, 1996.

Luong, Hy V., with the collaboration of Nguyen Dac Bang. *Revolution in the Village: Tradition and Transformation in North Vietnam, 1925-1988.* Honolulu: University of Hawaii Press, 1992.

Lynch, Frank, comp. *Four Readings on Philippine Values.* Quezon City: Ateneo de Manila University Press, 1968.

Macdonald, Sharon, Pat Holden, and Shirley Ardener. *Images of Women in Peace and War: Cross-Cultural and Historical Perspectives.* Oxford: Macmillan, 1987.

Maceda, Teresita. *Mga Tinig Mula Sa Ibaba: Kasaysayan ng Partido Komunista ng Pilipinas at Partido Sosialista ng Pilipinas sa Awit, 1930-1955* (Voices from Below: A History of the Communist Party and Socialist Party through Song, 1930-1955). Diliman: University of the Philippines Press, 1996.

Mallon, Florencia. *Peasant and Nation: The Making of Postcolonial Mexico and Peru.* Berkeley: University of California Press, 1995.

Mananzan, Mary John. *The Woman Question in the Philippines.* Pasay City: Daughters of Saint Paul, 1991.

Mananzan, Mary John, Asuncion Azcuna, and Fe Mangahas, eds. *Sarilaya: Women in Arts and Media.* Manila: Institute of Women's Studies, 1989.

Marr, David. *Vietnamese Tradition on Trial, 1920-1945.* Berkeley: University of California Press, 1981.

Martinez, Manuel F. *Magsaysay: The People's President.* Makati City: RMJ Development, 2005.

May, Elaine Tyler. *Homeward Bound: American Families in the Cold War Era.* New York: Basic Books, 1988.

May, Glenn. *Social Engineering in the Philippines: The Aims, Execution, and Impact of American Colonial Policy, 1900-1913.* Westport, CT: Greenwood, 1980.

McAdam, Doug. "Gender as Mediator of the Activist Experience." *American Journal of Sociology* 97, no. 5 (March 1992): 1211-40.

———. "Recruitment to High Risk Activism: The Case of Freedom Summer." *American Journal of Sociology* 92 (July 1986): 64-90.

McAdam, Doug, Sidney Tarrow, and Charles Tilly. "Towards an Integrated Perspective on Social Movements and Revolution." In *Comparative Politics: Rationality, Culture, and Structure,* ed. Marc Lichbach and Alan Zuckerman, 142-73. New York: Cambridge University Press, 1997.

McAdam, Doug, Charles Tilly, and Sidney Tarrow. *Dynamics of Contention.* New York: Cambridge University Press, 2001.

McCoy, Alfred W. "*Baylan:* Animist Religion and Philippine Peasant Ideology." In *Moral Order and the Question of Change,* ed. David Wyatt and Alexander Woodside, 338-408. New Haven, CT: Council on Southeast Asian Studies, Yale University, 1982.

———. *Closer Than Brothers: Manhood at the Philippine Military Academy.* New Haven, CT: Yale University Press, 1999.

———. "A Queen Dies Slowly: The Rise and Decline of Iloilo City." In *Philippine Social History: Global Trade and Local Transformations,* ed. Alfred W. McCoy and Ed. C. de Jesus, 297-358. Quezon City: Ateneo de Manila University Press, 1982.

———. "'Same Banana': Hazing and Honor at the Philippine Military Academy." *Journal of Asian Studies* 54, no. 3 (August 1995): 689–726.

McCoy, Alfred W., ed. *Southeast Asia under Japanese Occupation.* New Haven, CT: Yale University Press, 1980.

McCoy, Alfred W., and Ed. C. de Jesus, eds. *Philippine Social History: Global Trade and Local Transformations.* Quezon City: Ateneo de Manila University Press, 1982.

McDonald, Crispina S. "Educational Change in Barrio San Julian, Pangasinan, Philippines." In *Social Change in Modern Philippines: Perspectives, Problems, and Prospects,* ed. Mario Zamora, Donald Baxter, and Robert Lawless, 55–66. Norman: Department of Anthropology, University of Oklahoma, 1978.

McLennan, Marshall S. "Changing Human Ecology on the Central Luzon Plain: Nueva Ecija, 1705–1939." In *Philippine Social History: Global Trade and Local Transformations,* ed. Alfred W. McCoy and Ed. C. de Jesus, 57–90. Quezon City: Ateneo de Manila University Press, 1982.

———. "Land and Tenancy in Central Luzon Plain." *Philippine Studies* 17 (October 1969): 651–82.

McVey, Ruth T. "The Southeast Asian Insurrectionary Movements." In *Communism and Revolution: The Strategic Uses of Political Violence,* ed. Cyril Black and Thomas Thornton, 145–84. Princeton, NJ: Princeton University Press, 1964.

Meintjes, Sheila, Anu Pillay, and Meredith Turshen, eds. *The Aftermath: Women in Post-conflict Transformation.* London: Zed, 2001.

Melucci, Alberto. "The New Social Movements: A Theoretical Approach." *Social Science Information* 19 (1980): 199–226.

———. "The Symbolic Challenge of Contemporary Movements." *Social Research* 52 (1985): 789–815.

Mendoza-Guazon, Maria Paz. *The Development and Progress of the Filipino Woman.* Manila: Kiko, 1951.

Migdal, Joel. *Peasants, Politics, and Revolution: Pressures Toward Political and Social Change in the Third World.* Princeton, NJ: Princeton University Press, 1974.

Misra, Geentanjali, and Radhika Chandiramani, eds. *Sexuality, Gender, and Rights: Exploring Theory and Practice in South and Southeast Asia.* New Delhi: Sage, 2005.

Montiel, Cristina, and Mary Racelis Hollnsteiner. *The Filipino Woman: Her Role and Status in Philippine Society.* Quezon City: Institute of Philippine Culture, Ateneo de Manila University, 1976.

Moore, Barrington. *Social Origins of Democracy and Dictatorship: Lord and Peasant in the Making of the Modern World.* Boston: Beacon, 1967.

Morais, Robert J. *Social Relations in a Philippine Town.* Special Report 19. [DeKalb]: Center for Southeast Asian Studies, Northern Illinois University, 1981.

Mullaney, Marie Marmo. *Revolutionary Women: Gender and the Socialist Revolutionary Role*. New York: Praeger, 1983.

Murray, Francis J., Jr. "Lowland Social Organization I: Local Kin Groups in a Central Luzon Barrio." *Philippine Sociological Review* 21 (1973): 29–36.

Nakano Satoshi. "Appeasement and Coercion." In *The Philippines under Japan: Occupation Policy and Reaction*, ed. Ikehata Setsuho and Ricardo Jose, 21–58. Quezon City: Ateneo de Manila University Press, 1999.

Orozco, Wilhelmina. *Feminist Objectives in the Third World and Other Writings*. Manila: Philippine Women's Research Collective, 1987.

Osborne, Milton. *Region of Revolt: Focus on Southeast Asia*. New York: Penguin, 1971.

———. *Southeast Asia: An Introductory History*. St. Leonardo, NSW, Australia: Allen & Unwin, 1997.

Owen, Norman, ed. *Compadre Colonialism: Studies on the Philippines under American Rule*. Ann Arbor: Center for South and Southeast Asian Studies, University of Michigan, 1971.

———. *The Emergence of Modern Southeast Asia: A New History*. Honolulu: University of Hawaii Press, 2005.

Paige, Jeffrey. *Agrarian Revolution: Social Movements and Export Agriculture in the Underdeveloped World*. 1975. New York: Free Press, 1978.

Paredes, Ruby, ed. *Philippine Colonial Democracy*. New Haven, CT: Council on Southeast Asian Studies, Yale University, 1989.

Parker, Andrew, Mary Russo, Doris Summer, and Patricia Yaeger, eds. *Nationalisms and Sexualities*. New York: Routledge, 1992.

Parsa, Misagh. *States, Ideologies, and Social Revolutions: A Comparative Analysis of Iran, Nicaragua, and the Philippines*. New York: Cambridge University Press, 2000.

Pluvier, Jan. *South-East Asia from Colonialism to Independence*. Kuala Lumpur: Oxford University Press, 1974.

Pomeroy, William. *An American Made Tragedy: Neo-colonialism and Dictatorship in the Philippines*. New York: International Publishers, 1974.

———. *American Neo-colonialism: Its Emergence in the Philippines and Asia*. New York: International Publishers, 1970.

———. *The Forest: A Personal Record of the Huk Guerilla Struggle in the Philippines*. 1963. New York: International Publishers, 1978.

———. "The Philippine Peasantry and the Huk Revolt." *Journal of Peasant Studies* 5 (1978): 497–517.

———. *The Philippines: Colonialism, Collaboration, and Resistance*. New York: International Publishers, 1992.

Popkin, Samuel. *The Rational Peasant: The Political Economy of Rural Society in Vietnam*. Berkeley: University of California Press, 1977.

Porio, Emma, Frank Lynch, and Mary R. Hollnsteiner. *The Filipino Family, Community, and Nation: The Same Yesterday, Today, and Tomorrow*. Quezon City: Institute of Philippine Culture, Ateneo de Manila University, 1975.

Portelli, Alessandro. *The Death of Luigi Trastulli and Other Stories: Form and Meaning in Oral History.* Albany: State University of New York Press, 1991.

Presley, Cora Ann. *Kikuyu Women, the Mau Mau Rebellion, and Social Change in Kenya.* Boulder: Westview, 1992.

Pulang Mandirigma: Images of the New People's Army. Manila: Information Bureau, Communist Party of the Philippines, 2004.

Quibuyen, Floro C. *A Nation Aborted: Rizal, American Hegemony, and Philippine Nationalism.* Quezon City: Ateneo De Manila University Press, 1999.

Quinn-Judge, Sophie. "Women in the Early Vietnamese Communist Movement: Sex, Lies, and Liberation." *South East Asia Research* 9, no. 3 (November 2001): 245–69.

Rafael, Vicente. "Anticipating Nationhood: Identification, Collaboration, and Rumor in Filipino Responses to Japan." In *White Love and Other Events in Filipino History*, 103–21. Durham, NC: Duke University Press, 2000.

———. *White Love and Other Events in Philippine History.* Durham, NC: Duke University Press, 2000.

Randall, Margaret. *Sandino's Daughters: Testimonies of Nicaraguan Women in Struggle.* Vancouver, Canada: New Star Books, 1981.

———. *Sandino's Daughters Revisited: Feminism in Nicaragua.* New Brunswick, NJ: Rutgers University Press, 1994.

Reid, Anthony. *Southeast Asia in the Age of Commerce, 1450–1680.* Vol. 1, *The Lands Below the Winds.* New Haven, CT: Yale University Press, 1988.

Reif, Linda. "Women in Latin American Guerilla Movements: A Comparative Perspective." *Comparative Politics* 8, no. 2 (1986): 134–48.

Reinharz, Shulamit, with assistance from Lynn Davidman. *Feminist Methods in Social Research.* New York: Oxford University Press, 1992.

Reyes, Felina. *Filipino Women: Their Role in the Progress of Their Nation.* Washington, DC: Women's Bureau, U.S. Department of Labor, 1951.

Rivera, Generoso, and Robert McMillan. *An Economic and Social Survey of Rural Households in Central Luzon.* Manila: Cooperative Research Project of the Philippine Council for United States Aid and the United States of America Operations Missions to the Philippines, 1954.

Roces, Mina. "Is the Suffragist an American Colonial Construct? Defining 'the Filipino Woman' in the Colonial Philippines." In *Women's Suffrage in Asia: Gender, Nationalism, and Democracy*, ed. Louise Edwards and Mina Roces, 24–58. New York: RoutledgeCurzon, 2004.

———. "Negotiating Modernities: Filipino Women, 1970–2000." In *Women in Asia: Tradition, Modernity, and Globalisation*, ed. Louise Edwards and Mina Roces, 112–38. Ann Arbor: University of Michigan Press, 2000.

———. *Women, Power, and Kinship Politics: Female Power in Post-war Philippines.* Westport, CT: Praeger, 1998.

Rodgers, Susan. *Telling Lives, Telling History: Autobiography and Historical Imagination in Modern Indonesia.* Berkeley: University of California Press, 1995.

Rojas-Aleta, Isabel, Teresita Silva, and Christine Eleazar. *A Profile of Filipino Women: Their Status and Role.* Manila: Philippine Business for Social Progress, 1977.

Romani, John H. "The Philippine Barrio." *Far Eastern Quarterly* 15 (February 1956): 229–37.

Romulo, Carlos P., and Marvin M. Gray. *The Magsaysay Story.* New York: Pocket, 1957.

Rowbotham, Sheila. *Hidden from History: Rediscovering Women in History from the 17th Century to the Present.* New York: Pantheon, 1975.

———. *Women, Resistance, and Revolution: A History of Women and Revolution in the Modern World.* New York: Pantheon, 1972.

Salazar, Zeus. "Ang Babaylan sa Kasaysayan ng Pilipinas" (The Babaylan in Philippine History). In *Women's Role in Philippine History: Selected Essays,* 52–72. 2nd ed. Quezon City: Center for Women's Studies, University of the Philippines, 1996.

Santos, Alfred. *Heroic Virgins and Women Patriots.* Quezon City: Kalayaan, 1977.

Santos-Maranan, Aida. "Do Women Really Hold Up Half the Sky? Notes on the Women's Movement in the Philippines." In *Essays on Women,* ed. Mary John Mananzan, 36–51. Manila: Institute of Women's Studies, St. Scholastica's College, 1987.

Sargent, Lydia, ed. *Women and Revolution: A Discussion of the Unhappy Marriage of Marxism and Feminism.* Boston: South End Press, 1981.

Saulo, Alfredo. *Communism in the Philippines: An Introduction.* Quezon City: Ateneo de Manila University Press, 1990.

Scaff, Alvin. *The Philippine Answer to Communism.* Stanford: Stanford University Press, 1955.

Schellstede, Sangmie Choi, ed. *Comfort Women Speak: Testimony by Sex Slaves of the Japanese Military.* New York: Holmes & Meier, 2000.

Schirmer, Daniel B., and Stephen Shalom, eds. *The Philippines Reader: A History of Colonialism, Neocolonialism, Dictatorship, and Resistance.* Boston: South End, 1987.

Schumacher, John. *The Making of a Nation: Essays on Nineteenth-Century Filipino Nationalism.* Quezon City: Ateneo de Manila University Press, 1991.

———. *The Propaganda Movement: The Creation of a Filipino Consciousness, the Making of the Revolution.* Rev. ed. Quezon City: Ateneo de Manila University Press, 1997.

Scott, James. *Domination and the Arts of Resistance: Hidden Transcripts.* New Haven, CT: Yale University Press, 1990.

———. *The Moral Economy of the Peasant: Rebellion and Subsistence in Southeast Asia.* 1976. New Haven, CT: Yale University Press, 1990.

———. *Weapons of the Weak: Everyday Forms of Peasant Resistance.* New Haven, CT: Yale University Press, 1985.

Scott, Joan. "Gender: A Useful Category of Historical Analysis." In *Gender and the Politics of History,* 28–52. New York: Columbia University Press, 1988.

———. *Gender and the Politics of History.* New York: Columbia University Press, 1988.

Shalom, Stephen R. *The United States and the Philippines: A Study of Neocolonialism.* Quezon City: New Day Publishers, 1986.

Siapno, Jacqueline. *Gender, Islam, Nationalism, and the State in Aceh: The Paradox of Power, Co-optation, and Resistance.* New York: RoutledgeCurzon, 2002.

Silverstein, Josef, ed. *Southeast Asia in World War II: Four Essays.* New Haven, CT: Southeast Asia Studies, Yale University, 1966.

Skocpol, Theda. *States and Social Revolutions: A Comparative Analysis of France, Russia, and China.* Cambridge: Cambridge University Press, 1979.

———. "What Makes Peasants Revolutionary?" In *Power and Protest in the Countryside,* ed. Robert P. Weller and Scott E. Guggenheim, 157–79. Durham, NC: Duke University Press, 1982.

Smedley, Agnes. *Portraits of Chinese Women in Revolution.* Edited with an introduction by Jan MacKinnon and Steve MacKinnon. Old Westbury, NY: Feminist Press, 1976.

Smith, Lois. *Sex in Revolution: Gender, Politics, and Power in Modern Mexico.* New York: Oxford University Press, 1996.

Snow, David A., Louis A. Zurcher Jr., and Sheldon Ekland-Olson. "Social Networks and Social Movements: A Microstructural Approach to Differential Recruitment." *American Sociological Review* 45 (October 1980): 787–801.

Snow, Edgar. *Red Star over China.* New York: Random House, 1938.

Sobritchea, Carolyn I. "American Colonial Education and Its Impact on the Status of Filipino Women." In *Women's Role in Philippine History: Selected Essays,* 79–108. 2nd ed. Quezon City: Center for Women's Studies, University of the Philippines, 1996.

———. "Gender Ideology and the Status of Women in a Philippine Rural Community." In *Essays on Women,* ed. Mary John Mananzan, 90–103. Manila: Institute of Women's Studies, Saint Scholastica's College, 1989.

Soriano, Rafaelita H. *Women in the Philippine Revolution.* Quezon City: Printon, 1995.

Stacey, Judith. *Patriarchy and Socialist Revolution in China.* Berkeley: University of California Press, 1983.

Stanley, Peter. *A Nation in the Making: the Philippines and the United States, 1899–1921.* Cambridge, MA: Harvard University Press, 1974.

Starner, Frances L. *Magsaysay and the Philippine Peasantry.* Berkeley, CA: University of California Press, 1961.

Steinberg, David Joel. *Philippine Collaboration in World War II.* Ann Arbor: University of Michigan Press, 1967.

———. *The Philippines: A Singular and a Plural Place.* 4th ed. Boulder: Westview, 2000.

Stetz, Margaret, and Bonnie B. C. Oh, eds. *Legacies of the Comfort Women of World War II.* New York: M. E. Sharpe, 2001.

Stoler, Ann Laura. *Capitalism and Confrontation in Sumatra's Plantation Belt, 1870–1979.* New Haven, CT: Yale University Press, 1985.

Sturtevant, David R. *Agrarian Unrest in the Philippines.* Athens: Center for International Studies, Ohio University, 1969.

———. *Popular Uprisings in the Philippines, 1840–1940.* Ithaca, NY: Cornell University Press, 1976.

Syjuco, Maria Felisa A. *The Kempei Tai in the Philippines, 1941–1945.* Quezon City: Ateneo de Manila University Press, 1988.

Tai, Hue-Tam Ho. *Millenarianism and Peasant Politics in Vietnam.* Cambridge, MA: Harvard University Press, 1983.

———. *Radicalism and the Origins of the Vietnamese Revolution.* Cambridge, MA: Harvard University Press, 1992.

Takahashi, Akira. *Land and Peasants in Central Luzon: Socio-economic Structure of a Philippine Village.* Honolulu: East-West Center Press, 1970.

Tanaka, Yuki. *Japan's Comfort Women: Sexual Slavery and Prostitution during World War II and the U.S. Occupation.* New York: Routledge, 2002.

Tarrow, Sidney. *Power in Movement: Social Movements, Collective Action, and Politics.* New York: Cambridge University Press, 1998.

Taruc, Luis. *Born of the People.* 1953. Westport, CT: Greenwood, 1973.

———. *He Who Rides the Tiger: The Story of an Asian Guerrilla Leader.* New York: Praeger, 1967.

Taylor, Sandra. *Vietnamese Women at War.* Lawrence: University Press of Kansas, 1999.

Tenney, Lester. *My Hitch in Hell: The Bataan Death March.* Washington, DC: Potomac, 1995.

Terami-Wada, Motoe. "The Cultural Front in the Philippines, 1942–1945: Japanese Propaganda and Filipino Resistance in Mass Media." M.A. thesis, University of the Philippines, 1984.

———. "The Filipino Volunteer Armies." In *The Philippines under Japan: Occupation Policy and Reaction,* ed. Ikehata Setsuho and Ricardo Jose, 59–98. Quezon City: Ateneo de Manila University Press, 1988.

Tetrault, Mary Ann, ed. *Women and Revolution in Africa, Asia, and the New World.* Columbia: University of South Carolina Press, 1994.

Thompson, Paul. *The Voice of the Past, Oral History.* 3rd ed. Oxford: Oxford University Press, 1988.

Tiffany, Sharon W., and Kathleen J. Adams. *The Wild Woman: An Inquiry into the Anthropology of an Idea.* Cambridge, MA: Schenkman, 1985.

Tilly, Charles. "Contentious Action." In *Dynamics of Contention,* ed. Doug McAdam, Sidney Tarrow, and Charles Tilly, 124–59. New York: Cambridge University Press, 2001.

———. *Identities, Boundaries, and Social Ties.* New York: Paradigm, 2006.

———. *From Mobilization to Revolution.* Reading, MA: Addison Wesley, 1978.
———. *Stories, Identities, and Political Change.* Lanham, MD: Rowman and Littlefield, 2002.
Tilly, Louise, and Joan Scott. *Women, Work, and Family.* New York: Routledge, 1989.
Tirona, Mary Grace Ampil. *"Panuelo* Activism." In *Women's Role in Philippine History: Selected Essays,* 63–74. 2nd ed. Quezon City: Center for Women's Studies, University of the Philippines, 1996.
Torres, Amaryllis T. *The Filipina Looks at Herself: A Review of Women's Studies in the Philippines.* Diliman: Research and Extension for Development Office, College of Social Work and Community Development, University of the Philippines, 1992.
Tria Kerkvliet, Melinda. *Manila's Workers' Unions, 1900–1950.* Quezon City: New Day, 1992.
Turner, Karen Gottschang, with Phan Thanh Hao. *Even the Women Must Fight: Memories of War from North Vietnam.* New York: Wiley, 1998.
Vespa, Amleto. *Secret Agent of Japan.* New York: Garden City Pub. Co., 1941.
Villanueva-Kalaw, Pura. *How Women Got the Vote.* Manila: Free Press, 1952.
Vogel, Lise. *Marxism and the Oppression of Women: Toward a Unitary Theory.* New Brunswick, NJ: Rutgers University Press, 1983.
Walton, John. *Reluctant Rebels: Comparative Studies of Revolution and Underdevelopment.* New York: Columbia University Press, 1984.
War Crimes on Asian Women: Military Sexual Slavery by Japan during World War II—The Case of the Filipino Comfort Women. Manila: Asian Women Human Rights Council, 1998.
Waterson, Roxana, ed. *Southeast Asian Lives, Personal Narrative, and Historical Experience.* Singapore: National University of Singapore Press, 2007.
Watson, C. W. *Of Self and Nation: Autobiography and the Representation of Modern Indonesia.* Honolulu: University of Hawaii Press, 2000.
Weekley, Kathleen. *The Communist Party of the Philippines, 1968–1993: A Story of its Theory and Practice.* Diliman, Quezon City: University of the Philippines Press, 2001.
West, Guida, and Rhoda Lois Blumberg, eds. *Women and Social Protest.* New York: Oxford University Press, 1990.
White, Luise. "Separating Men from the Boys: Constructions of Gender, Sexuality, and Terrorism in Central Kenya, 1939–1959." *International Journal of African Historical Studies* 23, no. 1 (1990): 1–25.
Wieringa, Saskia. *Sexual Politics in Indonesia.* New York: Palgrave/Macmillan, 2002.
Wilde, Lyn W. *On the Trail of The Women Warriors: The Amazons in Myth and History.* New York: Thomas Dunne, 2000.
Wolf, Eric. *Peasant Wars of the Twentieth Century.* New York: Harper & Row, 1969.

Women's Role in Philippine History: Selected Essays. 2nd ed. Quezon City: Center for Women's Studies, University of the Philippines, 1996.

The Woman Question: Selections from the Writings of Karl Marx, Frederick Engels, V.I. Lenin, Joseph Stalin. New York: International Publishers, 1951.

Yoshimi, Yoshiaki. *Comfort Women: Sexual Slavery in the Japanese Military during World War II.* Trans. Suzanne O'Brien. New York: Columbia University Press, 2000.

Young, Helen P. *Choosing Revolution: Chinese Women Soldiers on the Long March.* Urbana: University of Illinois Press, 2001.

Zamora, Mario, Donald Baxter, and Robert Lawless, eds. *Social Change in Modern Philippines: Perspectives, Problems, and Prospects.* Norman: Department of Anthropology, University of Oklahoma, 1978.

Zetkin, Clara. *Clara Zetkin: Selected Writings.* New York: International Publishers, 1984.

———. "Lenin on the Woman Question." In *The Emancipation of Women: From the Writings of V.I. Lenin,* by V.I. Lenin, 95–123. New York: International Publishing, 1966.

Index

tenant farming, 24–27, 82, 285–86nn11–15, 301n26. *See also* land

Titis (newspaper), 99, 101, 164, 241

Tolentino, Filomena, 21, 29, 33, 52, 59–60, 68, 88, 95, 97, 111, 115, 208–9, 210, 270, 321n72

Torres, Rosenda, 33, 53–54, 91, 99, 115, 116, 188, 190, 213–14, 241–42, 271

Union of the Toiling Masses. *See* AMT

United Front: organization, 38, 148–49, 156, 299–300n16; policy, 29–30, 37–38, 50, 57, 80, 82, 97, 288n36

University of the Philippines, 19, 43, 146, 163, 171, 308n7

USAFFE (U.S. Armed Forces in the Far East), 31

U.S. colonialism/imperialism, 27–28, 68, 77, 78–79, 82–84, 123–24, 127, 128, 131–32, 175, 258, 287n26, 299n10, 301n30, 307–8nn6–8

Valerio, Amparo, 49, 62, 86

Valerio, Belen, 49, 61, 62, 86

Valerio, Teofista (alias Estrella), 4–5, 41, 43–44, 49, 55, 91–93, 106–7, 114, 171–72, 197–203, 244, 269–70, 303n60, 320n48

Vietnam, 72, 73, 118, 244–45, 331n55

Waling-Waling (Coronacion Chival), 135–36, 143

wedding ceremonies, 181–82, *184*, 193–95, 268, 273–74

"woman question," 175–76, 218–19, 237–44, 248

women's history, 8–10. *See also* gender: and history

women's organizations, 123–24, 129, 267, 308nn10–12, 309n19, 310n37, 310n40, 316n146; Gabriela, 310n43, 333n78; KaBaPa, 16, 270, 271–72, 333n78; National Council of Women, 125; NAW, 271; Philippine Women's Society, 99; SPKP, 270; Women's Forum, 240, 326n169

women's suffrage, 11, 123–26, 128–29, 241, 308nn10–12

Zetkin, Clara, 219, 239, 323n106, 323n109

NEW PERSPECTIVES IN
SOUTHEAST ASIAN STUDIES